365

Meike Peters

365

A Year of Everyday Cooking & Baking

PRESTEL

MUNICH · LONDON · NEW YORK

In memory of
Daphne Caruana Galizia
and her work

BURLÓ

Contents

Introduction

What shall we cook tonight? Let's take the pressure off—the kitchen isn't a place where we have to perform. It's our choice what we eat, how we eat, and how we feel when we prepare it. The kitchen is the best place to take it easy, to forget about duties, and to wind down the pace. Let's enjoy, yes, let's celebrate our food 365 days a year.

So what shall we cook tonight? In my home, dinner plans often start with this question, discussed over our morning espresso at the tiny bistro table in the kitchen. Pondering our mood and what's stocked in the fridge and pantry, we plan the dishes that will turn every evening into our own little feast. During a busy week, I often keep it simple. I use quick and comforting recipes, fresh vegetables, leftovers, pasta, and convenient helpers like pesto, good olive oil, and tasty flaky sea salt to tweak and turn frugal dishes into scrumptious treats.

I love to cook—I dive into it with passion every day, and I want to eat well—but there are times when I need some structure to make it work. A weekly shopping and cooking plan is the easiest thing to do. It doesn't spoil the fun, but saves time and prevents waste. I still follow the seasons and my mood, and feel inspired by the produce at the farmers' market, yet using my creativity in a moment of peace and quiet over a cup of tea to set up a rough culinary plan for the next seven days gives the weary weekday-mind a break.

My cooking is very much guided by the seasonal calendar. I love having nature's wide spectrum of colors and flavors on my plate, but this only truly works when fruits and vegetables are at their best, at their peak. This, and paying attention to their origin. Over the years, I simplified many of my recipes, reducing the number of ingredients to focus on their individual qualities rather than distracting from them. This can enhance the taste of a dish, and make for recipes that don't take long to prepare.

When I buy tomatoes, beans, zucchini, or eggplant, I buy plenty so that I can double recipes and enjoy them, and their leftovers, for more than a day. A sweet-and-sour caponata can become a Palermo-style dish when I top it with octopus (recipe no. 243), a juicy sandwich with chorizo sausage (recipe no. 227), or a frugal summer snack on its own. Grilling a bunch of bell peppers and storing them in spiced olive oil makes a handy topping for bread and adds sweetness to salads and pasta on another day. Homemade pesto can be enjoyed for days, helping potatoes, spaghetti, seafood, and poultry excite the palate. I like to stretch the term "pesto" in my kitchen and use it for every vegetable, legume, herb, fruit, and nut that my food processor can turn into something dollop-able.

My home country's comfort food is food for the soul. Traditional German dishes can lift the moody blanket on a gloomy day, turning the cold outside into a welcoming invitation to get cozy inside, relaxing over a warming stew or fragrant cake. My second home and adopted country, Malta, opened the doors to bright flavors, bold combinations, and dishes that are so simple that you sometimes only need three ingredients. Lunch is ready within seconds—and nothing but heavenly—when boiled potatoes, beets, oranges, or slices of warm sourdough bread meet the best olive oil and tasty, crunchy sea salt flakes. It can be that simple. Thanks to my Maltese-American partner's home country, I embrace the deep flavors of citrus fruits, spices, and herbs growing under the Mediterranean sun and I make use of them abundantly. Yet his and my culinary roots have one thing in common: both cuisines embrace our grandmothers' style of cooking and baking, which is unbeatably delicious, heartwarming, and frugal.

The fruitful dialogue with the readers of my blog, *Eat In My Kitchen*, confirmed my feeling that Mondays, Wednesdays, Fridays, and Sundays call for different recipes. It all comes down to our mood. We often start a new week with sleepy eyes. Our schedule is tight yet our mind is still caught up in lazy weekend memories and desperately in need of a little *dolce vita*. The sweet prospect of a bowl of steaming spaghetti mingling with ricotta, orange zest, and crispy sage (*recipe no. 2*) on a Monday evening can help to smooth the rugged transition. There are also many ways to take away the weight of weekday cooking. A vibrant salad can excite the taste buds with unusual combinations. A comforting soup can turn into two different meals just by shifting from a poached egg on top the first day, to a grilled pecorino crostini on the side the second day. With my blog's Sandwich Wednesday series, initiated by my partner's love for opulent creations involving bread, came a new view on the popular German *Butterbrot*. I drew on my grandmother's tradition of having bread with cheese or ham for dinner, but we often pack a whole meal between two slices of sourdough bread. Nothing beats a schnitzel and *Krautsalat* sandwich in the middle of the week!

If the week is for the simple recipes, the weekend is made to indulge in more luscious pleasures. I can't think of a better way to recharge the batteries than by taking a late Saturday morning stroll through the farmers' market, followed by a Mediterranean-style lunch prepared with all the delicious finds: a crunchy baguette, aromatic cheese, and a bowl of fresh mussels steamed in grape broth (*recipe no. 257*), accompanied by a glass of crisp white wine. That's my treat. On Saturdays and Sundays, I take my time in the kitchen. I make Sicilian tangerine jam (*recipe no. 333*), a Maltese pasta pie called *timpana* (*recipe no. 112 and no. 231*), or a fluffy babka with poppy seeds and white chocolate (*recipe no. 62*) to sweeten the air with the aroma of fragrant yeast bread while I sing happy tunes. A wintry Sunday roast is the celebration of everything that I love about the kitchen: my mother's traditional countryside cooking and honest comfort food shared with family and friends at one long table. A tender roast isn't labor- but time-intensive, and while the cook reads on the sofa, it fills the house with the heavy perfume of spices, herbs, and roasting juices. It was a conscious decision that we made a while back to cut down on meat and seafood and to only bring them to the table once a week. Hearty roasts and summery fish dishes aren't fast meals, these are special treats calling for high quality ingredients and plenty of time to enjoy them. To our surprise, it was much easier to reset our meaty habit than expected, maybe because we introduced another tradition to end the week. Every Sunday evening, we bake pizza from scratch and enjoy our crunchy masterpiece on the sofa while watching an old movie from the sixties or seventies. It became a date night.

Pizza, along with lasagna and other dishes made with dough and pastry, is the ultimate comfort food, creating instant happiness. As much as I'm in awe of flavor, I was always fascinated by this aspect of cooking and eating. Food goes beyond necessity, even beyond flavor—it creates the most special moments with only a few ingredients. I chose to have a quiche on the cover of this book because it was one of the first dishes that I learned to bake and eventually master as I moved out into the world during my university years. Since then, various quiche recipes have consistently helped me to celebrate the ups and overcome the downs in my life. They taught me one important lesson: there's no reason why I shouldn't have these special moments 365 days a year. I just need a table long enough to share them at. Food is pure bliss, transformed by and in our kitchens.

Notes on Equipment, Kitchen Specifics, and Ingredients

A dish is shaped by the person who cooks it, by the ingredients that it's made of, and by the equipment the cook uses. Every day, I choose what I cook and eat, I choose the ingredients, tools, and recipes. Paying attention to every single detail, even the most basic ones like salt and pepper or knives and pans, has a strong impact on the experience and the result. The decision to buy ORGANIC PRODUCE, EGGS, and DAIRY PRODUCTS and to be more discerning about the origin of MEAT and SEAFOOD was inevitable and came out of a growing awareness of our environmental responsibility. I trust nature. We often find SMALL LOCAL PRODUCERS during our travels whom we keep going back to for spices, dried herbs, tomatoes, and legumes, for capers and olive oil. The flavors nourish our holiday memories, and we get to support farmers who focus on quality rather than massive growth.

My collection of necessary—and admittedly unnecessary—kitchen equipment has grown over the years, and makes prepping and cooking simply more enjoyable. My wooden CUTTING BOARD is large, thick, and old, my KNIVES are always sharp, and my marble kitchen countertops are forgiving. I've been kneading dough and cutting cookies on the white stone tops for more than twenty years until they've become scratched up and dull, which only makes them more beautiful and my favorite surface to work on.

POTS should be large enough to avoid frustration—mine are stainless steel—and I have a weak spot for heavy cast iron PANS and COCOTTES. I use them all on an ELECTRIC STOVE and in a conventional OVEN, unless stated as convection setting or broiler. When it comes to COOKING TIMES and TEMPERATURE, the attentive cook should keep in mind that all electronic devices work differently and different materials don't conduct heat in the same way.

Attention and all the senses are needed in the kitchen, especially when it comes to the fine ADJUSTMENTS of a recipe. Our preferences vary, pantry products differ in their quality, and fresh produce from different places never tastes the same. I trust my eyes, nose, and taste buds—that's all we have and they will never let us down. The quantities in this cookbook are based on personal habits. My appetite is healthy, yet not excessive, and that's the guideline for my recipes.

VEGETABLES and FRUITS are rinsed and scrubbed, if not explicitly stated as peeled. Their WEIGHT indicates the amount after peeling, coring, and pitting. ONIONS and GARLIC are peeled, unless otherwise stated. If using the peel, CITRUS fruits should be organic and rinsed and scrubbed with a brush. MEAT and SEAFOOD are rinsed under cold water and dried well with paper towels.

I have a soft spot for flavorful CHEESES; they take up quite some space in our fridge. I grate them fresh and never buy pre-packed products. Paying attention to the quality—and spending a little more on a nice chunky piece—means using less, but tastier cheese in your dishes.

The baking recipes in this book call for all-purpose FLOUR. Unbleached all-purpose wheat flour weighs as much as white spelt flour (1 CUP EQUALS 130G /4 1/2 OUNCES), and both have almost the same qualities in taste and texture. I use white spelt flour, as I prefer its nutritional value.

I use two kinds of extra-virgin OLIVE OIL: a simple one for cooking, and a finer one for dressings, sandwiches, and for refining dishes at the table. When it comes to VINEGAR, I keep it simple: a dark and a white balsamic vinegar work perfectly for dressings and to deglaze seared fruits and vegetables. The BROTH I use for soups, sauces, and grains is homemade and stored in handy portions in my freezer, but it can be replaced with quality products from the store.

You might call it a quirk but I strongly believe that good sea SALT does make a difference in a dish. Mine is flaky and from the ancient Xwejni Salt Pans at the coast of Malta's sister island, Gozo. The salt is harvested by the Cini family in the fifth generation, and makes the most simple dishes taste out of this world. For fine salt, I use the same flakes but ground with a mortar and pestle.

PEPPERCORNS are black in my recipes, unless otherwise stated. I prefer to use a mortar and pestle to grind and crush whole SPICES, but you can replace them with ground spices. However, keep in mind that their taste tends to be less fine and complex.

Although I only have window sills and a balcony, not a garden, I try to keep as many fresh HERBS as possible. Apart from the classics, like basil, marjoram, rosemary, thyme, and sage, I love to experiment with tarragon, savory, or chervil. It's a very simple way to add exciting and surprising flavors.

January

It's the 1st of January, and nature is still in its deep winter sleep. A vibrant, reinvigorating caprese salad can easily help us forget that summer is still far away. Let's replace the familiar tomatoes with earthy beet and sweet blood orange and start dreaming of blue skies and sunshine.

Winter Caprese with Blood Orange, Beet, and Mozzarella di Bufala

Serves 2 to 4

For the salad

1 large beet, scrubbed
1 bay leaf
4 small blood oranges, peeled
(skin and white pith removed)
and cut into thick slices
4 ounces (110 g) mozzarella di
bufala, drained and torn into
2 to 4 pieces
1 small handful fresh basil leaves

For the dressing

3 tbsp olive oil
1 tbsp balsamic vinegar
1 tbsp white balsamic vinegar
½ to 1 tsp date syrup
(or maple syrup)
Fine sea salt
Finely ground pepper

For the salad, bring a medium pot of salted water to a boil and add the beet and bay leaf then reduce the heat, cover, and simmer for about 45 to 50 minutes or until tender. Drain the beet and quickly rinse with cold water. When it's cool enough to handle, peel off the skin, and cut into thick slices.

For the dressing, whisk together the olive oil, both vinegars, and $1/2$ teaspoon of the date syrup in a small bowl. Season to taste with salt, pepper, and additional date syrup.

Arrange the beet and blood orange slices in overlapping circles on individual plates and place mozzarella in the middle of each. Drizzle with the dressing, sprinkle with basil, and serve immediately.

Serves 2

⅓ cup (75 ml) olive oil
16 large fresh sage leaves
7 ounces (200 g) dried spaghetti
6 heaping tbsp fresh ricotta
2 to 4 tsp freshly grated
orange zest
About 4 tbsp finely grated
Parmesan
Flaky sea salt
Coarsely ground pepper

Picture opposite, top left

This is a variation of my beloved Maltese Lemon Ricotta Pasta with Basil from my first book, *Eat In My Kitchen*. I like replacing the yellow citrus with orange, and sneaking in crispy fried sage leaves, which lend darker, slightly bitter woody tones to this smooth composition.

Spaghetti with Ricotta, Orange, and Crispy Sage

In a small saucepan, heat the olive oil over high heat. Add the sage and cook, stirring gently, for 10 to 20 seconds or until golden, green, and crispy—mind that the leaves don't burn. Transfer the sage leaves to a plate, reserving the sage oil.

Bring a large pot of salted water to a boil and cook the spaghetti, according to the package instructions, until al dente. Drain the spaghetti and return it to the pot. Add the reserved sage oil and toss to coat. Divide the spaghetti among plates, top with dollops of ricotta, and sprinkle with a little orange zest, crispy sage, and Parmesan. Season to taste with salt and pepper and enjoy.

Makes 2 sandwiches

4 slices ham
2 rustic white buns, cut in half
1 large ripe persimmon,
peeled and torn into chunks
4 to 6 thick slices aromatic cheese
that melts well, such as Raclette,
Comté, or Gruyère
Coarsely ground pepper
6 fresh basil leaves

Picture opposite, top right

Hawaii toast is actually a German classic, despite its name. This staple of my early years—ham, pineapple, and melted cheese layered on toast—is easy to prepare and never disappoints. I love adding soft, honey-gold persimmon and skipping the pineapple, shifting this iconic sandwich away from the usual trio and turning it into a more exciting version of itself.

Grilled Persimmon, Ham, and Cheese Sandwich

Set the oven to broil (quicker method) or preheat to 500°F (260°C).

Place 2 slices of ham on the bottom half of each bun. Arrange the persimmon on top and cover with the cheese. Place the sandwiches on a broiler pan or baking sheet. Put the sandwiches under the broiler, or roast at 500°F (260°C) for a few minutes or until the cheese starts to melt—mind that the cheese doesn't burn or slip off the fruit. Sprinkle the sandwiches with pepper and basil, place top of bun on each sandwich, and enjoy.

Candied orange peel gives sweet potatoes a unique sticky-sweet feel, while Kalamata olives play a soothing role, making sure the flavors are kept in balance. It's one of those combinations that is hard to imagine, but exciting for the taste buds.

Coriander-Braised Sweet Potatoes with Black Olives and Candied Orange Peel

Serves 2 to 4

For the candied orange peel
3 long strips fresh orange peel
(white pith removed),
about ½-inch wide (1.25 cm)
and cut into very thin strips
⅓ cup (75 ml) freshly squeezed
orange juice
3 tbsp water
1 tbsp honey

For the sweet potatoes
Olive oil
1 tsp coriander seeds, finely
crushed with a mortar and pestle
2 medium red onions,
each cut into 12 chunks
1 pound (450 g)
peeled sweet potatoes,
cut into ⅔-inch (1.5 cm) cubes
⅓ cup (75 ml) freshly squeezed
orange juice
⅓ cup (75 ml) water
Fine sea salt
Finely ground pepper
12 to 16 black olives,
preferably Kalamata

For the candied orange peel, in a small saucepan, bring the orange peel, orange juice, water, and honey to a boil then reduce the heat to medium-low and simmer for about 15 minutes or until the orange peel is golden and soft. Mind that the peel doesn't get dark and add a little more water or reduce the heat if necessary. Cover to keep warm and set aside.

When the candied orange peel is done, cook the sweet potatoes: In a large, heavy pan with a tight fitting lid, heat a generous splash of olive oil and the coriander seeds over medium-high heat for 15 seconds or until fragrant. Add the onions and sauté, stirring occasionally, for 5 minutes or until golden and soft. Add another splash of olive oil and the sweet potatoes and sauté for 2 minutes. Add the orange juice, water, and about 2 teaspoons of the candied orange peel. Season to taste with salt and pepper, cover the pan, and cook, stirring occasionally, for 10 to 15 minutes or until the sweet potatoes are tender, but still hold their shape. Stir in the olives and add a little more candied orange peel to taste. Serve immediately or as a cold salad.

5

week 1 / friday

Osso buco is a beloved classic from my mama's kitchen, the kind of cooking that smells so good that it makes your mouth water hours before you get to sit at the table. This slow-roasted stew from northern Italy will bring joy to any hungry crowd, spoiling it with tender meat, a beautifully fragrant sauce, and bone marrow that, when spread on warm, crusty bruschetta, tastes so unbelievably delicious that you won't need a side dish.

Osso Buco
with Bone Marrow Bruschetta

Serves 4

Olive oil
4 crosscut veal shanks,
each about ½ to ⅔ pound
(225 to 300 g)
Fine sea salt
Finely ground pepper
3 medium carrots, cut in half
lengthwise and sliced
1 celery stalk, cut into small cubes
1 medium onion, finely chopped
1 large clove garlic, cut in half
½ cup (120 ml) dry white wine
3 medium tomatoes, chopped
4 ¼ cups (1 liter) homemade
or quality store-bought vegetable
broth
7 slices dried porcini
1 large bay leaf
1 long strip fresh lemon peel
(white pith removed)
3 fresh sage leaves
1 medium sprig fresh thyme
1 medium sprig fresh rosemary
1 large loaf ciabatta bread,
cut into slices, for serving

Preheat the oven to 325°F (160°C).

In a Dutch oven, large enough to fit the meat and with a tight-fitting lid, heat a splash of olive oil over high heat. Working in batches, sear the veal shanks for 1 to 2 minutes per side or until evenly browned. Season to taste with salt and pepper and transfer to a plate.

Add another splash of olive oil to the Dutch oven, reduce the heat to medium, and sauté the carrots, celery, onion, and garlic for 3 minutes or until golden. Add the white wine and deglaze the pan, using a spatula to scrape any bits and pieces off the bottom. Return the veal to the Dutch oven and add the tomatoes, broth, dried porcini, bay leaf, lemon peel, sage, thyme, and rosemary. Stir, season to taste with salt and pepper, and bring to a boil. Cover the Dutch oven, transfer to the oven, and cook for 1½ hours or until the meat is tender. Take the veal shanks out of the sauce, transfer to a plate, and cover. Remove and discard the herbs then reduce the sauce over high heat until it has the desired taste and texture. Season to taste with salt and pepper. Return the veal shanks to the Dutch oven and keep warm.

Set the oven to broil (quicker method) or preheat to 425°F (220°C).

Drizzle the ciabatta slices with olive oil and put under the broiler for 1 to 2 minutes, or roast at 425°F (220°C) for about 2 minutes or until golden brown.

To serve, divide the veal shanks with sauce among plates. Let each guest scrape the marrow out of the bones then spread it onto the warm bruschetta, season with a little salt, and enjoy alongside the veal.

Somewhere in the snowy mountains of the Italian Dolomites lies a tiny and picturesque village that you can only reach via a dangerously narrow road. Surrounded by dark fir trees on one side and a deep gorge on the other, this daunting ascent will make you murmur a hurried prayer once you reach the village of Corvara safely. This is the ideal place to eat *Germknödel*, a mountain treat of spongy steamed yeast dumplings filled with plums and topped with vanilla custard and poppy seeds.

Germknödel
Plum-Filled Yeast Dumplings with Vanilla Custard and Poppy Seeds

Serves 4

For the dumplings

2 cups plus 1 tbsp (270 g)
all-purpose flour
2 tbsp granulated sugar
2 tsp fast-acting yeast
½ tsp ground cinnamon,
plus more for the plums
¼ tsp fine sea salt
½ cup (120 ml) whole milk,
lukewarm
3 tbsp (45 g) unsalted butter,
melted and cooled
1 large egg
2 small preserved, fresh, or frozen
plums, pitted and cut in half
4 tbsp ground poppy seeds

For the vanilla custard

2 cups plus 2 tbsp (510 ml)
whole milk
4 large egg yolks
½ cup (100 g) granulated sugar
¼ cup (30 g) cornstarch
⅛ tsp fine sea salt
1 vanilla bean, split lengthwise

9½-inch-wide (24 cm),
6-inch-tall (15 cm) pot
Cotton or linen tea towel
4 clothespins
9½-inch-wide (24 cm) metal
or heat-resistant bowl

For the dumplings, whisk together the flour, sugar, yeast, cinnamon, and salt in the bowl of a stand mixer fitted with the dough hook attachment. Whisk together the lukewarm milk, melted butter, and egg and add to the flour mixture then mix with the hook for 5 minutes or until smooth and well combined. Transfer the dough to a work surface and continue kneading with your hands for 4 minutes or until you have a soft and silky ball of dough. Place the dough back in the bowl, cover with a tea towel, and let rise in a warm place, or preferably in a 100°F (35°C) warm oven, for about 70 minutes or until doubled in size.

When the dough has doubled in size, punch it down, take it out of the bowl, and knead for about 30 seconds. Divide the dough into 4 equal parts and use your hands to form each into a 4-inch (10 cm) disc. Lay 1 plum half in the middle of each disc and sprinkle with a little cinnamon. Fold the sides up and around the plums and use your fingers to squeeze the dough together to close the dumplings and seal the plums tightly inside. Roll into balls and transfer the dumplings to a lightly floured baking dish or baking sheet. Cover with a tea towel and let rise in a warm place for about 20 minutes or until puffy.

Fill the tall pot about a third of the way full with water and bring to a boil. Take the pot off the heat, place a cotton or linen tea towel over the pot—mind the hot steam—and secure the towel with clothespins at the handles so that the towel hangs over the water without touching it. Mind that the towel is strong enough to hold the dumplings above the water. Arrange the dumplings tightly next to each other on the towel; they shouldn't touch the water. Place a metal or heat-resistant bowl upside down over the pot to create a tight fitting lid, turn the heat to a low simmer, and steam the dumplings for 20 minutes without lifting the bowl.

For the vanilla custard, in a small bowl, whisk ¼ cup (60 ml) of the milk with the egg yolks, sugar, cornstarch, and salt until well combined. In a medium saucepan, bring the remaining milk and the vanilla bean halves to a boil. Take the vanilla bean out and scrape the seeds from the pod into the milk. Whisking constantly, add the egg yolk mixture to the hot milk and bring to a boil. Take the saucepan off the heat and continue whisking for 2 minutes.

When the dumplings are done, lift the bowl, but mind the hot steam. Carefully transfer the towel with the dumplings to a work surface. Wait about 2 minutes, then use a knife to peel the dumplings off the towel. Separate the dumplings and serve, drizzled with the warm vanilla custard and sprinkled with the poppy seeds.

Here's a new discovery, made in Berlin, and thanks to some late night munchies after a concert. It's a perfect pizza bianca, topped with mozzarella di bufala, pecorino, guanciale (Italian cured pork cheek), and — to my big surprise — fresh mint leaves. Pizza heaven.

Pizza Bianca with Pecorino, Guanciale, and Mint

Makes 2 (11-inch / 28-cm) pizzas

For the dough

2⅔ cups (350 g)
all-purpose flour
1 (¼-ounce / 7-g) envelope
fast-acting yeast
1 tsp fine sea salt
¾ cup (180 ml) water, lukewarm
4 tbsp olive oil

For the topping

9 ounces (250 g) mozzarella di
bufala, drained and cut into
small cubes
7 ounces (200 g) aged pecorino,
coarsely grated
18 very thin slices guanciale
(or 12 slices prosciutto di Parma)
1 small handful fresh mint leaves
Coarsely ground pepper

Start the preparations about 2 hours before you want to enjoy the pizza. I bake it on a baking sheet that's been heated on the bottom of the oven like a pizza stone to help create a crunchy crust.

For the dough, combine the flour, yeast, and salt in the bowl of a stand mixer fitted with the dough hook attachment. Add the lukewarm water and olive oil and mix with the hook for a few minutes or until well combined. If the dough is too sticky, add more flour. Transfer the dough to a work surface and continue kneading and punching it down with your hands for about 4 minutes or until you have a smooth and elastic ball of dough. Place the dough back in the bowl, cover with a tea towel, and let rise in a warm place, or preferably in a 100°F (35°C) warm oven, for 50 to 60 minutes or until doubled in size.

When the dough has doubled in size, punch it down, take it out of the bowl, and divide into 2 equal parts. On a well-floured work surface or pizza peel, stretch and roll each piece of dough into an 11-inch (28 cm) disc. Cover with a tea towel and let rise in a warm place for about 20 minutes or until puffy.

Place a baking sheet (or pizza stone) on the bottom of the oven and preheat the oven to the highest temperature, 500°F (260°C) or higher.

Once the baking sheet is hot, carefully take it out of the oven, flip it over, and place it on a trivet or other heat-safe surface. Arrange 1 of the dough discs on the baking sheet and spread $1/2$ of the mozzarella and $1/3$ of the pecorino on the dough. Bake on the bottom of the oven for 8 to 9 minutes or until golden brown. Spread $1/2$ of the guanciale on top of the hot pizza and transfer to a plate. Repeat to make the second pizza. Sprinkle each pizza with $1/2$ of the remaining pecorino and $1/2$ of the mint, season to taste with pepper, and serve hot.

Whenever I hear Italian music, watch Fellini's *La Dolce Vita*, or open a bottle of dark Tuscan red wine, I feel like going straight to my kitchen to cook like an Italian mama. This hearty lasagna, filled with fennel and bacon, helps me embody this role gracefully.

Fennel and Tomato Lasagna with Crunchy Bacon

Serves 4 to 6

For the béchamel sauce

3 cups (720 ml) whole milk

1 large bay leaf

Nutmeg, preferably freshly grated

Fine sea salt

Finely ground pepper

2 tbsp (30 g) unsalted butter

¼ cup (30 g) all-purpose flour

For the lasagna

Olive oil

1 (¾-pound / 340-g) fennel bulb, cut in half lengthwise, cored, and thinly sliced lengthwise

Fine sea salt

Finely ground pepper

7 ounces (200 g) thick-cut bacon, cut into very small cubes

3 large cloves garlic, crushed

2 small dried chiles

2 tbsp fennel seeds

2 ⅔ pounds (1.2 kg) canned whole peeled tomatoes, chopped

About 9 ounces (250 g) no-boil lasagna noodles

4 ounces (110 g) Parmesan, coarsely grated

Picture page 14, bottom left

For the béchamel sauce, combine the milk, bay leaf, $1/4$ teaspoon of ground or freshly grated nutmeg, $1/4$ teaspoon of salt, and a pinch of pepper in a medium saucepan and bring to a boil. Immediately take the pan off the heat, remove and discard the bay leaf, and set aside. To make the roux for the béchamel, melt the butter in a separate medium saucepan over medium-high heat and as soon as it's sizzling hot, whisk in the flour. Slowly pour the hot milk mixture into the roux and whisk until smooth. Simmer on low, whisking occasionally, for 2 to 3 minutes or until the sauce starts to thicken. Season to taste with nutmeg, salt, and pepper and set aside.

Preheat the oven to 350°F (180°C). Butter a 10 x 8-inch (25 x 20 cm) baking dish (or a dish of roughly this size).

For the lasagna, in a large, heavy pan, heat a generous splash of olive oil over medium-high heat. Working in batches, arrange the fennel slices, side by side, in the pan and sauté for 1 to 2 minutes per side or until golden brown and al dente. Season to taste with salt and pepper and transfer to a plate, but leave the pan on the heat.

Add a little olive oil and the bacon to the pan and cook, stirring occasionally, over medium-high heat for about 7 minutes or until golden brown and crispy. Scrape the bacon to the sides of the pan. If the pan is too dry, add a little olive oil. Add the garlic, chile peppers, and fennel seeds and cook for 15 seconds then add the tomatoes, season to taste with salt and pepper, and cook, stirring occasionally, for about 10 minutes or until the sauce starts to thicken. Taste and season again with salt and pepper and take the pan off the heat. Reserve 3 tablespoons of the sauce.

Arrange a layer of lasagna noodles on the bottom of the prepared baking dish, spread with $1/3$ of the tomato-bacon sauce, followed by $1/4$ of the béchamel. Top with $1/3$ of the sautéed fennel and $1/4$ of the Parmesan. Repeat to make 2 more layers and top the last layer with lasagna noodles. Top the noodles with the reserved 3 tablespoons of tomato-bacon sauce, followed by the remaining béchamel and Parmesan. Bake for 35 to 45 minutes, depending on the lasagna package instructions, or until the pasta is al dente. To brown the cheese a little, you can switch on the broiler for the last 1 to 2 minutes. Let the lasagna sit for 5 to 10 minutes then divide among plates, sprinkle with pepper, and serve.

Celeriac is a neglected vegetable in my kitchen. I mainly use it to make broth, but rarely give it enough attention otherwise. With that in mind, here's a recipe that lets celeriac shine like a star. It's just a salad, but the cardamom-yogurt dressing, caramelized kumquats, and crunchy walnuts thrust it into the spotlight.

Celeriac Salad with Cardamom-Yogurt Dressing, Caramelized Honey Kumquats, and Walnuts

Serves 3 to 4

For the dressing

1 cup (220 g) full-fat plain
Greek yogurt
2 tbsp olive oil
½ tsp freshly grated orange zest,
plus 1 tsp for the topping
1 tbsp freshly squeezed
orange juice
¼ tsp ground cardamom,
plus more to taste
Fine sea salt
Finely ground pepper

For the salad

9 ounces (250 g) peeled celeriac,
grated
1 tbsp freshly squeezed
lemon juice
1 tbsp honey,
plus 1 to 2 tbsp for the topping
12 kumquats, cut in half lengthwise and seeds removed
(or 2 small oranges, peeled
and cut into segments)
¼ cup (60 ml) freshly squeezed
orange juice
1 large handful walnuts
Coarsely ground pepper

Picture page 14, bottom right

For the dressing, whisk together the yogurt, olive oil, 1/2 teaspoon of orange zest, orange juice, and cardamom. Season to taste with salt and finely ground pepper.

For the salad, mix the celeriac and lemon juice in a large bowl until well combined then drizzle with the dressing.

In a small, heavy pan, heat 1 tablespoon of honey over high heat until bubbling. Add the kumquats and orange juice and cook, turning once, for 3 to 4 minutes or until golden brown and soft—mind that they don't burn.

Season the celeriac to taste with additional cardamom and salt and arrange the kumquats on top. Sprinkle with the walnuts, coarsely ground pepper, and additional orange zest then drizzle with honey. Enjoy immediately or let the salad sit for up to 3 to 4 hours (it won't look as pretty).

Makes 4 to 6 crostini

4 to 6 thick slices ciabatta
(or baguette)
Olive oil
20 large cloves garlic,
preferably young, unpeeled
¼ to ½ tsp finely chopped fresh
rosemary needles
Fine sea salt
Finely ground pepper
12 to 18 small cherry tomatoes,
cut in half lengthwise

Oven-roasted garlic reveals different qualities from the raw bulb. It's more subtle, sweet, and even slightly smoky. Eating twenty roasted cloves at once is no problem at all, especially when they're mixed with rosemary and turned into a velvety paste that's scrumptiously spread on crostini.

Roasted Garlic and Rosemary Crostini with Cherry Tomatoes

Preheat the oven to 425°F (220°C).

Brush one side of the ciabatta slices with olive oil. Spread the bread, oiled-side up, and garlic in a large baking dish. Roast for a few minutes or until the bread is golden brown then remove it from the oven. Continue roasting the garlic, turning occasionally, for 20 to 25 minutes or until soft enough to mash with a fork — mind that it doesn't burn. Let the garlic cool for a few minutes then peel the cloves.

In a food processor or blender, purée the roasted garlic, 2 tablespoons of olive oil, and 1/4 teaspoon of the rosemary until smooth. Season to taste with salt, pepper, and additional rosemary.

Spread the garlic paste onto the ciabatta, arrange the tomatoes on top, drizzle with a little olive oil, and enjoy.

Serves 2 to 4

7 ounces (200 g)
fresh or frozen peas
3 tbsp olive oil
½ tsp honey
¼ tsp ground cumin,
plus more to taste
4 ounces (110 g)
pomegranate seeds
Fine sea salt
Finely ground pepper

Bright colors and flavors come together in a bowl full of green peas and pink pomegranate seeds, refined with a little cumin, olive oil, and honey. The preparation only takes a few minutes, which makes it a convenient choice for a veggie-packed breakfast or a quick lunch or dinner.

Peas and Pomegranate with Cumin Oil

Bring a small pot of salted water to a boil and blanch the peas for about 1 minute or until al dente. Drain and quickly rinse with cold water.

In small, heavy pan, heat the olive oil, honey, and cumin over medium heat for about 2 minutes or until fragrant. Add the peas and pomegranate seeds, stir to combine, and season to taste with salt, pepper, and additional cumin. Transfer to a medium bowl and serve warm or cold.

A chicken recipe can't really go wrong when you pull the five tasty Cs out of your spice box. Coriander, cumin, *curcuma longa* (turmeric), cardamom, and cayenne pepper add character to the bird, and the butter beans that cook alongside. Thirty minutes in the oven, a drizzle of lemon juice, and dinner's done. The magic of this complex quintet and the kitchen's heavenly aroma will have your guests begging for more.

Spice-Roasted Chicken with Butter Beans and Mint

Serves 2 to 4

4 whole chicken legs
Olive oil
1 tbsp freshly squeezed
lemon juice
1 tsp coriander seeds,
crushed with a mortar and pestle
1 tsp ground cumin
½ tsp ground turmeric
¼ tsp ground cardamom
¼ tsp ground cayenne pepper
¼ tsp coarsely ground pepper
Flaky sea salt
1¼ cups (250 g) drained
and rinsed canned butter
or cannellini beans
1 medium lemon,
cut into thin slices
1 small handful fresh mint leaves

Preheat the oven to 425°F (220°C).

Cut off and discard any large chunks of fat from the chicken legs and arrange in a baking dish just large enough to fit them in.

Whisk 3 tablespoons of olive oil with the lemon juice, coriander seeds, cumin, turmeric, cardamom, cayenne pepper, and pepper and pour over the chicken. Using your fingers, rub the marinade into the chicken skin until well coated. (If you have the time, cover the chicken and let it marinate in the refrigerator for 30 minutes or longer.) Season the chicken to taste with salt then spread the butter beans around the legs. Drizzle the beans with a little olive oil and season to taste with salt and pepper. Place the lemon slices on top of the chicken legs. Roast, spooning the juices from the pan over the chicken every 10 minutes or so, for 25 to 30 minutes or until the juices run clear when you prick the thickest part of a leg with a skewer. Turn on the broiler for 1 to 2 minutes or until the chicken skin is golden and starts sizzling, but mind that the beans don't burn.

Sprinkle with fresh mint and serve immediately. You can use leftovers to make sandwiches the next day.

A cozy soup with kale and beans cooked in a hot, clear broth is the perfect cure for winter blues. I use duck broth to add richness and flavor, and add poached eggs to crown this wholesome treat. When you cut through the yolk, the golden liquid sinks into the vegetables, lending an almost creamy feel to the soup. And you can turn any leftover kale leaves into a beautiful pesto (*recipe no. 15*).

Kale and Borlotti Bean Soup with Poached Eggs

Serves 4

For the soup
Olive oil
1 medium onion, cut into quarters
2 large cloves garlic, cut in half
7 ounces (200 g) trimmed kale leaves, cut into strips
5 ¼ cups (1.25 liters) homemade or quality store-bought duck, chicken, or vegetable broth, hot
1 small bunch fresh thyme
1 medium sprig fresh rosemary
1 large bay leaf
Fine sea salt
Finely ground pepper
1 ¼ cups (250 g) drained and rinsed canned borlotti (cranberry) or pinto beans

For the topping
4 to 8 large eggs
Coarsely ground pepper

For the soup, in a large pot, heat a splash of olive oil over medium heat and sauté the onion and garlic, stirring, for a few minutes or until golden and soft. Add the kale, stir, and cook for 1 minute then add the hot broth, thyme, rosemary, and bay leaf. Season to taste with salt and finely ground pepper, reduce the heat, and simmer for 20 minutes or until the kale is tender. Remove and discard the herbs then add the borlotti beans and cook for 1 minute. Season to taste with salt and finely ground pepper and keep warm.

For the topping, bring a small saucepan of salted water to a low simmer. Crack 1 egg into a small bowl. Hold a large spoon just over the surface of the water and gently pour the egg onto the spoon. Lower the spoon into the water and hold until the egg white starts to turn white then use a tablespoon to gently scoop the egg off the large spoon. Poach the egg for 3 minutes. Using a slotted ladle or spoon, transfer the egg to a plate. Poach the remaining eggs the same way, adjusting the heat as needed to maintain a low simmer. It's best to poach 1 egg at a time, but you can cook 2 at once.

Divide the soup among bowls, place 1 to 2 eggs in the middle of each bowl, and sprinkle with a little coarsely ground pepper. Cut the tops of the eggs with a sharp knife and serve immediately.

This glorious pink beauty is the successful fusion of my beloved teenage cake crush, red wine cake, combined with the classic German marbled chocolate Bundt cake. Airy and fluffy, with hints of bittersweet chocolate and a sticky, boozy glaze — it's a beautiful Sunday teatime treat.

Marbled Red Wine and Chocolate Bundt Cake

Serves 12

For the cake
Dry breadcrumbs,
for sprinkling the Bundt pan
6 large eggs, separated
⅛ tsp fine sea salt
2⅓ cups (300 g) all-purpose flour
1 tbsp baking powder
2 tsp ground cinnamon
2 tsp Dutch-process
or natural unsweetened
cocoa powder,
plus ⅓ cup (30 g) for
the chocolate batter
¾ cup plus 2 tbsp (200 g)
unsalted butter,
at room temperature
1¼ cups (250 g) granulated sugar,
plus 1 heaping tbsp
for the chocolate batter
½ cup (120 ml) dry red wine

For the icing
2¼ cups (225 g)
confectioners' sugar
¼ to ⅓ cup (60 to 75 ml)
dry red wine
1 tbsp finely grated
bittersweet chocolate

Preheat the oven to 350°F / 180°C (preferably convection setting). Butter a 7½-cup (1.75 liters) Bundt pan and sprinkle lightly with breadcrumbs.

For the cake, whisk the egg whites and salt in the bowl of a stand mixer fitted with the whisk attachment for a few minutes or until stiff. Transfer to a bowl and set aside.

In a large bowl, whisk together the flour, baking powder, cinnamon, and 2 teaspoons of cocoa powder.

In the bowl of a stand mixer fitted with the paddle attachment, beat the butter and 1¼ cups (250 g) of granulated sugar for 2 minutes or until fluffy. Add the egg yolks, 1 at a time, incorporating each yolk before adding the next one, and continue beating for a few minutes or until thick and creamy. Add the red wine and mix until well combined. With a wooden spoon, gently fold ⅓ of the egg white mixture into the butter mixture, followed by ⅓ of the flour mixture. Repeat with the remaining egg white and flour mixtures, folding until combined. Scrape half the red wine batter into the prepared Bundt pan.

For the chocolate batter, add the remaining ⅓ cup (30 g) of cocoa powder and the remaining 1 heaping tablespoon of granulated sugar to the remaining red wine batter and mix gently until well combined. Dollop the chocolate batter on top of the lighter batter in the pan and spread a little. Using a fork, swirl through the 2 batters from top to bottom, carefully pulling once all the way through the pan. Bake for about 40 minutes (slightly longer if using a conventional oven) or until golden and spongy. If you insert a skewer into the center of the cake, it should come out clean. Let cool for a few minutes then shake the Bundt pan a little and turn the cake out onto a plate. Let cool completely.

For the icing, whisk the confectioners' sugar with ¼ cup (60 ml) of the red wine in a medium bowl until smooth. If the icing is too thick, add more wine. Drizzle the icing over the cooled cake and sprinkle with the grated chocolate while the icing is still soft.

Inviting hard goat cheese and garlic to mingle with the earthy-green taste of kale transforms the blanched leaves into a proper pesto.

Spaghetti with Kale-Goat Gouda Pesto and Lemon

Serves 4

For the pesto

10 ounces (280 g) trimmed kale leaves

4 large cloves garlic

1 ounce (30 g) finely grated medium-aged goat's milk Gouda (or pecorino), plus more for serving

Olive oil

Fine sea salt

Finely ground pepper

For the pasta

14 ounces (400 g) dried spaghetti

1 to 2 tbsp freshly grated lemon zest

Coarsely ground pepper

For the pesto, bring a large pot of salted water to a boil and blanch the kale and garlic for 5 minutes or until the kale is tender. Using a slotted ladle or spoon, remove the kale and garlic from the pot and transfer to a large colander, reserving 1/2 cup (120 ml) of the cooking water. Quickly rinse the kale and garlic with cold water then squeeze the kale gently.

For the pasta, refill the pot used to cook the kale with water, add salt, and bring to a boil. Cook the spaghetti, according to the package instructions, until al dente. Drain the spaghetti, return it to the pot, and drizzle with a little olive oil.

While the pasta is boiling, purée the kale, garlic, 3 tablespoons of the reserved cooking water, 1 ounce (30 g) of grated cheese, and 3 tablespoons of olive oil in a food processor or blender until smooth. If the pesto is too thick, add more of the reserved cooking water and a little more olive oil. Season to taste with salt and finely ground pepper.

Divide the spaghetti among plates, add a generous dollop of the pesto, and sprinkle with cheese, a little lemon zest, and coarsely ground pepper. Serve immediately. You can also mix the pasta and pesto in the pot before you serve it, but I prefer to adjust the amount of pesto individually.

I love simple salads—the more bold the individual components, the fewer ingredients you need for the bowl. Dukkah, the Egyptian spice mixture made of nuts, seeds, and peppercorns, is a brilliant way to add a little heat and complexity to this quick salad made of velvety artichoke hearts and bittersweet pink grapefruit.

Preserved Artichokes with Pink Grapefruit and Dukkah

Serves 2 to 4

For the dukkah*
1 ounce (30 g) skin-on hazelnuts
1 ounce (30 g) salted pistachios
1 ounce (30 g) white
sesame seeds
1 ounce (30 g) unsalted
sunflower seeds
1 tsp fennel seeds,
crushed with a mortar and pestle
1 tsp coriander seeds,
crushed with a mortar and pestle
½ tsp black peppercorns,
crushed with a mortar and pestle
½ tsp flaky sea salt
¼ tsp ground cumin

For the salad
4 large artichoke hearts,
preserved in olive oil,
cut into quarters lengthwise
1 large grapefruit,
peeled (skin and white pith
removed) and cut into segments
2 tbsp olive oil
Flaky sea salt

For the dukkah, pulse the hazelnuts, pistachios, sesame seeds, sunflower seeds, fennel seeds, coriander seeds, crushed black peppercorns, salt, and cumin in a food processor or blender until crumbly then transfer to a bowl or an airtight jar.

For the salad, arrange the artichoke hearts and grapefruit segments on a large plate, or divide among small plates, drizzle with olive oil, and sprinkle generously with the dukkah. Season to taste with salt and serve immediately.

* You can use leftover dukkah for salads and soups and store it in an airtight container for about 1 month.

The smoky baked eggplant topping pairs so well with the balsamic-basil ricotta spread. Either dip would be delicious on its own, but as a duo they are unbeatable. Prepare a big batch to keep in the fridge for those spontaneous sandwich cravings.

Baked Eggplant and Balsamic-Basil Ricotta Tartine

Makes 8 small tartines

For the eggplant dip

1 medium eggplant,
cut in half lengthwise
3 tbsp olive oil
Flaky sea salt
Finely ground pepper
2 medium sprigs fresh rosemary
4 large cloves garlic, unpeeled
Fine sea salt

For the ricotta dip

4 ounces (110 g) fresh ricotta,
drained
1 tsp balsamic vinegar
16 large fresh basil leaves,
finely chopped
Fine sea salt
Finely ground pepper

For the tartines

8 thick slices baguette

Preheat the oven to 400°F (200°C).

For the eggplant dip, line a medium baking dish with a piece of aluminum foil large enough to wrap the eggplant in. Place the eggplant in the middle of the aluminum foil then coat with the olive oil and season to taste with flaky sea salt and pepper. Lay the eggplant halves next to each other, cut-side down, and tuck 1 sprig of rosemary underneath each half. Arrange the garlic around the eggplant. Wrap and close the foil package and bake for 40 minutes or until the eggplant pulp is soft—you should be able to scrape it out of its skin with a spoon. Peel the garlic and transfer to a medium bowl then chop 4 of the rosemary needles very finely and add to the bowl with the garlic; reserve the remaining rosemary. Scrape out the eggplant pulp with a spoon, add to the garlic, and mix and mash with a fork until soft and chunky. Season to taste with fine sea salt and pepper and set aside.

For the ricotta dip, in a small bowl, whisk together the ricotta, vinegar, and basil. Season to taste with fine sea salt and pepper.

For the tartines, spread the ricotta dip onto the baguette slices, add generous dollops of the eggplant dip, sprinkle with a little of the reserved baked rosemary, and serve.

With a jar of fresh ricotta, plus some fresh ginger, lemon zest, and Parmesan, you can easily transform simple cabbage leaves into surprisingly exciting parcels—just be a little patient when it's time to wrap it all up.

Ginger and Ricotta-Stuffed Cabbage Parcels with Lemon Butter

Serves 2

For the cabbage parcels
7 ounces (200 g) fresh ricotta, drained
2 large eggs
1 ounce (30 g) Parmesan, finely grated, plus more for the topping
2 tsp freshly grated ginger
1¼ tsp freshly grated lemon zest, plus more for the topping
Fine sea salt
Finely ground pepper
8 large white or green cabbage leaves
About ½ cup (120 ml) dry white wine

For the lemon butter
¼ cup (60 g) unsalted butter
1 tbsp freshly squeezed lemon juice
Fine sea salt
Finely ground pepper

Preheat the oven to 400°F (200°C). Butter a baking dish just large enough to fit 8 small cabbage parcels.

For the cabbage parcels, whisk together the ricotta, eggs, Parmesan, ginger, and lemon zest. Season to taste with salt and pepper.

Bring a large pot of salted water to a boil and blanch the cabbage leaves for 5 to 8 minutes or until tender. Drain and quickly rinse with cold water then dry with paper towels and cut out the thick, hard stalks (just at the bottom). Spread the cabbage leaves on a work surface and season to taste with salt and pepper. Divide the ricotta filling among the cabbage leaves, placing it in the center of each cabbage leaf. Working quickly, as the filling will spread, fold the 4 sides of each cabbage leaf up and over the ricotta filling, overlapping them on the top, then flip the cabbage parcels over and transfer, seam-side down, to the prepared baking dish. Add enough white wine to cover the bottom of the dish then bake for 45 to 50 minutes or until golden and the ricotta is set.

For the lemon butter, heat the butter and lemon juice, whisking constantly, in a small saucepan over high heat until it starts sizzling. Season to taste with salt and pepper.

Divide the cabbage parcels among plates, cut in half, and drizzle with the lemon butter. Sprinkle with a little lemon zest and Parmesan, season to taste with pepper, and serve.

20

21

22

25

Olive oil
1 tbsp freshly squeezed
orange juice
1 tbsp white balsamic vinegar
¼ tsp freshly grated lemon zest
¾ tsp freshly grated ginger
Fine sea salt
Finely ground pepper
1¼ cups (250 g) drained
and rinsed canned butter
or cannellini beans
1 small red onion,
cut in half and very thinly sliced
1 (9-ounce / 250-g) tuna steak,
about 1-inch thick (2.5 cm)

Seared tuna steaks should only touch the pan for a few minutes and stay a little pink inside, or they'll dry out. The preparation of the butter bean salad with red onion doesn't take much longer, making this just the right meal for those hectic, busy times in life.

Ginger-Lemon Tuna with Butter Beans and Red Onion

In a medium bowl, whisk together 3 tablespoons of olive oil, the orange juice, vinegar, 1/8 teaspoon of the lemon zest, and 1/2 teaspoon of the ginger. Season to taste with salt and pepper. Add the butter beans and onion, toss to combine, and season to taste with salt and pepper.

In a small, heavy pan, heat a splash of olive oil over high heat and sear the tuna for 1 to 11/2 minutes per side or until flaky but still pink inside. Season to taste with salt and pepper and sprinkle with the remaining lemon zest and ginger.

Divide the beans among plates, cut the tuna in half, and serve on top of the beans.

Butter, to butter the pan
3 cups plus 2 tbsp (350 g)
ground skin-on almonds
(or hazelnuts)
2 tbsp freshly grated blood
orange zest
1 tbsp ground cinnamon
7 large eggs
1¾ cups (350 g) granulated sugar
2 tbsp freshly squeezed
blood orange juice
Confectioners' sugar,
to dust the cake

Picture opposite, top left

Traditional Galician *Torta de Santiago* originated in the Middle Ages, when no one was thinking about gluten or fat-free baking. It contains no butter or flour, and relies on just three main ingredients: almonds, sugar, and eggs. The inside is almost fudgy, but before you carve a path to the scrumptious core, you have to break through the crispy crust, delicately cracking it like a French macaron.

Spanish Almond Tart with Blood Orange

Preheat the oven to 350°F (180°C). Butter an 8-inch (20 cm) springform pan.

In a large bowl, combine the ground almonds, blood orange zest, and cinnamon.

In the bowl of a stand mixer fitted with the whisk attachment, whisk the eggs and granulated sugar for 1 to 2 minutes or until light and fluffy.

Gently fold the almond mixture and blood orange juice into the egg mixture until just combined. Scrape the batter into the prepared pan and bake for about 55 minutes or until golden brown and springy on top. If you insert a skewer into the cake, it should come out almost clean, but mind that the center should be a little fudgy. Let the cake cool for 10 minutes then transfer to a large plate and dust with a little confectioners' sugar for serving.

At least once a month you'll find a buttery golden quiche bubbling and baking in my oven. The pastry base is a trusted recipe that hasn't changed over the years, but the topping varies, depending on what I find in my fridge or pantry. Fennel bulbs help fill the gap before spring's greens are back and their subtle hint of licorice goes well with the eggy filling.

Fennel Tart

Serves 4 to 8

For the pastry

2 cups (260 g) all-purpose flour
1 tsp fine sea salt
½ cup plus 1 tbsp (130 g) unsalted butter, cold
1 large egg

For the filling

Olive oil
1 (14-ounce / 400-g) fennel bulb, cut in half lengthwise, cored, and very thinly sliced lengthwise
3 large eggs
½ cup (120 ml) heavy cream
½ cup (120 g) sour cream (or crème fraîche)
2 heaping tbsp finely grated Parmesan
¾ tsp fine sea salt
Finely ground pepper
Nutmeg, preferably freshly grated

Picture page 34, top right

For the pastry, combine the flour and salt in the bowl of a stand mixer fitted with the dough hook attachment. Add the butter and use a knife to cut it into the flour until there are just small pieces left. Quickly rub the butter into the flour with your fingers until combined. Add the egg and mix with the hook until crumbly. Form the dough into a thick disc, wrap it in plastic wrap, and freeze for 10 minutes.

Preheat the oven to 400°F (200°C).

On a work surface, place the dough between 2 sheets of plastic wrap and use a rolling pin to roll out into a disc, large enough to line the bottom and sides of a 12-inch (30 cm) quiche dish. Fit the dough into the quiche dish, pushing it into the dish, especially along the edges. Let the dough hang over the rim a little or trim with a knife. Use a fork to prick the dough all over. Bake for 15 minutes or until golden. If the dough bubbles up, push it down with a fork. Take the quiche dish out of the oven and reduce the heat to 350°F (180°C).

While the pastry is baking, prepare the filling: In a large, heavy pan, heat a splash of olive oil over medium-high heat. Add the fennel and sauté, stirring occasionally, for about 5 minutes or until golden and tender. Season to taste with salt and pepper and let cool for a few minutes.

In a medium bowl, whisk together the eggs, heavy cream, sour cream, Parmesan, salt, and generous amounts of pepper and nutmeg.

Arrange the fennel on top of the pre-baked pastry. Slowly pour the egg mixture over the fennel and bake for about 40 to 50 minutes or until the top is golden and firm and the pastry is crispy. Let it cool for 10 minutes. Serve warm or cold.

My mother's meatloaf is one of my favorite dishes. Moist and almost gooey, refined with fresh herbs, and so easy to prepare—it's the perfect tidbit for family parties and picnics. I fell for it with my very first bite, greedily wolfing it down with joy and pleasure. Here I pick up on my mother's tradition, while adding lots of coriander, cumin, juicy dates, and fruity orange, transforming this vintage German recipe into a fragrant loaf.

Coriander-Cumin Meatloaf with Dates and Orange

Serves 6 to 8

1½ cups plus 1 tbsp (375 ml) whole milk
⅓ cup (50 g) dry breadcrumbs
2 ¼ pounds (1 kg) ground beef
8 ounces (225 g) pitted dates, cut into small cubes
2 large eggs
3 large cloves garlic, crushed
3 tbsp fresh thyme leaves, plus 10 small sprigs for the topping
2 tbsp finely chopped fresh rosemary needles
1 tbsp freshly grated orange zest
Finely ground pepper
3½ tsp fine sea salt
1 tbsp ground cumin
1 tbsp coriander seeds, crushed with a mortar and pestle
1 orange, cut into thin slices

Picture page 34, bottom left

Preheat the oven to 350°F (180°C).

In a medium bowl, stir together the milk and breadcrumbs and let soak for 5 minutes.

In a large bowl, combine the beef, dates, eggs, garlic, thyme leaves, rosemary, orange zest, and a generous amount of pepper. In a small bowl, whisk together the salt, cumin, and coriander seeds and add to the meat mixture then add the breadcrumb mixture and mix together with your hands until well combined. Transfer the meatloaf mixture to a baking dish and form into a 10 x 5-inch (25 x 12.5 cm) loaf. Arrange the orange slices and a few thyme sprigs on top then sprinkle the remaining thyme sprigs around the meatloaf. Bake for about 1 hour and 20 minutes or until golden brown and cooked through; serve warm or cold.

23

Serves 2 to 4

For the dressing
3 tbsp olive oil
1 tbsp balsamic vinegar
1 tbsp white balsamic vinegar
Fine sea salt
Finely ground pepper

For the salad
2 small heads Belgian endive,
cut in half lengthwise and sliced
2 large ripe persimmons,
peeled and torn into chunks
About 1 tsp pink peppercorns,
lightly crushed with a mortar
and pestle

Give this salad a try and bitter endive and sweet persimmon will melt delicately in your mouth, while the subtle heat and crunch of pink peppercorns will gently invigorate your taste buds.

Belgian Endive and Persimmon Salad with Pink Peppercorns

For the dressing, whisk together the olive oil and both vinegars. Season to taste with salt and pepper.

For the salad, arrange the endives and persimmons on a large platter or individual plates. Drizzle with the dressing, sprinkle with the crushed pink peppercorns, and serve immediately.

24

Makes 2 sandwiches

For the pesto
1 ounce (30 g) fresh basil leaves
1 ounce (30 g) Parmesan,
finely grated
1 ounce (30 g) pine nuts, toasted
⅓ cup (75 ml) olive oil
1 clove garlic
Fine sea salt

For the sandwiches
8 thin slices prosciutto di Parma
4 ounces (110 g) mozzarella di
bufala, drained and cut into slices
2 round focaccia buns, cut in half
1 small handful pine nuts, toasted

Prosciutto, mozzarella, and pesto are a divine trio. Stuff these Italian gems inside oily focaccia and you'll jump with joy.

Prosciutto di Parma and Mozzarella di Bufala Focaccia with Basil Pesto

For the pesto, purée the basil, Parmesan, pine nuts, olive oil, and garlic in a food processor or blender until smooth. Season to taste with salt and set aside.

For the sandwiches, place half the prosciutto and mozzarella on the bottom half of each bun, then drizzle with the pesto and sprinkle with pine nuts. Place a top on each bun and enjoy.

Smooth polenta refined with a bunch of fresh herbs creates a beautifully fluffy bed for crunchy parsnip chips. Drizzling sticky maple butter over the composition creates an unusual yet comforting meal, perfect for one of those cozy nights when dinner shifts from the table to the sofa.

Fresh Herb Polenta with Parsnip Chips and Maple Butter

Serves 2

For the polenta
1 cup (240 ml) whole milk
1 cup (240 ml) water,
plus more as needed
1 tsp fine sea salt
2 tbsp olive oil
¾ cup (120 g) fine polenta

For the parsnip chips
Sunflower oil
7 ounces (200 g) peeled parsnips,
very thinly sliced on a mandoline
Fine sea salt

For the maple butter
2 tbsp (30 g) unsalted butter
½ to 1 tbsp maple syrup

For the topping
1 to 2 tsp finely chopped fresh
rosemary needles
1 to 2 tsp finely chopped fresh
thyme leaves
Finely ground pepper

Picture page 34, bottom right

For the polenta, bring the milk, water, and salt to a boil in a medium saucepan. Take the pan off the heat, add the olive oil and polenta, and whisk until combined. Place the saucepan over the lowest heat setting and cook the polenta like a risotto, stirring occasionally and adding a little more water whenever the polenta starts to thicken, for 10 minutes or until smooth and creamy. Cover and set aside.

For the parsnip chips, cover the bottom of a large, heavy sauté pan generously with sunflower oil and place over medium-high heat. When the oil is hot, in batches, arrange the parsnip slices, side by side, in the pan and fry for a few seconds per side or until golden and crispy. Reduce the heat if they brown too quickly. Transfer to paper towels to drain and season to taste with salt. Repeat with the remaining parsnip, adding more oil if necessary.

For the maple butter, melt the butter in a small saucepan over medium-high heat. When the butter starts sizzling, add 1/2 tablespoon of the maple syrup and whisk until smooth. Season to taste with additional maple syrup.

Divide the polenta among the bowls and drizzle with the maple butter. Arrange the parsnip chips on top, sprinkle with a little rosemary and thyme, and season to taste with pepper. Serve immediately.

Beef rolls were my granny's signature dish, the highlight of her scrumptious Sunday lunches. The thin meat was so tender that you could cut it with a fork. This German delicacy is wrapped around a hearty filling made of gherkins and prosciutto, then cooked in a whole bottle of dark red wine. Because you end up with a lot of sauce, we love to serve beef roulades with spongy potato dumplings, creating a meal of German favorites — meat, carbs, and sauce.

German Beef Roulades with Potato Dumplings

Serves 4

For the beef roulades

4 large, ¼-inch-thick (0.5 cm) beef round steaks (each roughly 12 × 4-inches / 30 x 10-cm, about 1½ pounds / 680 g total)

Fine sea salt

Finely ground pepper

6 tsp tomato paste

4 tsp Dijon mustard

8 thin slices Tyrolean prosciutto (or prosciutto di Parma)

4 large pickled gherkins, thinly sliced lengthwise

Olive oil

2 medium carrots, cut in half lengthwise and sliced

1 celery stalk, cut into cubes

⅓ leek (white and light green parts only), thinly sliced

¼ medium celeriac, peeled and cut in half

2 large cloves garlic, cut in half

¼ cup (60 ml) brandy (or port)

1 (750-ml) bottle full-bodied red wine

1 small bunch fresh thyme

3 fresh sage leaves

5 juniper berries, crushed

5 allspice berries

5 whole cloves

1 large bay leaf

Elderflower syrup (or any flowery syrup), for the sauce

8 toothpicks (or ovenproof cotton string), to tie the roulades

For the beef roulades, place a large piece of plastic wrap on a work surface. Arrange the steaks, side by side, on top of the plastic wrap and season to taste with salt and pepper. Spread 1 teaspoon of the tomato paste and 1 teaspoon of the mustard evenly onto each steak. Top each steak with 2 slices of prosciutto and ¼ of the gherkins. Roll up the steaks tightly and secure each roulade with 2 toothpicks or cotton string wrapped around each roulade.

In a Dutch oven large enough to fit the meat and with a tight-fitting lid, heat a splash of olive oil over medium-high heat. Working in batches, sear the roulades, turning them once, for 1 to 2 minutes or until evenly browned. Season the meat to taste with salt and pepper then transfer to a plate, but leave the Dutch oven on the heat. Add the carrots, celery, leek, celeriac, and garlic and sauté for 1 minute. Add the remaining 2 teaspoons of the tomato paste, stir, and cook for 1 minute then add the brandy and deglaze the pan, using a spatula to scrape any bits and pieces off the bottom. Return the meat to the Dutch oven, add the red wine, thyme, sage, juniper berries, allspice berries, cloves, and bay leaf and season to taste with salt and pepper—the meat should be almost covered with wine. Cover the Dutch oven and bring to a boil, then reduce the heat and simmer gently over medium-low heat for 2½ to 3 hours or until the meat is tender. Remove and discard the herbs then transfer the meat to a plate and cover. Bring the sauce to a boil and reduce for 1 to 2 minutes or until it reaches the desired taste and texture. Season to taste with salt, pepper, and a dash of elderflower syrup and return the meat to the Dutch oven.

While the meat is cooking, prepare the potato dumplings: Bring a large pot of salted water to a boil and cook the potatoes for 15 to 18 minutes or until very soft. Use a slotted ladle or spoon to transfer the potatoes to a colander. Drain and leave in the colander for 2 minutes. Press the warm potatoes through a potato ricer into a large bowl; if there's any water in the bowl, use a spoon to remove it. Add the butter and egg yolks, stir to combine, and let cool at room temperature for 30 minutes or until completely cool, or refrigerate for about 15 minutes.

Once the potato mixture is completely cool, add the flour, salt, nutmeg, and a generous amount of pepper then quickly stir to combine. If the mixture is too soft and not firm enough to roll into a ball, gradually add more flour. Lightly dust your hands and a work surface with flour. Take a heaping tablespoon of the potato mixture into your fingers and form into a thick disc. Gently press 3 cubes of bread in the center of the disc then roll into a ball to seal the bread inside the dumpling. Repeat with the remaining dough to make 10 to 12 dumplings.

For the potato dumplings

1 pound (450 g) peeled
starchy potatoes, cut into cubes
2 tbsp (30 g) unsalted butter
2 large egg yolks
1 cup (130 g) all-purpose flour
1½ tsp fine sea salt
½ tsp nutmeg, preferably
freshly grated
Finely ground pepper
3 slices soft white bread,
cut into ½-inch (1.25 cm) cubes

Bring a large pot of salted water to a boil. Working in batches, add the dumplings and simmer for about 10 minutes or until they float to the top—mind that they don't stick to the bottom of the pot. Use a slotted ladle or spoon to scoop the dumplings out of the water then drain and place them in an ovenproof dish. Cover and keep them in a warm oven while you cook the remaining dumplings, bringing the water back to a boil between the batches.

Serve the beef roulades with the potato dumplings and a small ladleful of the sauce.

For years I happily baked peanut butter cookies following the recipe from my partner's granny in the U.S. and never thought anything could improve on this trusted formula. However, when you add chunky bittersweet chocolate and chopped peanuts, you open entirely new doors to peanut butter heaven.

Peanut Butter-Chocolate Chunk Cookies

Makes about 40 cookies

2 cups plus 2 tbsp (275 g) all-purpose flour
2 tsp baking soda
¼ tsp fine sea salt
1⅓ cups (350 g) smooth peanut butter, at room temperature
1 cup plus 2 tbsp (250 g) unsalted butter, at room temperature
1¼ cups (280 g) light brown sugar
2 large eggs
6 ounces (170 g) bittersweet chocolate, roughly chopped
3 ounces (85 g) unsalted roasted peanuts, roughly chopped

Preheat the oven to 350°F / 180°C (preferably convection setting). Line 2 baking sheets with parchment paper.

In a medium bowl, whisk together the flour, baking soda, and salt.

In the bowl of a stand mixer fitted with the paddle attachment, beat the peanut butter, butter, and light brown sugar until light and fluffy. Add the eggs, 1 at a time, incorporating each egg before adding the next one, and continue beating for 1 minute. Gradually add the flour mixture and mix until combined then fold in the chocolate.

Shovel a large spoonful of dough into one hand, form into a $1^1/_2$-inch (4 cm) ball, and transfer to a lined baking sheet. Gently flatten the dough a little with a fork. Repeat to make 11 more cookies, arranging them on 1 lined baking sheet and leaving a roughly $1^1/_2$-inch (4 cm) space in between them. Sprinkle the cookies with a small spoonful of chopped peanuts and push the nuts gently into the dough. Bake for 10 to 11 minutes (slightly longer if using a conventional oven) or until golden but still a little soft in the center. Let the cookies cool for 2 minutes. When they are firm enough to be moved, carefully transfer them to a rack to cool completely. Continue shaping the remaining dough and bake 1 sheet at a time.

Once the cookies are completely cool, store in an airtight container for up to 1 week.

Cauliflower can be a little much when its cabbagey side overwhelms the taste buds. This vegetable needs to be kept in its place by partners with bright flavors, such as gremolata, a fresh Italian condiment made with parsley, lemon, and garlic. A little tahini stirred into this warming soup also does a great job taming and enhancing this knobbly vegetable.

Cauliflower Soup with Tahini and Gremolata

Serves 2 to 4

For the gremolata
4 tbsp finely chopped fresh
flat-leaf parsley leaves
1 small clove garlic, crushed
2 tsp freshly grated lemon zest
½ tsp freshly squeezed
lemon juice

For the soup
Olive oil
1 medium onion, chopped
1 clove garlic, crushed
1 pound (450 g) cored cauliflower,
cut into 2-inch (5 cm) florets
3⅓ cups (800 ml) homemade
or quality store-bought
vegetable broth, hot
2 long strips fresh lemon peel
(white pith removed)
2 tbsp freshly squeezed
lemon juice
1 bay leaf
Nutmeg, preferably freshly grated
Fine sea salt
Finely ground pepper
2 to 3 tbsp light tahini

For the gremolata, mix the parsley, garlic, lemon zest, and lemon juice in a small bowl.

For the soup, in a large pot, heat a splash of olive oil over medium heat. Add the onion and garlic and sauté, stirring, for a few minutes or until golden and soft. Add the cauliflower, hot broth, lemon peel, lemon juice, and bay leaf and stir to combine. Season to taste with nutmeg, salt, and pepper. Bring to a boil then reduce the heat, cover, and simmer for about 10 minutes or until the cauliflower is tender. Remove the bay leaf and lemon peel and discard. Use a slotted ladle or spoon to remove about 3 ounces (85 g) of the cauliflower florets, break or cut them into bite-size florets, and set aside. Add 2 tablespoons of the tahini to the soup and purée in a food processor or blender, or with an immersion blender, until smooth. Season to taste with additional tahini, nutmeg, salt, and pepper.

Divide the soup and reserved cauliflower florets among bowls, sprinkle with the gremolata and some pepper, and drizzle with a little olive oil.

Making your own gnocchi takes a little longer than cooking pasta, but it's definitely worth the effort. Once the work is done, it's unbelievably satisfying to enjoy a plate of these fluffy pillows, each one shaped with love, patience, and affection. Spinach is an earthy, green alternative to potato gnocchi and it goes perfectly with a creamy mushroom and bacon sauce.

Spinach Gnocchi with Mushrooms and Bacon

Serves 3 to 4

For the gnocchi
18 ounces (500 g) trimmed spinach leaves
9 ounces (250 g) fresh white bread, finely ground in a blender or food processor
About ½ cup (65 g) all-purpose flour, plus more as needed
2 ounces (60 g) finely grated Parmesan, plus more for serving
2 large egg yolks
1½ tsp fine sea salt
Nutmeg, preferably freshly grated
Finely ground pepper

For the mushroom-bacon sauce
Olive oil
2 ounces (60 g) thick-cut bacon, cut into very small cubes
10 ounces (280 g) trimmed cremini mushrooms, cut into slices
Fine sea salt
Finely ground pepper
¼ cup (60 ml) brandy (or port)
¾ cup (180 ml) heavy cream

For the gnocchi, bring a large pot of salted water to a boil and blanch the spinach for about 1½ minutes or until tender. Transfer to a colander, drain, and quickly rinse with cold water. Leave the spinach in the colander to cool for 5 minutes then squeeze until it's quite dry. Transfer to a food processor or blender and purée finely.

Bring a large pot of salted water to a boil.

In a large bowl, mix the puréed spinach, fresh breadcrumbs, flour, Parmesan, egg yolks, salt, and generous amounts of nutmeg and pepper until well combined. If the mixture is too soft and not firm enough to roll into a log, gradually add more flour. Lightly dust your hands and a work surface with flour. Roll a quarter of the dough into a 1-inch-thick (2.5 cm) log. Cut the log into 1-inch (2.5 cm) pieces and transfer to a well-floured baking sheet. Repeat with the remaining dough to make more gnocchi.

Working in batches, add the gnocchi to the boiling water and simmer, reducing the heat if necessary, for about 4 minutes or until they float to the top—mind that they don't stick to the bottom of the pot. Use a slotted ladle or spoon to scoop the gnocchi out of the water then quickly drain and place them in an ovenproof dish. Cover and keep them in a warm oven while you finish cooking the gnocchi, bringing the water back to a boil between batches.

For the mushroom-bacon sauce, heat a splash of olive oil in a large, heavy pan over medium-high heat. Add the bacon and cook for 5 to 7 minutes or until golden brown and crispy. Transfer the bacon to a plate, but leave the pan on the heat. If the pan is dry, add a little more olive oil, then add the mushrooms and sauté over high heat, turning occasionally, for 2 to 3 minutes or until golden brown and al dente. Season to taste with salt and pepper then add the brandy, stir, and cook for 15 seconds. Add the heavy cream and bring to a boil, stirring gently. Season to taste with salt and pepper and take the pan off the heat.

Divide the gnocchi among plates, arrange the mushrooms and bacon on top, and drizzle with the sauce. Sprinkle with a little Parmesan and pepper and serve immediately.

A plate of colorful rainbow potatoes, looking pretty in purple, pink, and yellow, plus a juicy cucumber and a vibrant green dill-pistachio pesto, brightens up even the gloomiest of January days.

Rainbow Potato and Cucumber Salad with Dill-Pistachio Pesto

Serves 2 to 4

For the pesto

1 ounce (30 g) salted pistachios
1 ounce (30 g) fresh dill
¼ cup (15 g) finely grated
mild pecorino
⅓ cup (75 ml) olive oil
Fine sea salt

For the salad

13 ounces (370 g) small rainbow
potatoes, preferably purple, pink,
and yellow, scrubbed and boiled
½ large English cucumber,
scrubbed and sliced
2 tbsp olive oil
Fine sea salt
Coarsely ground pepper
1 large sprig fresh dill,
roughly chopped
1 small handful salted pistachios,
roughly chopped

For the pesto, purée the pistachios, dill, pecorino, and olive oil in a food processor or blender until smooth. Season to taste with salt and transfer to a small bowl.

For the salad, cut the boiled potatoes in half lengthwise and arrange, along with the cucumber, on a large platter. Drizzle with the pesto and olive oil and season to taste with salt and pepper. Sprinkle with the chopped dill and pistachios and serve.

Classic crostini is the easiest way to have a delicious little nibble at hand in the kitchen, while you're chopping and stirring, listening to music, and sipping a glass of wine. It's just toasted white bread, rubbed with garlic and drizzled with olive oil. Try replacing the white bread with dark spelt or rye bread and you'll have a treat that's a bit heartier.

Garlic-Rubbed Spelt Crostini

Serves 1

2 thick slices dark spelt
or rye bread
1 large clove garlic,
preferably from a very fresh bulb
Olive oil
Flaky sea salt
Coarsely ground pepper

Toast the bread under the broiler, or make your life easier and use a toaster, until golden brown and crunchy. Rub the warm bread with the garlic, squeezing the clove so that its juices melt into the bread. Drizzle with a little olive oil, season to taste with salt and pepper, and enjoy.

February

Lentils tend to get lost and forgotten in the dark corners of my pantry for months, sometimes even years. The entire family of tiny legumes, whether red, green, yellow, or black, offers so many possibilities to create an exciting lunch or dinner. The nuttiness and glowing shades of red lentils, for example, pair beautifully with harissa, tahini sauce, and candy-sweet caramelized onions.

Spicy Harissa Lentils with Lemon Tahini and Sweet Onions

Serves 2

For the lentils

1 cup (220 g) red lentils
(no soaking required)
2 cups plus 2 tbsp (510 ml)
homemade or quality store-
bought unsalted vegetable broth
1 tbsp olive oil
1 tsp harissa paste,
plus more to taste
Fine sea salt
Finely ground pepper

For the topping

Olive oil
2 medium onions,
cut in half and thinly sliced
¼ tsp granulated sugar
Coarsely ground pepper
12 fresh flat-leaf parsley leaves,
roughly chopped

For the tahini sauce

3 tbsp olive oil
2 large cloves garlic, crushed
1½ tbsp light tahini
1 to 2 tsp freshly squeezed
lemon juice
Fine sea salt
Finely ground pepper

For the lentils, in a medium saucepan, bring the lentils and broth to a boil then reduce the heat and simmer, adding more water if necessary, for 8 minutes or until tender (or follow the package instructions). There should be almost no cooking liquid left when the lentils are done. Add the olive oil and harissa, stir, and season to taste with salt, finely ground pepper, and additional harissa.

For the topping, in a medium, heavy pan, heat a splash of olive oil over medium-high heat and cook the onions, stirring occasionally, for about 12 minutes or until golden brown and soft. Add the sugar, stir, and caramelize the onions for 1 minute.

For the tahini sauce, heat the olive oil and garlic in a small saucepan over medium heat for about 2 minutes or until the garlic is golden. Transfer to a medium bowl and let cool for 2 minutes. Add the tahini and 1 teaspoon of the lemon juice and whisk until combined then season to taste with salt, finely ground pepper, and additional lemon juice.

Divide the lentils among bowls and drizzle with the tahini sauce and a little harissa. Sprinkle with the onions, coarsely ground pepper, and parsley and serve.

Lapskaus is a traditional northern German stew that embodies comfort food in all its glory. Don't be misled by the fact that the dish is not aesthetically appealing. The taste and the unusual combination of ground beef, beet, and gherkins is definitely one to fall for and a reminder that looks are not everything.

Lapskaus—German Beef, Beet, and Potato Stew with Pickled Gherkins and Fried Eggs

Serves 4 to 6

Olive oil
2 medium onions, finely chopped
2 cloves garlic, cut in half
1⅓ pounds (600 g) ground beef
1 pound (450 g)
peeled waxy potatoes,
cut into ¾-inch (2 cm) cubes
1 pound (450 g) peeled beets,
cut into ¾-inch (2 cm) cubes
4¼ cups (1 liter) homemade
or quality store-bought vegetable
or chicken broth
8 whole cloves
6 allspice berries
2 bay leaves
¼ tsp ground nutmeg, preferably
freshly grated
Fine sea salt
Finely ground pepper
10 pickled gherkins,
cut into very small cubes
⅓ cup plus 1 tbsp (90 ml)
pickling liquid from the gherkins,
plus more to taste
About 1 tbsp unsalted butter,
to cook the eggs
4 to 6 large eggs

Picture opposite, top left

In a large pot, heat a splash of olive oil over medium heat. Add the onions and garlic and sauté for a few minutes or until golden and soft. Add a little more olive oil and the beef and cook, stirring to break up the meat, for a few minutes or until no more liquid comes out and the meat is browned. Add the potatoes, beets, broth, cloves, allspice, bay leaves, and nutmeg and season to taste with salt and pepper. Bring to a boil, reduce the heat, and simmer for 60 minutes.

Reserve 2 tablespoons of the gherkins and set aside. Add the remaining gherkins and the pickling liquid to the stew. Season to taste with salt, pepper, nutmeg, and additional pickling liquid, aiming for a subtle sweet-and-sour touch.

In a large, heavy pan, heat the butter over medium heat and fry the eggs to the desired doneness—the yolks should be runny.

Divide the lapskaus among bowls, sprinkle with the reserved gherkins, and place the fried eggs on top. Sprinkle with a little pepper and serve.

33

34

35

36

Rather than showing off the fruit in all its baked beauty on top of the loaf, this sticky banana gingerbread swallows it instead. It might look less pretty, but you'll be rewarded with an intense banana flavor found deep inside the loaf, combined with a heavenly soft and gooey texture. I use sugar beet syrup for this recipe—a popular German breakfast spread with a deep malty caramel taste—but you can substitute it with dark molasses.

Sticky Banana Gingerbread

Serves 4 to 6

3 ripe bananas
2 cups (260 g) all-purpose flour
1½ tsp baking powder
1 tsp baking soda
⅛ tsp fine sea salt
½ cup (115 g) unsalted butter,
at room temperature
½ cup plus 2 tbsp (200 g)
sugar beet syrup
(or dark molasses)
½ cup (110 g) light brown sugar
2 tsp ground cinnamon
1½ tbsp freshly grated ginger
3 large eggs
¼ cup (60 ml) whole milk

Picture page 53, top right

Preheat the oven to 325°F / 160°C (preferably convection setting). Butter a 9 x 4-inch (23 x 10 cm) loaf pan and line with parchment paper.

Cut 1 banana in half lengthwise and set aside. Mash the other 2 bananas with a fork until smooth then measure ⅔ cup (175 g), and set aside; reserve any remaining mashed banana for another use.

In a medium bowl, whisk together the flour, baking powder, baking soda, and salt.

In the bowl of a stand mixer fitted with the paddle attachment, beat the butter, mashed bananas, sugar beet syrup, light brown sugar, cinnamon, and ginger until light and fluffy. Add the eggs, 1 at a time, incorporating each egg before adding the next one, and continue beating for 1 minute or until creamy. With a wooden spoon, gently fold ⅓ of the flour mixture into the butter-banana mixture, followed by ⅓ of the milk. Repeat with the remaining flour mixture and milk, mixing until combined. Spread the batter evenly in the prepared pan, place the banana halves, cut-side up, on top, and bake for 65 to 70 minutes (slightly longer if using a conventional oven) or until golden brown and firm on top. If you insert a skewer into the center of the cake, it should come out clean.

Let the cake cool for at least 15 minutes then take it out of the pan, transfer to a wire rack, and let cool for another 15 minutes before removing the parchment paper and serving.

I adore this dish: It's simple, quick, and brings out the best in salmon. Don't shy away from being playful; feel free to compose any kind of spice mixture to top the fish—just be sure to use whole seeds. The fennel used here lets your taste buds travel to the peak of a Mediterranean summer, but white, green, or black peppercorns, along with coriander or cumin seeds, all add their own unique touch. *Mediterranean Lemon Mashed Potatoes (recipe no. 163)* is my favorite side dish for this kind of seafood recipe.

35

Serves 2

1 tbsp fennel seeds,
lightly crushed with a mortar
and pestle
1 (12-ounce / 340-g)
skin-on salmon fillet
1 large egg, beaten
Olive oil
Fine sea salt

Picture page 53, bottom left

Fennel-Crusted Salmon

Spread the fennel seeds on a plate. Dip the skin-less side of the salmon in the egg wash then dip the same side into the fennel seeds, pushing gently to make sure the seeds cover the salmon evenly.

In a medium, heavy pan, heat a splash of olive oil over medium-high heat. Add the salmon, skin-side down, and cook for about 5 minutes or until almost halfway cooked through. Carefully turn the salmon over—mind that the fennel seeds don't fall off. Add a little more oil to the pan and reduce the heat to medium-low. Cook the salmon for 2 to 3 more minutes, depending on its thickness, or until flaky but still pink inside.

Lightly season the salmon with salt, cut in half, and divide among plates.

Skordalia is a wonderful Greek dip made of puréed boiled garlic, potatoes, and olive oil. Despite my long-standing fascination with Greece's honest cuisine, this dip has somehow managed to slip under my radar—I only discovered it a few years ago. Although somewhat lighter, this Hellenic treat mimics the look and feel of mayonnaise and it works beautifully with oven-roasted vegetables.

36

Serves 2 to 4

For the carrots
¾ pound (340 g) rainbow carrots
(or regular carrots),
cut in half lengthwise
Olive oil
Flaky sea salt
Coarsely ground pepper

For the skordalia
½ pound (225 g) peeled starchy
potatoes, cut into small cubes
6 large cloves garlic, unpeeled
¼ cup (60 ml) olive oil
Flaky sea salt

Picture page 53, bottom right

Roasted Carrots with Greek Skordalia Garlic-Potato Dip

Preheat the oven to 400°F (200°C).

Spread the carrots in a medium baking dish, drizzle generously with olive oil, and season to taste with salt and pepper. Toss to combine and roast, turning once, for about 40 minutes or until golden brown and tender.

For the skordalia, in a medium saucepan, cover the potatoes with salted water and bring to a boil. Cook for 10 minutes then add the garlic and cook for another 5 minutes or until the potatoes are soft. Drain and quickly rinse with cold water. Peel the garlic and transfer to a blender or food processor. Add the potatoes and olive oil, pulse until smooth, and season to taste with salt.

Divide the carrots among plates and top generously with the skordalia or serve the skordalia on the side. Enjoy warm or cold.

There isn't much couscous happening in my kitchen, but this recipe is the result of one of my many culinary phone calls with my mother. We often chat for an hour or so, exchanging inspiring recipes over a glass of wine. This refreshing supper is one of the great outcomes of our creative encounters, and combines couscous, licorice-y fennel, juicy orange, and flowery orange blossom water.

Fennel-Orange Couscous with Orange Blossom Water and Mint

Serves 3 to 4

6 slim, long strips fresh
orange peel (white pith removed)
Olive oil
1 ½ cups (280 g) couscous
About 2 ¼ cups (530 ml) water
Fine sea salt
1 (⅔-pound / 300-g) fennel bulb,
cut in half lengthwise, cored,
and very thinly sliced, plus a few
chopped fennel fronds for serving
3 large oranges, peeled
(skin and white pith removed)
and cut into segments
¼ cup (60 ml) freshly squeezed
orange juice, plus more to taste
1 to 3 tbsp high-quality orange
blossom water, preferably organic
Finely ground pepper
1 small handful small fresh mint
leaves, for serving

Preheat the oven to 425°F (220°C).

In a small baking dish, toss the orange peel with ¼ cup (60 ml) of olive oil and roast for 6 to 7 minutes or until the peel turns crisp and golden brown—mind that it doesn't get dark. Remove the dish from the oven, break the orange peel into small pieces, and set aside with the orange oil.

Put the couscous in a large pot. In a kettle, bring the water to a boil (or adjust to the package instructions) and pour over the couscous. Stir in ⅛ teaspoon of salt, cover the pot immediately, and let sit for 5 minutes.

Transfer the couscous to a large, deep bowl. Gently fold in the fennel, oranges, reserved orange oil, orange juice, and 1 tablespoon of the orange blossom water. Season to taste with salt, pepper, and additional orange blossom water and orange juice. Drizzle with a little more olive oil if necessary and sprinkle with the roasted orange peel, mint, and fennel fronds. Serve warm or as a cold salad.

I tasted my first chowder at the tiny Luke's Lobster in Manhattan's East Village, on a gray and rainy afternoon just a few years ago. It was a late but nevertheless mind-blowing discovery. With seafood sinking into creamy potato soup and subtle hints of smoky bacon, it's the kind of heart-warming dish that both body and mind long for when fighting the cold.

Fish Chowder with Purple Potatoes and Marjoram

Serves 3 to 4

Olive oil
3 ounces (85 g) leek
(white and light green parts only),
very thinly sliced
2 large cloves garlic,
cut into quarters
10 ounces (280 g) peeled
purple or waxy potatoes,
cut into ½-inch (1.25 cm) cubes
1 celery stalk, very thinly sliced
1 (2-ounce / 60-g) piece bacon
3¾ cups (900 ml) homemade
or quality store-bought fish broth
1 small bunch fresh marjoram,
tied together, plus 1 tbsp fresh
marjoram leaves for serving
1 large bay leaf
Fine sea salt
Finely ground pepper
18 ounces (500 g) thick firm
fish fillets, such as halibut, cod,
or monkfish, cut into 1½ x 1½-inch
(4 x 4 cm) chunks
¼ cup (60 ml) heavy cream

In a large pot, heat a splash of olive oil over medium-high heat. Add the leek and garlic and sauté, stirring occasionally, for 1 minute. Add the potatoes and celery, stir, and cook for 1 minute then add the bacon, broth, marjoram, and bay leaf and season to taste with salt and pepper. Bring to a boil and simmer for 15 minutes or until the potatoes are tender. Remove and discard the marjoram and bay leaf. Add the fish then reduce the heat to medium-low and cook, just below simmering, for 5 minutes or until the fish is flaky and just cooked through. Add the heavy cream, stir, and season to taste with salt and pepper. Divide the soup among bowls, sprinkle with a little marjoram, and serve.

Brighten the mood during the short and gray days of winter with an extra splash of color on your plate. Ruby-colored pomegranate seeds burst with sweet juices and make a chicken sandwich with bacon and red coleslaw feel fresh and thrilling.

Pomegranate-Chicken Sandwich with Red Coleslaw, Orange, and Bacon

Makes 6 sandwiches

For the coleslaw
Fine sea salt
½ pound (225 g) cored red cabbage, shredded
⅓ cup plus 1 tbsp (90 g) full-fat plain Greek yogurt
1 tbsp freshly squeezed orange juice, plus more to taste
Finely ground pepper

For the pomegranate syrup
¾ cup (180 ml) pomegranate juice
⅓ cup (65 g) granulated sugar

For the sandwiches
Olive oil
14 ounces (400 g) boneless, skinless chicken breasts
Fine sea salt
Finely ground pepper
6 slices bacon
6 medium leaves lettuce
6 large white sandwich buns, cut in half
2 small oranges, peeled (skin and white pith removed) and cut into segments
Seeds from 1 medium pomegranate
1 spring onion (green part only), thinly sliced
1 tbsp freshly grated orange zest

Preheat the oven to 400°F (200°C).

For the coleslaw, in a large bowl, sprinkle ¼ teaspoon of salt over the cabbage, rub it in with your fingers for about 1 minute, and let it sit for 10 minutes to soften the cabbage. Add the yogurt and orange juice, stir to combine, and season to taste with additional orange juice and salt, plus pepper.

For the pomegranate syrup, bring the pomegranate juice and sugar to a boil in a small saucepan and cook over medium-high heat for 5 to 7 minutes or until syrupy.

For the sandwiches, in a medium, heavy pan, heat a splash of olive oil over medium-high heat and sear the chicken breasts for 1 to 2 minutes per side or until golden. Season to taste with salt and pepper, transfer to a medium baking dish, and roast for about 8 minutes or until the juices run clear when you prick the thickest part with a skewer. Transfer to a piece of aluminum foil, wrap, and let rest for 5 minutes then cut into slices.

In a large, heavy pan, heat a splash of olive oil over medium-high heat and cook the bacon for a few minutes per side or until golden brown and crispy. Transfer to a plate and break into pieces.

To assemble the sandwiches, divide the lettuce among the bottom halves of the buns, arrange the chicken on top, and drizzle with the pomegranate syrup. Arrange 1 heaping tablespoon of coleslaw, 3 orange segments, and some pomegranate seeds on top of each sandwich then sprinkle with the bacon, spring onion, and orange zest. Place a top on each bun, pressing on sandwich a little, and enjoy.

Serves 2 to 4

½ large cauliflower, cored
and broken into large chunks
¼ cup (60 ml) mild olive oil,
plus more as needed
1 tbsp freshly grated ginger
¼ to ½ tbsp freshly grated
lemon zest, plus more for serving
1 large clove garlic, crushed
Fine sea salt
Finely ground pepper
24 large pitted green olives,
rinsed, drained, and chopped

Serves 4 to 6

⅓ cup plus 1 tbsp (90 ml)
buttermilk
⅓ tsp saffron threads
1⅔ cups (210 g) all-purpose flour
½ cup plus 1 tbsp (70 g) cornstarch
1 tbsp baking powder
¼ tsp fine sea salt
¾ cup plus 1 tbsp (180 g) unsalted
butter, at room temperature
¾ cup plus 2 tbsp (175 g)
granulated sugar
3 large eggs
3 tbsp freshly grated
clementine zest
6 tbsp freshly squeezed
clementine juice
2 tbsp confectioners' sugar

Thanks to ginger, lemon, and green olives, cauliflower cultivates a deep, Mediterranean accent in this chunky mash. Warm or cold, it makes for a delicious, quick lunch or a light side dish for seafood or richly spiced Sunday roasts.

Mashed Ginger and Lemon Cauliflower with Green Olives

Bring a large pot of salted water to a boil, add the cauliflower, and cook for 10 to 15 minutes or until tender. Drain and quickly rinse with cold water then return it to the pot.

In a small saucepan, heat the olive oil, ginger, 1/4 tablespoon of the lemon zest, and the garlic over high heat until it starts sizzling. Take the pan off the heat then pour the warm ginger-lemon oil over the cauliflower and add a little salt. With a butter knife, break and chop the cauliflower until it resembles a chunky mash. If the mash is too dry, add 1 to 2 tablespoons of olive oil. Season to taste with salt, pepper, and additional lemon zest and divide among bowls. Sprinkle with the green olives, pepper, and a little lemon zest and serve warm or cold.

Saffron tastes unique and eccentric. I only use this polarizing, confident spice if I want it to be prominent, like in this teatime loaf cake. If clementines aren't available, replace them with oranges or tangerines.

Saffron and Clementine Cake

Preheat the oven to 325°F / 160°C (preferably convection setting). Butter a 9 x 4-inch (23 x 10 cm) loaf pan.

In a small bowl, whisk together the buttermilk and saffron. In a medium bowl, combine the flour, cornstarch, baking powder, and salt. In the bowl of a stand mixer fitted with the paddle attachment, beat the butter and granulated sugar until fluffy. Add the eggs, 1 at a time, incorporating each egg before adding the next one, and continue beating for 1 minute or until thick and creamy. Add 2 tablespoons of the clementine zest and 3 tablespoons of the juice and mix until well combined. With a wooden spoon, gently fold 1/3 of the flour mixture into the butter mixture, followed by 1/3 of the buttermilk mixture. Repeat with the remaining flour and buttermilk mixtures, mixing well until combined. Spread the batter evenly in the prepared pan and bake for about 50 minutes (slightly longer if using a conventional oven) or until golden and firm on top. If you insert a skewer in the center of the cake, it should come out clean.

In a small bowl, whisk together remaining 3 tablespoons of clementine juice and the confectioners' sugar until smooth. While the cake is still warm, prick the top all over with a skewer. Pour the syrup over the cake and let cool for 10 minutes then take it out of the pan and sprinkle with the remaining clementine zest.

Loukoumades, cute little Greek doughnuts soaked in sugary syrup, are an ancient treat that's also popular in Turkish cuisine. I cut down on the sugar, and make the syrup with honey, plus orange juice and zest. It's a little thicker and focuses on flavor rather than aggressive sweetness.

Loukoumades Greek Doughnuts with Honey, Cinnamon, and Pistachios

Serves 4 to 6

For the doughnuts

3 cups plus 1 tbsp (400 g) all-purpose flour

2 (¼-ounce / 7-g) envelopes fast-acting yeast

1 tbsp granulated sugar

1 tsp fine sea salt

⅔ cup (150 ml) whole milk, lukewarm

½ cup (120 ml) water, lukewarm

1 tbsp honey

1 heaping tsp freshly grated orange zest

6 cups (1.4 liters) sunflower oil, to fry the doughnuts

2 ounces (60 g) unsalted pistachios, roughly chopped, for serving

Ground cinnamon, for serving

For the syrup

⅓ cup plus 2 tbsp (140 g) honey

¼ cup (60 ml) freshly squeezed orange juice

1 tbsp granulated sugar

1 tsp freshly grated orange zest

For the doughnuts, combine the flour, yeast, sugar, and salt in the bowl of a stand mixer fitted with the dough hook attachment. In a medium bowl, whisk the lukewarm milk and water with the honey and orange zest then add to the flour mixture, and mix with the hook for about 5 minutes or until the dough is elastic and comes off the sides of the bowl—it will be a little sticky. Cover with a tea towel and let rise in a warm place, or preferably in a 100°F (35°C) warm oven, for about 50 minutes or until doubled in size.

For the syrup, in a small saucepan, bring the honey, orange juice, and sugar to a boil and cook over medium-high heat for about 5 minutes or until syrupy. Add the orange zest, stir, cover, and keep warm.

In a large, heavy pot, heat the sunflower oil over medium-high heat. Line a large baking dish with paper towels.

To see if the oil is hot enough, dip the bottom of a wooden spoon into the oil; tiny bubbles should form around it. Start with 1 doughnut to test the oil. Scoop out a tablespoonful of the dough and use a second tablespoon to form a roughly 1½-inch (4 cm) ball. Carefully drop the dough into the hot oil and fry, turning occasionally, for 3 to 4 minutes or until golden and cooked through, adjusting the heat if the doughnuts brown too quickly. Use a slotted ladle or spoon to transfer the doughnut to the prepared baking dish. Working in batches, fry more doughnuts with the remaining dough. This makes about 24 doughnuts.

Divide the doughnuts among small plates, drizzle with the warm syrup, and sprinkle with the pistachios and cinnamon.

Vibrant spices add a warming bouquet to colorful rainbow chard. The mix of coriander, cumin, cardamom, and fennel doesn't overpower and still allows the vegetable's flavor to come through. It also blends in perfectly with the sweet juice of an orange and the crunch of cashews. You can enjoy the spiced greens without spaghetti, but then you'd miss out on a great pasta dish.

Spaghetti with Spiced Rainbow Chard, Orange, and Cashews

Serves 3 to 4

For the spice mixture

2 tsp coriander seeds, finely crushed with a mortar and pestle

1½ tsp ground cumin

¾ tsp ground cardamom

½ tsp fennel seeds, finely crushed with a mortar and pestle

For the pasta

1 pound (450 g) trimmed rainbow chard (or regular chard)

10 ounces (280 g) dried spaghetti

Olive oil

1½ tbsp freshly grated orange zest

⅔ cup (150 ml) freshly squeezed orange juice

1 tbsp balsamic vinegar

Fine sea salt

Finely ground pepper

2 handfuls unsalted cashews, toasted and roughly chopped

For the spice mixture, in a small bowl, mix the coriander seeds, cumin, cardamom, and fennel seeds.

For the pasta, thinly slice the chard stalks and roughly chop the leaves.

Bring a large pot of salted water to a boil and cook the spaghetti, according to the package instructions, until al dente. Drain the spaghetti and return it to the pot.

In a large, heavy pan, heat a generous splash of olive oil and the spice mixture over medium-high heat for 15 seconds or until fragrant. Add the chard stalks and sauté, stirring occasionally, for about 8 minutes or until al dente. Add the chard leaves, stir, and sauté for 3 minutes, reducing the heat if necessary. Add 1 teaspoon of the orange zest, the orange juice, and vinegar, stir, and season to taste with salt, pepper, and additional orange zest. Cook for about 2 minutes or until the stalks are tender.

Add the spaghetti and a splash of olive oil to the chard, toss to combine, and season to taste with salt and pepper. Divide the pasta among plates, sprinkle with the cashews and a little orange zest, and serve.

Some days call for a cozy and comforting soup to put both mind and soul at ease. For this one, I cook canned chickpeas and potatoes in a clear vegetable broth. Puréeing the soup turns it smooth and velvety, and then it's sprinkled with arugula pesto and crispy fried chickpeas.

Chickpea-Potato Soup with Arugula Pesto and Fried Chickpeas

Serves 2 to 4

For the pesto*
2 ounces (60 g) arugula leaves
1 ounce (30 g) Parmesan, finely grated
1 ounce (30 g) pine nuts
⅓ cup (75 ml) olive oil
Fine sea salt

For the soup
1 ¼ cups (250 g) drained and rinsed canned chickpeas
Olive oil
1 medium onion, chopped
2 large cloves garlic, crushed
9 ounces (250 g) peeled starchy potatoes, cut into cubes
3 ¾ cups (900 ml) homemade or quality store-bought vegetable broth
1 bay leaf
¼ tsp ground cumin, plus more to taste
Nutmeg, preferably freshly grated
Fine sea salt
Finely ground pepper

For the topping
1 tbsp freshly grated lemon zest
Coarsely ground pepper

For the pesto, in a food processor or blender, purée the arugula, Parmesan, pine nuts, and olive oil until smooth. Season to taste with salt and set aside.

For the soup, reserve 4 tablespoons of the chickpeas for the topping and set aside.

In a large pot, heat a splash of olive oil over medium heat and sauté the onion for 5 minutes or until golden and soft then add the garlic and sauté for 1 minute. Add the potatoes and chickpeas, stir, and sauté for 1 minute. Add the broth, bay leaf, cumin, and a generous amount of nutmeg, season to taste with salt and finely ground pepper, and bring to a boil. Reduce the heat and simmer for 20 minutes or until the potatoes are soft. Remove and discard the bay leaf. In a food processor or blender, or with an immersion blender, purée the soup until smooth then return it to the pot. Season to taste with cumin, nutmeg, salt, and finely ground pepper, bring to a boil, and cook, stirring constantly, for 1 minute.

For the topping, heat a generous splash of olive oil in a small, heavy pan over high heat. Add the reserved chickpeas, cover (the chickpeas will pop), and fry for 45 to 60 seconds or until golden.

Divide the soup among bowls and sprinkle with the chickpeas, pesto, lemon zest, and a little coarsely ground pepper.

* You can use leftover pesto for pasta or as a spread on bread.

It doesn't get more German than thin golden schnitzel with caraway seed and cabbage salad stuffed between two thick slices of dark spelt bread.

Schnitzel Sandwich with German Caraway Seed-Cabbage Salad

Makes 2 sandwiches

For the cabbage salad

Fine sea salt
½ pound (225 g) cored white or green cabbage, shredded
2 tbsp olive oil
1½ tbsp white balsamic vinegar
¾ tsp caraway seeds
Finely ground pepper

For the schnitzel

2 large, ¼-inch-thick (0.5 cm) pork cutlets, about ¾ pound (340 g) total
About ½ cup (65 g) all-purpose flour
1 large egg, beaten
About ½ cup (70 g) dry breadcrumbs
Unsalted butter, to cook the schnitzel
Olive oil
Fine sea salt
Finely ground pepper

For the sandwiches

4 thick slices dark bread, preferably spelt or rye
1 small bunch fresh chives, finely chopped

Picture page 69, top left

For the salad, in a medium bowl, sprinkle $1/4$ teaspoon of salt over the cabbage and rub it in with your fingers for about 1 minute. Let it sit for 10 minutes to soften the cabbage. Add the olive oil, vinegar, and caraway seeds, mix until combined, and season to taste with salt and pepper; set aside.

For the schnitzel, on a work surface, arrange the pork between 2 sheets of plastic wrap. Use a meat pounder or your fist to tenderize and slightly flatten the meat.

Place the flour, egg, and breadcrumbs in 3 separate deep, wide plates.

In a large, heavy pan, heat 2 tablespoons of butter and a generous splash of olive oil over high heat. Season the meat on both sides with salt and pepper. Lightly dredge the meat in the flour then dip it in the egg and dredge it in the breadcrumbs, making sure it's evenly covered. Immediately place the meat in the hot pan. Reduce the heat to medium-high and cook, turning once, for about $1\,1/2$ minutes per side or until golden brown and just cooked through. Set the pan aside and cut the schnitzel in half.

For the sandwiches, drizzle the cooking juices from the pan over 2 slices of bread. Spread a few tablespoons of the cabbage salad on the bread and arrange the schnitzel on top. Sprinkle with chives and place a slice of bread on top of each sandwich then squeeze and enjoy.

The colors and flavors in this salad are loud, while the play of contrasts — smooth and sharp, sweet and bitter—will seize your taste buds and make your mouth water. The combination is inspired by a traditional Sicilian salad, featuring blood orange, olives, and onion. Its bright citrus looks like the glowing sun rising over the Mediterranean Sea, which is pleasantly uplifting during the short, gray days of February.

Serves 2 to 4

2 handfuls arugula leaves
4 small blood oranges,
   peeled (skin and white pith
   removed) and thinly sliced
2 small red onions, thinly sliced
12 to 16 black olives,
   preferably Kalamata
Olive oil
Flaky sea salt
Coarsely ground pepper

Picture opposite, top right

Blood Orange and Arugula Salad with Black Olives and Onion

Divide the arugula among plates. Arrange the blood oranges, onions, and olives on top. Drizzle with olive oil, season to taste with salt and pepper, and serve immediately.

One shouldn't underestimate the assertiveness of mussels. A little sweet, with a hint of the sea, they might seem a bit shy, but there's no doubt they can handle strong partners. I've mixed seafood with spices, fruits, and vegetables in the past, but I wasn't sure how it would react to the heat of chorizo and chile. The result was clear: Mussels love it!

Serves 2 to 3

2¼ pounds (1 kg) fresh mussels
1 cup (240 ml) dry white wine
¼ cup (60 ml) freshly squeezed
   orange juice
3 ounces (85 g) strong
   Spanish chorizo salami,
   cut into very small cubes
1 medium tomato,
   cut into small cubes
1 medium, fresh red chile, seeded
   and cut into very small cubes
1 small bunch fresh marjoram
1 large bay leaf
½ tsp fine sea salt
1 baguette, for serving (optional)

Picture opposite, bottom left

Spicy Chorizo Mussels with Chile and Marjoram

Rinse and scrub the mussels with cold water and cut off the beards. Discard any broken mussels.

In a large pot, combine the white wine, orange juice, chorizo, tomato, chile, marjoram, bay leaf, and salt and bring to a boil. Add the mussels, reduce the heat to medium, cover, and cook for 5 minutes or until the shells open. Shake the pot once or twice while the mussels are cooking or gently stir them with a slotted ladle or spoon. Discard any mussels that don't open.

Divide the mussels, chorizo, and broth among bowls and serve with a fresh baguette.

45

46

47

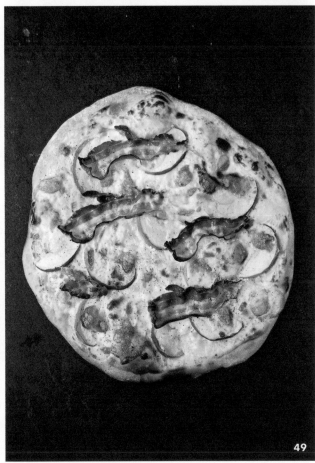

49

Olive oil is a great substitute for butter when baking. It produces a lighter texture and makes the cake a little more moist. If you mix the oil with tahini, you bring in a nutty tone—add this to a fruitcake and you'll be smitten. Tahini whipped cream is just the right topping for this rustic-looking weekend baking project.

Tahini-Date Cake

Serves 6 to 8

For the cake
2 cups (260 g) all-purpose flour
1 tbsp baking powder
1 tbsp freshly grated orange zest
1 tsp ground cinnamon
⅛ tsp fine sea salt
⅓ cup plus 1 tbsp (90 ml) whole milk
⅓ cup (75 ml) mild olive oil
⅓ cup (75 g) light tahini
1 cup (200 g) granulated sugar
4 large eggs
4 ounces (110 g) pitted dates, roughly chopped
1 tbsp white sesame seeds
Butter, to butter the pan

For the whipped cream
1¼ cups (300 ml) heavy cream
Granulated sugar, to taste
1½ to 2 tbsp light tahini

For the topping
6 pitted dates, roughly chopped
2 tbsp sesame seeds

Preheat the oven to 350°F / 180°C (preferably convection setting) and butter an 8-inch (20 cm) springform pan.

For the cake, in a large bowl, combine the flour, baking powder, orange zest, cinnamon, and salt.

In the bowl of a stand mixer fitted with the paddle attachment, beat the milk, olive oil, tahini, sugar, and eggs for 1 minute or until well combined. Add the flour mixture and mix quickly until combined. Stir in the dates then spread the batter evenly in the prepared pan. Sprinkle with the sesame seeds and bake for about 45 minutes (slightly longer if using a conventional oven) or until golden and spongy. If you insert a skewer in the center of the cake, it should come out almost clean. Let the cake cool for 2 minutes then take it out of the pan.

Whip the heavy cream until stiff and sweeten to taste with sugar. Add the tahini and whip for a few seconds or until well combined.

Serve the cake with generous dollops of the whipped cream and sprinkle with chopped dates and sesame seeds.

Tarte flambée is one of the most famous—and most genius—inventions among Alsace's wonderfully rich and hearty cuisine. This thin-crusted treat is like a pizza, just more delicate and with a lighter and less opulent topping. The classic version shines with crème fraîche, bacon, and onions, but I like my German and Italian-style tarte flambée topped with Taleggio cheese, apples, and, of course, bacon.

Tarte Flambée with Taleggio, Apples, and Bacon

Makes 1 (12-inch / 30-cm) tarte flambée

For the dough
2 cups (260 g) all-purpose flour
1 (¼-ounce / 7-g) envelope fast-acting yeast
½ tsp granulated sugar
¼ tsp fine sea salt
½ cup (120 ml) whole milk, lukewarm
2 tbsp olive oil

For the topping
4 ounces (110 g) sour cream (or crème fraîche)
1 large egg yolk
⅛ tsp fine sea salt
1 medium, tart baking apple, cored and cut into thin wedges
3 ounces (85 g) mild, sweet cheese that melts well, such as Taleggio, fontina, or Robiola, cut into small cubes
Coarsely ground pepper
6 slices bacon

Picture page 69, bottom right

Start the preparations about 1 1/2 hours before you want to enjoy the tarte flambée. I bake it on a baking sheet that's been heated on the bottom of the oven like a pizza stone to help create a crunchy crust.

For the dough, combine the flour, yeast, sugar, and salt in the bowl of a stand mixer fitted with the dough hook attachment. Add the lukewarm milk and the olive oil and mix with the hook for a few minutes or until well combined. If the dough is too sticky, add more flour. Transfer the dough to a work surface and continue kneading and punching it down with your hands for about 4 minutes or until you have a smooth and elastic ball of dough. Place the dough back in the bowl, cover with a tea towel, and let rise in a warm place, or preferably in a 100°F (35°C) warm oven, for 60 minutes or until doubled in size.

Place a baking sheet (or pizza stone) on the bottom of the oven and preheat the oven to the highest temperature, 500°F (260°C) or higher.

For the topping, whisk together the sour cream, egg yolk, and salt until smooth.

When the dough has doubled in size, punch it down and take it out of the bowl. On a well-floured work surface or pizza peel, stretch and roll the dough into a 12-inch (30 cm) disc.

Carefully take the hot baking sheet out of the oven, flip it over, and place it on a trivet or other heat-safe surface. Arrange the dough disc on the baking sheet and spread the sour cream mixture on top. Place the apple and Taleggio on top and season to taste with pepper. Arrange the bacon on top and bake on the bottom of the oven for 7 to 9 minutes or until the crust is golden brown and crisp and the cheese has melted; serve immediately.

Minestrone is one of my first choices when it's time to clear out the vegetable drawer. This recipe turns long-forgotten squash, roots, and cabbages into a hearty soup with a comforting broth that's easy to refine with just a little creativity. Add some pesto—I like the garlicky edge of ramp pesto—stir in colorful borlotti beans, sprinkle it with Parmesan, and you'll have a Genovese-style minestrone, completely made of leftovers.

Genovese Minestrone with Borlotti Beans and Pesto

Serves 4 to 6

For the soup
1 ½ pounds (680 g) peeled, cored, and trimmed mixed vegetables, such as squash, fennel bulb, sweet potato, carrots, white or green cabbage, kale, or chard
Olive oil
1 medium onion, finely chopped
2 large cloves garlic, cut in half
1 celery stalk, cut in half
½ leek, cut in half
½ medium parsnip
(or parsley root), cut into half
⅛ medium celeriac, cut in half
6 ½ cups (1.5 liters) water, hot
1 medium tomato,
cut into small cubes
6 sprigs fresh thyme
1 bay leaf
Fine sea salt
Finely ground pepper
1 ¼ cups (250 g) drained
and rinsed canned borlotti
(cranberry) or pinto beans

For the topping
⅓ cup (80 g) green pesto,
such as ramp or basil pesto
(recipe no. 102)
4 to 6 heaping tbsp
finely grated Parmesan
Coarsely ground pepper

For the soup, cut the leafy vegetables into small square shapes and the remaining vegetables into very small cubes.

In a large pot, heat a splash of olive oil over medium heat. Add the onion and garlic and sauté, stirring, for 5 minutes or until golden and soft. Add a little more oil and the mixed vegetables, along with the celery, leek, parsnip, and celeriac, stir, and cook for 1 minute. Add the hot water, the tomato, thyme, and bay leaf and season to taste with salt and finely ground pepper. Bring to a boil then reduce the heat and simmer for 15 minutes or until the vegetables are tender. Remove and discard the celery, leek, parsnip, and celeriac. Add the borlotti beans and cook for 1 minute then season to taste with salt and finely ground pepper.

Divide the soup among bowls and sprinkle with pesto, Parmesan, and a little coarsely ground pepper.

Serves 2

3 tbsp olive oil

½ tsp freshly grated lime zest,
plus ½ tsp for the topping

2 tbsp freshly squeezed lime juice

Fine sea salt

Finely ground pepper

1 large handful fresh cilantro
stalks and leaves

½ medium red onion, thinly sliced

A trip to Tokyo—and a late night visit to an *izakaya*, or Japanese pub—brought this supremely minimalist salad into my life. Cilantro leaves and stalks are treated like a vegetable rather than an herb and paired with red onion and lime. Add a little olive oil, salt, and pepper and you've found the secret to an easy, fresh, and delicious lunch or side dish. As much as I'm fascinated by complex creations in the kitchen, I'm deeply awestruck by genius simplicity.

Cilantro and Red Onion Salad with Lime

Whisk together the olive oil, $1/2$ teaspoon of lime zest, and the lime juice. Season to taste with salt and pepper.

Arrange the cilantro and red onion in a medium bowl and drizzle with the dressing. Toss to combine, sprinkle with additional lime zest, and serve immediately.

Makes 4 sandwiches

1 (6-ounce / 170-g) can tuna
in water, drained and squeezed

5 ounces (140 g) fresh ricotta,
drained

1 large hard-boiled egg,
finely chopped

3 medium pickled gherkins,
cut into small cubes

10 large capers, rinsed, dried,
and finely chopped

1 tbsp olive oil

1 tsp Dijon mustard

1 tsp tomato paste

Fine sea salt

Finely ground pepper

4 to 8 slices ciabatta

7 ounces (200 g) aromatic cheese
that melts well, such as Raclette,
Comté, or Gruyère, thinly sliced

When I was a child, my mother often mixed canned tuna, yogurt, hard-boiled eggs, capers, and gherkins to make a spread for sandwiches. Years later, I realized this combination that I love so much would be just perfect for a tuna melt. In my version, the yogurt gives way for ricotta, and melted Raclette spreads its hearty qualities all over tuna and crusty ciabatta.

Raclette Tuna Melt Sandwich

Set the oven to broil (quicker method) or preheat to 500°F (260°C).

In a medium bowl, stir together the tuna, ricotta, hard-boiled egg, 2/3 of the gherkins, capers, olive oil, mustard, and tomato paste and season to taste with salt and pepper.

Divide the tuna mixture among 4 slices of ciabatta. Spread the cheese slices on top and put the sandwiches under the broiler, or roast at 500°F (260°C) for a few minutes or until the cheese starts to melt. Sprinkle with a little pepper and the remaining gherkin, place a slice of ciabatta on top to close each sandwich (optional), and serve.

Bitter endive, sweet apple, salty bacon, and flowery marjoram are a harmonic quartet. Mix them together in a pan, and you'll have a quick and comforting warm lunch that only takes a few minutes to prepare.

Sautéed Belgian Endive and Apple Wedges with Bacon and Marjoram

Serves 2

Olive oil
2 ounces (60 g) thick-cut bacon, cut into very small cubes
2 medium, tart baking apples, peeled, cored, and each cut into 8 wedges
2 medium heads Belgian endive, cut in half lengthwise and thickly sliced
1 tsp finely chopped fresh marjoram leaves
Fine sea salt
Finely ground pepper

In a medium, heavy pan, heat a splash of olive oil over medium-high heat and cook the bacon, stirring occasionally, for 3 to 4 minutes or until golden brown and crispy. Transfer the bacon to a plate, but leave the pan on the heat.

Add the apples to the pan and sauté over medium-high heat, flipping once or twice and adding more olive oil if necessary, for a few minutes or until golden brown. Transfer the apples to a plate, but leave the pan on the heat.

Add a little more olive oil and the endives to the pan and sauté over medium-high heat, stirring occasionally, for 3 minutes or until golden and tender. Add the apples, bacon, and marjoram, mix until combined, and season to taste with salt and pepper. Serve immediately.

54

week 8 / friday

I'm a huge fan of anything made with ground beef. Offer me a hearty meatloaf or experimental burger creation and I'll be there, no matter how or when. *Polpette* can be a mouthful of delicious happiness, but it's important to keep the tiny meatballs juicy and your mind open to uncharted territories. Sneak tahini, pistachios, cilantro, and spices into the beef mixture—the taste and texture are divine—and serve this crowd-pleaser at your next meze party. If you fill the table with lots of small dishes for guests to nibble, you get to sit back and relax.

Spiced Tahini-Cilantro Meatballs with Tomato Salad

Serves 2 to 4

For the meatballs

14 ounces (400 g) ground beef
1 small shallot
(or ½ medium onion),
finely chopped
1 large clove garlic, crushed
⅓ cup (75 g) light tahini
1 ounce (30 g) salted pistachios,
roughly chopped,
plus 1 small handful for serving
1 large handful fresh
cilantro leaves, roughly chopped
1 allspice berry, finely crushed
with a mortar and pestle
½ tsp ground cumin
½ tsp ground cinnamon
1 ½ tsp fine sea salt
Finely ground pepper
Unsalted butter,
to cook the meatballs
Olive oil

For the tomato salad

3 tbsp olive oil
2 tbsp white balsamic vinegar
Fine sea salt
Finely ground pepper
12 to 16 small cherry tomatoes,
cut in half
1 large handful fresh
cilantro leaves

For the meatballs, combine the beef, shallot, garlic, tahini, pistachios, cilantro, allspice, cumin, cinnamon, salt, and a generous amount of pepper in a large bowl and mix with your hands until well combined. Wet your hands and form the mixture into 16 roughly 1 ½-inch (4 cm) meatballs.

In a large, heavy pan, heat 2 tablespoons of butter and a generous splash of olive oil over medium-high heat. Reduce the heat to medium and cook the meatballs, turning occasionally, for 8 to 10 minutes or until evenly browned and just cooked through.

For the salad, whisk together the olive oil and vinegar and season to taste with salt and pepper. Divide the tomatoes and cilantro among plates and sprinkle with the dressing.

Arrange the meatballs next to the tomatoes, sprinkle with chopped pistachios, and serve.

Muffins are the quickest way to satisfy sudden weekend cravings for something sweet and cakey. Imagine a cold Saturday morning and pulling out of the oven warm and fluffy pistachio-orange blossom muffins topped with crunchy caramelized nuts. Trust me: You'll be eating them straight from the pan.

Pistachio-Orange Blossom Muffins

Makes 12 muffins

For the batter

1 cup (120 g) unsalted pistachios

2 ½ cups (325 g) all-purpose flour

¾ cup (150 g) granulated sugar

1 tbsp baking powder

½ tsp baking soda

⅛ tsp fine sea salt

½ cup (115 g) unsalted butter, melted and cooled

1 tsp freshly grated orange zest

½ vanilla bean, split and scraped

¾ cup plus 2 tbsp (210 ml) whole milk

2 large eggs

3 tbsp high-quality orange blossom water, preferably organic

12 paper muffin pan liners

For the topping

2 tbsp granulated sugar

2 tbsp water

1 tsp honey

1 small handful unsalted pistachios

Preheat the oven to 400°F / 200°C (preferably convection setting). Line a 12-cup muffin pan with paper liners.

For the batter, in a food processor or blender, finely grind 3 ounces (85 g) of the pistachios; roughly chop the remaining pistachios and reserve for the batter.

In a large bowl, whisk together the ground pistachios, flour, sugar, baking powder, baking soda, and salt.

In a medium bowl, whisk together the melted butter, orange zest, and vanilla seeds then add the milk, eggs, and orange blossom water. Add to the flour mixture and stir with a wooden spoon until the batter is lumpy with a few bits of flour here and there. Gently fold in the reserved chopped pistachios. Mind that if you mix too much, the muffins will lose their light texture.

Spoon the batter into the muffin cups and bake for about 14 minutes (slightly longer if using a conventional oven) or until golden and baked through. Let them cool for 5 minutes.

For the topping, in a small saucepan, bring the sugar, water, and honey to a boil and cook, without stirring, for a few minutes or until golden brown and caramelized. Add the pistachios, stir, and quickly divide among the tops of the muffins (before the caramel becomes hard again). The muffins taste best on the first day.

A savory tart is perfect for a picnic in summer, but even better for a romantic rendez-vous when it's still frosty outside. This one features pastry that's crisp, crumbly, and almost flaky. The potato, chèvre, and rosemary filling sounds frugal but looks surprisingly elegant and festive. So, pretend you're in France, bring out a good bottle of red Bordeaux, light some candles, and get cozy with your loved one.

Potato Tart
with Chèvre and Rosemary

Serves 4 to 8

For the pastry

2 cups (260 g) all-purpose flour

1 tsp fine sea salt

½ cup plus 1 tbsp (130 g)
unsalted butter, cold

1 large egg

For the filling

4 large eggs

¾ cup (175 g) sour cream
(or crème fraîche)

½ cup (120 ml) heavy cream

1 tsp fine sea salt

Nutmeg, preferably freshly grated

Finely ground pepper

18 ounces (500 g) peeled
waxy potatoes, boiled and sliced

4 ounces (110 g) soft chèvre,
broken into chunks

1 small handful fresh
rosemary needles

For the pastry, combine the flour and salt in the bowl of a stand mixer fitted with the dough hook attachment. Add the butter and use a knife to cut it into the flour until there are just small pieces left. Quickly rub the butter into the flour with your fingers until combined. Add the egg and mix with the hook until crumbly. Form the dough into a thick disc, wrap it in plastic wrap, and freeze for 10 minutes.

Preheat the oven to 400°F (200°C).

On a work surface, place the dough between 2 sheets of plastic wrap and use a rolling pin to roll out into a disc, large enough to line the bottom and sides of a 12-inch (30 cm) quiche dish. Fit the dough into the quiche dish, pushing it into the dish, especially along the edges. Let the dough hang over the rim a little or trim with a knife. Use a fork to prick the dough all over. Bake for 15 minutes or until golden. If the dough bubbles up, push it down with a fork. Take the quiche dish out of the oven and reduce the temperature to 350°F (180°C).

For the filling, whisk together the eggs, sour cream, heavy cream, salt, and gener-ous amounts of nutmeg and pepper.

Arrange the potatoes on top of the pre-baked pastry and season to taste with nut-meg, salt, and pepper. Sprinkle the chèvre, followed by the rosemary on top of the potatoes then pour the egg mixture into the pastry. Bake for 50 to 55 minutes or until the top is golden and firm and the pastry is crispy. Let the tart cool for 10 minutes. Serve warm or cold, preferably with a glass of Bordeaux.

Makes 2 sandwiches

8 medium shallots, unpeeled
Olive oil
¼ pound (110 g) peeled beets
3 ounces (85 g) fresh ricotta
1 tsp freshly squeezed lemon juice
1 heaping tsp fresh thyme leaves,
plus 8 small sprigs young thyme
Fine sea salt
Finely ground pepper
2 to 4 slices dark bread,
such as spelt or rye
4 medium leaves regular spinach,
trimmed (or 1 small handful baby
spinach leaves)

There are always beets on my kitchen counter during winter. I usually boil or bake these purple roots and enjoy their honest, earthy taste—and their vitamins—in salads or roasted vegetable dishes. I hardly ever prepare them raw, but pulsing and mixing them with ricotta as a dip for sandwiches convinced me to add this technique to my beet repertoire.

Beet-Ricotta Sandwich with Roasted Shallots, Spinach, and Fried Thyme

Preheat the oven to 425°F (220°C).

In a medium baking dish, toss the shallots with 1 tablespoon of olive oil. Roast for 15 minutes then turn them over and roast for 15 minutes on the other side or until the shallots feel soft.

In a food processor or blender, purée the beets, ricotta, 3 tablespoons of olive oil, the lemon juice, and thyme leaves until smooth, adding more olive oil if the dip is too dry. Season to taste with salt and pepper.

In a small saucepan, heat 3 tablespoons of olive oil over high heat, add the thyme sprigs, and immediately take the pan off the heat.

Brush 2 slices of bread with the thyme oil, arrange the spinach on top, and then sprinkle with generous dollops of the beet-ricotta dip. Cut the ends off the shallots and squeeze them out of their skins and onto the dip. Sprinkle with the fried thyme leaves and a little pepper, place a second slice of bread on top of each sandwich (optional), and enjoy.

Serves 2

¼ to ⅓ cup (60 to 75 ml) water,
warm
3 tbsp light tahini
1 to 2 tbsp freshly squeezed
lemon juice
Fine sea salt
3 medium blood oranges,
peeled (skin and white pith
removed) and cut into slices
or segments

Nutty, bitter tahini melts smoothly into the sweet juice of dark blood oranges. You only need a tiny drizzle of the sesame sauce, as you don't want it to overwhelm this wintry composition. It's a perfect snack for long days and weary minds.

Blood Oranges with Tahini-Lemon Sauce

In a medium bowl, whisk together 1/4 cup (60 ml) of warm water, the tahini, and 1 tablespoon of the lemon juice until smooth. If the sauce is too thick, add more water. Season to taste with additional lemon juice and salt.

Spread the oranges on a large platter and drizzle with the tahini-lemon sauce, or serve separately and dip the citrus fruit into the tahini-lemon sauce.

You can use leftover tahini-lemon sauce for roasted vegetables or as a spread for toasted dark bread.

There's a tall jar of sun-dried tomatoes in my pantry, always filled to the brim and sadly, often ignored. It's lucky that these shriveled red fruits stay fresh forever, because when a craving strikes, I always want a lot of them. I like to boil the tomatoes first to soften them and remove the salt and pulse them with pistachios to make a beautiful pesto—it's quite the stunner on a pile of warm spaghetti.

Spaghetti with Sun-Dried Tomato and Pistachio Pesto

Serves 2

For the pesto*
2 ounces (60 g) sun-dried tomatoes, preserved in salt
2 ounces (60 g) salted pistachios, plus 1 to 2 tbsp chopped pistachios for the topping
¼ cup (60 ml) olive oil
1 large clove garlic, crushed

For the pasta
7 ounces (200 g) dried spaghetti
Olive oil
Coarsely ground pepper

For the pesto, bring a small pot of water to a boil and cook the sun-dried tomatoes for 3 to 4 minutes or until soft. Remove the tomatoes with a slotted ladle or spoon and transfer to a plate; reserve the cooking water.

Drain and rinse the sun-dried tomatoes under cold water, dry with paper towels, and transfer to a food processor or blender. Add 4 tablespoons of the cooking water, 2 ounces (60 g) of pistachios, the olive oil, and garlic and purée until smooth. If the pesto is too dry, add a little more of the cooking water.

For the pasta, bring a large pot of salted water to a boil and cook the spaghetti, according to the package instructions, until al dente. Drain the spaghetti, divide among plates, and drizzle with a little olive oil. Sprinkle with the pesto, chopped pistachios, and a little pepper and serve warm.

* You can use leftover pesto as a spread on bread.

March

A potato and radish salad is like a glimpse into the slowly approaching greener season. The combination of colorful rainbow potatoes, Swabian warm shallot vinaigrette, horseradish, and watercress, all topped with a poached egg, feels like a spring feast in the midst of March.

Rainbow Potato Salad with Radishes, Shallot Vinaigrette, and Poached Eggs

Serves 2 to 4

For the dressing

¼ cup (60 ml) white balsamic vinegar, plus more to taste
¼ cup (60 ml) water
1 large shallot, very finely chopped

For the salad

13 ounces (370 g) small rainbow potatoes, preferably purple, pink, and yellow, scrubbed, boiled, and sliced
8 large radishes, cut in half
1 large handful arugula leaves
2 to 4 large eggs
Olive oil
Fine sea salt
Finely ground pepper
1 small handful watercress
1 to 2 tsp freshly grated horseradish

For the dressing, in a small saucepan, bring the vinegar, water, and shallot to a boil. Reduce the heat and simmer for 4 minutes or until the shallot is tender. Remove from the heat, cover, and keep warm.

For the salad, arrange the potatoes, radishes, and arugula in a large bowl.

Bring a small saucepan of salted water to a low simmer. Crack 1 egg into a small bowl. Hold a large spoon just over the surface of the water and gently pour the egg onto the spoon. Lower the spoon into the water and hold until the egg white starts to turn white then use a tablespoon to gently scoop the egg off the large spoon. Poach the egg for 3 minutes. Using a slotted ladle or spoon, transfer the egg to a plate and cover. Poach the remaining eggs the same way, adjusting the heat as needed to maintain a low simmer. It's best to poach 1 egg at a time, but you can cook 2 at once.

Drizzle the salad with the warm dressing and a little olive oil and season to taste with salt and pepper. Sprinkle with the watercress and horseradish. Divide the salad among plates, place a poached egg on top of each, and serve immediately.

Fennel and butter beans were meant to merge in a soup — together, they're like velvet on a spoon. A roughly chopped black olive–parsley pesto disrupts the harmony with its harsh fruitiness, but in precisely the right way.

Fennel and Butter Bean Soup with Black Olive–Parsley Pesto

Serves 3 to 4

For the pesto
10 large black olives,
preferably Kalamata,
pitted and finely chopped
2 tbsp roughly chopped
fresh flat-leaf parsley leaves
¼ cup (60 ml) olive oil

For the soup
Olive oil
1 medium onion,
roughly chopped
2 large cloves garlic,
cut into quarters
¾ pound (340 g) fennel bulb,
cut in half lengthwise, cored,
and very thinly sliced
1¼ cups (250 g) drained
and rinsed canned butter
or cannellini beans
3¾ cups (900 ml) homemade
or quality store-bought
vegetable broth, hot
1 large bay leaf
Nutmeg, preferably freshly grated
Fine sea salt
Finely ground pepper

For the pesto, whisk together the olives, parsley, and olive oil in a medium bowl.

For the soup, heat a splash of olive oil in a large pot over medium heat and sauté the onion and garlic, stirring occasionally, for 5 minutes or until golden and soft. Add a little more olive oil and the fennel and sauté, stirring occasionally, for 5 minutes or until golden and al dente. Add the beans, hot broth, and bay leaf, season to taste with nutmeg, salt, and pepper, and bring to a boil. Reduce the heat and simmer for 5 minutes. Remove and discard the bay leaf. In a food processor or blender, or with an immersion blender, purée the soup until smooth then return it to the pot. Bring to a boil then reduce over high heat until the soup has the desired taste and texture. Season to taste with nutmeg, salt, and pepper and divide among bowls. Sprinkle with a little pesto and serve immediately.

Sometimes, all I want to do is sink my hands into a ball of dough and knead until I let out all my energy and the pale ball slowly softens between my fingers—and I calm down. Babka is a good recipe for this kind of relaxing endeavor—it's the perfect exercise to reenergize on the weekend. A good babka can't be done in a rush, so make sure to give yourself enough time. If you're not into poppy seeds, try blueberry and lemon cream cheese for the filling (recipe no. 286).

Poppy Seed and White Chocolate Babka

Serves 6

For the dough

2 cups plus 2 tbsp (275 g) all-purpose flour
¼ cup (50 g) granulated sugar
1½ tsp fast-acting yeast
¼ tsp fine sea salt
¼ cup (60 ml) whole milk, lukewarm
1 large egg
1 large egg yolk
⅓ cup (75 g) unsalted butter, at room temperature, cut into cubes
Sunflower oil, to grease the bowl

For the filling

2 ounces (60 g) raisins
¾ cup plus 2 tbsp (210 ml) whole milk
¼ cup (50 g) granulated sugar
1 tsp ground cinnamon
1 tsp freshly grated orange zest
1¼ cups (125 g) ground poppy seeds
4 ounces (110 g) white chocolate, roughly chopped

For the glaze

¼ cup (60 ml) water
½ cup (100 g) granulated sugar

Picture page 88

Mind that the dough has to rise twice, the first time overnight, for about 8 hours.

For the dough, whisk together the flour, sugar, yeast, and salt in the bowl of a stand mixer fitted with the dough hook attachment.

In a medium bowl, whisk together the lukewarm milk, egg, and egg yolk. Add the milk mixture and butter to the flour mixture and mix with the hook for 5 minutes or until smooth and well combined. Transfer to a work surface and continue kneading and punching it down with your hands for 5 minutes or until you have a soft and silky ball of dough. If the dough is too sticky, add a little more flour, but mind that it stays soft. Brush a large bowl with a little sunflower oil, add the dough, cover with plastic wrap, and leave it in the fridge overnight, or for about 8 hours (don't be alarmed, the dough will only rise a little).

Take the dough out of the fridge and let it sit in the bowl at room temperature for about 1 hour.

For the filling, fill a medium bowl with warm water. Add the raisins and soak for 5 minutes then drain. In a medium saucepan, bring the milk, sugar, cinnamon, and orange zest to a boil. Take the pan off the heat then add the poppy seeds, stir, and soak for 5 minutes. Stir in the raisins and let cool completely.

Butter a 9 x 4-inch (23 x 10 cm) loaf pan and line the bottom with a piece of parchment paper.

Punch the dough down, take it out of the bowl, and knead for 30 seconds. Lightly flour a work surface and roll the dough with a rolling pin into a 16 x 11-inch (40 x 28 cm) rectangle. Spread the filling on top of the dough, leaving a 3/4-inch (2 cm) border, then sprinkle with the white chocolate. Starting from one long side, carefully roll the dough up into a log. Use your fingers to squeeze the overlapping dough then flip the roll over so that the seam is at the bottom. Cut the roll in half lengthwise with a sharp knife, place both pieces next to each other (cut-side up) then lift one half over the other, repeating to form a twist. Tuck the ends underneath the babka and quickly transfer to the prepared pan—you can use the blade of a large knife to lift it. Cover with a tea towel and let rise in a warm place for 60 to 90 minutes or until puffy.

→

Preheat the oven to 375°F (190°C).

For the glaze, bring the water and sugar to a boil in a small saucepan and cook for 2 minutes or until syrupy.

Bake the babka for 30 to 35 minutes or until golden brown. If you insert a skewer in the middle of the babka, it should come out almost clean. As soon as the babka is done, brush the top with the syrup, using up all the syrup. Let cool for 15 minutes then transfer to a plate and serve, or let cool completely.

Whenever we visit the island of Gozo, one of my favorite Mediterranean beach treats is the local cheese galette pizza from Maxokk Bakery in Nadur. It's filled with goat's milk cheese and eggs, all framed by a circle of hearty potatoes, and the Gozitan baker uses the most delicious sourdough base. Since patience is not always my virtue, I simply use yeast for my homemade version.

Gozitan Pizza with Ricotta, Goat Cheese, and Potatoes

Makes 2 (11-inch / 28-cm) pizzas

For the dough

2⅔ cups (350 g) all-purpose flour
1 (¼-ounce / 7-g) envelope fast-acting yeast
1 tsp fine sea salt
¾ cup (180 ml) water, lukewarm
4 tbsp olive oil

For the topping

18 ounces (500 g) fresh ricotta, drained
5 ounces (140 g) aromatic goat's milk cheese, finely grated
3 ounces (85 g) Parmesan, finely grated
Fine sea salt
Coarsely ground pepper
2 large eggs
1⅓ pounds (600 g) peeled waxy potatoes, boiled and sliced
Olive oil
12 fresh basil leaves

Start the preparations about 2 hours before you want to enjoy the pizza. I bake it on a baking sheet that's been heated on the bottom of the oven like a pizza stone to help create a crunchy crust.

For the dough, combine the flour, yeast, and salt in the bowl of a stand mixer fitted with the dough hook attachment. Add the lukewarm water and the olive oil and mix with the hook for a few minutes or until well combined. If the dough is too sticky, add more flour. Transfer the dough to a work surface and continue kneading and punching it down with your hands for about 4 minutes or until you have a smooth and elastic ball of dough. Place the dough back in the bowl, cover with a tea towel, and let rise in a warm place, or preferably in a 100°F (35°C) warm oven, for 50 to 60 minutes or until doubled in size.

While the dough is rising, prepare the topping: In a medium bowl, whisk together the ricotta, goat's milk cheese, and Parmesan and season to taste with salt and pepper. Add the eggs and whisk until smooth.

When the dough has doubled in size, punch it down, take it out of the bowl, and divide into 2 equal parts. On a well-floured work surface or pizza peel, stretch and roll each piece of dough into a 13-inch (33 cm) disc. Cover with a tea towel and let rise in a warm place for about 20 minutes or until puffy.

Place a baking sheet (or pizza stone) on the bottom of the oven and preheat the oven to the highest temperature, 500°F (260°C) or higher.

Once the baking sheet is hot, carefully take it out of the oven, flip it over, and place it on a trivet or other heat-safe surface. Arrange 1 of the dough discs on the baking sheet and spread 1/2 of the ricotta mixture on top, leaving a 11/2-inch (4 cm) border. Working quickly, arrange 1/2 of the potato slices in an overlapping circle around the edge of the pizza but still on top of the ricotta mixture. Fold the edges of the dough up and press firmly onto the potatoes. Drizzle with a little olive oil and bake on the bottom of the oven for 8 to 9 minutes or until the crust is golden brown and crisp and the ricotta is set. Repeat to make the second pizza. Sprinkle with basil and pepper and serve immediately.

I prefer my bread crunchy, so the famous French onion soup, topped with a slice of cheesy toast softening in the warm liquid, was never my thing. Instead, I opt for *cipollata*, an Italian tomato-based onion and prosciutto soup, served with grilled pecorino crostini on the side.

Cipollata—Italian Onion and Tomato Soup with Crispy Prosciutto and Pecorino Crostini

Serves 4

For the soup
Olive oil
4 ounces (110 g) thick-cut
Tyrolean prosciutto
(or prosciutto di Parma),
cut into short, thin strips
18 ounces (500 g) onions,
cut in half and thinly sliced
1 large clove garlic, cut in half
1 tbsp granulated sugar
14 ounces (400 g) canned
whole peeled tomatoes, chopped
4 ¼ cups (1 liter) homemade
or quality store-bought vegetable
broth, hot
3 whole cloves
1 large bay leaf
1 small sprig fresh rosemary
Fine sea salt
Finely ground pepper

For the crostini
4 ounces (110 g) young pecorino,
coarsely grated
4 thick slices ciabatta bread
Coarsely ground pepper

For the soup, heat a splash of olive oil in a large pot over medium-high heat. Add the prosciutto and cook, stirring, for a few minutes or until golden and crispy. Transfer the prosciutto to a plate, but leave the pot on the heat.

Add a little more olive oil, the onions, garlic, and sugar to the pot, reduce the heat to medium, and cook, stirring occasionally, for 15 minutes or until the onions are golden and soft. Add the tomatoes, hot broth, cloves, bay leaf, and rosemary and season to taste with salt and finely ground pepper. Bring to a boil then reduce the heat and simmer for 30 minutes. Remove and discard the herbs then add the prosciutto and season to taste with salt and finely ground pepper.

Set the oven to broil (quicker method) or preheat to 500°F (260°C).

For the crostini, divide the pecorino among the slices of bread and put the crostini under the broiler, or roast at 500°F (260°C), for 1 to 2 minutes or until the cheese starts to melt; sprinkle with coarsely ground pepper.

Divide the soup among bowls and serve with the warm pecorino crostini.

Serves 2

22 large cloves garlic,
preferably young, unpeeled
2 tbsp (30 g) unsalted butter,
at room temperature
Fine sea salt
7 ounces (200 g) dried spaghetti
2 to 3 tbsp finely grated
young pecorino
2 tbsp fresh thyme leaves
Coarsely ground pepper

The amount of garlic used for this fragrant, velvety butter sounds excessive, almost intimidating. Just let go of the idea of harsh, raw garlic and think of smooth, oven-roasted cloves instead.

Spaghetti with Roasted Garlic Butter and Thyme

Preheat the oven to 425°F (220°C).

Spread the garlic cloves in a medium baking dish and roast, turning occasionally, for about 25 minutes or until soft enough to mash with a fork—mind that the garlic doesn't burn. Let the garlic cool for a few minutes then peel the cloves and transfer to a food processor or blender. Add the butter, purée until smooth, and season to taste with salt.

Bring a large pot of salted water to a boil and cook the spaghetti, according to the package instructions, until al dente. Drain the spaghetti and return it to the pot.

Mix the warm spaghetti with the garlic butter and divide among plates. Sprinkle with pecorino and thyme and season to taste with salt and pepper.

Makes 6 small sandwiches

1 allspice berry
½ tsp coriander seeds
½ tsp fennel seeds
½ tsp ground cumin
2 large eggs
¼ cup (60 ml) whole milk
Fine sea salt
Finely ground pepper
3 tbsp all-purpose flour
2 ounces (60 g) Taleggio, fontina,
or Robiola, coarsely grated
6 slices soft white bread
Unsalted butter,
to cook the sandwiches

Picture page 92, top left

The *mozzarella in carrozza*, which translates to "mozzarella in a carriage," is an Italian snack classic and an exciting playground to experiment with flavors. Here, fruity Taleggio cheese creates harmonic fusion with the complex tones of cumin, coriander, allspice, and fennel seeds. It's a keeper for breakfast and brunch, especially if you happen to have guests over that don't have a sweet tooth.

Spices and Taleggio in Carrozza

Combine the allspice, coriander seeds, fennel seeds, and cumin and grind with a mortar and pestle.

In a shallow bowl, whisk together the eggs and milk and season to taste with salt and pepper. Spread the flour on a flat plate.

Divide the cheese and spice mixture among 3 slices of bread, leaving a thin border around the edges. Top each sandwich with a second slice of bread and press together. Dip both sides of each sandwich in the flour until lightly coated then carefully dip each sandwich in the egg mixture, continuing to dip until all the liquid is soaked up.

In a large, heavy pan, heat 1 tablespoon of butter over medium-high heat and cook the sandwiches for a few minutes or until golden brown and crispy. Reduce the heat and add 1/2 tablespoon of butter then flip the sandwiches over and cook for 1 to 2 minutes or until golden brown. Cut the sandwiches in half diagonally and serve immediately.

66

67

68

69

Rutabaga is another neglected root in many kitchens, often overlooked and underappreciated. It looks unspectacular, but its subtle, earthy taste is pleasantly unique if you give it a chance and a little attention. Sauté the yellow root, deglaze it with orange juice and Grand Marnier liqueur, and it will be the star on top of a bowl of black beluga lentils.

Beluga Lentils with Orange-Grand Marnier Rutabaga

Serves 3 to 4

1 cup (220 g) lentils, preferably beluga (no soaking required)
1 small bunch fresh thyme, plus 6 sprigs for the rutabaga, and 1 tbsp fresh thyme leaves for the topping
1 bay leaf
Olive oil
Fine sea salt
Finely ground pepper
⅔ pound (300 g) peeled rutabaga, cut into ⅓-inch (7.5 mm) cubes
⅓ cup (75 ml) orange-flavored liqueur, such as Grand Marnier
½ tsp freshly grated orange zest, plus 2 tsp for the topping
⅓ cup (75 ml) freshly squeezed orange juice

Picture opposite, top right

Place the lentils in a medium saucepan with plenty of (unsalted) water, add the bunch of thyme and the bay leaf, and bring to a boil. Reduce the heat and simmer, adding more water if necessary, for about 20 minutes or until al dente (or follow the package instructions). There should be a little cooking liquid left when the lentils are done. Remove and discard the herbs then stir in a generous splash of olive oil and season to taste with salt and pepper.

While the lentils are cooking, prepare the rutabaga: In a large, heavy pan, heat a generous splash of olive oil over medium-high heat and sauté the rutabaga, stirring occasionally, for about 6 minutes or until golden and tender. Add the orange-flavored liqueur and 6 thyme sprigs and deglaze the pan, using a spatula to scrape any bits and pieces off the bottom. Cook for 20 seconds then add 1/2 teaspoon of orange zest and the orange juice and cook for 1 minute; season to taste with salt and pepper.

Divide the lentils among small bowls and arrange the rutabaga on top. Sprinkle with the rutabaga juices from the pan, a little orange zest, and thyme leaves and serve warm.

Whenever my partner gets a chance to take over the kitchen, he closes the door to make sure he's in complete control of the room, and gets experimental. On one such occasion, he impressed me with juicy meatballs cooked in a fruity cumin-tomato sauce. He had the genius idea to mix mashed kidney beans into the tiny meatballs, not only enhancing their flavor but also giving them a lighter texture. Fluffy flatbread or *Torta al Testo (recipe no. 125)* stuffed with the meatballs and aromatic sauce is absolutely delicious.

Kidney Bean and Beef Meatballs with Tomato Sauce and Cilantro

Serves 3 to 4

1 ¼ cups (250 g) drained
and rinsed canned kidney beans
14 ounces (400 g) ground beef
2 large handfuls fresh
cilantro leaves
1 medium red onion,
finely chopped
2 large cloves garlic, crushed
1 medium, fresh red chile,
seeded and very finely chopped
Ground cumin
Fine sea salt
Finely ground pepper
Olive oil
14 ounces (400 g) canned
whole peeled tomatoes, chopped
⅛ tsp granulated sugar
6 small flatbreads

Picture page 92, bottom left

Squeeze a handful of the kidney beans until mushy and transfer to a large bowl; reserve the remaining beans and set aside. Add the ground beef, $1/2$ the cilantro, $3/4$ of the onion, the garlic, $1/4$ of the chile, 1 teaspoon of cumin, $1 1/4$ teaspoons of salt, and a generous amount of pepper to the bowl and mix with your hands until well combined. Wet your hands and form the mixture into 16 roughly $1 1/2$-inch (4 cm) meatballs.

Reserve 10 cilantro leaves and set aside for the topping then roughly chop the remaining cilantro.

In a large, heavy pan, heat a generous splash of olive oil over medium heat. Add the meatballs and the remaining chopped onions and cook, turning the meatballs occasionally, for about 6 minutes or until the meatballs are light brown. Transfer the meatballs and onions to a plate, but leave the pan on the heat. Add a splash of olive oil and the reserved beans to the pan, and sear over high heat for 1 minute, stirring constantly. Add the tomatoes, the chopped cilantro, $1/4$ of the chile, $1/4$ teaspoon of cumin, and the sugar, stir, and season to taste with salt and pepper. Return the meatballs to the pan and stir until they are coated in sauce. Cover and simmer over medium-low heat for 3 minutes or until the meatballs are just cooked through. Season to taste with salt and pepper, sprinkle with the reserved cilantro leaves and the remaining chile, and serve with flatbread.

Finding inspiring seasonal produce in early March can be somewhat tricky, but restrictions and limitations often lead to creative inspiration. Belgian endive stays firm and crisp when you roast it in the oven, and this texture, along with its bitter taste, is a welcome contrast to the creamy, sweet softness of a potato gratin that is flecked with chèvre and thyme. I use sliced boiled potatoes, which makes it a quick lunch or dinner.

Potato-Belgian Endive Gratin with Chèvre and Thyme

Serves 3 to 6

Olive oil
4 medium heads Belgian endive, cut in half lengthwise
Fine sea salt
Finely ground pepper
½ cup (120 ml) heavy cream
½ cup (120 ml) whole milk
Nutmeg, preferably freshly grated
1⅔ pounds (750 g) peeled waxy potatoes, boiled and sliced
4 ounces (110 g) soft chèvre, crumbled
1 small bunch fresh thyme, leaves only
Butter, to butter the quiche dish

Picture page 92, bottom right

Preheat the oven to 400°F (200°C) and butter a 12-inch (30 cm) quiche dish.

In a large, heavy pan, heat a splash of olive oil over medium-high heat and sauté the endive for 1 ½ to 2 minutes per side or until golden brown and al dente. Season to taste with salt and pepper.

In a medium bowl, whisk together the heavy cream, milk, 1 teaspoon of salt, and generous amounts of nutmeg and pepper.

Arrange the potatoes in overlapping circles in the prepared quiche dish. Place the endive, like rays, on top of the potatoes then pour the cream mixture over the vegetables. Sprinkle with the chèvre and thyme and bake for 25 to 30 minutes or until golden brown and bubbling. Let the gratin cool for 5 minutes then sprinkle with a little pepper and serve.

Filling brownies with jam elevates their fudgy gooeyness to new heights. Although raspberry jam brownies—with all their deep red fruitiness wrapped in dense, dark chocolate—were my indulgence of choice for years, a jar of leftover home-made tangerine jam was a game changer. Bittersweet chocolate complemented by this sticky citrus spread is a match made in heaven.

Tangerine Jam Chocolate Brownies

Serves 8 to 12

1½ cups plus 1 tbsp (350 g) unsalted butter
12 ounces (340 g) bittersweet chocolate
1 vanilla bean, split and scraped
6 large eggs
1¼ cups (250 g) granulated sugar
2 cups (260 g) all-purpose flour
1 tsp fine sea salt
1 cup (300 g) thick and chunky tangerine jam *(recipe no. 333)* or orange marmalade, whisked*

Preheat the oven to 350°F / 180°C (preferably convection setting). Butter a 9 x 11-inch (23 x 28 cm) cake pan or baking dish and line with parchment paper.

In a medium saucepan, melt the butter, chocolate, and vanilla seeds, stirring constantly, over medium heat. Set the pan aside and let the mixture cool for 5 minutes.

In the bowl of a stand mixer fitted with the whisk attachment, whisk together the eggs and sugar for 4 minutes or until thick and fluffy. Add the cooled chocolate mixture and mix for 1 minute or until combined.

Whisk together the flour and salt, fold into the chocolate batter, and mix for 1 minute or until combined. Scrape half the batter into the lined cake pan and even out the top. Drizzle the jam all over the batter and spread it carefully, so that the layers stay separate. Add the remaining batter and even out the top. Bake for 50 to 55 minutes (slightly longer if using a conventional oven) or until the top is golden and spongy. Let it cool for at least 10 minutes then cut into small brownies.

The brownies taste best on the first and second day.

* If your jam is too loose, cook it in a saucepan over high heat, stirring constantly, until thick.

This recipe is dedicated to my beautiful friend Aylin, who always asks her dear partner, Jan, to cook this dish for her when she's feeling the blues. Juicy eggplant, paired with cumin, cinnamon, capers, and orange juice, sits on a dollop of smooth polenta. It's so easy to create a bite of happiness.

Cumin-Cinnamon Eggplant with Capers and Orange Polenta

Serves 2

For the polenta

1 cup (240 ml) milk

1 cup (240 ml) water, plus more as needed

1 tsp fine sea salt

2 tbsp olive oil

¾ cup (120 g) fine polenta

3 long strips fresh orange peel (white pith removed)

For the eggplant

Olive oil

2 large cloves garlic, crushed

1 tbsp capers, preferably preserved in salt, rinsed, drained, and dried

¼ tsp ground cumin

¼ tsp ground cinnamon

7 ounces (200 g) eggplant, cut into ¼-inch (0.5 cm) cubes

¼ cup (60 ml) freshly squeezed orange juice

1 tsp balsamic vinegar, plus more to taste

Fine sea salt

Finely ground pepper

½ to 1 tsp freshly grated orange zest

For the polenta, bring the milk, water, and salt to a boil in a medium saucepan. Take the pan off the heat, add the olive oil, polenta, and orange peel and whisk until combined. Place the saucepan over the lowest heat setting and cook the polenta like a risotto, stirring occasionally and adding a little more water whenever the polenta starts to thicken, for 10 minutes or until smooth and creamy. Remove and discard the orange peel, cover, and set aside.

For the eggplant, heat a generous splash of olive oil in a large, heavy pan set over medium heat. Add the garlic, capers, cumin, and cinnamon and cook, stirring, for 1 minute. Add the eggplant and sauté, stirring and adding a little more oil if necessary, for 5 minutes or until golden and soft. Add the orange juice and deglaze the pan, using a spatula to scrape any bits and pieces off the bottom. Add the vinegar and season to taste with salt, pepper, and additional vinegar. Sprinkle with a little orange zest and serve on top of the warm polenta.

Serves 2 to 4

1 large beet, scrubbed
1 bay leaf
3 tbsp olive oil
1 tbsp balsamic vinegar
1 tbsp white balsamic vinegar
Fine sea salt
Finely ground pepper
1 large, firm apple, cored
and cut into very thin wedges
1 handful pomegranate seeds

Whenever my mother calls me to rave excitedly about one of her new creations, I can't help but go straight to the kitchen. Her enthusiasm for her "red carpaccio" was infectious, so I got started right away, boiling beets and peeling a ruby-red pomegranate, and was immediately smitten by this vibrant vegetable creation.

Beet and Apple Carpaccio with Pomegranate

Bring a medium pot of salted water to a boil and add the beet and bay leaf then reduce the heat, cover, and simmer for 45 to 50 minutes or until it's tender. Drain the beet and quickly rinse with cold water. When it's cool enough to handle, peel off the skin, and thinly slice on a mandoline.

Whisk together the olive oil and both vinegars and season to taste with salt and pepper.

Arrange the beet and apple slices in overlapping circles on a large plate then sprinkle with the pomegranate seeds, drizzle with the dressing, and serve immediately.

Makes 2 sandwiches

1 large or 2 small ripe avocados,
peeled and pitted
3 heaping tbsp chopped fresh
cilantro leaves, plus a few leaves
for the topping
2 to 3 tbsp sour cream
1 tbsp freshly squeezed
lemon juice
Ground cumin
Fine sea salt
Finely ground pepper
Olive oil
4 slices bacon
2 large dark rustic buns,
such as spelt or rye, cut in half
¼ medium, fresh red chile,
seeded and thinly sliced

I might be one of the few people on this planet who isn't totally crazy about avocados, but I would never, ever reject a bowl of good guacamole. My version has hints of lemon, cilantro, and hot chile, but when I want to switch things up, I stir in some cumin, spread the dip on a crusty bun, and top it off with crispy bacon.

Cumin Guacamole Sandwich with Bacon

In a medium bowl, gently mash the avocado until smooth but still chunky. Add the cilantro, 2 tablespoons of sour cream, and the lemon juice and mix until combined. Season to taste with cumin, salt, pepper, and additional sour cream.

In a large, heavy pan, heat a splash of olive oil over medium heat and cook the bacon, turning occasionally, for a few minutes or until golden and crisp; reserve the bacon juices from the pan.

Spread the guacamole on the bottom of each bun and sprinkle with the chile. Place 2 slices of bacon on top of each sandwich and drizzle with the bacon juices. Sprinkle with a few cilantro leaves, place a top on each bun, and enjoy.

My grandmother Lisa's potato latkes—called *Kartoffelpuffer* in Germany—were my favorite food as a child. Whenever I visited her for a few days, she asked me for a list of dishes I'd like to eat during my short holiday. She'd cook for me and I'd sit, daydreaming on the swing tied to a thick branch of an old cherry tree in her garden. I treasure this memory, but I also believe we have to let recipes evolve in order to keep traditions alive. I add celeriac and carrots to my latkes and top them with a smoked trout dip.

Potato, Celeriac, and Carrot Latkes with Smoked Trout Dip

Serves 3 to 4

For the smoked trout dip

3 ounces (85 g) smoked trout fillet (or smoked mackerel fillet)
3 ounces (85 g) cream cheese
3 tbsp chopped fresh chives, plus 3 tbsp for serving
Fine sea salt
Finely ground pepper

For the latkes

1½ pounds (680 g) peeled waxy potatoes, grated in a food processor
⅓ pound (150 g) peeled celeriac, grated in a food processor
7 ounces (200 g) peeled carrots, grated in a food processor
2 large onions, grated in a food processor
1 cup (130 g) all-purpose flour
2 ½ tsp fine sea salt
Finely ground pepper
Sunflower oil, to fry the latkes

For the dip, purée the smoked trout, cream cheese, and 3 tablespoons of chives in a food processor or blender until smooth. Season to taste with salt and pepper.

For the latkes, squeeze as much liquid as possible out of the grated potatoes, celeriac, and carrots then mix them together and spread them out on paper towels. Top with a second layer of paper towels and press out any remaining moisture. Transfer to a large bowl. Squeeze the onions between two layers of paper towels and add to the potato mixture. Add the flour, salt, and a generous amount of pepper and use your hands to mix it together until well combined.

Fill a large, heavy sauté pan with about 1/3 inch (7.5 mm) of sunflower oil and place over medium-high heat. Take 2 to 3 tablespoons of the potato mixture into your fingers and form it into a thin, small pancake-shaped latke. Mind that the latkes are thin enough to get crispy when fried. Repeat with the remaining latke mixture. Working in batches, fry the latkes for 3 to 4 minutes per side or until golden brown and crispy. Reduce the heat if they brown too quickly. Transfer to paper towels to drain and repeat with the remaining latkes, adding more oil if necessary. This makes 12 to 14 latkes.

Enjoy the latkes warm with a dollop of the smoked trout dip and a sprinkle of chives.

Monkfish has two great qualities: Its flavor is strong and its texture is firmer than many other fish. You can roll, roast, and wrap it and it will still look as pretty as ever. Wrapping monkfish in garlicky ramp leaves and prosciutto gives it a festive appearance, but doesn't take long at all, which makes this an easy weekday dinner.

Ramp and Prosciutto-Wrapped Monkfish with Lemony Peas

Serves 2

26 large fresh ramp
or ramson leaves
(the European cousin of ramps)
1 (10-ounce / 280-g)
monkfish fillet, preferably
a thick center piece
Olive oil
Fine sea salt
Finely ground pepper
10 very thin slices
prosciutto di Parma
(or prosciutto di San Daniele)
6 ounces (170 g) fresh
or frozen peas
1 to 2 tsp freshly squeezed
lemon juice

Preheat the oven to 400°F (200°C). Brush the bottom of a medium baking dish with olive oil.

Thinly slice 12 ramp leaves and set aside.

Cut the monkfish in half lengthwise, coat both pieces in a little olive oil, and season to taste with salt and pepper.

Place a large piece of plastic wrap on a work surface. Arrange 5 slices of prosciutto, slightly overlapping, on top of the plastic wrap then arrange 7 ramp leaves cross-wise on top of the prosciutto. Place 1 piece of monkfish on top of and parallel to the ramp leaves. Roll and wrap the fish tightly in the ramp leaves and prosciutto and transfer to the prepared baking dish, leaving the plastic wrap on the work surface. Prepare the second piece of monkfish the same way. Brush both pieces of wrapped monkfish with a little olive oil and bake for about 15 minutes or until the monkfish is just cooked through.

While the fish is baking, bring a small pot of salted water to a boil and blanch the peas for about 1 minute or until al dente. Drain and quickly rinse with cold water.

In a small saucepan, heat a splash of olive over high heat. Add 1/2 of the reserved ramp leaves then take the pan off the heat and add the peas and 1 teaspoon of the lemon juice. Stir and season to taste with salt, pepper, and additional lemon juice.

Cut the monkfish into thick slices with a very sharp knife and divide among plates. Sprinkle with the remaining ramp leaves and serve with the peas.

My taste buds and rice never really found common ground to develop a close relationship. But thanks to this recipe, my attitude is slowly changing. Cloves, allspice berries, and bay leaf enliven the simple white grains, and when crispy broccoli and sesame seeds pitch in, I can feel the tender beginning of a new era of rice cooking in my kitchen.

Spiced Rice with Broccoli and Sesame Seeds

Serves 2 to 3

For the rice
5 whole cloves, finely ground with a mortar and pestle
2 allspice berries, finely ground with a mortar and pestle
1 small bay leaf, finely ground with a mortar and pestle
1 cup (190 g) parboiled (converted) rice
Olive oil
Fine sea salt
Finely ground pepper

For the broccoli
1 small head broccoli, trimmed
Olive oil
Fine sea salt
Finely ground pepper
2 tbsp white sesame seeds, toasted
Piment d'Espelette (optional)

For the rice, whisk together the cloves, allspice, and bay leaf and set aside.

Bring a medium pot of salted water to a boil and cook the rice for 15 to 20 minutes or until tender (or follow the package instructions). Drain the rice and return to the pot. Add a splash of olive oil and the spice mixture, mix until combined, and season to taste with salt and pepper.

While the rice is cooking, blanch the broccoli: Bring a large pot of salted water to a boil and blanch the broccoli for a few minutes or until al dente. Drain and quickly rinse with cold water then break or cut the broccoli into bite-size florets. In a large, heavy pan, heat a splash of olive oil over high heat and sear the broccoli, turning once, for 1 1/2 to 2 minutes or until golden brown—mind that it doesn't get too soft. Season to taste with salt and pepper.

Divide the rice and broccoli among plates, sprinkle with sesame seeds and a little piment d'Espelette or pepper, and serve immediately.

During a trip to Le Touquet, a seaside village on Normandy's stormy coast, I ended up at Crêperie Aux Mignardises Saint-Jean, looking for food and shelter from heavy wind and rain. They served me a crêpe that was so simple and genius. You cook thin crêpes, sprinkle them with a little sugar, and generously squeeze fresh lemon over each pancake. This is a perfect dessert for a dinner party with friends.

Crêpes au Citron

Serves 3 to 6

2 cups plus 2 tbsp (510 ml) whole milk

4 large eggs

2 cups (260 g) all-purpose flour, sifted

¼ cup (50 g) granulated sugar, plus more for serving

⅛ tsp fine sea salt

Unsalted butter, to cook the crêpes

About 4 large lemons, cut in half

1 small handful small fresh mint leaves, for the topping (optional)

In the bowl of a stand mixer fitted with the whisk attachment, whisk together the milk, eggs, flour, sugar, and salt until smooth. Let the batter sit for about 10 minutes before you cook the crêpes.

In a large cast-iron pan or nonstick skillet, melt $1/2$ teaspoon of the butter over medium-high heat. Pour in a ladle of the batter, tilting and turning the pan, so that the batter spreads evenly and very thinly. Cook the crêpe, flipping once, for about 30 to 60 seconds per side or until golden then sprinkle with a little sugar. Carefully fold the crêpe in half twice, so it forms a triangle then transfer to a plate and cover to keep warm. Finish making crêpes with the remaining batter, adding a little more butter to the pan between crêpes and adjusting the heat as necessary; this makes 15 to 18 crêpes.

Divide the warm crêpes among individual plates then drizzle each crêpe with a generous amount of freshly squeezed lemon juice, sprinkle with a little sugar, and decorate with a few mint leaves. Bon appétit!

Maltese *zeppoli*, also known as *sfineġ*, are traditionally made on March 19th to celebrate the feast of St. Joseph. The village bakers fry tiny, puffy balls of choux pastry to golden perfection and fill them with fresh ricotta, chocolate, and candied citrus peel. In Sicily and other parts of Europe, you can also find them plain, rolled in sugar, or dipped in melted chocolate. I follow the Maltese tradition and go for ricotta, but I use fresh berries instead of chocolate.

Maltese Zeppoli
Fried Cream Puffs with Vanilla Ricotta and Fresh Berries

Serves 4 to 6

For the filling

9 ounces (250 g) fresh ricotta, drained
1 tbsp honey, plus more to taste
1 tbsp freshly squeezed orange juice
½ vanilla bean, split and scraped
2 handfuls mixed fresh berries, such as raspberries and blueberries

For the pastry

6 cups (1.4 liters) sunflower oil, to fry the pastry
½ cup (115 g) unsalted butter
½ cup (120 ml) water
¼ cup (50 g) granulated sugar
⅛ tsp fine sea salt
1 cup (130 g) all-purpose flour, sifted
3 large eggs

For the topping

About 4 tbsp confectioners' sugar

For the filling, whisk together the ricotta, honey, orange juice, and vanilla seeds in a medium bowl until creamy. Sweeten to taste with additional honey.

In a large, heavy pot, heat the sunflower oil over medium-high heat. Line a large baking dish with paper towels.

For the pastry, in a medium pot, bring the butter, water, granulated sugar, and salt to a boil. Reduce the heat to medium-low, add the flour, and stir vigorously with a wooden spoon until the dough is smooth and comes away from the sides of the pot. Transfer the dough to a large bowl and let cool for about 10 minutes. Add the eggs, 1 at a time, beating with a wooden spoon and incorporating each egg before adding the next one, and continue beating until well combined.

To see if the oil is hot enough, dip the bottom of a wooden spoon into the oil; tiny bubbles should form around it. Start with 2 balls of dough to test the oil. Scoop out a heaping teaspoon of the dough and use a second teaspoon to form a small ball. Repeat to make a second ball of dough. Carefully drop the balls of dough into the hot oil and fry for about 4 to 6 minutes or until they are golden and cooked through, adjusting the heat if the pastry browns too quickly. Use a slotted ladle or spoon to transfer the puffy balls to the prepared baking dish. Working in batches, fry more puffs with the remaining dough. This makes about 26 puffs.

Let the puffy balls cool completely then cut a wide slit into each ball and fill with a small spoonful of the ricotta filling and 2 to 3 berries. Dust with a little confectioners' sugar and serve.

Froga tat-Tarja is a popular weekday classic in Malta, mastered by every nanna and mama on the islands, and praised and cherished by the Maltese people. It's a leftover spaghetti omelet, and provides pure and satisfying comfort. Mixing in pesto and spring onions balances any heaviness from the pasta.

Froga tat-Tarja
Maltese Pasta Frittata with Pesto and Spring Onions

Serves 1 to 2

2 large eggs
3 tbsp green pesto,
such as ramp or basil pesto
(recipe no. 102)
4 tbsp finely grated Parmesan
1 handful thinly sliced
spring onions (white and light
green parts only)
3 ounces (85 g) leftover
cooked spaghetti, cold
Fine sea salt
Coarsely ground pepper
Olive oil

In a large bowl, whisk together the eggs, 2 tablespoons of the pesto, 3 tablespoons of the Parmesan, and 3/4 of the spring onions. Add the spaghetti, season to taste with salt and pepper, and toss to combine.

In a heavy 8-inch (20 cm) pan, heat a splash of olive oil over medium-high heat. Add the pasta mixture, pushing gently to even out the top and sides, and cook for about 2 minutes or until golden brown. Carefully flip the frittata over and cook for 2 more minutes or until golden brown and just cooked through. Sprinkle with the remaining pesto, Parmesan, and spring onions and season to taste with salt and pepper. Cut into wedges and serve warm.

The sharpness of blue cheese cuts boldly through the creaminess of an omelet, and together, they call out to be made into a breakfast sandwich. This is a quick and simple recipe: You only need a few very thin slices of Italian rosemary ham, a little arugula, and fresh spongy ciabatta bread. By lunchtime, you'll be craving more and wishing you had made an extra sandwich.

Blue Cheese Omelet Sandwich with Rosemary Ham

Makes 2 sandwiches

3 large eggs
¼ cup (60 ml) heavy cream
Nutmeg, preferably freshly grated
Fine sea salt
Finely ground pepper
Unsalted butter
2 ounces (60 g) blue cheese
1 small handful arugula leaves
1 medium loaf ciabatta, cut into 2
buns and each cut in half
4 slices Italian rosemary ham
1 tbsp finely chopped fresh
rosemary needles

In a medium bowl, whisk together the eggs and heavy cream and season to taste with nutmeg, salt, and pepper. In a small cast-iron pan or nonstick skillet, heat 1 teaspoon of butter over medium-high heat. Pour the egg mixture into the pan and stir 3 to 4 times. Mind to not scramble the eggs and to just fluff them up a bit; reduce the heat if they brown too quickly. When the bottom side is golden, flip the omelet and cook the other side for 1 to 2 minutes or until golden and just set. Take the pan off the heat. Crumble the blue cheese over the omelet then cut it in half. Layer the two halves on top of each other and cut the omelet in half again.

Divide the arugula among the bottom halves of the buns and place the warm omelet on top. Arrange the ham on top of the omelet and sprinkle with a little rosemary and pepper. Place a top on each bun, squeeze a little, and enjoy.

I've added all kinds of pesto to my burger mixtures and sneaked dried dates into meatloaf *(recipe no. 22)*. Now it's time for sticky prunes to show what they can do to refine ground beef. Dark and shriveled and not as sweet as dates, prunes bring a subtle hint of fruit, but also add juiciness to burger patties. Golden brown sautéed onions, finished with a dash of elderflower syrup, are a scrumptious topping for this meaty treat.

Prune Burgers with Elderflower Onions and Pan-Roasted Potatoes

Serves 4

For the elderflower onions

Unsalted butter,
to cook the onions
Olive oil
2 medium onions,
cut in half and thinly sliced
1 tbsp elderflower syrup
(or maple syrup)

For the burgers and potatoes

18 ounces (500 g) ground beef
3 ounces (85 g) pitted prunes,
roughly chopped
¼ cup (40 g) dry breadcrumbs
1 large egg
1 medium onion, finely chopped
1 large clove garlic, crushed
2 tbsp fresh thyme leaves
Olive oil
1½ tsp coriander seeds, crushed
with a mortar and pestle
½ tsp freshly grated orange zest
Fine sea salt
Finely ground pepper
Unsalted butter,
to cook the burgers
12 small waxy potatoes, scrubbed,
boiled, and cut in half lengthwise

For the onions, in a small, heavy pan, heat 1 teaspoon of butter and a splash of olive oil over medium heat. Add the onions and cook, stirring occasionally, for 15 minutes or until golden and soft. Stir in the elderflower syrup, cover, and set aside.

For the burgers, combine the ground beef, prunes, breadcrumbs, egg, onion, garlic, thyme, 1 tablespoon of olive oil, coriander seeds, orange zest, 2 teaspoons of salt, and a generous amount of pepper in a large bowl and mix with your hands until well combined. Form the mixture into 4 large burgers, flattening them just a little.

In a large, heavy pan, heat 2 tablespoons of butter and a generous splash of olive oil over medium heat. Cook the burgers, turning occasionally, for about 14 minutes or until just cooked through. Transfer the burgers to a plate and cover, but leave the pan on the heat. Add the potatoes to the pan and roast over medium-high heat, turning them once or twice, for 6 to 8 minutes or until golden brown. Season to taste with salt and pepper.

Divide the burgers and potatoes among plates and sprinkle with the onions.

Once a week, I boil a batch of beets and keep them in the refrigerator for salads, dips, and quick lunch nibbles. Sprinkling this root with olive oil and flaky sea salt is the most minimalistic way to enjoy them, but it's also my favorite. It's a pure and honest dish, uniting earthy, sweet, and salty in a single bite. Just keep in mind that the fewer ingredients you use, the more attention you have to pay to their quality.

Serves 2 to 4

2 medium beets, scrubbed
2 large bay leaves
High-quality olive oil
Flaky sea salt

Beets with Olive Oil and Flaky Sea Salt

Bring a medium pot of salted water to a boil and add the beets and bay leaves then reduce the heat, cover, and simmer for about 45 minutes or until tender. Drain the beets and quickly rinse with cold water. When they are cool enough to handle, peel off the skin and cut into chunky cubes. Drizzle the beets with olive oil and season to taste with salt.

Combining pan-seared prawns, sautéed fennel, and creamy polenta began as one of my mother's late-winter projects. She cooked and refined this trilogy three nights in a row before I got involved, but after a productive phone call, dissecting all the details, I went straight to the kitchen to do my own homework.

Serves 2

For the polenta
1 cup (240 ml) homemade
or quality store-bought
vegetable broth
1 cup (240 ml) water
1 tsp fine sea salt
2 tbsp olive oil
¾ cup (120 g) fine polenta

For the prawns and fennel
Olive oil
8 large shell-on prawns
without heads
1 small fennel bulb,
cut in half lengthwise, cored,
and very thinly sliced lengthwise
Fine sea salt
Finely ground pepper
¼ cup (60 ml) pastis, Ricard,
or Pernod

Prawns, Pastis, and Fennel with Polenta

For the polenta, bring the broth, water, and salt to a boil in a medium saucepan. Take the pan off the heat, add the olive oil and polenta, and whisk until combined. Place the saucepan over the lowest heat setting and cook the polenta like a risotto, stirring occasionally and adding a little more water when it starts to thicken, for 10 minutes or until smooth and creamy. Season to taste with salt, cover, and set aside.

For the prawns and fennel, in a medium, heavy pan, heat a splash of olive oil over medium-high heat. Add the prawns and sear, turning occasionally, for 5 minutes or until golden brown and cooked through. Transfer the prawns to a plate but leave the pan on the heat. Add a splash of olive oil and the fennel to the pan and sauté, stirring, for about 3 minutes or until golden and al dente; season to taste with salt and pepper. Pour the pastis over the fennel and deglaze the pan, using a spatula to scrape any bits and pieces off the bottom. Cook for 1 minute then return the prawns to the pan and stir to combine. Divide the polenta among plates, arrange the prawns and fennel on top, and serve.

When berries and other juicy fruits aren't in season yet and it's time for citrus to say goodbye, there's no need to be melancholy. Chocolate and peanut butter will easily satisfy any weekend cravings for a sweet treat. Ripe banana joins the peanut filling for these gooey chocolate baby cakes, and while they may sound like treats for a kid's birthday party, deep down, we know that, luckily, we never fully grow up.

Chocolate Baby Cakes with Peanut Butter and Banana

Serves 6

¼ cup (60 g) unsalted butter, at room temperature

⅓ cup (65 g) granulated sugar

½ vanilla bean, split and scraped

⅛ tsp fine sea salt

4 large eggs

10 ounces (280 g) bittersweet chocolate, melted and cooled

⅓ cup (45 g) all-purpose flour

⅓ cup (85 g) smooth peanut butter, at room temperature

2 ounces (60 g) ripe banana

Picture opposite, top left

Preheat the oven to 400°F / 200°C (preferably convection setting). Butter 6 (4-ounce / 120-ml) ramekins.

In the bowl of a stand mixer fitted with the paddle attachment, beat the butter, sugar, vanilla seeds, and salt until fluffy. Add the eggs, 1 at a time, incorporating each egg before adding the next one, and continue beating for 1 minute or until thick and creamy. Add the chocolate and mix until combined then add the flour and mix for 1 minute or until combined.

In a food processor or blender, purée the peanut butter and banana until smooth.

Divide about ²/₃ of the chocolate batter among the prepared ramekins. Place 1 heaping teaspoon of the peanut butter mixture in the center of each ramekin, softly pushing it into the batter. Scrape the remaining batter on top of the filling and even it out. Bake for 12 to 14 minutes (slightly longer if using a conventional oven) or until the tops of the cakes start to become spongy but still feel slightly wobbly underneath. The batter should still be partially liquid in the center. Remove the cakes from the ramekins and serve warm or cold.

84

85

86

89

Seeing the first asparagus of the year spread out on the kitchen table is exciting—it feels like the official beginning of spring. There are many recipes to herald the start of the season, including ones that are elegant and complex, as well as time- and labor-intensive. But the week has just begun, so let's take it easy for now. A Spanish tortilla, refined with aromatic cheese and tarragon, and crowned with crisp green asparagus, sounds just right. It's a main dish for two or makes for a nice nibble when you have a few friends over to enjoy a bottle of wine.

Asparagus Tortilla with Mountain Cheese and Tarragon

Serves 2 to 4

14 ounces (400 g) trimmed green asparagus
1 pound (450 g) peeled waxy potatoes, very thinly sliced on a mandoline
Olive oil
1 medium onion, cut in half and thinly sliced
4 large eggs
Fine sea salt
Nutmeg, preferably freshly grated
Finely ground pepper
2 ounces (60 g) aromatic mountain cheese that melts well, such as Appenzeller, Comté, or Gruyère, coarsely grated
1 small handful fresh tarragon leaves

Picture page 113, top right

Set the oven to broil (quicker method) or preheat to 500°F (260°C).

Bring a large pot of salted water to a boil and blanch the asparagus for about 1 1/2 minutes or until al dente. Drain, quickly rinse with cold water, and set aside.

Spread the potatoes, side by side, between 2 layers of paper towels and pat them dry.

In a heavy, ovenproof 10-inch (25 cm) skillet, heat a splash of olive oil over medium heat and sauté the onions, stirring occasionally, for 5 minutes or until golden and soft. Transfer the onions to a large plate, but leave the pan on the heat. Add a generous splash of olive oil to the pan then add the potatoes, spreading them evenly. Cover and cook the potatoes over medium heat for about 12 minutes or until golden. If the potatoes brown too quickly, reduce the heat. Using a spatula, loosen the potatoes from the sides of the pan and lift gently off the bottom. Cover the pan with a large lid then carefully and quickly flip the pan over. Keep the potatoes on the lid while you add 1 tablespoon of olive oil to the pan then slide the potatoes off the lid into the pan. Spread the onions on top of the potatoes, cover, and cook for 2 minutes. Whisk the eggs with 1 teaspoon of salt, season to taste with nutmeg and pepper, and pour over the potatoes. Cover and cook for 2 minutes. Spread the asparagus on top of the tortilla, cover, and cook for 4 minutes or until the egg is just set. Sprinkle with the cheese and put the tortilla under the broiler, or roast at 500°F (260°C) for a few minutes or until the cheese starts to melt. Sprinkle with tarragon, season to taste with salt and pepper, and serve immediately.

This fresh cucumber salad with dill, ginger, and lime is a five-minute solution for when you're longing for a green boost, and need some vibrant flavor and vitamins.

Cucumber Carpaccio with Dill, Ginger, and Lime

Serves 1 to 2

For the dressing

2 tbsp olive oil

½ tsp freshly grated lime zest

1 tbsp freshly squeezed lime juice

1 ½ tbsp finely chopped fresh dill

1 tsp freshly grated ginger

Fine sea salt

Finely ground pepper

For the salad

½ large Englisch cucumber, scrubbed and very thinly sliced on a mandoline

1 small spring onion (green part only), thinly sliced

Picture page 113, bottom left

For the dressing, whisk together the olive oil, lime zest, lime juice, dill, and ginger. Season to taste with salt and pepper.

Arrange the cucumber and spring onion on a large plate, drizzle with the dressing, and serve immediately.

A fried egg is like a good friend—it doesn't take much to have a good time. You can keep it plain, or pick some fresh herbs, like the delicate leaves of parsley, dill, basil, tarragon, cilantro, or chives, and sprinkle them on top while the egg is cooking. The tasty greens merge with the setting egg white and yolk, adding a little excitement to this rather frugal dish.

Herb-Fried Egg on Toast

Makes 1 toast

Unsalted butter, to cook the egg

1 slice dark bread, such as spelt or rye

1 large egg

6 leaves mixed fresh herbs, such as parsley, dill, basil, tarragon, cilantro, or chives

Fine sea salt

Finely ground pepper

In a small, heavy pan, heat 1½ teaspoons of butter over medium-high heat. Add the bread and toast for 1 to 2 minutes per side or until golden and crisp. Transfer the toast to a plate, but leave the pan on the heat. Add 1 teaspoon of butter to the pan and as soon as it starts sizzling, crack the egg into the pan. Sprinkle the herbs over the egg and cook for 2 to 3 minutes or until the egg white is just set, the edges are crispy, and the yolk is still runny. Season to taste with salt and pepper. Place the egg on top of the toast and enjoy.

A golden rösti is quick Swiss comfort food: It takes only ten minute to turn raw potatoes into hearty pan-roasted deliciousness. Depending on the topping, rösti can be rich and filling, but if you plop a dollop of herb feta dip on top, it tastes green and fresh.

Potato Rösti with Sorrel, Parsley, and Dill Feta Dip

Serves 2 to 4

For the feta dip*

5 ounces (140 g) feta
⅓ cup (75 ml) olive oil
1 ounce (30 g) fresh sorrel leaves,
plus 8 chopped leaves
for the topping
1 handful fresh dill
1 handful fresh flat-leaf
parsley leaves
Fine sea salt
Finely ground pepper

For the potato rösti

Olive oil
15 ounces (420 g) peeled
waxy potatoes,
cut into thin matchsticks
Flaky sea salt
Coarsely ground pepper

For the dip, purée the feta, olive oil, sorrel, dill, and parsley in a food processor or blender until smooth. Season to taste with fine sea salt and finely ground pepper and set aside.

For the rösti, in a 10-inch (25 cm) cast-iron pan, heat 5 tablespoons of olive oil over high heat. Add the potatoes, spreading them evenly and gently pushing them down with a spatula. Turn the heat down to medium-high and cook for 5 minutes, reducing the heat if the potatoes brown too quickly. Using a spatula, loosen the rösti from the sides of the pan and lift gently off the bottom. Cover the pan with a large lid then carefully and quickly flip the pan over. Keep the rösti on the lid while you add 1 tablespoon of olive oil to the pan then slide the rösti off the lid into the pan. Cook for 5 minutes or until the potatoes are golden brown and crispy on the bottom. Loosen the rösti from the sides and the bottom of the pan and slide it onto a large plate. Season to taste with flaky sea salt and coarsely ground pepper. Serve the rösti with a generous dollop of the feta dip and sprinkle with chopped sorrel.

* You can use leftover feta dip as a spread on bread.

Baking salmon in a thick crust of flaky sea salt is the best way to infuse it with flavor and guarantees perfectly juicy, tender fillets. You'll find two recipes in this book that use this technique: this dill and juniper version for traditionalists and a blood orange and turmeric combination for more adventurous cooks (*recipe no. 355*). You can use other fish, but I find the strong taste and oiliness of salmon's pink fillets ideal for this recipe.

Salt-Baked Salmon with Dill and Juniper

Serves 2 to 3

For the salt crust
2 ¼ pounds (1 kg) flaky sea salt
¾ cup (100 g) all-purpose flour
¼ cup (30 g) cornstarch
2 large egg whites
About ⅓ cup (75 ml) water, cold

For the salmon
2 (10-ounce / 280-g)
skin-on salmon fillets
8 juniper berries, crushed
with a mortar and pestle
½ tsp black peppercorns,
crushed with a mortar and pestle
1 small bunch fresh dill,
plus 1 tbsp chopped fresh dill
for serving

Ovenproof cotton string

Picture page 113, bottom right

Preheat the oven to 400°F (200°C). Line a medium baking dish with parchment paper.

For the salt crust, combine the salt, flour, cornstarch, egg whites, and cold water in a large bowl and use your fingers or a tablespoon to quickly mix until combined. Spread a thin layer of the salt mixture, roughly the size of 1 salmon fillet, in the middle of the lined baking dish.

For the salmon, rub the pink side of each salmon fillet with half the juniper berries and crushed black peppercorns. Place the bunch of dill on top of 1 salmon fillet and top with the second fillet, so that the skin side of each fillet is on the outside. Carefully tie the salmon fillets together with ovenproof cotton string and arrange on top of the salt mixture in the baking dish. Using your fingers, gently pack the remaining salt mixture over and around the salmon until it's covered. If the salt mixture is too dry, add a little more water. The salt may slide down a little and have some cracks, but that's fine—just try to seal the fish inside the crust as much as possible. Bake for 55 minutes or until a metal skewer, poked through the crust into the thickest part of the salmon, is warm to the touch when you pull it out of the salmon.

Let the salt crust cool for 2 minutes then carefully break it open with a sharp bread knife. Scrape the salt off the salmon then divide the fillets among plates, sprinkle with a little dill, and serve immediately.

Russischer Zupfkuchen is a German classic, and popular for Sunday coffee table gatherings. Although the cake is a relatively recent creation, its origin and history are somewhat murky. The name is misleading, as the cake has no connection to Russia. Zupfkuchen means "plucked cake," and refers to the chocolate pastry pattern on top of the cheese filling. The same pastry is used for the crumbly base, adding depth to balance the creamy filling. Traditionally, the cake is made with cream cheese, but I prefer a slightly lighter combination of ricotta and mascarpone.

Russischer Zupfkuchen
German Chocolate
and Ricotta Cheesecake

Serves 8 to 12

For the pastry

2⅓ cups (300 g) all-purpose flour

⅓ cup plus 1 tbsp (80 g) granulated sugar

½ cup (50 g) Dutch-process or natural unsweetened cocoa powder

1½ tsp baking powder

⅛ tsp fine sea salt

¾ cup (170 g) unsalted butter, cold

1 large egg

1 tbsp whole milk, cold

For the filling

⅔ cup (125 g) granulated sugar

½ cup (60 g) cornstarch

1 tsp baking powder

⅛ tsp fine sea salt

1 vanilla bean, split and scraped

18 ounces (500 g) fresh ricotta, drained

9 ounces (250 g) mascarpone

4 large eggs

1 tbsp whole milk, cold

Preheat the oven to 350°F (180°C) and butter a 10-inch (25 cm) springform pan.

For the pastry, combine the flour, sugar, cocoa powder, baking powder, and salt in the bowl of a stand mixer fitted with the dough hook attachment. Add the butter and use a knife to cut it into the flour until there are just small pieces left. Quickly rub the butter into the flour with your fingers until combined. Add the egg and cold milk and mix with the hook until crumbly. Form the dough into a thick disc, wrap in plastic wrap, and chill in the fridge while you prepare the filling.

For the filling, whisk together the sugar, cornstarch, baking powder, salt, and vanilla seeds in the bowl of a stand mixer fitted with the whisk attachment. Add the ricotta, mascarpone, eggs, and milk and whisk until smooth.

On a work surface, place ²/₃ of the dough between 2 sheets of plastic wrap and use a rolling pin to roll out into a disc, large enough to line the bottom and go ²/₃ of the way up the sides of the springform pan. Fit the dough into the springform pan. Place the remaining dough between the 2 sheets of plastic wrap and roll out into a 1/₄-inch-thick (0.5 cm) circle. Pluck, or cut, the dough into 1¹/₂-inch (4 cm) rounds and set aside. Scrape the filling on top of the pastry base and bake for 20 minutes then place the plucked rounds of dough on top of the filling and bake for another 35 minutes or until golden and firm. Turn off the oven, prop the door partially open, and leave the cake inside for another 10 minutes. Take the cake out of the oven and let it cool for 15 minutes then transfer to a large plate, remove the sides of the pan, and serve.

April

Many cultures around the world celebrate the Easter feast with a lamb dish. Some recipes are frugal, some like *Roasted Rosemary Lamb with Garlic and Tomatoes (recipe no.196)* are opulent, and others are just delicious and quick like these seared lamb chops that only take a few minutes to cook. If you serve them with a syrupy pomegranate-port sauce and sprinkle some crunchy green pistachios on top, no one will believe that you only spent fifteen minutes in the kitchen to create this stunner.

Lamb Chops with Port Sauce, Pomegranate, and Pistachios

Serves 2

Olive oil
6 lamb chops,
about 1 pound (450 g) total
Fine sea salt
Finely ground pepper
¼ cup (60 ml) port (or brandy)
½ cup (120 ml) pomegranate juice
1 tbsp balsamic vinegar
1 tsp honey
1 medium sprig fresh thyme
½ tsp freshly grated orange zest
2 tbsp pomegranate seeds
1 tbsp roughly chopped
unsalted pistachios

Place a piece of aluminum foil, large enough to wrap the lamb chops, on a plate.

In a large, heavy pan, heat a splash of olive oil over medium-high heat. Add the lamb chops and sear for 1 1/2 minutes per side—the meat should still be pink inside. Season the lamb chops to taste with salt and pepper then transfer to the prepared plate, loosely wrap them in the foil, and let rest for 3 minutes. Leave the pan on the heat.

Turn the heat up to high, add the port, and deglaze the pan, using a spatula to scrape any bits and pieces off the bottom. Cook for 20 seconds then add the pomegranate juice, vinegar, honey, thyme, and orange zest and reduce the sauce for 1 to 2 minutes or until it reaches the desired taste and texture; it should be syrupy, but not thick. Remove and discard the thyme, season the sauce to taste with salt and pepper, and stir in the pomegranate seeds.

Divide the lamb chops among plates, drizzle with the sauce, and sprinkle with the pomegranate seeds and pistachios.

Baking braided yeast bread takes time and challenges a hungry baker's patience, but every minute put into this creation, every time you punch and knead the smooth dough, will be worth it. I like to bake fragrant *tsoureki* during the holidays. It's a Greek Easter bread, rich like a brioche, that I flavor with orange and aniseed. And if you happen to have a bottle of orange blossom water in your pantry, here's a recipe to use it in.

Tsoureki—Greek Easter Bread with Aniseed and Orange Blossom Water

Serves 4 to 6

For the dough

4 cups (520 g) all-purpose flour
½ cup (100 g) granulated sugar
1 (¼-ounce / 7-g) envelope fast-acting yeast
1 ½ tbsp freshly grated orange zest
2 tsp aniseed, lightly crushed with a mortar and pestle
½ tsp fine sea salt
⅔ cup (150 ml) whole milk, lukewarm
2 large eggs
2 tbsp high-quality orange blossom water, preferably organic
½ cup (115 g) unsalted butter, melted and cooled
2 tbsp sesame seeds, for the topping

For the glaze

1 large egg yolk
1 tbsp water

Picture page 127, top left

For the dough, combine the flour, sugar, yeast, orange zest, aniseed, and salt in the bowl of a stand mixer fitted with the dough hook attachment. Whisk together the lukewarm milk, eggs, orange blossom water, and butter and add to the flour mixture then mix with the hook for 5 minutes or until well combined. Transfer the dough to a work surface and continue kneading it with your hands for about 7 minutes or until you have a soft and silky ball of dough. Place the dough back in the bowl, cover with a tea towel, and let it rise in a warm place, or preferably in a 100°F (35°C) warm oven, for about 1 hour and 40 minutes or until puffy (it won't double in size).

Line a baking sheet with parchment paper.

When the dough is puffy, punch it down, take it out of the bowl, and knead for about 30 seconds. Divide the dough into 3 equal parts, roll them into long sausage shapes, and braid them tightly into a loaf. Tuck both ends underneath the loaf then transfer to the lined baking sheet, cover with a tea towel, and let it rise in a warm place for 50 minutes or until puffy.

Preheat the oven to 350°F (180°C).

For the glaze, whisk together the egg yolk and water then brush on top of the loaf and sprinkle with sesame seeds. Bake for 15 minutes then cover the bread with aluminum foil so it doesn't brown too quickly. Continue baking for 25 to 35 minutes or until the bread is golden brown and sounds hollow when you knock on its bottom. Let it cool for 10 minutes then cut into thick slices and enjoy with butter.

Green asparagus finds a surprisingly harmonic companion in this screaming-pink hummus. You achieve this gorgeous color by adding a generous amount of boiled beets, with the earthy-sweet root enhancing the nutty tahini-chickpea dip not just visually, but also in taste.

Green Asparagus with Pink Beet and Chickpea Hummus

Serves 3 to 4

For the hummus*
2 large beets, scrubbed
2 large bay leaves
2 tsp olive oil
1 ¼ cups (250 g) drained
and rinsed canned chickpeas
⅔ cup (150 g) light tahini
½ cup (120 ml) water
2 large cloves garlic, crushed
About 6 tbsp freshly squeezed
lemon juice
About 1 ¼ tsp fine sea salt
¼ to ½ tsp ground cumin

For the asparagus
2 ¼ pounds (1 kg) trimmed
green asparagus
Olive oil
About 3 tbsp white sesame seeds
Flaky sea salt

Picture page 127, top right

For the hummus, bring a medium pot of salted water to a boil and add the beets and bay leaves then reduce the heat, cover, and simmer for 45 to 50 minutes or until tender. Drain the beets and quickly rinse with cold water. When they are cool enough to handle, peel off the skin. Measure 7 ounces (200 g) and reserve any remaining beets for another use. Purée the beets and olive oil in a food processor or blender until smooth then transfer to a medium bowl and set aside.

Add the chickpeas, tahini, water, garlic, 5 tablespoons of the lemon juice, the fine sea salt, and 1/4 teaspoon of the cumin to the food processor or blender and purée until smooth. Add half the beet mixture to the hummus and purée until well combined, adding more puréed beet until it reaches the desired taste. Season to taste with additional lemon juice, fine sea salt, and cumin and set aside.

For the asparagus, bring a large pot of salted water to a boil and blanch the stalks for about 3 minutes or until al dente. Drain and quickly rinse with cold water then transfer to a large platter or divide among individual plates. Drizzle the asparagus with a little olive oil and sprinkle with sesame seeds and flaky sea salt. Sprinkle a few spoonfuls of the hummus over the green stalks and enjoy warm or cold.

* *You can use leftover hummus as a spread on bread.*

¾ cup (160 g) yellow split peas
(no soaking required)
2 large cloves garlic
½ medium shallot
1½ tbsp capers, preferably
preserved in salt, rinsed and dried
⅓ cup plus 1 tbsp (90 ml) olive oil
2 tbsp freshly squeezed
lemon juice
Finely ground pepper
6 thick slices white
sourdough bread

My friend Alex loves and celebrates the beauty of life. He lives in the most gorgeous old house in Malta, throws the island's best lunch and dinner parties, and always manages to surprise me with delicious dishes of striking simplicity. His marvelous yellow split pea dip with capers, spread generously onto thick slices of Maltese sourdough bread, is a creation I always dream of when I think of him.

Yellow Split Pea and Caper Dip on Sourdough

Place the yellow split peas in a large saucepan with plenty of (unsalted) water and bring to a boil. Reduce the heat and simmer for 15 to 20 minutes or until tender (or follow the package instructions). Drain the split peas, let cool for 5 minutes, and transfer to a food processor or blender. Add the garlic, shallot, capers, olive oil, and lemon juice and purée until smooth. Season to taste with pepper and transfer to a medium bowl.

Spread the dip generously onto thick slices of white sourdough bread and enjoy.

1 small bunch fresh cilantro,
plus 1 tsp chopped cilantro leaves
for serving
Olive oil
1 tbsp freshly grated horseradish,
plus 1 tsp for serving
1 (10-ounce / 280-g) swordfish
fillet, about 1¼-inch thick (3 cm)
Fine sea salt
Finely ground pepper
1 lime, very thinly sliced
⅓ cup plus 1 tbsp (90 ml)
dry white wine

Picture opposite, bottom left

Swordfish fillets are easy to cook, and won't hassle the bustling cook. It's also the right fish for experimenting with new ingredient combinations. Lay swordfish on a bed of cilantro, bring in spicy horseradish and floral lime, and surprise your taste buds with fresh and pungent flavors.

Swordfish with Cilantro, Horseradish, and Lime

Preheat the oven to 400°F (200°C). Brush the bottom of a medium baking dish with olive oil and place the bunch of cilantro in the middle of the baking dish.

Whisk together 2 tablespoons of olive oil and 1 tablespoon of horseradish in a medium bowl, add the swordfish, and toss to coat. Arrange the swordfish on top of the cilantro in the baking dish, pour any remaining horseradish oil on top, and season to taste with salt and pepper. Place the lime slices on top of the swordfish, pour the white wine over the swordfish and cilantro, and roast for 20 to 23 minutes or until you can flake the fish with a fork. Cut the swordfish in half, sprinkle with the chopped cilantro and the horseradish, and serve immediately.

92

93

95

98

Minestrone made with green beans, peas, and zucchini tastes crisp and fresh, but it's still a soup that should warm the soul, so I'm adding tiny meatballs, refined with arugula and lime, for that cozy, hearty feeling. It's the German in me. I can't help it.

Green Minestrone with Lime-Arugula Meatballs

Serves 2 to 4

14 ounces (400 g) ground beef
2 large cloves garlic, crushed, plus 1 large clove garlic, cut in half
2 ounces (60 g) arugula leaves, finely chopped
1 heaping tsp freshly grated lime zest
Fine sea salt
Finely ground pepper
Olive oil
¾ pound (340 g) trimmed mixed green vegetables*
4¼ cups (1 liter) homemade or quality store-bought vegetable broth, hot
1 tbsp freshly squeezed lime juice
1 bay leaf
1 spring onion (green part only), thinly sliced

Combine the ground beef, crushed garlic, arugula, lime zest, 1 teaspoon of salt, and a generous amount of pepper in a large bowl and mix with your hands until well combined. Form the mixture into 38 roughly 1-inch (2.5 cm) meatballs.

Heat a splash of olive oil in a large pot over medium heat. Add the garlic and sauté for 1 minute. Add a little more oil and the vegetables and sauté, stirring, for 1 minute. Add the hot vegetable broth, lime juice, and bay leaf, season to taste with salt and pepper, and bring to a boil. Add the meatballs then reduce the heat, cover, and simmer gently for 4 to 6 minutes or until the meatballs are just cooked through and the vegetables are tender. Season to taste with salt, pepper, and additional lime juice.

Divide the soup among deep bowls, sprinkle with the spring onion, and serve immediately.

* *Such as green beans, peas, and zucchini, cut into bite-size pieces if necessary.*

When it's time for lunch, and you only have a few moments, but you're also desperately in need of a little *dolce vita*, boil pasta, zest a lemon, and melt butter. It's that easy to create a taste of the sweet life, Italian-style.

Spaghetti with Lemon Butter and Basil

Serves 1

3 ounces (85 g) dried spaghetti
2 tbsp (30 g) unsalted butter
2 tsp freshly grated lemon zest
Fine sea salt
Coarsely ground pepper
10 fresh small basil leaves
2 tbsp finely grated Parmesan

Bring a medium pot of salted water to a boil and cook the spaghetti, according to the package instructions, until al dente. Drain the spaghetti and return it to the pot.

In a medium saucepan, heat the butter and $1\frac{1}{2}$ teaspoons of the lemon zest over medium-high heat and cook until it starts sizzling. Take the pan off the heat, add the spaghetti, and mix until combined. Season to taste with salt and pepper, transfer to a plate, and sprinkle with basil, Parmesan, and the remaining lemon zest. Buon appetito!

The first rhubarb of the year deserves a celebration. This pink meringue pie is lusciously filled with cinnamon-scented rhubarb curd, the wobbly filling lying gracefully on a flaky pastry base. It tastes divine and looks wonderfully opulent.

Rhubarb Meringue Pie

Serves 6 to 8

For the rhubarb curd

1 ½ pounds (680 g) trimmed rhubarb, cut into ¼-inch (0.5 cm) slices

¾ cup plus 2 tbsp (175 g) granulated sugar

⅓ cup plus 1 tbsp (90 ml) water

¼ tsp ground cinnamon

1 tbsp (15 g) unsalted butter

½ cup (60 g) cornstarch

⅛ tsp fine sea salt

3 large egg yolks, beaten

For the pastry

1 ¼ cups (160 g) all-purpose flour

1 tbsp granulated sugar

¼ tsp fine sea salt

⅓ cup plus 1 tbsp (90 g) unsalted butter, cold

1 tbsp water, cold

For the meringue

3 large egg whites

⅛ tsp fine sea salt

⅓ cup plus 1 tbsp (80 g) granulated sugar

Picture page 127, bottom right

For the curd, cook the rhubarb, 3/4 cup (150 g) of the sugar, 1 tablespoon of the water, and the cinnamon in a large pot over medium heat until the sugar dissolves. Increase the heat to medium-high and cook, stirring occasionally, for 10 minutes or until thick. Add the butter and whisk until combined. Whisk together the remaining ⅓ cup (75 ml) of the water, the cornstarch, the remaining 2 tablespoons (25 g) of the sugar, and the salt and add to the rhubarb mixture. Bring to a boil and cook, stirring constantly, over medium heat for 3 minutes. Whisk together 1 tablespoon of the rhubarb mixture and the egg yolks and add to the rhubarb mixture then bring to a boil and cook, stirring constantly, for 30 seconds. Pour the curd into a large bowl and let it cool completely.

For the pastry, combine the flour, sugar, and salt in the bowl of a stand mixer fitted with the dough hook attachment. Add the butter and use a knife to cut it into the flour until there are just small pieces left. Quickly rub the butter into the flour with your fingers until combined. Add the cold water and mix with the hook until crumbly. Form the dough into a thick disc, wrap it in plastic wrap, and freeze for 10 minutes.

Preheat the oven to 400°F (200°C).

On a work surface, place the dough between 2 sheets of plastic wrap and use a rolling pin to roll out into a disc, large enough to line the bottom and sides of a 9-inch (23 cm) pie dish. Fit the dough into the pie dish, pushing it into the dish, especially along the edges. Let the dough hang over the rim a little or trim with a knife. Use a fork to prick the dough all over. Bake for 15 to 17 minutes or until golden and crisp. If the dough bubbles up, push it down with a fork. Take the pie dish out of the oven and let it cool for at least 10 minutes.

For the meringue, whisk the egg whites and salt in the bowl of a stand mixer fitted with the whisk attachment for 30 seconds. Continue whisking, while gradually adding the sugar, for a few minutes or until stiff.

Spread the rhubarb curd on top of the pre-baked pastry then spread the egg white on top, forming peaks with a knife. Bake for 6 to 7 minutes or until the meringue is golden and crispy. Let the pie sit at least 10 minutes or until the rhubarb curd is set then cut into pieces and serve.

My April quiche features legumes and leaves. The green beans are crisp and taste of spring, while ramp's short season will soon come to an end, which is reason enough to highlight the garlicky flavor in the eggy filling of this quiche.

Green Bean and Ramp Quiche

Serves 4 to 8

For the pastry

2 cups (260 g) all-purpose flour
1 tsp fine sea salt
½ cup plus 1 tbsp (130 g) unsalted butter, cold
1 large egg

For the filling

7 ounces (200 g) trimmed green beans
3 large eggs
½ cup (120 ml) heavy cream
½ cup (120 g) sour cream (or crème fraîche)
1 tsp fine sea salt
Finely ground pepper
Nutmeg, preferably freshly grated
1 ounce (30 g) fresh ramp or ramson leaves, sliced
1 spring onion (green part only), thinly sliced

For the pastry, combine the flour and salt in the bowl of a stand mixer fitted with the dough hook attachment. Add the butter and use a knife to cut it into the flour until there are just small pieces left. Quickly rub the butter into the flour with your fingers until well combined. Add the egg and mix with the hook until crumbly. Form the dough into a thick disc, wrap it in plastic wrap, and freeze for 10 minutes.

Preheat the oven to 400°F (200°C).

On a work surface, place the dough between 2 sheets of plastic wrap and use a rolling pin to roll out into a disc, large enough to line the bottom and sides of a 12-inch (30 cm) quiche dish. Fit the dough into the quiche dish, pushing it into the dish, especially along the edges. Let the dough hang over the rim a little or trim with a knife. Use a fork to prick the dough all over. Bake for 15 minutes or until golden. If the dough bubbles up, push it down with a fork. Take the quiche dish out of the oven and reduce the heat to 350°F (180°C).

For the filling, bring a large pot of salted water to a boil and blanch the green beans for 2 to 5 minutes or until al dente. Drain and quickly rinse with cold water.

In a medium bowl, whisk together the eggs, heavy cream, sour cream, salt, and generous amounts of pepper and nutmeg.

Arrange the green beans, ramp leaves, and spring onion on top of the pre-baked pastry. Slowly pour the egg mixture over the vegetables and bake for 40 to 50 minutes or until the top is golden and firm and the pastry is crisp. Let it cool for 10 minutes. Serve warm or cold.

100

week 15 / tuesday

Serves 2

Olive oil
2 medium Persian cucumbers,
scrubbed and very thinly sliced
on a mandoline
⅓ cup (75 ml) dry white wine
2 tsp unsalted butter
High-quality soy sauce
1 to 2 tbsp white sesame seeds,
toasted

101

week 15 / wednesday

Makes 2 sandwiches

For the pesto*
2 ounces (60 g) ramp
or ramson leaves
1 ounce (30 g) Parmesan,
finely grated
¼ cup (60 ml) olive oil
¼ tsp fine sea salt

For the sandwiches
2 rustic white buns, cut in half
3 high-quality canned sardines,
boned and each cut into 2 fillets
1 small handful arugula leaves
2 cherry tomatoes,
cut into quarters
⅛ preserved lemon,
very thinly sliced
(or ¼ tsp freshly grated
lemon zest)

Picture page 132, top left

This is a quick lunch recipe, using a condiment that, until recently, barely saw the light in my kitchen: soy sauce. But that was before visiting Japan! I found a traditional brewery, where the sauce is still handcrafted, and the experience was a true game changer. I immediately felt inspired by the finesse and complexity of the various soy sauces. So, thanks to Japanese soy sauce, this dish was born: sautéed cucumber, enhanced by the dark fermented sauce, melted butter, and sesame seeds.

Sautéed Cucumber with Soy Sauce and Sesame Seeds

In a large, heavy pan, heat a splash of olive oil over medium-high heat. Add the cucumbers, spreading them evenly, and sauté, stirring occasionally, for 2 to 3 minutes or until they start to soften. Add the white wine and cook for 20 seconds. Take the pan off the heat then add the butter and stir gently until melted. Divide the cucumbers among plates, drizzle with a little soy sauce, sprinkle with sesame seeds, and serve warm.

The best canned sardines come from Belle-Île-en-Mer, a picturesque island off the coast of Brittany. The cans are colorfully painted while the fish is tender and tasty and paired with lemon, Muscadet wine, or dark olive tapenade. They're so good that you don't want to deviate from their flavor too much, so just put them in a sandwich with a little pesto, fresh tomato, and preserved lemon.

Sardine and Lemon Sandwich with Ramp Pesto and Tomatoes

For the pesto, purée the ramp leaves, Parmesan, olive oil, and salt in a food processor or blender until smooth.

For the sandwiches, brush the bottom half of each bun with a little oil from the canned sardines, or use olive oil. Divide the arugula among the buns, place 3 sardine fillets on top of the greens, and sprinkle with the tomatoes, a little pesto, and the preserved lemon. Place a top on each bun, squeeze, and enjoy.

* *You can double the recipe and use the leftover pesto for spaghetti (recipe no. 102).*

101

102

104

107

The change of seasons can be drastic and abrupt, especially the arrival of spring. All of a sudden, nature sprouts and flourishes, with a burst of energy from one day to the next. The trilogy of asparagus, ramp pesto, and burrata pays homage to the beginning of spring and the produce that it finally brings back to our plates.

Spaghetti with Asparagus, Burrata, and Ramp Pesto

Serves 2

For the pesto*
2 ounces (60 g) ramp
or ramson leaves
1 ounce (30 g) Parmesan,
finely grated
¼ cup (60 ml) olive oil
¼ tsp fine sea salt

For the pasta
1 pound (450 g) trimmed
green asparagus
6 ounces (170 g) dried spaghetti
Olive oil
7 ounces (200 g) burrata
(or mozzarella di bufala),
torn in half
Fine sea salt
Coarsely ground pepper

Picture opposite, top right

For the pesto, purée the ramp leaves, Parmesan, olive oil, and salt in a food processor or blender until smooth.

For the pasta, bring a large pot of salted water to a boil and blanch the asparagus for about 3 minutes or until al dente. Using a slotted ladle or spoon, transfer the asparagus to a colander, reserving the cooking water in the pot, then drain and quickly rinse with cold water. Cut each stalk into quarters lengthwise.

Put the pot used to cook the asparagus back on the heat, adding more water if necessary, and bring to a boil. Cook the spaghetti, according to the package instructions, until al dente. Drain the spaghetti and return it to the pot. Add a splash of olive oil and toss to coat.

Divide the spaghetti and asparagus among the plates. Add the buratta and drizzle with the pesto. Season to taste with salt and pepper and serve immediately.

* You can double the recipe and use the leftover pesto for sandwiches (recipe no. 101).

The famous Austrian *Kaiserschmarrn* is a fluffy pancake that's torn into pieces. It is named after Emperor Franz Joseph I—kaiser means "emperor" in German—a man with a sweet tooth who deeply admired this cozy dessert. It's the kind of dish you'd want to eat straight out of the pan. I like to replace the traditional raisins with caramelized apple deglazed with a splash of orange-flavored liqueur.

Kaiserschmarrn
Torn Pancake with Caramelized Grand Marnier Apple

Serves 2 to 4

For the apple

1 tbsp (15 g) unsalted butter
1 tbsp granulated sugar
1 large, tart baking apple, peeled, cored, and cut into 8 wedges
⅓ cup (75 ml) orange-flavored liqueur, such as Grand Marnier

For the pancake

3 large eggs, separated
⅛ tsp fine sea salt
1½ cups (360 ml) whole milk
¼ cup (50 g) granulated sugar
1 tsp freshly grated orange zest
1 cup (130 g) all-purpose flour
Unsalted butter,
to cook the pancake
Confectioners' sugar

For the apple, in a small, heavy pan, heat the butter and sugar over medium-high heat for about 1 minute or until golden brown. Add the apple wedges, and sear for $1\frac{1}{2}$ minutes per side or until golden brown. Add the liqueur and cook, turning the apple wedges occasionally, for 2 minutes or until syrupy. Cover, keep warm, and set aside.

For the pancake, in the bowl of a stand mixer fitted with the whisk attachment, whisk the egg whites and salt until stiff then transfer to a large bowl.

In the same bowl of the stand mixer fitted with the whisk attachment, whisk together the milk, egg yolks, granulated sugar, and orange zest. Sift the flour, add to the milk mixture, and whisk until well combined and smooth. Gently fold the egg whites into the batter with a wooden spoon. Mind that you don't over-mix, as it should be fluffy and just combined.

In a 12-inch (30 cm) cast-iron pan or nonstick skillet, heat 2 tablespoons of butter over medium heat. Add all of the pancake batter and cook for 4 to 6 minutes or until the bottom is golden and the pancake is just set but still soft. Flip the pancake over, or cut it in half first and turn both sides separately. Add 1 tablespoon of butter to the pan, letting it melt underneath the pancake, and continue cooking the pancake for 4 to 6 minutes or until the other side is golden. Carefully tear the pancake into chunks with two forks then add 1 tablespoon of butter and cook, stirring, over medium-high heat for about 2 minutes or until starting to crisp.

Transfer the Kaiserschmarrn to a large platter, dust generously with confectioners' sugar, and serve with the warm apple.

Let winter and spring mingle in a bowl during the short period when the seasons overlap. Winter contributes little kumquats, sweet and tart, and warming turmeric root, while Romano beans and peas scream spring, and together they make a beautiful, vibrant salad.

Romano Bean, Pea, and Kumquat Salad with Turmeric and Mint

Serves 2 to 4

For the dressing
3 tbsp olive oil
3 tbsp freshly squeezed
orange juice
⅛ to ¼ tsp freshly grated turmeric
root (or ginger), plus more for
serving
Fine sea salt
Finely ground pepper

For the salad
¾ pound (340 g) trimmed
Romano beans
⅓ pound (150 g) fresh
or frozen peas
4 kumquats, very thinly sliced
and seeds removed
1 small handful fresh mint leaves

Picture page 132, bottom left

For the dressing, whisk together the olive oil, orange juice, and 1/8 teaspoon of the turmeric. Season to taste with salt, pepper, and additional turmeric.

For the salad, bring a large pot of salted water to a boil and blanch the beans for about 3 minutes or until al dente. Using a slotted ladle or spoon, transfer the beans to a colander, reserving the cooking water in the pot, then drain and quickly rinse with cold water. Bring the water back to a boil then blanch the peas for about 1 minute or until al dente. Drain and quickly rinse with cold water.

Arrange the beans and peas on a large plate, drizzle with the dressing, and sprinkle with the kumquat, mint, and a little turmeric. Enjoy warm or cold.

The kitchen of a food-loving mother is the best cooking class in the world, the place to learn all the tricks and secrets passed from one generation to the next. My mother taught me all the important cooking techniques, but she also encouraged me to trust my own taste and never be intimidated by a recipe, including French classics like coq au vin. They often turn out to be much simpler than expected.

Coq au Vin

Serves 4

For the bouquet garni
1 small bunch fresh
flat-leaf parsley
1 small bunch fresh thyme
3 leaves fresh sage
1 large bay leaf

For the coq au vin
Olive oil
3½ pounds (1.6 kg) whole
chicken legs
Fine sea salt
Finely ground pepper
2 ounces (60 g) thick-cut bacon,
cut into small cubes
2 medium carrots, peeled and
cut into thin matchsticks
1 celery stalk, cut into 3 pieces
½ large leek (white part only),
cut into thin matchsticks
2 large cloves garlic, crushed
1 (750-ml) bottle light red wine
14 ounces (400 g) trimmed
small cremini mushrooms
(or medium mushrooms,
cut in half)
1 small handful fresh
flat-leaf parsley leaves
1 large baguette, for serving

For the bouquet garni, tie the parsley, thyme, sage, and bay leaf together with cotton string.

For the coq au vin, in a Dutch oven, large enough to fit the chicken and mushrooms and with a tight-fitting lid, heat a splash of olive oil over high heat. Working in batches, sear the chicken legs for 1 to 2 minutes per side or until golden brown. Season to taste with salt and pepper and transfer to a plate. Reduce the heat to medium-high then add the bacon and cook, stirring, for about 3 minutes or until golden and crispy. Add the carrots, celery, leek, and garlic and sauté, stirring constantly, for 2 minutes. Return the chicken to the Dutch oven, add the bouquet garni and red wine, and season to taste with salt and pepper. Cover the Dutch oven and bring to a boil then reduce the heat and simmer gently for 30 minutes or until the chicken is cooked through. Arrange the mushrooms on top of the chicken, gently pushing them into the sauce, cover the Dutch oven, and cook for 10 minutes or until the mushrooms are al dente but not soft. Remove and discard the bouquet garni and celery then season to taste with salt and pepper and sprinkle with parsley.

Divide the chicken, mushrooms, and sauce among plates and serve with a crunchy baguette.

Serves 2 to 4

Olive oil

1 shallot, chopped

¾ pound (340 g) peeled
starchy potatoes, cut into cubes

1¼ cups (250 g) drained
and rinsed canned butter beans

¼ pound (110 g) leek (white
and light green parts only), sliced

3 ¾ cups (900 ml)
vegetable broth, hot

1 large bay leaf

Nutmeg, preferably freshly grated

Fine sea salt

Finely ground pepper

¼ cup (60 ml) heavy cream

2 tbsp chopped fresh chives,
for the topping

Vichyssoise is a wonderful, simple French classic. It's relatively mild and perfect for experimenting. The traditional recipe is made with potatoes and leek, and served cold in summer. It's sweet and smooth, so you can sneak in velvety butter beans; they won't disturb the harmony, and will just make it a little richer and heartier. I enjoy serving this soup warm, which I prefer for vichyssoise anyway.

Butter Bean Vichyssoise with Chives

In a large pot, heat a splash of olive oil over medium heat. Add the shallot and sauté for 2 minutes. Add the potatoes, butter beans, and leek and sauté, stirring, for 2 minutes. Add the hot broth and bay leaf, season to taste with nutmeg, salt, and pepper, and bring to a boil. Reduce the heat and simmer for 15 minutes or until the potatoes are tender. Remove and discard the bay leaf then purée the soup in a food processor or blender, or with an immersion blender, until smooth. Return it to the pot, add the heavy cream, and whisk until smooth. Season to taste with salt, pepper, and nutmeg.

Serve the vichyssoise in wide, shallow bowls and sprinkle with chives.

Serves 2 to 4

1 small spring onion

3 tbsp olive oil

2 tbsp white balsamic vinegar

Fine sea salt

Finely ground pepper

½ red and ½ yellow bell pepper

1 medium tomato

1 large preserved artichoke heart

1 ounce (30 g) flat-leaf parsley
leaves

Picture page 132, bottom right

There's a tiny Tunisian restaurant in Berlin that I adore for their fantastic falafel, hummus, and especially their parsley salad. It's basically a pile of fresh parsley leaves topped with tomatoes and red onion. For my version, I add chopped red and yellow bell peppers and preserved artichoke hearts, and drizzle it with a light spring onion vinaigrette.

Parsley Salad with Tomato, Bell Pepper, and Artichoke

Thinly slice the spring onion then add, along with the olive oil and vinegar, to a small bowl, whisk, and season to taste with salt and pepper.

Cut the bell peppers into small cubes, cut the tomato into thin wedges, and cut the artichoke heart into quarters lengthwise. Arrange the vegetables and parsley on a large plate, sprinkle with the dressing, and serve immediately.

108

week 16 / wednesday

Makes 4 sandwiches

4 ounces (110 g) sheep's milk
cream cheese (or cow's milk
cream cheese)
1 tbsp olive oil
1 ½ tbsp finely chopped
fresh cilantro leaves
Fine sea salt
Finely ground pepper
4 slices baguette
¼ large red bell pepper,
coarsely grated

Sheep's milk cream cheese may sound a little extravagant—you can, of course, replace it with common cow's milk cream cheese—but if you can get a hold of it, give it a shot. The taste is surprisingly subtle and more refined, and it makes an especially scrumptious dip when you add chopped cilantro.

Fresh Baguette with Cilantro and Sheep's Milk Cream Cheese and Grated Bell Pepper

In a small bowl, whisk together the cream cheese, olive oil, and cilantro until smooth. Season to taste with salt and pepper.

Spread the dip on the baguette then pile the grated bell pepper on top and enjoy.

109

week 16 / thursday

Serves 2

Olive oil
1 (¾-pound / 340-g)
skin-on salmon fillet
12 juniper berries,
crushed with a mortar and pestle
1 bay leaf
Fine sea salt
Finely ground pepper
⅓ cup (75 ml) gin
1 tbsp (15 g) unsalted butter

Gin, juniper berry, and bay leaf have a similar effect on the palate, with a taste that's slightly resinous and piney, with subtle hints of citrus. They also bring out the best in one another. Mixed with sizzling butter, and drizzled over golden-seared salmon, this trio work wonders.

Salmon with Juniper-Gin Butter

In a medium, heavy pan, heat a splash of olive oil over medium-high heat. Add the salmon, skin-side down, along with the juniper berries and bay leaf, and cook for about 5 minutes or until almost halfway cooked through. If the spices brown too quickly, reduce the heat to medium. Turn the salmon over, adding a little more oil to the pan, reduce the heat to medium, and cook for 2 to 3 more minutes, or until flaky but still pink inside. Season to taste with salt and pepper then cut the fillet in half, transfer to plates, and cover to keep warm.

Place the same pan over high heat, add the gin, and deglaze the pan, using a spatula to scrape any bits and pieces off the bottom. Cook for 1 minute then add the butter and whisk until combined. Take the pan off the heat, season to taste with salt and pepper, drizzle over the salmon, and serve.

There are two reasons why I like to mix pesto into my burger mixture: The herb lends flavor and the oily sauce adds juice to the meat. Ground beef can easily become dry in the pan, or you can undercook it, which is equally unpleasant. You can also use the green dip as a topping. On the plate, it mixes well with the thick blueberry-port sauce, and will make you lick your fingers over and over again.

Basil Pesto Burgers with Blueberry-Port Sauce

Serves 4

For the pesto
1 ounce (30 g) fresh basil leaves
1 ounce (30 g) Parmesan, finely grated
1 ounce (30 g) pine nuts
1 clove garlic
⅓ cup (75 ml) olive oil
Fine sea salt

For the blueberry sauce
Olive oil
¾ medium red onion, very finely chopped
9 ounces (250 g) large fresh blueberries
1 tbsp maple syrup
1 tsp balsamic vinegar
⅓ cup (75 ml) port (or brandy)
6 small sprigs fresh thyme
Fine sea salt

For the burgers
18 ounces (500 g) ground beef
¼ cup (40 g) dry breadcrumbs
1 medium onion, finely chopped
2 large cloves garlic, crushed
1 large egg
2 tsp freshly grated lemon zest, plus 1 tsp for serving
1½ tsp fine sea salt
Finely ground pepper
Unsalted butter
Olive oil

For the pesto, purée the basil, Parmesan, pine nuts, garlic, and olive oil in a food processor or blender until smooth. Season to taste with salt.

For the blueberry sauce, in a small, heavy pan, heat a splash of olive oil over medium heat and sauté the onion for 5 minutes or until golden and soft. Add the blueberries, maple syrup, and vinegar and bring to a boil then add the port, thyme, and a little salt. Reduce the heat and simmer for 5 minutes or until the blueberries start to soften but still keep their shape; set aside.

For the burgers, combine 3 tablespoons of the pesto with the ground beef, breadcrumbs, onion, garlic, egg, lemon zest, salt, and a generous amount of pepper in a large bowl and mix with your hands until well combined. Form the mixture into 4 large burgers, flattening them just a little.

In a large, heavy pan, heat 2 tablespoons of butter and a generous splash of olive oil over medium heat. Cook the burgers, turning occasionally, for about 14 minutes or until just cooked through.

Divide the burgers among plates and add a little dollop of the pesto and a large spoonful of the blueberry sauce. Sprinkle with a little lemon zest and pepper and serve.

Dutch honey cake is a supermarket staple in Germany. This golden brown loaf, sealed in plastic wrap, isn't an eye-catcher, but it's so sticky, spongy, and moist, and packed with ginger and spices, that you can't help but love it. Baking Dutch honey cake at home allows it to unfold its full potential. Fragrant cinnamon, cloves, aniseed, and nutmeg are present, the flowery sweetness of the honey is fine and balanced. However, store-bought and homemade cake gets the same treatment in my kitchen: I cut it into thick slices and spread them with butter.

Dutch Honey Cake

Serves 4 to 6

2 cups (260 g) all-purpose flour
1½ tsp baking powder
1 tsp baking soda
⅛ tsp fine sea salt
3 tbsp (45 g) unsalted butter
½ cup (170 g) honey
½ cup (120 ml) whole milk
2 large eggs, beaten
2 tbsp (45 g) sugar beet syrup
(or dark molasses)
¼ cup (55 g) light brown sugar
¼ cup (60 ml) brewed strong
black tea
2 tsp ground cinnamon
1 tsp freshly grated ginger
½ tsp whole cloves,
ground with a mortar and pestle
⅓ tsp aniseed, ground
with a mortar and pestle
¼ tsp freshly grated nutmeg
Pearl sugar, for the topping
(optional)

Preheat the oven to 325°F / 160°C (preferably convection setting). Butter a 9 x 4-inch (23 x 10 cm) loaf pan and line with parchment paper.

In the bowl of a stand mixer fitted with the whisk attachment, whisk together the flour, baking powder, baking soda, and salt.

In a medium saucepan, melt the butter and let it cool for 2 minutes then add the honey, milk, eggs, sugar beet syrup, light brown sugar, tea, cinnamon, ginger, cloves, aniseed, and nutmeg and whisk until combined. Add to the flour mixture and whisk for 1 to 2 minutes or until well combined. Scrape the batter into the prepared pan, sprinkle with a little pearl sugar, and bake for about 45 minutes (slightly longer if using a conventional oven) or until golden and firm on top. If you insert a skewer into the center of the cake, it should come out clean. Let the cake cool for at least 10 minutes then take it out of the pan and transfer to a platter for serving.

You can't have more carbs in a meal than in a Maltese *timpana*. This buttery pie is filled with lots of short pasta freckled with rich Bolognese sauce. After some serious discussions with my Maltese man, I decided to break with tradition, going meat free, reducing the pasta, and introducing some greens to the mix. I use asparagus and peas for my spring timpana, and a mix of Mediterranean summer vegetables for my summer pasta pie *(recipe no. 231)*. It was a struggle to get there, but now the man is happy.

Spring Timpana
Maltese Pasta Pie
with Asparagus, Peas, and Leek

Serves 4 to 6

For the filling
9 ounces (250 g) dried penne
(or any short pasta)
7 ounces (200 g) fresh
or frozen peas
18 ounces (500 g) trimmed
green asparagus
Olive oil
7 ounces (200 g) leek,
very thinly sliced
1 tbsp Dijon mustard,
plus more to taste
Fine sea salt
Finely ground pepper
1 large egg, lightly beaten
4 ounces (110 g) Parmesan,
finely grated, plus
1 tbsp for the topping

For the pastry
2⅓ cups (300 g) all-purpose flour
1 tsp fine sea salt
⅔ cup (150 g) unsalted butter,
cold
2 large egg yolks
2 tbsp water, cold

For the glaze
1 large egg yolk
1 tbsp whole milk
⅛ tsp fine sea salt

For the filling, bring a large pot of salted water to a boil and cook the penne, according to the package instructions, until al dente. Drain the penne and let it cool completely.

Bring a large pot of salted water to a boil and blanch the peas for about 1 minute or until al dente. Using a slotted ladle or spoon, transfer the peas to a colander, reserving the cooking water in the pot, then drain and quickly rinse with cold water and set aside. Put the pot used to cook the peas back on the heat and bring to a boil. Add the asparagus and cook for about 3 minutes or until al dente. Reserve 1/2 cup (120 ml) of the cooking water and let it cool. Drain the asparagus, quickly rinse with cold water, and cut into penne-size pieces.

In a large, heavy pan, heat a splash of olive oil over medium-high heat and cook the leek, stirring occasionally, for about 10 minutes or until golden and soft. Transfer to a large bowl, add the asparagus and peas, mix, and let cool completely.

For the pastry, combine the flour and salt in the bowl of a stand mixer fitted with the dough hook attachment. Add the butter and use a knife to cut it into the flour until there are just small pieces left. Quickly rub the butter into the flour with your fingers until combined. Add the egg yolks and cold water and mix with the hook until crumbly. Form the dough into a ball. Remove 1/3 of the dough and form it into a thick disc. Form the rest of the dough into a second disc. Wrap both discs in plastic wrap and freeze for 10 minutes.

Preheat the oven to 400°F (200°C). For the glaze, whisk together the egg yolk, milk, and salt.

In a large bowl, combine the penne, the reserved asparagus water, the mustard, 1 teaspoon of salt, and a generous amount of pepper. Season to taste with additional mustard, salt, and pepper then add the egg and mix until well combined.

→

On a work surface, place both discs of dough between 2 sheets of plastic wrap and use a rolling pin to roll each disc into a circle, the larger disc for the bottom and sides of an 8-inch (20 cm) springform pan or a 9-inch (23 cm) shallow pie dish and the smaller disc to close the pie. Line the springform pan or pie dish with the larger disc of dough, pushing it into the dish, especially along the edges. Let the dough hang over the rim a little. Spread 1/3 of the penne mixture on top of the pastry, sprinkle with 1/3 of the Parmesan and 1/3 of the asparagus-pea mixture, and season to taste with salt and pepper. Repeat to make 2 more layers. Pour any remaining liquid from the penne mixture over the filling. Close the pie with the smaller disc of dough, gently pressing the edges of the pastry together to seal it. Use a skewer to make a few small holes in the top, brush with the glaze, and sprinkle with the remaining 1 tablespoon of Parmesan. Bake for 15 minutes then reduce the heat to 350°F (180°C) and continue baking for another 50 minutes or until the pie is golden and the pastry is baked through. Let the pie cool for at least 15 minutes before cutting into pieces and serving.

113
week 17/monday

Serves 2 to 4

For the dressing
3 tbsp olive oil
2 tbsp white balsamic vinegar
Fine sea salt
Finely ground pepper

For the salad
1 medium head lettuce,
such as red leaf or romaine,
torn into pieces
1¼ cups (250 g) drained
and rinsed canned cannelli beans
12 black olives,
preferably Kalamata
4 tbsp capers, preferably
preserved in salt, rinsed and dried
1 small handful fresh flat-leaf
parsley leaves

After days of labor-intensive kitchen projects, it's fine to be a bit lazy. It doesn't take much to throw together a quick salad of fresh greens and some pantry gems. All you need is a head of lettuce, a can of cannellini beans, capers, and olives.

Green Salad with Cannellini Beans, Capers, and Olives

For the dressing, whisk together the olive oil and vinegar and season to taste with salt and pepper.

For the salad, toss together the lettuce, cannellini beans, olives, and capers in a large bowl. Drizzle with the dressing, sprinkle with the parsley, and serve immediately.

Our grandmothers' food wins our hearts with comfort and simplicity. *My Oma Lisa* used to make boiled potatoes with a quark dip speckled with sweet paprika and chives and I'll never forget the taste. It can be difficult to find German quark outside my home country, so I make a version with feta and add some dill to pay homage to Lisa's wonderfully honest, down-to-earth cooking.

Potatoes with Dill-Feta Dip

Serves 2

4 medium waxy potatoes
5 ounces (140 g) feta
1 medium bunch fresh dill, trimmed
¾ tsp freshly grated lemon zest
¼ cup (60 ml) olive oil
Fine sea salt
Finely ground pepper

In a medium saucepan, boil the potatoes in plenty of salted water for 15 to 20 minutes or until tender. Drain the potatoes, quickly rinse with cold water, and peel.

In a food processor or blender, purée the feta, dill, and lemon zest until smooth. Gradually pour in the olive oil, adding oil just until it reaches the desired taste and texture, and purée until smooth. Season to taste with salt and pepper. Divide the warm potatoes among plates and serve with a generous dollop of the dill-feta dip.

I grew up thinking of German *Käsebrot*—basically cheese on bread—as a proper sandwich, but when my man came into my life, my standards changed. The American in him was disturbed and had different notions of what a sandwich should look and taste like. After years of coming up with a new sandwich idea every week for my blog, he finally started to approve my creations, and this one in particular.

Butter Bean Hummus and Coppa di Parma Baguette Sandwich with Chile Oil

Makes 10 sandwiches

1¼ cups (250 g) drained and rinsed canned butter beans
⅔ cup (150 g) light tahini
¼ cup (60 ml) water
3 tbsp freshly squeezed lemon juice
1 clove garlic, crushed
1 tsp fine sea salt
2 tbsp olive oil
½ medium, fresh red chile, seeded and very finely chopped
10 slices baguette
10 very thin slices coppa di Parma (or prosciutto di Parma)

In a food processor or blender, purée the butter beans, tahini, water, lemon juice, garlic, and salt until smooth. Season to taste with salt and transfer to a small bowl.

Heat the olive oil and chile in a small saucepan over high heat until it starts sizzling. Take the pan off the heat and set aside.

Generously spread the hummus on the baguette slices and arrange a slice of coppa di Parma on top. Drizzle with a little chile oil and serve.

Tuna has a strong taste and needs to partner with flavors that can handle its intensity. I prefer to add fewer ingredients and pick those that are potent enough to tango with the meaty fish. Pistachios, cucumber, and minty basil oil do just that, embracing pan-seared tuna steaks with their salty, fresh, and green composition.

Tuna with Basil-Mint Oil, Cucumber Salad, and Pistachios

Serves 2

For the basil-mint oil
1 large handful fresh basil leaves, roughly chopped
1 small handful fresh mint leaves, roughly chopped
¼ to ½ tsp freshly grated lemon zest
⅓ cup (75 ml) olive oil
Fine sea salt

For the tuna
Olive oil
1 (9-ounce / 250-g) tuna steak, about 1-inch thick (2.5 cm)
Fine sea salt
Finely ground pepper

For serving
½ large English cucumber, scrubbed and very thinly sliced on a mandoline
1 small handful salted pistachios, roughly chopped

For the basil-mint oil, whisk together the basil, mint, $1/4$ teaspoon of the lemon zest, and the olive oil. Season to taste with salt and additional lemon zest.

For the tuna, in a small, heavy pan, heat a splash of olive oil over high heat and sear the tuna for 1 to $11/2$ minutes per side or until flaky but still pink inside. Season to taste with salt and pepper, cut in half, and transfer to plates.

Arrange the cucumber slices around the tuna and season to taste with salt and pepper. Drizzle the tuna and cucumber with the basil-mint oil, sprinkle with pistachios, and serve.

For many, it comes as a surprise that rhubarb can be used for non-sweet dishes and treats. Its sour quality is usually reserved for pies, compotes, crumbles, or ice cream, but rarely shines in savory recipes. It's a pity, as these pink stalks create an exciting contrast to the heavy heartiness of meat. Here, for instance, I add a little ginger and elderflower syrup and use rhubarb to brighten up rustic veal schnitzel.

Schnitzel with Ginger-Elderflower Rhubarb and Crispy Bacon

Serves 2

For the rhubarb

1 pound (450 g) trimmed rhubarb, chopped
½ to ¾ tbsp freshly grated ginger
2 tbsp water
1 tsp granulated sugar
1 tbsp elderflower syrup (or maple syrup)
Fine sea salt
Finely ground pepper

For the schnitzel

Olive oil
1 large, ¼-inch-thick (0.5 cm) slice bacon, cut into very small cubes
2 large, ¼-inch-thick (0.5 cm) veal or pork cutlets, about ¾ pound (340 g) total
Fine sea salt
Finely ground pepper
About 2 heaping tbsp all-purpose flour
Unsalted butter, to cook the schnitzel

For the rhubarb, in a small saucepan, bring the rhubarb, 1/2 tablespoon of the ginger, the water, and sugar to a boil. Reduce the heat, cover, and simmer for 5 minutes or until the rhubarb starts to soften. Stir in the elderflower syrup and season to taste with salt, pepper, and additional ginger.

For the schnitzel, heat a splash of olive oil in a small, heavy pan over medium-high heat and cook the bacon, stirring occasionally, for a few minutes or until golden brown and crispy; set aside.

On a work surface, arrange the veal or pork between 2 sheets of plastic wrap. Use a meat pounder or your fist to tenderize and slightly flatten the meat. Season the cutlets to taste with salt and pepper on both sides and dust lightly with flour.

In a large, heavy pan, heat 2 tablespoons of butter and a generous splash of olive oil over medium-high heat. Add the cutlets and sear for about 1 minute per side or until golden brown and just cooked through.

Divide the schnitzel and rhubarb among plates, sprinkle with the bacon, and serve immediately.

These are very dark cookies, combining melted bittersweet chocolate and chocolate chunks. Citrusy-sharp ginger and fresh red chile infuse the crunchy brown bites with freshness and heat and help to keep the bitter to sweet ratio balanced. You can save the recipe for Christmas, but I love to have a jar of homemade cookies close to my teapot all year round.

Ginger and Chile Double Chocolate Cookies

Makes about 12 cookies

11 ounces (310 g) bittersweet chocolate
3 tbsp (45 g) unsalted butter
1 heaping tbsp freshly grated ginger
1 tsp ground cinnamon
½ cup (65 g) all-purpose flour
½ tsp baking powder
¼ tsp fine sea salt
2 large eggs
½ cup (100 g) granulated sugar
2 tsp seeded and finely chopped medium-hot fresh red chile

Preheat the oven to 350°F / 180°C (preferably convection setting). Line 1 baking sheet with parchment paper.

Roughly chop 1/3 of the chocolate and set aside. In a medium saucepan, melt the remaining chocolate with the butter, ginger, and cinnamon over low heat, stirring occasionally. Let it cool for 5 minutes.

In a medium bowl, whisk together the flour, baking powder, and salt.

In the bowl of a stand mixer fitted with the whisk attachment, whisk the eggs and sugar for 2 minutes or until light and fluffy. Add the melted chocolate mixture and mix until combined. Add the flour mixture, the reserved chopped chocolate, and the chile and use a wooden spoon to fold until just combined. Scoop heaping tablespoons of dough onto the lined baking sheet, leaving a roughly 11/2-inch (4 cm) space between the cookies; don't flatten the cookies. Bake for 11 to 12 minutes (slightly longer if using a conventional oven) or until crunchy, but still a little soft in the middle. Let them cool for 10 minutes then transfer to a wire rack to cool completely.

Once the cookies are completely cool, store in an airtight container for up to 1 week.

If you feel too tired to bake a layered Black Forest torte on a Sunday morning, but you're still in the mood for chocolate, cherry, cream, and Kirsch, whip up these luscious pancakes instead.

Black Forest Pancakes

Serves 3 to 4

For the cherry compote*
11 ounces (310 g) drained
canned pitted cherries in water
(or fresh or frozen pitted cherries)
3 tbsp water
2 tbsp granulated sugar
1 tbsp Kirsch
(German clear cherry brandy)
1 tsp cornstarch
¼ tsp ground cinnamon,
plus more to taste

For the topping
¾ cup (180 ml) heavy cream,
whipped to stiff peaks
Granulated sugar
4 tbsp (20 g) grated
bittersweet chocolate

For the pancakes
1⅓ cups (175 g) all-purpose flour
⅓ cup (30 g) Dutch-process
or natural unsweetened
cocoa powder
⅓ cup (65 g) granulated sugar
2 tsp baking powder
4 large eggs, separated
⅛ tsp fine sea salt
1 cup (240 ml) whole milk
Unsalted butter,
to cook the pancakes

For the cherry compote, in a medium saucepan, bring the cherries, water, sugar, Kirsch, cornstarch, and cinnamon to a boil. Cover and cook over medium heat for 5 to 7 minutes or until the cherries start to soften. Take the pan off the heat and season to taste with cinnamon then transfer to a bowl and set aside.

For the topping, sweeten the whipped cream to taste with sugar.

For the pancakes, whisk together the flour, cocoa powder, sugar, and baking powder in a medium bowl.

In the bowl of a stand mixer fitted with the whisk attachment, whisk the egg whites and salt until stiff then transfer to a large bowl. In the same bowl of the stand mixer, whisk together the egg yolks and milk until smooth. Add the flour mixture and mix until well combined. Gently fold the egg whites into the egg yolk mixture.

In a large cast-iron pan or nonstick skillet, melt 1 teaspoon of butter over medium heat. Working in batches of 2 to 3 pancakes, add 1 ladle of the batter to the pan for each pancake and cook for 1 to 2 minutes per side or until golden and cooked through. Adjust the heat as necessary and add a little more butter to the pan between batches. Stack the pancakes on a plate. This makes about 15 pancakes.

Arrange the whipped cream and cherry compote on top of the pancakes, letting it drip down the sides, and sprinkle with the grated chocolate, or serve the pancakes individually.

* You can also use store-bought cherry compote.

Let's chill a bottle of white wine, cook spaghetti, and bring a flamboyant green pea–marjoram pesto to the table to laugh in Monday's weary face. A bunch of oven-roasted garlic cloves crown the pesto with a rich, caramel sweetness.

Spaghetti with Pea Pesto, Roasted Garlic, and Fresh Marjoram

Serves 2

For the pasta
14 large cloves garlic,
preferably young, unpeeled
6 ounces (170 g) dried spaghetti
Olive oil
Coarsely ground pepper

For the pesto
7 ounces (200 g) fresh
or frozen peas
2 tsp fresh marjoram leaves,
plus 1 tbsp for the topping
3 tbsp olive oil
2 tsp freshly squeezed lemon juice
Fine sea salt
Finely ground pepper

Preheat the oven to 425°F (220°C).

For the pasta, spread the garlic cloves in a medium baking dish and roast, turning occasionally, for about 25 minutes or until soft enough to mash with a fork—mind that the garlic doesn't burn. Let the garlic cool for a few minutes then peel the cloves and roughly mash with a fork.

For the pea pesto, bring a small pot of salted water to a boil and blanch the peas for about 1 minute or until al dente. Reserve 1/2 cup (120 ml) of the cooking water then drain and quickly rinse the peas with cold water. In a food processor or blender, purée the peas, 1/2 of the cooking water, 2 teaspoons of marjoram, the olive oil, and lemon juice until smooth. If the pesto is too dry, add more of the cooking water. Season to taste with salt and finely ground pepper.

Bring a large pot of salted water to a boil and cook the spaghetti, according to the package instructions, until al dente. Drain the spaghetti and return it to the pot. Add a splash of olive oil and toss to coat.

Divide the spaghetti among plates and sprinkle generously with the pea pesto, coarsely ground pepper, and marjoram. Place the mashed garlic on top of the pasta and serve immediately.

May

When May comes knocking on the door, I jolt out of hibernation mode and let my adopted Mediterranean home inspire and guide my cooking. I leave wintry German comfort food behind and crave lighter, southern European dishes. Seafood cooked *al cartoccio* brings back summer memories. It only needs green olives, parsley, and lemon to turn the kitchen into a rustic trattoria.

Cod al Cartoccio with Olives, Parsley, and Lemon

Serves 2

Olive oil
1 medium bunch fresh
flat-leaf parsley
1 (14-ounce / 400-g) cod fillet
(or any firm white fish,
such as monkfish or halibut),
about 1-inch thick (2.5 cm)
Fine sea salt
Finely ground pepper
2 large lemon slices
14 green olives
2 tbsp dry white wine
1 tbsp freshly squeezed
lemon juice

Parchment paper

Preheat the oven to 400°F (200°C).

Cut 2 pieces of parchment paper large enough to wrap the fish like a package and lay them on top of each other. Brush the top sheet with olive oil. Reserve 1 sprig of parsley then place the remaining parsley in the middle of the parchment and lay the cod on top. Season to taste with salt and pepper and arrange the lemon slices and the reserved parsley sprig on top of the cod. Arrange the olives around the fish fillet. Whisk together the white wine, 2 tablespoons of olive oil, and the lemon juice and pour over the fish. To close the package, fold the sides over, twist both ends of the parchment and fold the top twice so it's well sealed. Place the parchment package in a baking dish and bake for 10 minutes or until you can flake the fish gently with a fork. If the fish isn't ready, close the parchment and continue baking for up to 5 minutes. The cooking time can vary depending on the kind of fish and the fillet's thickness, but mind that you don't overcook it.

Cut the cod in half and serve with the olives and lemon slices.

Makes 6 sandwiches

7 ounces (200 g) soft, mild chèvre
¼ cup (60 ml) heavy cream
¼ tsp freshly grated lime zest,
plus more for the topping
Fine sea salt
7 ounces (200 g) strawberries,
hulled and cut into quarters
6 slices ciabatta bread
1 small handful small fresh
basil leaves

Chèvre and lime are a scrumptious duo, and make a beautiful spread for fresh ciabatta, especially if you top it with ripe strawberries and fresh basil.

Lime Chèvre and Strawberry Ciabatta Sandwich with Basil

In a medium bowl, whisk together the chèvre, heavy cream, and lime zest and season to taste with salt.

Spread the lime chèvre on the ciabatta slices and sprinkle with the strawberries, basil, and a little lime zest. Enjoy.

Serves 3 to 4

Olive oil
3 medium onions, finely chopped
2 large cloves garlic, crushed
4 heaping tbsp finely chopped
fresh flat-leaf parsley leaves
(or 3 tbsp fresh marjoram leaves)
2 tsp freshly grated lemon zest
2¼ pounds (1 kg)
cored cauliflower,
cut into 1¼-inch (3 cm) wedges
Flaky sea salt
Coarsely ground pepper
4 ounces (110 g) Parmesan,
coarsely grated

The distinct cabbagey note of cruciferous vegetables becomes less intrusive when roasted in the oven. Roasted broccoli or Brussels sprouts tamed by lemon and ginger make a delicious lunch, and cauliflower topped with parsley, Parmesan, and onions is equally exciting.

Roasted Cauliflower with Parmesan, Parsley, and Onions

Preheat the oven to 425°F (220°C).

In a medium, heavy pan, heat a splash of olive oil over medium heat. Add the onions and sauté for 5 minutes or until golden and soft. Add the garlic and sauté for 1 minute then add the parsley and lemon zest, stir, and set aside.

Spread the cauliflower wedges on a baking sheet. Drizzle 1/3 cup (75 ml) of olive oil over the cauliflower and use your fingers to gently toss and coat the wedges. Season to taste with salt and pepper and roast for about 18 minutes or until the wedges turn golden. Flip the cauliflower over, add a little more salt and pepper, and roast for another 7 minutes. Sprinkle the cauliflower with the onion mixture and the Parmesan and roast for 5 to 7 minutes or until golden brown and al dente.

Serve the warm cauliflower for lunch, or as a side dish with schnitzel, steak, or burgers.

After years of unsuccessful attempts to cook a good, honest steak at home, we decided to step up our game. We took out the pan—or rather my partner did—and cooked our way through a week of steaks. We wanted it seared and crisp on the outside, with a smoky touch, as if it came right off the barbecue grill, and the meat had to be juicy, pink, and a little bloody in the center. We set the bar high, but my co-chef exceeded both of our expectations.

The Perfect Peppered Steak

Serves 2

2 (7-ounce / 200-g)
boneless rib-eye steaks,
about 1⅓-inch thick (3.5 cm)
2 tbsp (30 g) unsalted butter
Flaky sea salt
Coarsely ground pepper
½ baguette, for serving

Take the meat out of the refrigerator about 1 hour before you want to start cooking. Dry the steaks with paper towels just before you sear them in the pan.

Preheat the oven to 400°F (200°C). Spread a piece of aluminum foil, large enough to wrap both steaks, on a work surface.

Heat a medium cast-iron pan or ovenproof skillet over high heat, without adding any fat, until the pan is scorching hot and starts smoking. Sear the steaks for 1½ minutes per side then remove the pan from the heat. Place 1 tablespoon of butter on top of each steak, transfer to the oven, and bake for 3 minutes for rare or 4 minutes for medium-rare.

Transfer the steaks to the aluminum foil, reserving the cooking juices in the pan. Wrap the steaks and let them rest for 2 minutes.

Divide the steaks among plates and season to taste with salt and pepper. Drizzle with the buttery juices from the pan and serve with a fresh baguette.

Umbrian *torta al testo* has been a staple in Italy's baking culture for centuries. This round flatbread is traditionally baked on clay or stone discs—the *testo*—placed over hot coals, but a scorching hot cast-iron pan and a stove work perfectly for the home baker. The tortas can be served on the side of a warm meal, but they are at their best when filled like a sandwich.

Torta al Testo
with Mozzarella and Arugula

Makes 6 sandwiches

For the flatbread
2 cups (260 g) all-purpose flour
1 ½ tsp fast-acting yeast
¼ tsp fine sea salt
⅔ cup (150 ml) water, lukewarm

For the sandwiches
9 ounces (250 g) mozzarella di bufala, drained and cut into small cubes
1 large handful arugula leaves
Olive oil
White balsamic vinegar
Fine sea salt
Finely ground pepper

For the flatbread, combine the flour, yeast, and salt in the bowl of a stand mixer fitted with the dough hook attachment. Add the lukewarm water and mix with the hook for a few minutes or until well combined and elastic. On a work surface, continue kneading with your hands for 4 minutes or until you have a soft and silky ball of dough. Place the dough back in the bowl, cover with a tea towel, and let rise in a warm place, or preferably in a 100°F (35°C) warm oven, for 60 minutes or until almost doubled in size.

When the dough has almost doubled in size, punch it down, take it out of the bowl, and divide it into 6 equal parts. On a well-floured work surface, use a rolling pin to roll each piece into a 4-inch (10 cm) disc. Cover the dough with a tea towel and let rise in a warm place for 20 to 30 minutes or until puffy.

Heat a large cast-iron pan over high heat, without adding any fat, until the pan is scorching hot and starts smoking. Working in batches, arrange 2 to 3 discs of dough in the pan and cook, flipping once, for 45 seconds to 1 ½ minutes per side. The flatbread should be golden brown, freckled with black spots, puffed up, and baked through—mind that it doesn't burn. Repeat to bake the remaining flatbreads and let them cool for a few minutes.

For the sandwiches, cut each flatbread in half like a roll without cutting through it completely, so that you can stuff it like a pocket. Divide the mozzarella and arugula among the flatbreads, drizzle with a little olive oil and vinegar, and season to taste with salt and pepper. Serve immediately.

Recreating recipes from foreign cultures and countries can't replace the thrilling experience of travel, but it can soften the pain of wanderlust. Close your eyes and smell and taste this Provençal tart made with pine nuts, dates, and honey. It will carry you to the hilltop villages of Roussillon or Gordes, in the heart of Provence, where the sky is blue and magical, and the perfume of pine trees is enchanting.

Provençal Pine Nut, Date, and Honey Tart

Serves 6 to 8

For the pastry

1½ cups (200 g) all-purpose flour

⅓ cup (65 g) granulated sugar

⅛ tsp fine sea salt

½ cup (115 g) unsalted butter, cold

2 large egg yolks

For the filling

½ cup (115 g) unsalted butter, at room temperature

¼ cup (55 g) light brown sugar

3 tbsp (50 g) honey

1 tsp freshly grated orange zest

1 tbsp freshly squeezed orange juice

2 large eggs

1 cup (110 g) ground skin-on almonds

4 ounces (110 g) pitted dates, finely chopped

4 ounces (110 g) pine nuts

For the pastry, combine the flour, granulated sugar, and salt in the bowl of a stand mixer fitted with the dough hook attachment. Add the butter and use a knife to cut it into the flour until there are just small pieces left. Quickly rub the butter into the flour with your fingers until combined. Add the egg yolks and mix with the hook until crumbly. Form the dough into a thick disc, wrap it in plastic wrap, and freeze for 12 minutes.

Preheat the oven to 400°F (200°C).

On a work surface, place the dough between 2 sheets of plastic wrap and use a rolling pin to roll out into a disc, large enough to line the bottom and sides of a 9-inch (23 cm), preferably loose-bottom, tart pan. Fit the dough into the tart pan, pushing it into the pan, especially along the edges. Let the dough hang over the rim a little or trim with a knife. Use a fork to prick the dough all over. Bake for 10 minutes or until golden and crisp. If the dough bubbles up, push it down with a fork. Take the tart pan out of the oven and set it aside.

For the filling, beat the butter, light brown sugar, honey, orange zest, and orange juice in the bowl of a stand mixer fitted with the paddle attachment until creamy. Add the eggs, 1 at a time, incorporating each egg before adding the next one. Add the almonds and dates and mix for 1 minute or until combined. Spread the filling evenly on top of the pre-baked pastry and sprinkle with the pine nuts, pushing them gently into the filling. Bake for 15 minutes then reduce the heat to 350°F (180°C) and bake for another 10 to 12 minutes or until the top is golden brown and firm. Let the tart cool for 15 minutes then take it out of the pan, cut into slices, and serve.

Serves 2 to 4

¾ pound (340 g) trimmed
thin green asparagus
3 tbsp olive oil
Flaky sea salt
Coarsely ground pepper
2 large eggs, hard-boiled
and roughly chopped
8 large strawberries,
hulled and cut into quarters
1 small handful
fresh tarragon leaves

If you roast asparagus in the oven and crumble a hard-boiled egg over the oily stalks, they merge into a smooth, almost velvety sauce that gently mellows the acidity of fresh strawberries.

Roasted Asparagus with Strawberries, Tarragon, and Crumbled Eggs

Preheat the oven to 425°F (220°C).

Spread the asparagus in a medium baking dish, drizzle with the olive oil, and toss to coat. Season to taste with salt and pepper and roast for about 18 minutes or until tender.

Arrange the asparagus on a large platter, sprinkle with the eggs, strawberries, and tarragon and season to taste with salt and pepper. Serve warm or as a cold salad.

128

week 19 /tuesday

Serves 1 to 2

½ tsp flaky sea salt
¼ to ½ tsp freshly grated lime zest
14 cherry tomatoes, cut in half
¼ medium red onion,
very thinly sliced
1 ½ tbsp olive oil
Freshly squeezed lime juice,
to taste

A bite of this salad tastes like summer, or at the very least, the promise of a rapidly approaching sunny season. You could add fresh cilantro, but if you reduce the spectrum and focus only on tomato, lime, and red onion, you can enjoy each ingredient and allow them to create a very fine and subtle composition together. Needless to say, it's the quickest lunch during a busy week.

Cherry Tomatoes with Lime Salt and Red Onions

Whisk together the salt and $1/4$ teaspoon of the lime zest and grind with a mortar and pestle until fine.

Arrange the tomatoes and onion on a plate and drizzle with the olive oil and a squeeze of lime juice. Season to taste with the lime salt and additional lime zest and enjoy.

Whether risotto *alla Milanese* or with porcini or radicchio, if risotto is cooked well, with the grains al dente and the texture smooth, it's the kind of food that calms your soul and rewards your taste buds. And if you add mascarpone, lemon zest, and crispy fried sage leaves, it's a heavenly dish.

Lemon-Mascarpone Risotto with Crispy Sage

Serves 2

Olive oil
2 tbsp (30 g) unsalted butter
1 medium onion, finely chopped
7 ounces (200 g) risotto rice
¼ cup (60 ml) dry white wine
About 3 ¾ cups (900 ml)
vegetable broth
4 long strips fresh lemon peel
2 tbsp mascarpone
Fine sea salt
Finely ground pepper
12 large fresh sage leaves
1 to 2 tsp freshly grated
lemon zest
2 tbsp finely grated Parmesan

In a large pot, heat a splash of olive oil and 1 tablespoon of the butter over medium heat. Add the onion and sauté for 3 minutes or until golden. Add the rice and cook, stirring, for 1 minute. Add the white wine and a ladle of the broth to cover the rice then add the lemon peel. Cook the rice, stirring occasionally and adding more broth when necessary to keep the rice covered, until the broth is fully absorbed and the rice is al dente. Take the pot off the heat and stir in 1 tablespoon of the mascarpone. Season to taste with salt and pepper, cover, and let it sit for 1 minute.

In a small saucepan, heat the remaining 1 tablespoon of butter over high heat. Add the sage and cook, stirring gently, for 10 to 20 seconds or until golden, green, and crispy—mind that the leaves don't burn.

Divide the risotto among plates and drizzle with the sage butter. Sprinkle with the remaining mascarpone, the sage leaves, lemon zest, Parmesan, and a little pepper; serve immediately.

Cooking a whole sole isn't the most relaxing kitchen task. It's a delicate fish, and can easily be overcooked, but its fine taste more than makes up for any trouble. Try to use a pan that's large enough to fit the whole sole, but if the fish is too long, don't despair—just leave the tail hanging out. I'm not a big fan of rich sauces plopped onto crispy pan-seared fish, but I don't mind serving it with some fruity balsamic tomatoes with marjoram on the side.

Sole with Balsamic Cherry Tomatoes and Marjoram

Serves 2

For the tomatoes

Olive oil

2 large cloves garlic, thinly sliced

14 cherry tomatoes, cut in half

1 tsp balsamic vinegar

1 tbsp fresh marjoram leaves,

plus 1 tbsp for serving

Fine sea salt

Finely ground pepper

For the sole

Unsalted butter, to cook the sole

Olive oil

1 (18-ounce / 500-g) whole sole

or flounder, gutted and cleaned

Fine sea salt

Finely ground pepper

For the tomatoes, heat a splash of olive oil in a small, heavy pan over medium heat and sauté the garlic for 2 minutes or until golden. Add the tomatoes, vinegar, and 1 tablespoon of marjoram, season to taste with salt and pepper, and cook over medium-high heat for about 5 minutes or until the tomatoes are soft but still hold their shape. If the liquid cooks off too quickly, reduce the heat. Season to taste with salt and pepper and set aside.

In a heavy, preferably nonstick pan, large enough to fit the sole, heat 1 tablespoon of butter and a generous splash of olive oil over medium-high heat. Season the sole to taste with salt and pepper and sear, dark-side down, for 2 1/2 minutes. Using two spatulas, carefully flip the fish over and cook for 2 1/2 to 3 minutes or until just cooked through and you can flake the fish with a fork.

Divide the fish into 2 fillets and serve with the balsamic tomatoes on the side. Sprinkle the fish and tomatoes with a little marjoram.

This pleasantly sour rhubarb galette with a crunchy, golden cornmeal crust is the perfect spring tart. Saffron's vivid crimson threads infuse the baked rhubarb with their unusual and vibrant flavor, taking it to the next level of deliciousness.

Rhubarb-Corn Galette with Saffron Sugar

Serves 4

For the pastry

½ cup (90 g) very fine yellow cornmeal (or corn flour)

⅔ cup (90 g) all-purpose flour

1 tbsp granulated sugar

¼ tsp fine sea salt

½ cup plus 1 tbsp (125 g) unsalted butter, cold

2 tbsp water, cold

1 tsp cider vinegar

For the galette

⅓ cup plus 1 tbsp (80 g) granulated sugar, plus 1 tsp for the topping

½ vanilla bean, split and scraped

⅛ to ¼ tsp saffron threads

1 tbsp all-purpose flour

⅛ tsp fine sea salt

10 ounces (280 g) trimmed rhubarb

1 tbsp freshly squeezed lemon juice

1 large egg, beaten

For the pastry, combine the cornmeal, all-purpose flour, sugar, and salt in the bowl of a stand mixer fitted with the dough hook attachment. Add the butter and use a knife to cut it into the flour until there are just small pieces left. Quickly rub the butter into the flour with your fingers until combined. Add the cold water and the vinegar and mix with the hook until combined. Form the dough into a thick disc, wrap it in plastic wrap, and chill in the fridge overnight (or for a few hours), or freeze for 30 minutes or until firm.

On a work surface, place the dough between 2 sheets of plastic wrap and use a rolling pin to roll it out into a 12-inch (30 cm) circle. Pull off the top layer of plastic wrap and replace with a piece of parchment paper. Flip the pastry over then transfer to a wooden board or platter, pull off the plastic wrap, and chill in the fridge for 15 minutes or until firm.

Place a baking sheet in the middle of the oven and preheat to 400°F (200°C).

For the galette, finely grind 1/3 cup plus 1 tablespoon (80 g) of sugar, the vanilla seeds, and 1/8 teaspoon of the saffron with a mortar and pestle. Season to taste with additional saffron. Add the flour and salt and mix well.

Cut the rhubarb into 4-inch-long (10 cm) pieces and cut each piece into quarters lengthwise. In a large bowl, toss the rhubarb with the saffron sugar and lemon juice.

Arrange the rhubarb, like rays, on top of the pastry, leaving a 2-inch (5 cm) border and sprinkle with any remaining saffron sugar. Fold the edges of the pastry up and over the ends of the rhubarb then press the pastry firmly to seal the folds. Brush the pastry with the egg and sprinkle with 1 teaspoon of sugar. Use the parchment paper to carefully pull the galette onto the hot baking sheet and bake for 30 minutes or until golden brown. Let it cool for at least 10 minutes then cut into slices and serve.

This puréed soup, made of asparagus and fava beans cooked in a clear vegetable broth, focuses on the pure flavor of the vegetables. You could whisk in some cream, but it's not necessary. Add a poached egg instead and let the liquid yellow yolk run into the bright green soup. Go ahead and double the recipe. There'll be no regrets the next day, when you can enjoy the leftovers sprinkled with bacon, ricotta, and fresh tarragon.

Asparagus-Fava Bean Soup with Poached Egg and Chile Oil

Serves 3 to 4

For the soup
Olive oil
1 medium onion,
roughly chopped
2 large cloves garlic,
cut into quarters
10 ounces (280 g) trimmed
green asparagus, each stalk cut
into 3 pieces
10 ounces (280 g) fresh or frozen
shelled fava beans
3 ¾ cups (900 ml) homemade
or quality store-bought
vegetable broth, hot
1 large bay leaf
Nutmeg, preferably
freshly grated
Fine sea salt
Finely ground pepper

For the topping
3 tbsp olive oil
½ medium, fresh red chile,
seeded and finely chopped
3 to 4 large eggs

For the soup, in a large pot, heat a splash of olive oil over medium heat and sauté the onion and garlic, stirring occasionally, for 5 minutes or until golden and soft. Add the asparagus, fava beans, hot broth, and bay leaf. Season to taste with nutmeg, salt, and pepper and bring to a boil. Reduce the heat and simmer for 7 minutes or until the asparagus and beans are tender. Remove and discard the bay leaf. Transfer 8 asparagus tips to a cutting board, cut them in half lengthwise, and set aside. Purée the soup in a food processor or blender, or with an immersion blender, then season to taste with nutmeg, salt, and pepper and keep warm.

For the topping, heat the olive oil and chile in a small saucepan over high heat until sizzling then immediately take the pan off the heat.

Bring a small saucepan of salted water to a low simmer. Crack 1 egg into a small bowl. Hold a large spoon just over the surface of the water and gently pour the egg onto the spoon. Lower the spoon into the water and hold until the egg white starts to turn white then use a tablespoon to gently scoop the egg off the large spoon. Poach the egg for 3 minutes. Using a slotted ladle or spoon, transfer the egg to a plate. Poach the remaining eggs the same way, adjusting the heat as needed to maintain a low simmer. It's best to poach 1 egg at a time, but you can cook 2 at once.

Divide the soup among bowls, place 1 egg in the middle of each bowl, and arrange the reserved asparagus tips around it. Sprinkle with the chile oil, cut the tops of the eggs with a sharp knife, and serve immediately.

We bake pizza from scratch every Sunday and the toppings change according to our mood. I'm the pizza traditionalist in the family, while my partner is more experimental, and often convinces me to leave out the tomatoes and go for a pizza bianca. The individual ingredients get more attention without the dominant fruity sauce. And if you top the crunchy base with asparagus, salsiccia (Italian sausage), and mozzarella, you surely won't regret choosing white over red this time around.

Pizza Bianca with Green Asparagus, Salsiccia, and Mozzarella di Bufala

Makes 2 (11-inch / 28-cm) pizzas

For the dough
2 ⅔ cups (350 g) all-purpose flour
1 (¼-ounce / 7-g) envelope fast-acting yeast
1 tsp fine sea salt
¾ cup (180 ml) water, lukewarm
4 tbsp olive oil

For the topping
Olive oil
14 thin green asparagus stalks, trimmed
Fine sea salt
Finely ground pepper
1 large salsiccia (or any thick, coarse sausage), skin removed, cut into chunks
4 ounces (110 g) mozzarella di bufala, drained and cut into small cubes

Picture page 175, top left

Start the preparations about 2 hours before you want to enjoy the pizza. I bake it on a baking sheet that's been heated on the bottom of the oven like a pizza stone to help create a crunchy crust.

For the dough, combine the flour, yeast, and salt in the bowl of a stand mixer fitted with the dough hook attachment. Add the lukewarm water and the olive oil and mix with the hook for a few minutes or until well combined. If the dough is too sticky, add more flour. Transfer the dough to a work surface and continue kneading and punching it down with your hands for about 4 minutes or until you have a smooth and elastic ball of dough. Place the dough back in the bowl, cover with a tea towel, and let rise in a warm place, or preferably in a 100°F (35°C) warm oven, for 50 to 60 minutes or until doubled in size.

While the dough is rising, prepare the topping: Heat a generous splash of olive oil in a large, heavy pan over medium-high heat and sauté the asparagus, turning occasionally, for about 7 minutes or until golden brown and al dente. Season to taste with salt and pepper and set aside.

When the dough has doubled in size, punch it down, take it out of the bowl, and divide into 2 equal parts. On a well-floured work surface or pizza peel, stretch and roll each piece of dough into an 11-inch (28 cm) disc. Cover with a tea towel and let rise in a warm place for about 20 minutes or until puffy.

Place a baking sheet (or pizza stone) on the bottom of the oven and preheat the oven to the highest temperature, 500°F (260°C) or higher.

Once the baking sheet is hot, carefully take it out of the oven, flip it over, and place it on a trivet or other heat-safe surface. Arrange 1 of the dough discs on the baking sheet and spread 1/2 of the asparagus, salsiccia, and mozzarella on the dough. Push the asparagus gently into the dough. Sprinkle with 2 tablespoons of olive oil and some pepper and bake on the bottom of the oven for 9 to 10 minutes or until golden brown. Repeat to make the second pizza and serve hot.

You could argue that this is not a proper shakshuka in the classic sense, but sometimes I allow myself to be a bit silly in the kitchen and look at food with humor. For traditional shakshuka, the eggs are poached in a thick bed of tomatoes and vegetables. I dare to sneak in a crêpe, change the color from red to green, and skip the sauce. You can also call it green vegetables with an egg on a crêpe.

Green Shakshuka Crêpes

Serves 2 to 4

For the crêpes

1 cup plus 1 tbsp (255 ml) whole milk

2 large eggs

1 cup (130 g) all-purpose flour, sifted

½ tbsp granulated sugar

⅛ tsp fine sea salt

Unsalted butter, to cook the crêpes

For the filling

7 ounces (200 g) fresh or frozen peas

2 tbsp olive oil

1 large clove garlic, cut in half

¼ tsp ground cumin, plus more to taste

2 spring onions, very thinly sliced

1 small handful fresh flat-leaf parsley leaves, roughly chopped

Fine sea salt

Finely ground pepper

4 large eggs

3 ounces (85 g) aromatic cheese that melts well, such as Raclette, Comté, or Gruyère, finely grated

1 small handful arugula leaves

Piment d'Espelette (optional)

Picture opposite, top right

For the crêpes, in the bowl of a stand mixer fitted with the whisk attachment, whisk together the milk, eggs, flour, sugar, and salt until smooth. Let the batter sit for 10 minutes before you cook the crêpes.

For the filling, bring a small pot of salted water to a boil and blanch the peas for about 1 minute or until al dente. Drain and quickly rinse with cold water.

In a medium saucepan, heat the olive oil, garlic, and cumin over high heat until sizzling. Take the pan off the heat then add the peas, 3/4 of the spring onions, and the parsley, stir, and season to taste with salt, pepper, and additional cumin.

In a large cast-iron pan or nonstick skillet, melt about 1/2 teaspoon of butter over medium-high heat. Pour in a ladle of the crêpe batter, tilting and turning the pan, so that the batter spreads evenly and very thinly. Cook the crêpe for 30 to 60 seconds or until golden, flip, and take the pan off the heat. Carefully crack 1 egg in the middle of the crêpe. Spread 1/4 of the cheese, 1/4 of the pea mixture, and 1/4 of the arugula around the egg yolk then fold the 4 sides of the crêpe up and around the egg white to create a square, without covering the egg yolk. Place over medium-low heat and cook for 1 to 2 minutes or until the egg white is set and the yolk is still runny. Sprinkle with 1/4 of the remaining spring onion, season to taste with salt and piment d'Espelette, and serve warm. Repeat to make 3 more crêpes, adjusting the heat as necessary, and adding a little more butter to the pan between crêpes.

133

134

137

138

I ate my first Tuscan panzanella at the young age of six, right at this recipe's place of origin, an old farmhouse just outside Lucca. I will never forget the taste of the bread chunks soaked in oily balsamic juices, and tossed with sun-kissed tomatoes, onions, and basil. That's the classic version. Bacon, berries, figs, and rosemary pull the frugal salad in another direction and prove that you should never throw away stale bread. Just mix it with a light vinaigrette and whatever fruits and veggies you feel like and call it a panzanella.

Berry and Bacon Panzanella with Rosemary

Serves 2 to 4

For the dressing
3 tbsp olive oil
1 tbsp balsamic vinegar
1 tbsp white balsamic vinegar
2 tsp finely chopped
fresh rosemary needles
Fine sea salt
Finely ground pepper

For the salad
Olive oil
4 slices bacon
1 large handful arugula leaves
(or mixed lettuce leaves),
torn into pieces
2 large handfuls bite-size
chunky ciabatta cubes
(or any spongy white bread)
1 handful strawberries,
hulled and cut in half
1 handful blueberries
2 large fresh figs, cut into quarters

For the dressing, whisk together the olive oil, both vinegars, and the rosemary and season to taste with salt and pepper.

For the salad, heat a splash of olive oil in a large, heavy pan over medium-high heat and cook the bacon, turning occasionally, for a few minutes or until golden brown and crispy. Transfer the bacon to a plate, let it cool for a few minutes then break into pieces.

Arrange the arugula in a large bowl and add the ciabatta, strawberries, blueberries, figs, and bacon. Drizzle with the dressing, toss to combine, and let sit for 1 minute. If the salad is too dry, add a little more olive oil. Divide among plates and enjoy.

Makes 4 sandwiches

8 small spring onions,
cut in half lengthwise
Olive oil
Fine sea salt
Coarsely ground pepper
8 thin slices prosciutto di Parma
(or prosciutto di San Daniele)
4 rustic white buns, cut in half
4 ounces (110 g) mild,
sweet cheese that melts well,
such as Taleggio, fontina,
or Robiola, cut into slices

Taleggio tastes almost fruity, and has hints of flowers. Although this creamy cheese from the Val Taleggio is the best choice for this sandwich, you can, of course, replace it with fontina or Robiola.

Roasted Spring Onion and Prosciutto Sandwich with Taleggio

Preheat the oven to 425°F (220°C).

Spread the spring onions in a medium baking dish, drizzle with a little olive oil, and season to taste with salt and pepper. Roast for 10 minutes, flip, and roast for 5 to 10 minutes or until golden and soft.

Set the oven to broil (quicker method) or preheat to 500°F (260°C).

Arrange 2 slices of prosciutto on the bottom half of each bun then cover with the spring onions and cheese. Put the sandwiches under the broiler, or roast at 500°F (260°C) for a few minutes or until the cheese starts to melt. Sprinkle with pepper, place a top on each bun, and serve.

Serves 3 to 6

1 pound (450 g) trimmed rhubarb,
cut in half lengthwise and cut into
5-inch (12.5 cm) pieces
1 pound (450 g) leeks, cut in half
lengthwise and cut into 5-inch
(12.5 cm) pieces
¼ cup (60 ml) olive oil
Flaky sea salt
Coarsely ground pepper
1 tsp granulated sugar
1 small bunch fresh thyme

Picture page 175, bottom left

Sweet leeks take rhubarb by the hand and gently balance its sourness, but this is still a bold combination and not an easy pleaser. You have to be in the mood for an unusual flavor pairing. If you're up for it, this dish makes a refreshing lunch and a brave side dish for meaty meals. You could add some maple syrup to soften the duo, but that would feel like cheating—keep it sour.

Roasted Rhubarb and Leek with Thyme

Preheat the oven to 400°F (200°C).

In a medium baking dish, combine the rhubarb, leeks, and olive oil, toss to coat, and arrange in a tight alternating pattern next to each other. Season to taste with salt and pepper, sprinkle with the sugar and thyme, and roast for 20 minutes or until golden and tender. Serve warm or cold.

Tapenade, a Provençal dip made of black olives, onion, parsley, capers, and mustard, is usually put on the table for appetizers. Spreading it on bread is very common, but you can also use it for poultry or seafood. The taste is strong but not overpowering, and in this recipe, it merges beautifully with the chicken's roasting juices. Preserved lemon and whole garlic bulbs chime in and turn it into a French feast.

138

week 20 / friday

Serves 2 to 4

4 whole chicken legs
Tapenade (¼ recipe no. 182)
Flaky sea salt
Coarsely ground pepper
½ preserved lemon, thinly sliced
(or 1 tbsp freshly grated
lemon zest)
2 large bulbs garlic,
cut in half crosswise
⅓ cup (75 ml) fruity white wine
1 small handful fresh flat-leaf
parsley leaves

Picture page 175, bottom right

Tapenade Chicken with Roasted Garlic and Lemon

Preheat the oven to 425°F (220°C).

Cut off and discard any large chunks of fat from the chicken legs and arrange in a baking dish, just large enough to fit them in. Use your fingers to rub the tapenade into the legs until well coated. Season to taste with salt and pepper, sprinkle with the preserved lemon, and arrange the garlic bulbs in between the chicken legs. Add the white wine and roast, spooning the juices from the pan over the chicken every 10 minutes or so, for 25 to 30 minutes or until the juices run clear when you prick the thickest part of a thigh with a skewer. Turn on the broiler for 1 to 2 minutes or until the chicken skin is golden and starts sizzling. Sprinkle with the parsley and serve immediately.

139

week 20 / saturday

Serves 2 to 4

10 ounces (280 g) very fresh firm
white fish fillet, such as flounder,
sea bass, or halibut
Zest and juice of 2 medium limes
½ medium red onion, cut in half
and thinly sliced
About ¼ fresh Peruvian red aji
límo chile (or red habanero),
seeded and thinly sliced
About ¼ fresh Peruvian yellow aji
límo chile (or yellow habanero),
seeded and thinly sliced
Fine sea salt

Sheila is an American food lover and writer living in Peru and has been following the stories and recipes on Eat In My Kitchen since its early days in 2013. A few summers ago, she gave me her Peruvian ceviche recipe. It's the freshest, purest, and most delicious treat you can create with the fruits of the sea.

Sheila's Peruvian Ceviche

Cut the fish into $1/2$-inch (1.25 cm) pieces and transfer to a medium bowl. Add the lime juice, toss to coat, and marinate for 5 minutes. Remove excess lime juice (optional) and add the onion and $1/2$ of the chiles. Stir and season to taste with additional chiles, the lime zest, and salt. Divide among plates and serve immediately.

My friend Essa is a passionate baker. Once she made a cake for one of our family gatherings in Malta, and for months I couldn't get it out of my head. It was the most perfect Maltese ricotta pie, fluffier and lighter than a New York cheesecake, and topped with sticky lemon syrup and crunchy pistachios. It was love at first bite. After a year of begging, she gave me the recipe and let me play with it a bit.

Maltese Ricotta Pie with Lemon Syrup and Pistachios

Serves 6 to 8

For the pastry

1 ¼ cups (160 g) all-purpose flour
1 tbsp granulated sugar
¼ tsp fine sea salt
⅓ cup plus 1 tbsp (90 g) unsalted butter, cold
1 tbsp water, cold

For the filling

13 ounces (370 g) fresh ricotta, drained
½ cup (100 g) granulated sugar
3 large eggs
3 tbsp (45 g) unsalted butter, melted and cooled
1 ½ tbsp fine semolina
2 tsp freshly grated lemon zest

For the topping

⅓ cup (75 ml) freshly squeezed lemon juice
¼ cup (50 g) granulated sugar
1 ½ tbsp honey
2 ounces (60 g) unsalted pistachios, roughly chopped

For the pastry, combine the flour, sugar, and salt in the bowl of a stand mixer fitted with the dough hook attachment. Add the butter and use a knife to cut it into the flour until there are just small pieces left. Quickly rub the butter into the flour with your fingers until combined. Add the cold water and mix with the hook until crumbly. Form the dough into a thick disc, wrap it in plastic wrap, and freeze for 10 minutes.

Preheat the oven to 400°F (200°C).

On a work surface, place the dough between 2 sheets of plastic wrap and use a rolling pin to roll out into a disc, large enough to line the bottom and sides of a 9-inch (23 cm) pie dish. Fit the dough into the pie dish, pushing it into the dish, especially along the edges. Let the dough hang over the rim a little or trim with a knife. Use a fork to prick the dough all over. Bake for 15 minutes or until golden. If the dough bubbles up, push it down with a fork. Take the pie dish out of the oven then reduce the heat to 375°F (190°C).

For the filling, in a large bowl, whisk together the ricotta, sugar, eggs, butter, semolina, and lemon zest until well combined. Spread the filling on top of the pre-baked pastry and bake for 30 to 40 minutes or until the top is golden and firm.

For the topping, in a small saucepan, bring the lemon juice, sugar, and honey to a boil and cook, whisking occasionally, over medium-high heat for 4 to 5 minutes or until it starts to thicken. Let it cool for 5 minutes then drizzle over the pie, sprinkle with the pistachios, and serve.

Even if you're not the biggest fan of mayonnaise, give this recipe a try. When you whip up your own eggy dip at home and add a little tahini, lemon, and garlic, it has nothing in common with the heavy products that you see in stores. It's like a mix between hummus and Mediterranean aïoli. Drizzle it over a salad of blanched greens and see for yourself.

Green Beans and Peas with Tahini-Lemon Mayonnaise and Basil

Serves 2 to 4

For the mayonnaise

2 very fresh large egg yolks

⅓ cup (75 ml) mild olive oil

1 tbsp light tahini

1 large clove garlic, crushed

1 tbsp freshly grated lemon zest, plus more for serving

1 tbsp freshly squeezed lemon juice

Fine sea salt

For the salad

5 ounces (140 g) fresh or frozen peas

1¼ pounds (560 g) trimmed green beans

Olive oil

Fine sea salt

Finely ground pepper

1 small spring onion, very thinly sliced

12 small fresh basil leaves

For the mayonnaise, drop the egg yolks into a tall mug that's just large enough for an immersion blender. Start mixing and slowly pour in the olive oil. When it's thick and creamy, add the tahini, garlic, 1/2 tablespoon of the lemon zest, and 1/2 tablespoon of the lemon juice and stir to combine. Season to taste with salt and additional lemon zest and juice.

For the salad, bring a large pot of salted water to a boil and blanch the peas for about 1 minute or until al dente. Use a slotted ladle or spoon to transfer the peas to a colander, leaving the pot over high heat. Drain and quickly rinse the peas with cold water and transfer to a large platter. Add the green beans to the boiling water and blanch for 4 to 5 minutes or until al dente then drain, quickly rinse with cold water, and cut in half. Add the green beans to the platter, drizzle with 2 tablespoons of olive oil, and toss to coat. Season to taste with salt and pepper and sprinkle with the mayonnaise, spring onion, basil, and a little lemon zest; serve immediately.

Focaccia is a bit like summer pizza. Fewer toppings make it less heavy, but that doesn't diminish the cozy feeling it inspires or the sweet, tempting smell of baked yeast dough that fills the kitchen. Adding aromatic Gruyère and sharp red onions is a good choice, especially if you want to serve this spongy bread at a barbecue with crisp salads and some cheese and fruit on the side.

Gruyère and Red Onion Focaccia

Serves 3 to 6

3 ¾ cups plus 1 tbsp (500 g)
all-purpose flour
1 (¼-ounce / 7-g) envelope
fast-acting yeast
1 ½ tsp granulated sugar
1 tsp fine sea salt
1 cup plus 1 tbsp (255 ml) water,
lukewarm
½ cup (120 ml) olive oil
2 medium red onions,
cut into round slices
4 ounces (110 g) aromatic cheese
that melts well, such as Gruyère,
Raclette, or Comté,
coarsely grated
Flaky sea salt
Coarsely ground pepper

In the bowl of a stand mixer fitted with the dough hook attachment, combine the flour, yeast, sugar, and fine sea salt. Add the lukewarm water and ¼ cup (60 ml) of the olive oil and mix with the hook for 5 minutes or until well combined. If the dough is too sticky, add more flour. Transfer the dough to a work surface and continue kneading and punching it down with your hands for 4 minutes or until you have a smooth and elastic ball of dough. Place the dough back in the bowl, cover with a tea towel, and let rise in a warm place, or preferably in a 100°F (35°C) warm oven, for 60 minutes or until doubled in size.

Brush a baking sheet with olive oil. When the dough has doubled in size, punch it down, take it out of the bowl, and knead for 1 minute. On the prepared baking sheet, pull and stretch the dough into a 13 x 10-inch (33 x 25 cm) rectangle. Cover with a tea towel and let rise in a warm place for about 20 minutes or until puffy.

Preheat the oven to 425°F (220°C).

Using the bottom of a wooden spoon or your finger, push 6 rows of 7 holes into the dough. Arrange the onions on top, gently pushing them into the dough. Pour the remaining ¼ cup (60 ml) of olive oil over the dough and onions and into the holes. Sprinkle with the cheese and a little flaky sea salt and bake for 20 minutes or until golden and spongy. Season to taste with pepper and enjoy warm or cold.

Chorizo and strawberry make an unusual, albeit impressive match: The meaty heat of the salami and the juicy sweetness of the fruit merge marvelously. Ricotta whipped with basil and pink peppercorns, and spread on tiny crostini creates a perfect cradle for this delicacy.

Chorizo and Strawberry Crostini with Basil Ricotta and Pink Peppercorns

Makes 6 small sandwiches

For the ricotta dip

4 ounces (110 g) fresh ricotta
20 large fresh basil leaves, roughly chopped
1 ½ tsp pink peppercorns, crushed with a mortar and pestle
Fine sea salt
1 large strawberry, hulled and cut into very small cubes

For the sandwiches

6 slices baguette, toasted or grilled
18 small thick slices Spanish chorizo salami
3 large strawberries, hulled and cut into quarters
12 small fresh basil leaves

For the ricotta dip, whisk together the ricotta, basil, and crushed pink peppercorns in a medium bowl. Season to taste with salt and fold in the strawberry.

For the sandwiches, spread the ricotta dip onto the crostini, arrange 3 slices of chorizo and 2 pieces of strawberry on top of each, and decorate with 2 basil leaves. Serve immediately.

It's only May, but golden calamari, tossed in a hot pan with fresh red chile, lime, and cilantro, tastes like the height of summer.

Seared Calamari with Chile, Lime, and Cilantro

Serves 1 to 2

3 tbsp olive oil
2 tbsp seeded and finely chopped fresh red chile
8 small calamari, cleaned
Fine sea salt
Finely ground pepper
1 tsp freshly grated lime zest
2 tbsp freshly squeezed lime juice
1 small handful fresh cilantro leaves, roughly chopped

Picture page 187, top left

In a small, heavy pan, heat the olive oil over medium-high heat, add the chile, and cook for 10 seconds. Add the calamari, season to taste with salt and pepper, and sear, stirring constantly, for about 2 minutes or until golden and just cooked through—mind not to overcook the calamari or they become chewy. Add the lime zest and lime juice, stir, and take the pan off the heat. Sprinkle with the cilantro and enjoy with a fresh baguette for dipping in the pan juices.

Classic Roman saltimbocca only needs sage and prosciutto—basta! But a stroll through the farmers' market and a peek into the baskets filled with colorful berries can distract the mind and seduce the creative cook into ignoring tradition. Sweet raspberries soaked in dark red onion-port sauce flatter fine cutlets, no matter if it's veal or pork.

Saltimbocca alla Romana with Port Raspberries

Serves 2

For the raspberries

Olive oil

¼ medium red onion,
very finely chopped

½ cup (120 ml) port

2 tbsp freshly squeezed
orange juice

2 tsp honey

1 tsp balsamic vinegar

3 medium sprigs fresh thyme

2 long strips fresh orange peel
(white pith removed)

Fine sea salt

Finely ground pepper

¼ pound (110 g) fresh raspberries

For the saltimbocca

4 small, ¼-inch-thick (0.5 cm) veal
or pork cutlets, about ¾ pound
(340 g) total (or 2 large cutlets,
cut in half)

Fine sea salt

Finely ground pepper

About 2 heaping tbsp
all-purpose flour

24 fresh sage leaves

4 thin slices coppa di Parma
(or prosciutto di Parma)

Unsalted butter,
to cook the cutlets

Olive oil

Picture opposite, top right

For the raspberries, in a small, heavy pan, heat a splash of olive oil over medium heat and cook the onion for 10 minutes or until golden and soft. Set the heat to high, add the port, and cook for 15 seconds. Reduce the heat to medium and add the orange juice, honey, vinegar, thyme, and orange peel. Cook for 5 minutes then remove and discard the thyme and orange peel. Season to taste with salt and pepper and add the raspberries. Cook for 1 to 2 minutes or until the berries soften but still keep their shape. Cover and set aside.

For the saltimbocca, arrange the 4 cutlets on a work surface between 2 sheets of plastic wrap. Use a meat pounder or your fist to tenderize and slightly flatten the meat. Season to taste with salt and pepper on both sides then dust the upper side with flour. Flip the cutlets over and top each with 4 sage leaves and 1 slice of coppa di Parma, gently pressing the toppings into the meat.

In a large, heavy pan, heat 2 tablespoons of butter and a generous splash of olive oil over medium-high heat. Add the saltimbocca, coppa-side down, and sear for 1 minute then carefully flip the saltimbocca over, add the remaining sage, and cook for 1 minute or until golden brown and just cooked through. Divide the saltimbocca and sage among plates and drizzle with the juices from the pan. Arrange the raspberries and the port sauce around the meat and serve immediately.

144

145

146

150

Gathering friends around a long table filled with wine, bread, and platters of fruit, cheese, salads, and sweets feels like an indoor picnic. You sit and chat for hours and everybody picks and nibbles on whatever they feel like. A savory tart is a must for this type of meal. Imagine the famous caprese salad merged with a tart: tomato, mozzarella, and basil pesto baked on top of the flakiest pastry.

Tomato and Mozzarella Tart with Pesto

Serves 4 to 8

For the pastry

2 cups (260 g) all-purpose flour
1 tsp fine sea salt
½ cup (115 g) unsalted butter, cold
1 tbsp olive oil
1 large egg

For the pesto

1 ounce (30 g) fresh basil leaves
1 ounce (30 g) Parmesan, finely grated
1 ounce (30 g) pine nuts
⅓ cup (75 ml) olive oil
1 clove garlic
Fine sea salt

For the topping

4 ounces (110 g) mozzarella di bufala, drained and very thinly sliced
4 medium tomatoes, sliced
3 tbsp coarsely grated Parmesan
Fine sea salt
Finely ground pepper
8 small fresh basil leaves

Picture page 187, bottom left

For the pastry, combine the flour and salt in the bowl of a stand mixer fitted with the dough hook attachment. Add the butter and use a knife to cut it into the flour until there are just small pieces left. Quickly rub the butter into the flour with your fingers until combined. Add the olive oil and egg and mix with the hook until crumbly. Form the dough into a thick disc, wrap it in plastic wrap, and freeze for 10 minutes.

Preheat the oven to 400°F (200°C).

For the pesto, purée the basil, Parmesan, pine nuts, olive oil, and garlic in a food processor or blender until smooth and season to taste with salt.

On a work surface, place the dough between 2 sheets of plastic wrap and use a rolling pin to roll out into a disc, large enough to line the bottom and sides of a 12-inch (30 cm) quiche dish. Fit the dough into the quiche dish, pushing it into the dish, especially along the edges. Let the dough hang over the rim a little or trim with a knife. Use a fork to prick the dough all over. Bake for 15 to 17 minutes or until golden. If the dough bubbles up, push it down with a fork. Take the quiche dish out of the oven and reduce the heat to 350°F (180°C).

For the topping, brush the pre-baked pastry with a little olive oil and spread the mozzarella on top. Cover with the tomatoes, sprinkle with the Parmesan, and season to taste with salt and pepper. Sprinkle with 1/2 of the pesto and bake for 45 to 50 minutes or until the top is golden and the pastry is crisp. Sprinkle with basil and serve warm or cold with the remaining pesto.

This is such a kiddie cake, but one that adults love just as much. It's light and fluffy, sweet and juicy, and packed with strawberries and pockets of creamy white chocolate. And it's so easy to prepare that if you roll out of bed a tiny bit early on a Sunday morning, you can enjoy this mouthwatering treat for breakfast.

Strawberry-White Chocolate Breakfast Cake

Serves 6 to 8

For the cake
1 cup (130 g) all-purpose flour, plus 1 tbsp for the strawberries
¼ cup (30 g) cornstarch
1¼ tsp baking powder
⅛ tsp fine sea salt
⅔ cup plus 1 tbsp (160 g) unsalted butter, at room temperature
½ cup (100 g) granulated sugar
½ vanilla bean, split and scraped
3 large eggs
⅓ pound (150 g) fresh strawberries, hulled and cut into cubes
4 ounces (110 g) white chocolate, roughly chopped

For the topping
1 tbsp finely grated white chocolate
4 fresh strawberries, hulled and cut in half

Preheat the oven to 350°F / 180°C (preferably convection setting). Butter an 8-inch (20 cm) springform pan.

For the cake, whisk together the flour, cornstarch, baking powder, and salt in a large bowl.

In the bowl of a stand mixer fitted with the paddle attachment, beat the butter, sugar, and vanilla seeds for a few minutes or until light and fluffy. Add the eggs, 1 at a time, incorporating each egg before adding the next one, and beat for 2 minutes or until thick and creamy. Add the flour mixture and mix for 1 minute or until combined. Mix the strawberries with the remaining 1 tablespoon of flour and quickly fold, along with the white chocolate, into the batter.

Spread the batter in the prepared pan and bake for 40 to 45 minutes (slightly longer if using a conventional oven) or until golden and spongy. If you insert a skewer in the center of the cake, it should come out almost clean. Let the cake cool for 10 minutes then take it out of the pan. Decorate with the white chocolate and strawberries just before serving.

Fava beans make a fabulous pesto. I pair the blanched beans with fresh mint and lemon zest, plop it generously into a bowl of warm spaghetti, and for the final touch, sprinkle crunchy bacon on top.

Spaghetti with Fava Bean-Mint Pesto and Crunchy Bacon

Serves 2

For the pesto

½ pound (225 g) fresh or frozen shelled fava beans
1 large clove garlic, cut in half
2 tbsp olive oil
1 tbsp freshly squeezed lemon juice
2 tsp finely chopped fresh mint leaves
Fine sea salt
Finely ground pepper

For the pasta

6 ounces (170 g) dried spaghetti
Olive oil
1 handful tiny bacon cubes
1 tbsp roughly chopped fresh mint leaves
Coarsely ground pepper

For the pesto, bring a small pot of salted water to a boil and blanch the fava beans and garlic for about 5 minutes or until al dente. Reserve $1/2$ cup (120 ml) of the cooking water then drain and quickly rinse the fava beans and garlic with cold water. In a food processor or blender, purée the fava beans, garlic, the reserved cooking water, the olive oil, lemon juice, and mint until smooth. Season to taste with salt and finely ground pepper.

For the pasta, bring a large pot of salted water to a boil and cook the spaghetti, according to the package instructions, until al dente. Drain the spaghetti and return it to the pot. Add a splash of olive oil and toss to coat.

In a small, heavy pan, heat a splash of olive oil over medium-high heat and cook the bacon, stirring occasionally, for a few minutes or until golden brown and crunchy. Remove the bacon from the pan and reserve the bacon juices.

Divide the spaghetti among plates and sprinkle generously with the pesto, bacon, mint, and coarsely ground pepper. Drizzle with the bacon juices from the pan and serve immediately.

149

Serves 2 to 4

Olive oil
1 ounce (30 g) fresh flat-leaf
parsley leaves
24 large fresh mint leaves
⅛ medium red onion
1 (1-inch / 2.5-cm) piece fresh
red chile, seeded
Fine sea salt
10 small red radishes
1 large tomato
½ medium red bell pepper
½ medium cucumber, scrubbed
2 ounces (60 g) feta
1 large handful arugula leaves
Finely ground pepper

It's not hard to fall for a colorful Greek salad: It screams summer and bursts with freshness. Tomato, cucumber, and feta is the classic combination, but if you want to surprise your taste buds, toss in seared red radishes and a parsley-mint pesto.

Greek Salad with Seared Radishes and Parsley-Mint Pesto

Purée ⅓ cup (75 ml) of olive oil, the parsley, mint, onion, and chile in a food processor or blender until smooth and season to taste with salt.

Cut the radishes in half and set aside. Cut the tomato into wedges, the bell pepper into cubes, the cucumber into thick slices, and the feta into cubes, then arrange, along with the arugula, on a large plate. Drizzle with 4 tablespoons of olive oil and season to taste with salt and pepper.

In a small, heavy pan, heat a splash of olive oil over high heat and sear the radishes, stirring occasionally, for 1 to 2 minutes or until golden and al dente. Season to taste with salt and arrange on top of the salad. Sprinkle with pesto and serve immediately.

150

Serves 2 to 4

4 ounces (110 g) mild Camembert
3 ounces (85 g) cream cheese
1 tbsp heavy cream
1 small bunch fresh chives,
plus 2 tbsp chopped chives
for serving
Fine sea salt
Finely ground pepper
4 large pretzels
(or 4 thick slices dark spelt
or rye bread)
12 red radishes, cut in half

Picture page 187, bottom right

Obazda is a Bavarian beer garden staple. My version is fresh and green thanks to a bunch of chives mixed into the creamy mixture of mild Camembert and cream cheese. It's usually served with pretzels and a huge glass of chilled beer—*Maßkrug* in German—at least when you join the crowds at a Biergarten in Munich.

Obatzda Bavarian Camembert Dip with Chives and Radish

In a food processor or blender, purée the Camembert, cream cheese, heavy cream, and chives until smooth. Season to taste with salt and pepper, transfer to a medium bowl, and sprinkle with chopped chives.

Serve the pretzels with the Obatzda and radishes.

Having a variety of fresh herbs at hand is a wonderful luxury. In the city, the cook depends on windowsill gardens or the farmers' market. If all your herbs happen to wilt at the same time, throw them together and make a pesto celebrating all their individual qualities. It might taste different each time, but it will always go well with pan-roasted asparagus and new potatoes.

Pan-Roasted Asparagus and Potatoes with Leftover-Herb Pesto

Serves 2

For the pesto*
1 ounce (30 g) mixed fresh
herb leaves, preferably dill,
cilantro, basil, mint, and parsley
1 ounce (30 g) Parmesan,
finely grated
1 ounce (30 g) cashews
(or pine nuts)
⅓ cup (75 ml) olive oil
1 clove garlic
Fine sea salt

For the vegetables
⅔ pound (300 g) trimmed
and peeled white asparagus
(or trimmed green asparagus)
⅛ tsp granulated sugar
9 ounces (250 g) small
new potatoes, scrubbed,
boiled, and dried
Olive oil
Fine sea salt
Finely ground pepper
1 small handful small fresh
basil leaves

For the pesto, purée the mixed herbs, Parmesan, cashews, olive oil, and garlic in a food processor or blender until smooth and season to taste with salt.

For the vegetables, bring a large pot of water to a boil. Add the asparagus and sugar and cook for 8 to 10 minutes or until al dente. (If using green asparagus, cook for only 3 to 4 minutes.) Drain the asparagus and quickly rinse with cold water. Cut each stalk into 3 pieces and let them dry for 5 minutes.

Cut the potatoes in half lengthwise. In a large, heavy pan, heat a generous splash of olive oil over medium-high heat. Roast the potatoes, turning occasionally, for about 10 minutes or until golden brown and crispy. Season the potatoes to taste with salt and pepper and transfer to a plate. Add a little olive oil and the asparagus to the pan and roast, turning constantly, over high heat for 1 minute or until golden brown. Return the potatoes to the pan, stir gently, and season to taste with salt and pepper.

Arrange the vegetables on a large platter, sprinkle with the pesto and basil, and serve.

* You can use leftover pesto as a spread on bread.

June

Ask any Maltese person, and they will tell you that their nanna makes the best *bragoli* on the islands. My friend Joanna Bonnici, a fabulous cook, introduced me to the art of cooking these tenderly stewed cutlets stuffed with hard-boiled eggs, cheese, and parsley. She uses pork and adds fruity bell pepper to the sauce. For my adaptation, I sneak in fresh marjoram and lemon.

Bragoli—Maltese Egg and Cheese-Stuffed Meat Roulades with Bell Peppers

Serves 6

For the pork roulades

Olive oil

2 medium red onions,
finely chopped

6 large cloves garlic,
finely chopped

3 large hard-boiled eggs,
finely chopped,
plus 1 large raw egg

4 ounces (110 g) mild
goat's milk cheese, finely grated

2 ounces (60 g) fresh flat-leaf
parsley leaves, roughly chopped

¼ cup (35 g) dry breadcrumbs

2 tbsp finely chopped
fresh marjoram leaves

1 tsp freshly grated lemon zest

1 tsp fine sea salt

¾ tsp nutmeg, preferably
freshly grated

Finely ground pepper

About 4 tbsp (30 g)
all-purpose flour

6 large, ¼-inch-thick (0.5 cm)
pork cutlets, about
2 ¼ pounds (1 kg) total

6 large, thin slices
Tyrolean prosciutto
(or prosciutto di Parma)

12 toothpicks (or ovenproof
cotton string), to tie the roulades

For the pork roulades, heat a splash of olive oil in a medium, heavy pan over medium heat and sauté the onions and garlic for 5 minutes or until golden and soft. Transfer to a large bowl. Add the chopped hard-boiled eggs, raw egg, goat's milk cheese, parsley, breadcrumbs, marjoram, lemon zest, salt, nutmeg, and a generous amount of pepper and mix with your fingers until well combined. Spread the flour on a large plate.

Place a large piece of plastic wrap on a work surface. Arrange the pork cutlets side by side on top of the plastic wrap, season to taste with salt and pepper, and place 1 slice of prosciutto in the middle of each. Divide the filling among the cutlets, using about 3 generous tablespoons for each cutlet, and spread evenly, leaving a thin border around the edges. Roll up the cutlets tightly and secure each roll with 2 toothpicks or cotton string wrapped around each roll. Lightly dredge the roulades in the flour.

In a Dutch oven large enough to fit the meat and with a tight-fitting lid, heat a splash of olive oil over medium-high heat. Working in batches, sear the roulades, turning them once, for 1 to 2 minutes or until evenly browned then transfer to a plate, but leave the Dutch oven on the heat.

For the sauce

Olive oil

1 medium red onion, chopped

4 large cloves garlic, cut in half

2 medium green bell peppers,
cut into thick slices

2 medium red bell peppers,
cut into thick slices

1 ½ tbsp coriander seeds,
crushed with a mortar and pestle

3 tbsp tomato paste

1 ½ cups (360 ml) dry white wine

1 cup (240 ml) homemade
or quality store-bought
vegetable broth, hot

3 medium sprigs fresh marjoram

2 large bay leaves

Fine sea salt

Finely ground pepper

For the sauce, add a little olive oil to the Dutch oven and sauté the onion, garlic, bell peppers, and coriander over medium heat, stirring occasionally, for 1 minute. Add the tomato paste, stir, and cook for 1 minute then add the white wine, hot broth, marjoram, bay leaves, 1 teaspoon of salt, and a generous amount of pepper. Return the meat to the Dutch oven, cover, and bring to a boil then simmer gently over medium-low heat for 1 1/2 to 2 hours or until the meat is tender. Season the sauce to taste with salt and pepper.

Serve the bragoli, in one piece or cut into thick slices, with the bell peppers and sauce.

Serves 2 to 4

3 tbsp granulated sugar

¼ vanilla bean, split and scraped

⅛ tsp saffron threads

⅔ pound (300 g)
fresh strawberries,
hulled and cut into quarters

Hello there summer! Sweet and juicy strawberries refined with vanilla sugar are delicious, but adding saffron turns a good dish into a perfect one. The spice is strong, present, and confident, guiding the fruit into an exciting new realm.

Fresh Strawberries with Saffron-Vanilla Sugar

Finely grind the sugar, vanilla seeds, and saffron with a mortar and pestle.

Spread the strawberries on a large plate and sprinkle with the saffron sugar. Serve immediately or let sit for a little while to soften the fruit.

Serves 6

1 pound (450 g) trimmed rhubarb,
cut lengthwise into ½-inch-thick
(1.25 cm) stalks

5 ounces (140 g)
bittersweet chocolate

⅔ cup (150 g) unsalted butter

1 tsp ground cinnamon

½ tsp ground cardamom

4 large eggs, separated

⅛ tsp fine sea salt

¾ cup plus 2 tbsp (175 g)
granulated sugar

1 cup (130 g) all-purpose flour

Picture page 201, top left

My favorite chocolate cake is spongy, light, fluffy, and a bit moist. It has just the right amount of chocolate, and is neither too bitter nor too sweet. You can top it off with whipped cream and fruit (recipe no. 189), or stir rhubarb chunks into the batter. The pink and green stalks add juicy sourness to the dark chocolaty loaf—it's a genius flavor combo.

Rhubarb-Chocolate Cake

Preheat the oven to 350°F / 180°C (preferably convection setting) and butter a 9 x 4-inch (23 x 10 cm) loaf pan. Cut the rhubarb into five 9-inch-long (23 cm) pieces for the top of the cake and the remaining rhubarb into 3/4-inch-long (2 cm) pieces.

In a small saucepan, melt the chocolate, butter, cinnamon, and cardamom over low heat, whisking until smooth; let cool for a few minutes.

In the bowl of a stand mixer fitted with the whisk attachment, whisk the egg whites and salt for a few minutes or until stiff, and transfer to a large bowl.

In the same bowl of the stand mixer fitted with the paddle attachment, beat the egg yolks and sugar for 2 minutes or until thick and creamy. Add the chocolate mixture and mix for 1 minute or until well combined. Add the flour and mix until well combined then fold the egg whites into the batter. Gently fold the shorter rhubarb pieces into the batter. Spread the batter evenly in the prepared pan, arrange the longer rhubarb pieces, side by side, on top, and bake for 65 to 75 minutes (slightly longer if using a conventional oven) or until golden brown and spongy. If the top browns too quickly, cover with a piece of aluminum foil. If you insert a skewer in the center of the cake, it should come out almost clean. Let the cake cool for at least 1 hour before serving to cool the chocolate pockets around the rhubarb inside the cake.

If you spot guanciale, the Italian cured pork cheek that resembles fatty prosciutto, at your trusted butcher or Italian deli, grab a chunky piece and use it for pasta and pizza (recipe no. 7). You can replace it with bacon in this recipe, but guanciale is finer, not so harsh and salty, and it melts more smoothly into the fennel.

Fennel and Guanciale Pasta

Serves 2

6 ounces (170 g) dried spaghetti
Olive oil
1 tbsp fennel seeds,
crushed with a mortar and pestle
1 ounce (30 g) guanciale
(or mild bacon), cut into short,
thin strips
1 (7-ounce / 200-g) fennel bulb,
quartered, cored, and very
thinly sliced, plus 1 tbsp chopped
fennel fronds for serving
Fine sea salt
Coarsely ground pepper

Bring a large pot of salted water to a boil and cook the spaghetti, according to the package instructions, until al dente. Drain the spaghetti and return it to the pot.

In a small saucepan, heat 1 tablespoon of olive oil over medium-high heat. Add the fennel seeds and cook for 15 seconds or until fragrant—mind that they don't burn. Set aside.

In a large, heavy pan, heat a splash of olive oil over medium-high heat and cook the guanciale for 1 to 2 minutes or until soft and translucent. (If using bacon, it will need a little longer and should be golden brown and crispy.) Transfer the guanciale to a plate then add the fennel bulb to the pan and sauté, stirring occasionally and adding a splash of olive oil if the pan is dry, for 2 to 3 minutes or until golden and al dente. Add the spaghetti, guanciale, and fennel seeds and drizzle with a little olive oil. Season to taste with salt and pepper. Divide among plates, sprinkle with the fennel fronds, and serve.

The day I decided to combine roasted eggplant with ricotta, balsamic vinegar, and basil was a very good day. This stunning quartet never ceases to amaze me. You can turn this fabulous foursome into a luscious sandwich (*recipe no. 17*), roll the creamy cheese and smoky eggplant into handy vegetable wraps for cocktail parties, or assemble a meze plate and serve the dish with a generous dollop of the balsamic ricotta on the side.

Serves 2 to 4

For the ricotta dip

4 ounces (110 g) fresh ricotta, drained

1 tsp balsamic vinegar

15 large fresh basil leaves, roughly chopped, plus 12 small leaves for the topping

Fine sea salt

Finely ground pepper

For the eggplant

1 large eggplant, cut lengthwise into ¼-inch-thick (0.5 cm) slices

Olive oil

Flaky sea salt

Coarsely ground pepper

Picture opposite, top right

Roasted Eggplant with Basil Ricotta

For the ricotta dip, whisk together the ricotta, vinegar, and chopped basil. Season to taste with fine sea salt and finely ground pepper and set aside.

Set the oven to broil (quicker method) or preheat to 500°F (260°C).

For the eggplant, set a wire rack on a rimmed baking sheet and arrange the eggplant slices, side by side, on the rack. Brush both sides of the eggplant slices with olive oil and season to taste with flaky sea salt and coarsely ground pepper. Broil, turning once, for about 5 to 7 minutes per side, or roast at 500°F (260°C) for 15 minutes then flip and continue roasting for another 6 minutes. The eggplant should be golden and partly brown, but not black. Watch it closely, as the very thin parts tend to burn quickly. Stack the eggplant slices on a plate and let them sit for at least 2 minutes, or cover and keep them in the fridge for up to 1 day.

Divide the eggplant among plates, add a generous dollop of the balsamic ricotta, and sprinkle with the basil leaves.

This sandwich wraps up the culinary beauty of summer: The produce is fresh, the combination simple, and there's crunchy bread and cheese involved. Cherry tomatoes, seared for just a few minutes and drizzled with balsamic vinegar, soften over the heat but maintain their shape. You just have to plop them onto a bed of whipped basil chèvre.

Makes 2 sandwiches

4 ounces (110 g) soft, mild chèvre

¼ cup (60 ml) heavy cream

Olive oil

3 tbsp finely chopped fresh basil leaves, plus 6 leaves for the topping

Finely ground pepper

10 cherry tomatoes

2 tsp balsamic vinegar

2 crusty white buns, cut in half

Picture opposite, bottom left

Summer Sandwich with Balsamic Tomatoes and Whipped Chèvre

In a medium bowl, whisk together the chèvre, heavy cream, 1 tablespoon of olive oil, and 3 tablespoons of chopped basil and season to taste with pepper.

In a small, heavy pan, heat a splash of olive oil over high heat and sear the tomatoes, stirring occasionally, for 2 to 3 minutes or until they start to soften and their skin is freckled with black spots. Add the balsamic vinegar, stir, and take the pan off the heat. Spread the whipped chèvre on the bottom half of each bun. Arrange the tomatoes on top and sprinkle with the basil leaves and a little pepper. Place a top on each bun and enjoy.

154

156

157

162

When I visited my mother on the weekends during my university years, she'd often teach me quick and frugal recipes that wouldn't strain my tight student budget. Once she braised chicken breasts in white wine, nestled on a bunch of fresh herbs. Ten minutes later the meat was perfectly tender, and infused with the full bouquet of her herb garden.

Sorrel and Tarragon-Braised Chicken Breast with Watermelon and Feta

Serves 2

For the chicken
Olive oil
2 (6-ounce / 170-g) boneless, skinless chicken breasts
Flaky sea salt
Coarsely ground pepper
1 handful fresh tarragon sprigs, plus 12 chopped leaves for the topping
4 large fresh sorrel leaves, plus 2 thinly sliced leaves for the topping
1 small handful fresh flat-leaf parsley
3 medium sprigs fresh mint
¾ cup (180 ml) dry white wine

For the salad
¼ small watermelon, peeled and cut into cubes
4 ounces (110 g) feta, cut into cubes
Olive oil
Flaky sea salt

For the chicken, heat a splash of olive oil in a medium pot over medium-high heat. Sear the chicken breasts for 1 minute per side, season generously with salt and pepper, and transfer to a plate. Spread the herbs on the bottom of the pot, lay the chicken breasts on top, and add the white wine. Cover and bring to a boil then reduce the heat to a low simmer and cook for about 10 minutes or until the chicken is cooked through.

For the salad, divide the watermelon and feta among plates, drizzle with a little olive oil, and season to taste with salt. Arrange the chicken breasts and some of the cooked herbs next to the watermelon-feta salad, sprinkle with the fresh tarragon and sorrel leaves, and serve.

A delicious dip, served at a friend's lunch party in Malta, led to instant inspiration. My friend Alex cooks yellow split peas for his version (*recipe no. 94*), while mine is made for busy days and features canned cannellini beans. Refining the dip with capers and shallots is Alex's genius idea and it creates an unexpected yet pleasant taste that's hard to define. You can spread it on thick slices of ciabatta, or serve it with sautéed zucchini for a proper lunch or dinner.

Sautéed Zucchini with Bean-Caper Dip

Serves 2

1½ cups (300 g) drained and rinsed canned cannellini or butter beans
½ medium shallot
1½ tbsp capers, preferably preserved in salt, rinsed and dried
Olive oil
2 tbsp freshly squeezed lemon juice
Finely ground pepper
2 small zucchini
Fine sea salt

Purée the beans, shallot, capers, 1/3 cup (75 ml) of olive oil, and the lemon juice in a food processor or blender until smooth. Season to taste with pepper and transfer to a small bowl.

Cut the zucchini into 1/3-inch-thick (0.75 cm) round slices. In a large, heavy pan, heat a splash of olive oil over medium-high heat and sauté the zucchini, side by side and turning once, for 1 1/2 to 2 minutes per side or until golden brown and al dente. Season to taste with salt and pepper.

Divide the zucchini among plates and add a few spoonfuls of the dip. Sprinkle with a little pepper and enjoy.

You could whisk freshly chopped garlic into sizzling hot butter to drizzle over flaky swordfish, but if you take the time to roast the cloves first, you'll be rewarded with a finer—almost sweet—and smoother flavor.

Swordfish with Roasted Garlic Butter

Serves 2

For the garlic butter
6 large cloves garlic, preferably young, unpeeled
2 tbsp (30 g) unsalted butter

For the swordfish
Olive oil
1 (10-ounce / 280-g) swordfish fillet, about 1¼-inch thick (3 cm)
Flaky sea salt
Coarsely ground pepper

Preheat the oven to 425°F (220°C).

For the garlic butter, spread the garlic cloves in a small baking dish and roast, turning occasionally, for about 25 minutes or until the garlic is soft enough to mash with a fork—mind that it doesn't burn. Let the garlic cool for a few minutes then peel the cloves and roughly mash with a fork. Reduce the heat to 400°F (200°C).

For the swordfish, in a medium, heavy ovenproof pan, heat a splash of olive oil over medium-high heat. Sear the swordfish for 1 1/2 minutes per side. Season to taste with salt and pepper on both sides then transfer the pan to the oven and bake for 10 minutes or until you can flake the swordfish with a fork.

While the swordfish is baking, prepare the garlic butter: In a small saucepan, heat the butter over medium-high heat, add the roasted garlic, whisking constantly, and cook for 30 to 45 seconds or until golden, chunky, and combined.

Cut the swordfish in half and divide among plates. Drizzle with the roasted garlic butter and serve immediately.

There's no flour in this cake and you won't even notice. Ground almonds, polenta, and poppy seeds replace it, and with a few spoonfuls of ricotta, create a moist texture with a contrasting crunch.

Lemony Polenta-Almond Cake with Poppy Seeds and Ricotta

Serves 6 to 8

1 ¼ cups plus 1 tbsp (150 g) ground skin-on almonds
½ cup (80 g) fine polenta
½ cup (50 g) ground poppy seeds
2 tsp baking powder
⅛ tsp fine sea salt
⅓ cup plus 2 tbsp (100 g) unsalted butter, at room temperature
1 cup (200 g) granulated sugar
4 large eggs
4 ounces (110 g) fresh ricotta, drained
3 tbsp freshly grated lemon zest, plus 1 tsp for the topping
3 tbsp freshly squeezed lemon juice
Confectioners' sugar, for the topping

Preheat the oven to 350°F / 180°C (preferably convection setting). Butter an 8-inch (20 cm) springform pan.

In a large bowl, whisk together the ground almonds, polenta, poppy seeds, baking powder, and salt.

In the bowl of a stand mixer fitted with the paddle attachment, beat the butter and granulated sugar for a few minutes or until light and fluffy. Add the eggs, 1 at a time, incorporating each egg before adding the next one, and continue beating for 2 minutes or until creamy. Add the ricotta, lemon zest, and lemon juice and mix for 1 minute or until combined. With a wooden spoon, fold the almond mixture into the butter mixture, mixing until well combined. Scrape the batter into the prepared pan and bake for 35 to 40 minutes (slightly longer if using a conventional oven) or until golden brown and firm on top. If you insert a skewer in the center of the cake, it should come out clean. Let the cake cool for 10 minutes then take it out of the pan. Dust with confectioners' sugar, sprinkle with the lemon zest, and serve.

Serves 2 to 3

¾ pound (340 g) small potatoes,
scrubbed
7 ounces (200 g) fresh
or frozen shelled fava beans
4 medium carrots, peeled and
cut in half lengthwise
2 large bulbs garlic,
cut in half crosswise
1 medium bunch fresh marjoram
⅓ cup plus 1 tbsp (90 ml) olive oil
Flaky sea salt
Coarsely ground pepper

Picture page 201, bottom right

If you double this recipe for flavorful vegetables tossed and roasted with fresh marjoram, you'll create a colorful lunch for one day and a delicious side for poultry the next.

Roasted Potatoes, Carrots, and Fava Beans with Garlic

Preheat the oven to 400°F (200°C).

In a medium pot, cover the potatoes with cold salted water and bring to a boil. Reduce the heat, cover, and simmer for 10 minutes. Drain the potatoes and cut them in half lengthwise.

Bring a small saucepan of salted water to a boil and blanch the fava beans for about 5 minutes or until al dente. Drain and quickly rinse with cold water.

Arrange the potatoes, fava beans, carrots, garlic, and 2/3 of the marjoram in a medium baking dish. Add the olive oil, gently toss to coat, and season to taste with salt and pepper. Roast for about 40 minutes or until the vegetables are golden brown and partly crisp.

Pick the leaves off the remaining marjoram and sprinkle over the roasted vegetables; serve warm or cold.

Serves 2 to 4

⅓ cup (75 ml) olive oil,
plus more to taste
2 tsp freshly grated lemon zest,
plus more to taste
1¼ pounds (560 g) peeled
waxy potatoes
Flaky sea salt
1 tbsp freshly squeezed
lemon juice

Lemony mashed potatoes make a lovely light lunch and you only need five ingredients. You can also serve them with grilled seafood whenever it's warm enough to get a barbecue grill going.

Mediterranean Lemon Mashed Potatoes

In a small saucepan, heat the olive oil and lemon zest over medium heat for 2 minutes or until fragrant. Take the pan off the heat and set aside.

In a large pot, cover the potatoes with salted water and bring to a boil. Reduce the heat, cover, and simmer for 18 to 20 minutes or until tender. Drain the potatoes and return them to the pot.

Using a plain butter knife, break the potatoes into chunks, while gradually adding the lemon oil and a little salt until the desired taste and texture is achieved—the mash should be smooth but a little chunky. Stir in the lemon juice. If the potatoes are dry, add a little more olive oil. Season to taste with salt and additional lemon zest and serve warm or cold.

164

Makes 6 sandwiches

2 large white peaches,
preferably doughnut peaches,
pitted and each cut into 6 wedges
4 ounces (110 g)
aged Camembert,
cut into 12 thick slices
6 thick slices ciabatta
Coarsely ground pepper
1 tbsp finely chopped
fresh rosemary needles

Aged cheese and ripe fruit create stunning sandwiches, even more so when you put them under the broiler. White doughnut peaches and assertively strong, runny Camembert will melt every cheese lover's heart.

Grilled Peach and Camembert Sandwich

Set the oven to broil (quicker method) or preheat to 500°F (260°C).

Arrange 2 peach wedges on each slice of ciabatta and top with 2 slices of Camembert. Put the sandwiches under the broiler, or roast at 500°F (260°C) for 1 minute or until the cheese starts to melt. Season to taste with pepper, sprinkle with a little rosemary, and serve immediately.

165

Serves 2

3 tbsp olive oil
2 tbsp freshly squeezed orange juice
2 tsp high-quality orange blossom water, preferably organic
¼ tsp honey
Fine sea salt
Finely ground pepper
2 ounces (60 g) pecorino
10 young thin green asparagus stalks, trimmed
2 ripe peaches, pitted
1 small handful fresh small basil leaves

Only very young, fresh and juicy, slender green stalks work for a raw asparagus salad. Choose the crispest that you can find, and toss them with ripe peaches, pecorino, fragrant basil, and a fruity orange blossom dressing for this delightful lunch dish.

Raw Asparagus and Peach Salad with Orange Blossom Water and Pecorino

In a small bowl, whisk together the olive oil, orange juice, orange blossom water, and honey and season to taste with salt and pepper. Shave thin strips of pecorino.

Cut off the asparagus tips then cut them in half lengthwise and transfer to a large plate. Cut the remaining stalks lengthwise into thin slices on a mandoline. Cut the peaches into thin wedges and add, along with the sliced asparagus, to the asparagus tips. Sprinkle with the pecorino and basil and drizzle with the dressing then toss and serve immediately.

Seafood, parsley, garlic, and lemon define the culinary essence of the Mediterranean summer. The smell brings back memories of lush dinners at tiny trattorias with red and white checkered tablecloths swinging in the salty breeze and music and laughter filling the air. A whole grilled fish is always the star of the night, making the eyes of the hungry grow in excitement.

Oven-Roasted Sea Bream with Italian Gremolata

Serves 2

For the gremolata
About 4 tbsp finely chopped fresh flat-leaf parsley leaves
1 small clove garlic, crushed
2 tsp freshly grated lemon zest
½ tsp freshly squeezed lemon juice

For the sea bream
Olive oil
1 (1-pound / 450-g) whole sea bream (porgy), scaled, gutted, and cleaned
Fine sea salt
Finely ground pepper
1 lemon, very thinly sliced
3 sprigs fresh flat-leaf parsley
⅓ cup (75 ml) dry white wine

Picture opposite, top left

Preheat the oven to 400°F (200°C).

For the gremolata, in a small bowl, combine the parsley, garlic, lemon zest, and lemon juice.

For the sea bream, brush olive oil on the bottom of a baking dish large enough to fit the fish. Coat the sea bream with a little olive oil and season to taste with salt and pepper inside and out. Stuff the sea bream with ⅓ of the gremolata and place in the prepared baking dish. Sprinkle with 1/2 of the remaining gremolata and cover with the lemon slices. Arrange the parsley sprigs around the fish then pour the white wine into the baking dish. Roast for 20 to 23 minutes or until the fish is cooked through. To see if the fish is done, cut along the middle line on its side, from gill to tail. If you can lift the fillet off the bones with a fork, it's done. If not, rearrange the citrus slices and continue roasting.

Divide the fish into 2 fillets, sprinkle with the remaining gremolata, and serve each with a slice of the roasted lemon.

166

167

168

170

Almost every root, stalk, leaf, or fruit can be turned into something spreadable or dollop-able — in other words, a pesto. Mother nature provides plenty to experiment with and a blender takes care of the rest. Sweet peas and marjoram is a match made in heaven, producing a pesto that's thick, fresh, and green, and ready to enrich sandwiches, pasta, and salads.

Tomato Salad with Pea-Marjoram Pesto

Serves 2

For the pesto
¼ pound (110 g)
fresh or frozen peas
1 clove garlic
2 tbsp olive oil
1 tsp freshly squeezed lemon juice
1 ½ tsp chopped fresh
marjoram leaves
Fine sea salt
Finely ground pepper

For the salad
3 medium tomatoes, thinly sliced
2 tbsp fresh marjoram leaves
Olive oil
Fine sea salt
Finely ground pepper

Picture page 209, top right

For the pesto, bring a small pot of salted water to a boil and blanch the peas and garlic for about 1 minute or until the peas are al dente. Drain and quickly rinse with cold water. Reserve 2 tablespoons of the peas and set aside. In a food processor or blender, purée the remaining peas, the garlic, olive oil, lemon juice, and chopped marjoram until smooth. Season to taste with salt and pepper.

For the salad, divide the tomatoes among plates. Sprinkle with the reserved peas, the pesto, and marjoram leaves. Drizzle with a little olive oil, season to taste with salt and pepper, and serve immediately.

Red currants—plump, juicy, and bursting with sourness—will always be my first choice for these tender and cakey oat cookies, but if you can't find currants, use blueberries. Sometimes I buy frozen currants, a convenient solution for the colder months of the year.

Cakey Red Currant and Oat Cookies

Makes about 26 cookies

1½ cups (200 g) all-purpose flour
1⅔ cups (150 g) rolled oats
1 tsp fine sea salt
¾ tsp baking powder
½ tsp baking soda
¾ cup (170 g) unsalted butter,
at room temperature
1 cup (200 g) granulated sugar
4 ounces (110 g) mashed
ripe banana
1 large egg
¼ vanilla bean, split and scraped
7 ounces (200 g) fresh or frozen
red currants or blueberries*

Picture page 209, bottom left

Preheat the oven to 350°F / 180°C (preferably convection setting). Line 2 baking sheets with parchment paper.

In a large bowl, whisk together the flour, oats, salt, baking powder, and baking soda.

In the bowl of a stand mixer fitted with the paddle attachment, beat the butter and sugar until fluffy. Add the banana, egg, and vanilla seeds and mix for 1 minute or until well combined. Using a wooden spoon, fold in the flour mixture and mix until the dough is lumpy with a bit of flour here and there. Reserve 1 small handful of red currants and set aside. Gently fold the remaining berries into the dough—mind not to mix the dough more than 4 to 5 times to avoid damaging the berries. Scoop tablespoons of dough onto the lined baking sheets, leaving a roughly 1 1/2-inch (4 cm) space between the cookies. Gently flatten the cookies with a fork then sprinkle with the reserved red currants, gently pushing them into the dough. Bake, 1 baking sheet at a time, for about 13 minutes (slightly longer if using a conventional oven) or until golden but still soft. Let the cookies cool for a few minutes then transfer to a wire rack to cool completely.

The texture of the cookies is best the day they are baked, but they taste just as good on the second day.

* Don't defrost frozen currants or blueberries; it's easier to mix frozen berries into the dough.

Chef Salvatore Gambuzza is a lucky man. His kitchen and vegetable garden at the stunning Hotel Villa Athena in Agrigento are right in front of the splendid temples of Juno and Concordia in the Valle dei Templi. Salvatore introduced me to cherry tomatoes baked and candied with herbs, garlic, and sugar. The result is sweet and soft, a delicious nibble on bread or a topping for salads. You can also use the shriveled tomatoes for pasta *(recipe below)*.

Sicilian Candied Cherry Tomatoes

Makes 20 candied cherry tomatoes

20 cherry tomatoes
1 small bunch fresh marjoram
1 small bunch fresh thyme
4 large cloves garlic,
   unpeeled and cut in half
1 cup (100 g) confectioners' sugar
About ⅓ cup (75 ml) olive oil,
   to store the tomatoes

Preheat the oven to 200°F (100°C). Fill a large bowl with ice-cold water.

Bring a small pot of water to a boil. Add the tomatoes and use a slotted ladle or spoon to immediately transfer them to the bowl of ice water. Using your fingers, squeeze and peel the skins off the tomatoes. Cut off and discard a very thin layer from the tops of the tomatoes.

Spread the marjoram and thyme in a small baking dish, add the tomatoes and garlic, and sprinkle with the confectioners' sugar. Bake for about 2 hours and 15 minutes or until the tomatoes are soft and a little shriveled. Transfer the tomatoes and herbs to a small bowl and let them cool then cover completely with the olive oil.

You can use the tomatoes for up to 5 days, keeping them covered in the refrigerator; use any remaining oil for salads and pasta, or drizzle over bread.

This is one delicious way of using Salvatore Gambuzza's candied cherry tomatoes *(recipe above)*. The Sicilian chef adds them to a fruity caponata, but I turn them into the quickest lunch, stirring the candied bites and their sweet oil into warm spaghetti. Just add some fresh basil for the final touch.

Spaghetti with Sicilian Candied Cherry Tomatoes and Basil

Serves 2

7 ounces (200 g) dried spaghetti
About 4 tbsp candied cherry
tomato oil *(recipe above)*
20 candied cherry tomatoes
(recipe above)
Fine sea salt
Coarsely ground pepper
1 small handful fresh basil leaves

Picture page 209, bottom right

Bring a large pot of salted water to a boil and cook the spaghetti, according to the package instructions, until al dente. Drain the pasta and divide among plates. Drizzle with the candied cherry tomato oil and top with the candied cherry tomatoes. Season to taste with salt and pepper and sprinkle with basil. Buon appetito!

171

Makes 4 sandwiches

2 large bell peppers,
preferably 1 red and 1 yellow
1 tbsp olive oil
1 cup (230 g) full-fat plain
Greek yogurt
(or quark* plus 2 tbsp
heavy cream)
About ¼ pound (110 g) cucumber,
roughly grated, drained,
and squeezed
2 large cloves garlic, crushed
1 tsp finely chopped fresh
mint leaves
Fine sea salt
Finely ground pepper
1 large loaf ciabatta,
cut into 4 buns and each cut
in half

I always roast a bunch of bell peppers to use in salads and sandwiches, or to throw a quick lunch together. Preserved in olive oil, they last for days. I use the broiler or the barbecue grill, but I've seen brave Roman chefs scorch peppers straight in the flames of their gas stove.

Mint Tzatziki and Roasted Bell Pepper Sandwich

Set the oven to broil (quicker method) or preheat to 425°F (220°C).

Place the bell peppers in a broiler-proof baking dish and roast, turning twice so they cook on 3 sides, until the skin turns partly black. The peppers need about 22 minutes using the broil setting or 30 minutes at 425°F (220°C). Remove from the oven and immediately cover with a wet paper towel—this will make peeling easier. Let cool for 2 minutes. Use a sharp knife to peel the peppers then cut them in half, scrape out and discard any seeds and fibers, and cut into strips. Transfer to a small bowl and toss with the olive oil.

In a medium bowl, whisk together the yogurt, cucumber, garlic, and mint. Season to taste with salt and pepper. Spread the tzatziki generously on the bottom half of each bun. Arrange the roasted bell peppers on top, place a top on each bun, and serve immediately.

I prefer to make tzatziki with quark, but you can use Greek yogurt instead.

172

Serves 1 to 2

1 roasted large yellow bell pepper,
cut into strips *(recipe above)*
2 tbsp olive oil
1 tsp coriander seeds,
crushed with a mortar and pestle
Flaky sea salt

This is scrumptious simplicity. Roasted yellow bell pepper and coriander oil combine sweetness, smokiness, and lemony spiciness, and if you roast a bunch of peppers, you can also use them to make a sandwich *(recipe above)*.

Roasted Yellow Bell Pepper with Coriander Oil

Arrange the bell pepper on a plate.

In a small saucepan, heat the olive oil and coriander seeds over high heat until the oil starts sizzling. Take the pan off the heat and pour over the bell pepper. Season to taste with salt and serve warm or cold.

Pork tenderloin may sound a little hearty for late June, but it all depends on the preparation. Crushed pepper spices it up with heat and the quickest chutney made of apricot, peach, and red onion gives it a summery feeling. It's a dish that easily impresses guests — no one will suspect you only spent half an hour in the kitchen.

Peppered Pork Tenderloin with Apricot-Peach Chutney

Serves 3 to 4

For the chutney
Olive oil
1 medium red onion,
cut into 6 chunks
4 large apricots,
pitted and cut into quarters
1 large peach, peeled, pitted,
and roughly chopped
2 tbsp balsamic vinegar
2 tsp honey
Fine sea salt
Finely ground pepper

For the pork tenderloin
Olive oil
1 (1⅓-pound / 600-g)
pork tenderloin
Fine sea salt
2 tbsp black peppercorns,
crushed with a mortar and pestle
2 tbsp (30 g) unsalted butter,
cut into small cubes

Preheat the oven to 400°F (200°C).

For the chutney, heat a splash of olive oil in a small, heavy pan over medium heat and cook the onion, stirring occasionally, for 10 minutes or until golden and soft. Add the apricots and peach and cook, stirring constantly, over medium-high heat for 2 minutes. Add the vinegar and honey, stir, and cook for 2 minutes or until the fruit starts to soften. Season to taste with salt and finely ground pepper, cover, and set aside.

For the pork tenderloin, in a large, heavy ovenproof pan, heat a generous splash of olive oil over high heat. Season the pork to taste with salt and sear for 1 to 1 1/2 minutes per side or until golden brown. Take the pan off the heat, rub the tenderloin with the crushed black peppercorns then place the butter on top of the meat and roast for 12 minutes—it should still be pink inside. Take the meat out of the oven, cover with aluminum foil, and let rest for 2 minutes.

Cut the tenderloin into thick slices and serve with the chutney.

Flourishing nature is mesmerizing. Riding around the city on my bike, in the midst of June, I feel like I'm being embraced by a cloud of elderflower, acacia, and chestnut. The smell of elderflower is captivating and the sticky syrup made from the tiny white flowers transforms this quality into a concentrated cordial. You can use it instead of maple syrup, to sweeten and caramelize, or let it sink into a fragrant lime loaf cake.

Elderflower-Lime Cake

Serves 4 to 6

For the syrup
⅓ cup plus 2 tbsp (100 ml) elderflower syrup
3 tbsp freshly squeezed lime juice

For the cake
1 ⅔ cups (210 g) all-purpose flour
½ cup plus 1 tbsp (70 g) cornstarch
1 tbsp baking powder
¼ tsp fine sea salt
¾ cup plus 1 tbsp (180 g) unsalted butter, at room temperature
¾ cup plus 2 tbsp (175 g) granulated sugar
3 large eggs
2 tbsp freshly grated lime zest
3 tbsp freshly squeezed lime juice
⅓ cup plus 1 tbsp (90 ml) buttermilk

Preheat the oven to 325°F / 160°C (preferably convection setting). Butter a 9 x 4-inch (23 x 10 cm) loaf pan.

For the syrup, bring the elderflower syrup and lime juice to a boil in a small saucepan and cook for 1 minute; cover and set aside.

For the cake, whisk together the flour, cornstarch, baking powder, and salt in a medium bowl.

In the bowl of a stand mixer fitted with the paddle attachment, beat the butter and sugar until fluffy. Add the eggs, 1 at a time, incorporating each egg before adding the next one, and continue beating for 2 minutes or until creamy. Add the lime zest and juice and beat for 1 minute. With a wooden spoon, fold 1/3 of the flour mixture into the batter, followed by 1/3 of the buttermilk. Repeat with the remaining flour mixture and buttermilk, folding just until combined. Scrape the batter into the prepared pan and bake for about 50 minutes (slightly longer if using a conventional oven) or until golden and spongy. If you insert a skewer in the center of the cake, it should come out clean. Prick the warm cake all over with a skewer and slowly pour the syrup over the top. Let the cake cool for at least 10 minutes then take it out of the pan, transfer to a platter, and serve warm, or let it cool completely.

I love walking up and down the narrow streets of Malta's breathtakingly beautiful capital, Valletta, passing grocery stores that proudly present plump tomatoes in baskets and lush bundles of fragrant basil in buckets. I usually nibble on a snack while I discover hidden spots and places. *Qassatat*, a small Maltese ricotta pie, is one of my favorites. Strolling slowly and munching happily relaxes my mind and helps me come up with new recipes like this one.

Basil-Ricotta Pie with Cherry Tomatoes

Serves 3 to 6

For the pastry

1¼ cups (160 g) all-purpose flour
⅓ tsp fine sea salt
⅓ cup plus 1 tbsp (90 g)
unsalted butter, cold
1 tbsp water, cold

For the filling

14 ounces (400 g) fresh ricotta, drained
3 large eggs
2 tbsp (30 g) unsalted butter, melted and cooled
2 ounces (60 g) Parmesan, finely grated
1 ounce (30 g) finely chopped fresh basil leaves,
plus 8 small leaves for the topping
2 tsp freshly grated lemon zest
1 tsp fine sea salt
Finely ground pepper
6 cherry tomatoes, cut in half

For the pastry, combine the flour and salt in the bowl of a stand mixer fitted with the dough hook attachment. Add the butter and use a knife to cut it into the flour until there are just small pieces left. Quickly rub the butter into the flour with your fingers until combined. Add the cold water and mix with the hook until crumbly. Form the dough into a thick disc, wrap it in plastic wrap, and freeze for 10 minutes.

Preheat the oven to 400°F (200°C).

On a work surface, place the dough between 2 sheets of plastic wrap and use a rolling pin to roll out into a disc, large enough to line the bottom and sides of a 9-inch (23 cm) pie dish. Fit the dough into the pie dish, pushing it into the dish, especially along the edges. Let the dough hang over the rim a little or trim with a knife. Use a fork to prick the dough all over. Bake for 15 minutes or until golden. If the dough bubbles up, push it down with a fork. Take the pie dish out of the oven and reduce the heat to 375°F (190°C).

For the filling, in a medium bowl, whisk together the ricotta, eggs, butter, Parmesan, basil, lemon zest, salt, and a generous amount of pepper until well combined. Spread the filling on top of the pre-baked pastry and arrange the tomatoes, cut-side up, on top. Bake for 45 to 50 minutes or until the top is golden and firm.

Let the pie cool for 5 to 10 minutes, sprinkle with the basil leaves, and serve warm or cold.

It's so easy to turn ripe tomatoes into a tasty deep red soup. To let the concentrated fruitiness of these summer beauties shine bright, I cook them with skin and seeds for ten minutes in a little vegetable broth. Then you can refine them with other vegetables, herbs, or whatever comes to mind. Fresh cilantro and red chile are highly refreshing during the hotter months of the year (recipe no. 240), while celery and zucchini fit June, when the air is still moved by a gentle breeze.

Serves 2 to 4

1 large clove garlic
Fine sea salt
Olive oil
2 celery stalks, very thinly sliced
2¼ pounds (1 kg) tomatoes, roughly chopped
½ cup (120 ml) vegetable broth, hot
1 tbsp tomato paste
1 bay leaf
1 tbsp balsamic vinegar
Finely ground pepper
1 medium zucchini, very thinly sliced on a mandoline

Fruity Tomato-Celery Soup with Sautéed Zucchini

Roughly chop the garlic then sprinkle with ¼ teaspoon of salt and use the side of a large knife to press and rub the garlic and salt into a smooth paste.

In a large pot, heat a splash of olive oil over medium-high heat, add the garlic paste and celery, and sauté, stirring constantly, for 1 minute. Add the tomatoes and cook, stirring occasionally, for 4 minutes. Add the hot broth, tomato paste, bay leaf, and vinegar and season to taste with salt and pepper. Bring to a boil then reduce the heat and simmer for 5 minutes. Remove and discard the bay leaf then purée the soup in a food processor or blender until smooth. Season to taste with salt, pepper, and additional vinegar, cover, and keep warm.

In a medium, heavy pan, heat a splash of olive oil over medium-high heat and sauté the zucchini, stirring constantly, for a few minutes or until golden and soft then season to taste with salt and pepper. Divide the tomato soup among bowls, sprinkle with the zucchini and a little pepper, and serve.

Serves 4

4 medium red bell peppers
Fine sea salt
Finely ground pepper
9 ounces (250 g) feta, mashed with a fork
3 medium tomatoes, cut into small cubes
1 tbsp olive oil
4 tbsp finely chopped fresh flat-leaf parsley leaves
10 large mint leaves, finely chopped

Bell peppers and feta are a safe match. Stuffed and roasted in the oven, they'll bring the smell and taste of Greece straight to your kitchen.

Feta and Tomato-Stuffed Bell Peppers with Parsley and Mint

Preheat the oven to 425°F (220°C).

Cut the tops off the bell peppers and reserve. Scrape out and discard the seeds and fibers then rinse out the peppers, season to taste with salt and pepper, and set aside.

In a large bowl, combine the feta, tomatoes, olive oil, parsley, and mint and season to taste with salt and pepper. Using a large spoon, stuff the peppers with the feta mixture, pushing the filling into the peppers. Place the tops on the peppers and arrange the peppers in a baking dish. Add a splash of water to cover the bottom of the dish and roast for about 25 minutes or until the peppers are al dente and the tops turn dark. Take the peppers out of the oven and serve warm.

For many years, I didn't dare to poach eggs. It seemed complicated and stressful, an intimidating kitchen mystery I didn't want to learn. But once I balanced the first wobbly egg on a spoon set over simmering water, my fear disappeared and I was hooked. Perfectly poached eggs often crown my soups and salads, and when a sandwich calls for warm runny egg yolk, I forget the classic fried egg and bring out the poaching pot.

Roasted Eggplant and Bacon Baguette Sandwich with Poached Egg

Makes 2 sandwiches

1 small eggplant, cut lengthwise
into ¼-inch (0.5 cm) slices
Olive oil
Flaky sea salt
Coarsely ground pepper
4 slices bacon
2 to 4 large eggs
½ baguette, cut into 2 buns
and each cut in half
1 tbsp roughly chopped fresh
flat-leaf parsley leaves

Set the oven to broil (quicker method) or preheat to 500°F (260°C).

Set a wire rack on a rimmed baking sheet and arrange the eggplant slices, side by side, on the rack. Brush both sides of the eggplant slices with olive oil and season to taste with salt and pepper. Broil, turning once, for about 5 to 7 minutes per side, or roast at 500°F (260°C) for 15 minutes then flip and continue roasting for another 6 minutes. The eggplant should be golden and partly brown, but not black. Watch it closely, as the very thin parts tend to burn quickly. Stack the eggplant slices on a plate and set aside.

In a medium, heavy pan, heat a splash of olive oil over medium-high heat and cook the bacon, turning occasionally, for a few minutes or until golden brown and crispy.

Bring a small saucepan of salted water to a low simmer. Crack 1 egg into a small bowl. Hold a large spoon just over the surface of the water and gently pour the egg onto the spoon. Lower the spoon into the water and hold until the egg white starts to turn white then use a tablespoon to gently scoop the egg off the large spoon. Poach the egg for 3 minutes. Using a slotted ladle or spoon, transfer the egg to a plate. Poach the remaining eggs the same way, adjusting the heat as needed to maintain a low simmer. It's best to poach 1 egg at a time, but you can cook 2 at once.

Arrange 1/2 of the eggplant on the bottom of each bun and cover with 2 slices of bacon. Place 1 or 2 poached eggs on top of each sandwich and sprinkle with parsley and pepper. Cut the eggs open, place a top on each bun, and serve immediately.

See-through-thin sautéed zucchini slices are delicate and tender. Paired with juice-dripping melon and young pecorino, they make the perfect salad for those sun-kissed days of summer.

Sautéed Zucchini with Melon and Pecorino

Serves 2 to 4

Olive oil
7 ounces (200 g) zucchini,
cut lengthwise into very thin
slices on a mandoline
Flaky sea salt
Coarsely ground pepper
½ small Galia melon
(or cantaloupe), peeled
and cut into thin wedges
1 ounce (30 g) young pecorino,
thinly sliced

In a large, heavy pan, heat a splash of olive oil over medium-high heat. Working in batches, sauté the zucchini slices, side by side, for about 1 minute or until golden. Flip the slices over, season to taste with salt and pepper, and cook for another 30 seconds or until golden and soft. Transfer to a large plate and continue cooking the remaining zucchini, adding more olive oil before each batch.

Divide the zucchini and melon among plates, drizzle with 2 tablespoons of olive oil, and sprinkle with the pecorino. Season to taste with salt and pepper and serve warm or cold.

White fish is more common for classic Peruvian ceviche, but tuna tenderly marinated in flowery lime juice is a better match for watermelon. This recipe is a five-minute solution for summery seafood cravings.

Tuna and Watermelon Ceviche

Serves 2

6 ounces (170 g) sashimi-quality
tuna, cut into cubes
2 tsp freshly grated lime zest,
plus more for serving
¼ cup (60 ml) freshly squeezed
lime juice
¼ small watermelon, peeled
and cut into cubes
½ medium red onion, thinly sliced
⅓ medium, fresh red chile,
seeded and thinly sliced
1 small handful small fresh mint
leaves
Fine sea salt

Toss the tuna, lime zest, and lime juice in a medium bowl and marinate for 2 $\frac{1}{2}$ minutes.

Add the watermelon, onion, chile, and mint, stir to combine, and season to taste with salt. Sprinkle with a little lime zest and serve immediately.

According to my man, this is the best tart he's ever had—but he's biased. Fruity-sour apricots, sprinkled with crunchy cinnamon crumble, soften on a buttery flaky pastry and make for a wonderful summer tart. The pleasure never lasts long, so I always bake two tarts right from the start.

Apricot Crumble Tart

Serves 12 to 16 (Makes 2 tarts)

For the pastry

3 cups (390 g) all-purpose flour

½ cup (100 g) granulated sugar

¼ tsp fine sea salt

¾ cup plus 2 tbsp (200 g)
unsalted butter, cold

3 large egg yolks

2 tbsp water

For the topping

2 ¼ pounds (1 kg) pitted apricots,
cut in half

⅔ cup (125 g) granulated sugar,
plus 2 tbsp for the apricots

1 ½ cups (200 g) all-purpose flour,
plus more as needed

¼ vanilla bean, split and scraped

2 tsp ground cinnamon

½ cup plus 1 tbsp (125 g)
unsalted butter, melted
and cooled, plus more as needed

For the pastry, combine the flour, sugar, and salt in the bowl of a stand mixer fitted with the dough hook attachment. Add the butter and use a knife to cut it into the flour until there are just small pieces left. Quickly rub the butter into the flour with your fingers until combined. Add the egg yolks and water and mix with the hook until crumbly. Form the dough into 2 thick discs, wrap them in plastic wrap, and freeze for 20 minutes.

Preheat the oven to 400°F (200°C).

On a work surface, place 1 disc of dough between 2 sheets of plastic wrap and use a rolling pin to roll out into a disc, large enough to line the bottom and sides of a 9-inch (23 cm), preferably loose-bottom, tart pan. Fit the dough into the tart pan, pushing it into the pan, especially along the edges. Let the dough hang over the rim a little or trim with a knife. Use a fork to prick the dough all over. Repeat with the other disc of dough and a second tart pan. Bake for 12 minutes or until golden. If the dough bubbles up, push it down with a fork. Take the pans out of the oven.

For the topping, arrange the apricots, cut-side up, in circles on top of the pre-baked tarts and sprinkle each tart with 1 tablespoon of sugar then prepare the crumble immediately.

For the crumble, whisk together the remaining 2/3 cup (125 g) of sugar, the flour, vanilla seeds, and cinnamon in the bowl of a stand mixer fitted with the dough hook attachment. Add the butter and mix with the hook just until it forms crumbles. If the crumbles are too moist and sticky, add more flour; if they're too small and don't form large crumbles, add more melted butter. Immediately spread the crumble over the fruit, using your fingers to separate any large crumbles, and bake for 30 to 35 minutes or until golden brown. Serve the tarts warm or cold, plain or with vanilla ice cream or whipped cream.

July

Lahmacun is a Turkish-style pizza that's thin and crunchy, with a dough made of only flour, water, and salt. It's a much quicker treat than the Italian equivalent—there's no yeast, so there's no rising period—yet has the same crispiness. The base for this pizza is inspired by Turkey, but the topping is borrowed from Provençal cuisine. Black olive tapenade and thin slices of aged Sainte-Maure de Touraine chèvre turn it into a perfect picnic dish.

Lahmacun Thin-Crust Pizza with Tapenade and Chèvre

Makes 4 (9-inch / 23-cm) pizzas

For the pizza
2 cups (260 g) all-purpose flour
1 tsp fine sea salt
½ cup (120 ml) water, lukewarm
4 ounces (110 g) aged chèvre, preferably Sainte-Maure de Touraine, cut into 20 thin slices
4 small sprigs fresh flat-leaf parsley

For the tapenade*
7 ounces (200 g) pitted black olives, preferably Kalamata
1 large handful fresh flat-leaf parsley leaves
½ medium red onion
2 tbsp capers, preferably preserved in salt, rinsed and dried
½ cup (120 ml) olive oil
2 tbsp freshly squeezed lemon juice
2 tsp Dijon mustard
Finely ground pepper

I bake my pizza on a baking sheet that's been heated on the bottom of the oven like a pizza stone to help create a crunchy crust.

Place a baking sheet (or pizza stone) on the bottom of the oven and preheat the oven to the highest temperature, 500°F (260°C) or higher.

For the dough, combine the flour and salt in the bowl of a stand mixer fitted with the dough hook attachment. Add the lukewarm water and mix with the hook for a few minutes or until well combined. If the dough is too sticky, add more flour. Transfer the dough to a work surface and continue kneading and punching it with your hands for about 4 minutes or until you have a smooth and elastic ball of dough. Divide the dough into 4 equal parts, cover with a damp tea towel, and let rest while you prepare the tapenade.

For the tapenade, in a food processor or blender, purée the olives, parsley, onion, capers, olive oil, lemon juice, and mustard until smooth and season to taste with pepper. Transfer about 1/3 of the dip to a small bowl, cover with olive oil then plastic wrap, and keep in the fridge for up to 3 days to use for other recipes. Transfer the remaining tapenade to a medium bowl.

On a well-floured work surface stretch and roll the dough into four 9-inch (23 cm) discs and cover with a tea towel. Transfer 1 of the dough discs to a well-floured pizza peel or large cutting board, spread about 2 heaping tablespoons of the tapenade on top, and arrange 5 slices of chèvre and 1 parsley sprig on top of the tapenade. Once the baking sheet is hot, carefully take it out of the oven, flip it over, and place it on a trivet or other heat-safe surface. Immediately and quickly slide and pull the pizza onto the hot baking sheet and bake on the bottom of the oven for about 4 minutes or until golden and crisp then transfer to a large plate and drizzle with a little olive oil. Repeat to make 3 more pizzas. Serve hot or as a cold snack.

* You'll only need about 2/3 of the tapenade. You can use any remaining tapenade for chicken (recipe no. 138), pasta (recipe no. 211), and mozzarella (recipe no. 296).

Serves 2

6 ounces (170 g) dried spaghetti
Olive oil
1 ¼ tsp black peppercorns,
lightly crushed with a mortar
and pestle
1 tsp fennel seeds, lightly crushed
with a mortar and pestle
¼ tsp ground cumin
¼ preserved lemon,
finely chopped
(or 1 ½ tsp freshly grated
lemon zest)
14 ounces (400 g) cherry tomatoes,
cut in half
Fine sea salt
4 ounces (110 g) fresh ricotta
1 small handful fresh flat-leaf
parsley leaves

I barely plan my pasta meals in advance. Instead, I look in the fridge, and then smell the spice jars to see which aroma is the best match for my finds. Ricotta, cherry tomatoes, and lemon are a good start and a fragrant spice oil, infused with crushed peppercorns, fennel seeds, and cumin, wraps it up.

Spice Oil Spaghetti with Tomatoes, Ricotta, and Lemon

Bring a large pot of salted water to a boil and cook the spaghetti, according to the package instructions, until al dente. Drain the spaghetti and return it to the pot.

In a large, heavy pan, heat a generous splash of olive oil over medium heat and cook the crushed black peppercorns, fennel seeds, and cumin, stirring constantly, for 15 seconds or until fragrant. Add the preserved lemon and cook for 5 seconds then add the tomatoes and cook, stirring occasionally, for about 2 minutes or until they start to soften. Take the pan off the heat then add the spaghetti, stir to combine, and season to taste with salt. Sprinkle with the ricotta and parsley, divide among plates, and serve.

Serves 2 to 4

10 ounces (280 g) radicchio
4 large strawberries, hulled
Olive oil
Flaky sea salt
Coarsely ground pepper
2 tbsp balsamic vinegar
3 tbsp chopped fresh
marjoram leaves

Picture page 234, top left

Radicchio is charmingly bitter, which helps add depth to light summer salads. If you sear the purple lettuce first, you soften it, but don't interfere with its taste. Deglaze the hot pan with a splash of balsamic vinegar, stir in sweet strawberries, and you'll have a complex salad that plays with contrasting textures and flavors.

Balsamic Radicchio and Strawberries with Marjoram

Cut the radicchio into thin wedges and cut each strawberry into 6 pieces.

In a large, heavy pan, heat a splash of olive oil over high heat. Add the radicchio, reduce the heat to medium-high, and sear for 1 minute or until golden and partly brown but not black. Season to taste with salt and pepper, flip the radicchio over, and cook for 1 minute or until golden and tender. Add the vinegar and cook for 10 seconds then add the strawberries, gently shake the pan, and cook for 5 seconds. Season to taste with salt and pepper, drizzle with 1 tablespoon of olive oil, and sprinkle with the marjoram. Serve as a warm or cold salad.

185

Makes 2 sandwiches

Olive oil
6 slices bacon
4 large eggs
Fine sea salt
Finely ground pepper
5 ounces (140 g) mild,
hard cheese, very thinly sliced
2 large rustic buns, cut in half
1 small red bell pepper,
cut into rings
1 Persian cucumber, scrubbed
and very thinly sliced lengthwise
on a mandoline
1 avocado, peeled, pitted,
and very thinly sliced

Picture page 234, top right

A bacon and egg sandwich satisfies hearty breakfast appetites, but it can also adapt to the seasons. July screams out for more colorful creations, so pile a stack of fresh garden vegetables underneath the smoked meat. Juicy bell pepper and cucumber, smooth avocado, and thin slices of cheese are a blissful combination, but fennel, tomato, carrots, or mushrooms would make a vegetable-craving sandwich lover just as happy.

Bacon and Egg Sandwich with Garden Vegetables

In a medium, heavy pan, heat a splash of olive oil over medium-high heat and cook the bacon, turning occasionally, for a few minutes or until golden brown and crispy. Transfer the bacon to a plate, but leave the pan on the heat. Crack the eggs into the pan and cook to the desired doneness. Season to taste with salt and pepper.

Divide the cheese among the bottom halves of the buns and layer the bell pepper, cucumber, avocado, and bacon on top. Drizzle the vegetables with a little olive oil and season to taste with salt and pepper. Arrange 2 eggs on top of each sandwich then place a top on each bun. Squeeze and enjoy—it'll be messy.

186

Serves 2

Olive oil
1 large zucchini,
cut into thick round slices
Flaky sea salt
Coarsely ground pepper
4 large artichoke hearts,
preserved in olive oil,
cut into quarters lengthwise
1 small focaccia (or ciabatta),
for serving

This is the simplest lunch, focusing on the subtle sweetness of seared zucchini and artichoke hearts, without any unnecessary distraction. If your appetite asks for more, you can add pan-roasted potatoes.

Pan-Roasted Zucchini and Artichokes

In a large, heavy pan, heat a splash of olive oil over high heat and sauté the zucchini, turning once, for $1\frac{1}{2}$ to 2 minutes per side or until golden brown and al dente. Season to taste with salt and pepper. Stack the zucchini on a plate, but leave the pan on the heat. Add the artichoke hearts and sauté, turning occasionally, for 2 minutes or until golden and partly brown. Return the zucchini to the pan, stirring gently, and season to taste with salt and pepper.

Divide the zucchini and artichoke hearts among plates and serve with the focaccia, or ciabatta drizzled with olive oil.

184

185

188

189

Sometimes I like to treat myself to a special meal that I cook just for me. I put on a crackling vinyl, nibble on some cheese and Kalamata olives—strategically positioned next to the chopping board—and chill a bottle of rosé. Pork chops are a good choice for this kind of evening. Just two minutes in the hot pan and the meat is ready for a velvety sauce of balsamic fig butter.

Pork Chop with Balsamic Fig Butter

Serves 1

For the fig butter
Olive oil
3 fresh figs, cut into quarters
2 tsp balsamic vinegar
1 tbsp (15 g) unsalted butter
Fine sea salt
Finely ground pepper

For the pork chop
Unsalted butter,
to cook the pork chop
Olive oil
1 (6-ounce / 170-g) pork chop
Fine sea salt
Finely ground pepper

For the balsamic fig butter, in a small, heavy pan, heat a splash of olive oil over medium-high heat. Add the figs and sear, turning twice, for 1 1/2 minutes or until golden brown on all sides. Add the vinegar, cook for 10 seconds, then add the butter, stir, and season to taste with salt and pepper; set the pan aside.

For the pork chop, in a medium, heavy pan, heat 1 tablespoon of butter and a splash of olive oil over medium-high heat. Add the pork chop and sear for about 1 minute per side or until golden brown and just cooked through. Season to taste with salt and pepper and transfer to a plate. Drizzle the pork chop with the meaty cooking juices from the pan and the balsamic butter and arrange the figs on top— enjoy.

Pink prawns are sprawled on the grill and served on a minimalist potato salad in this recipe. Reducing the number of ingredients only works when you truly cherish their quality and freshness. When I'm in Malta, I buy the prawns from my trusted fishmonger. The local potatoes are sweet and earthy and only need a drizzle of olive oil, flaky sea salt, and fragrant marjoram from my Maltese mama's garden.

Grilled Prawns with Herbed Potato Salad

Serves 2

8 large shell-on prawns
without heads
4 large waxy potatoes, scrubbed,
boiled, and cut into slices
Olive oil
2 to 3 tbsp fresh marjoram
or oregano leaves
Flaky sea salt
Coarsely ground pepper

Picture opposite, bottom left

You can cook the prawns on the barbecue grill for 2 to 3 minutes per side or until golden brown and cooked through. Alternatively, cook the crustaceans on the stovetop: In a medium, heavy pan, heat a splash of olive oil over high heat and sear the prawns, turning occasionally, for 3 to 5 minutes or until golden brown and cooked through.

Divide the potatoes among plates then drizzle with olive oil, sprinkle with some marjoram, and season to taste with salt and pepper. Arrange the prawns on top of the potatoes and serve immediately.

This chocolate cake gives me goose bumps. Let the marbled raspberry whipped cream drip lusciously off the spongy, dark top and eat a big forkful—it's divine. You can also turn it into a fruity chocolate loaf and stir berries or rhubarb into the batter (recipe no. 154).

The Best Chocolate Cake with Raspberry Whipped Cream

Serves 6 to 8

For the cake
5 ounces (140 g) bittersweet chocolate
⅔ cup (150 g) unsalted butter
¼ tsp ground cinnamon
¼ tsp ground cardamom
4 large eggs, separated
⅛ tsp fine sea salt
¾ cup plus 2 tbsp (175 g) granulated sugar
1 cup (130 g) all-purpose flour

For the whipped cream
5 ounces (140 g) raspberries, plus 8 raspberries for serving
⅔ cup (150 ml) heavy cream
2 tbsp granulated sugar
1 vanilla bean, split and scraped

Picture page 234, bottom right

Preheat the oven to 350°F / 180°C (preferably convection setting). Butter an 8-inch (20 cm) springform pan.

For the cake, melt the chocolate, butter, cinnamon, and cardamom in a small saucepan over low heat, whisking until smooth; let cool for a few minutes.

In the bowl of a stand mixer fitted with the whisk attachment, whisk the egg whites and salt for a few minutes or until stiff, transfer to a large bowl, and set aside.

In the same bowl of the stand mixer fitted with the paddle attachment, beat the egg yolks and sugar for 2 minutes or until thick and creamy. Add the chocolate mixture and mix for 1 minute or until well combined. Add the flour and mix until well combined then fold the egg whites into the batter. Spread the batter evenly in the prepared pan and bake for 30 to 35 minutes (slightly longer if using a conventional oven) or until golden brown and spongy. If you insert a skewer in the center of the cake, it should come out clean. Let the cake cool for 10 minutes then take it out of the pan.

For the whipped cream, purée 5 ounces (140 g) of raspberries in a food processor or blender. Whip the heavy cream, sugar, and vanilla seeds until stiff then fold the puréed raspberries into the cream, leaving a marbled effect.

Serve the cake with a dollop of the raspberry whipped cream and top with the raspberries.

An apricot isn't honey-sweet like a peach. This small fuzzy stone fruit is a bit tart, with a texture that's firm, less juicy, and it easily pairs with vegetables. Its silky orange flesh melts smoothly into this green pea soup that's topped off with caramelized onions and ricotta.

Pea Soup with Apricots, Caramelized Onions, and Ricotta

Serves 2

For the soup
Olive oil
½ medium onion,
roughly chopped
1 large clove garlic, cut in half
2 ounces (60 g) leek
(white and light green parts only),
cut into slices
3 large apricots, pitted
and cut into quarters
10 ounces (280 g) fresh
or frozen peas
2 cups (480 ml) homemade
or quality store-bought
vegetable broth, hot
8 medium sprigs fresh marjoram
1 large bay leaf
Fine sea salt
Finely ground pepper

For the topping
Olive oil
1 medium red onion,
cut in half and thinly sliced
¾ tsp granulated sugar
2 large apricots, pitted
and cut into quarters
4 tsp fresh ricotta
1 tbsp fresh marjoram leaves

For the soup, in a medium pot, heat a splash of olive oil over medium heat and sauté the onion and garlic, stirring occasionally, for a few minutes or until golden and soft. Add the leek and cook for 1 minute then add the apricots, stir, and cook for 1 minute. Add the peas, hot broth, marjoram, and bay leaf. Season to taste with salt and pepper and bring to a boil. Reduce the heat and simmer for 5 minutes. Remove and discard the marjoram and bay leaf. In a food processor or blender, or with an immersion blender, purée the soup until smooth then return it to the pot. Season to taste with salt and pepper, cover, and keep warm.

For the topping, in a medium, heavy pan, heat a splash of olive oil over medium-high heat. Add the onion and cook, stirring occasionally, for 10 minutes or until golden brown and soft. Add 1/4 teaspoon of the sugar, stir, and cook for 2 more minutes.

In a small, heavy pan, heat a splash of olive oil over high heat and sear the apricots, turning once, for 30 to 40 seconds or until golden brown and partly charred. Add the remaining sugar, stir, and cook for 5 seconds then take the pan off the heat.

Divide the soup among bowls and arrange the apricots, onions, and ricotta on top. Sprinkle with marjoram and serve immediately.

Cherry season is short and sweet, so grab these pretty fruits by the bucket and have a feast. There's more to this dark red stone fruit than jams, cakes, and ice cream. Instead, let them unfold their juicy summer taste in savory dishes. They are lovely paired with Stilton and thyme and if you happen to have ciabatta or sourdough bread lying on your kitchen counter, make a panzanella.

Cherry Panzanella with Stilton, Shallots, and Thyme

Serves 2 to 4

For the dressing
3 tbsp olive oil
1 tbsp balsamic vinegar
1 tbsp white balsamic vinegar
2 tsp finely chopped fresh
thyme leaves
Fine sea salt
Finely ground pepper

For the salad
¾ pound (340 g) fresh cherries,
pitted
1 large handful arugula leaves
1 large handful bite-size
chunky ciabatta cubes
(or any spongy white bread)
2 medium shallots,
very thinly sliced
2 ounces (60 g) Stilton
(or any crumbly blue cheese),
crumbled

For the dressing, whisk together the olive oil, both vinegars, and the thyme and season to taste with salt and pepper.

For the salad, arrange the cherries, arugula, ciabatta, and shallots in a large bowl. Drizzle with the dressing, sprinkle with the Stilton, and enjoy.

Exchanging recipes with friends, family, or strangers is a great source of inspiration. To talk about a single ingredient, a whole recipe, or family traditions around the table, makes me want to go straight to my kitchen and bring out my pots and pans. A few years ago, one of the readers of my blog mentioned an omelet made with preserved artichoke. It immediately caught my attention and led me to create this sandwich.

Artichoke-Omelet Sandwich with Basil Pesto

Makes 2 sandwiches

For the pesto

1 ounce (30 g) fresh basil leaves
2 fresh mint leaves
2 tbsp finely grated Parmesan
1 tbsp pine nuts
1 small clove garlic
¼ cup (60 ml) olive oil
Fine sea salt

For the omelet

3 large eggs
¼ cup (60 ml) heavy cream
Nutmeg, preferably freshly grated
Fine sea salt
Finely ground pepper
Unsalted butter,
to cook the omelet
2 large artichoke hearts,
preserved in olive oil,
cut into quarters lengthwise

For the sandwiches

1 small handful fresh
arugula leaves
1 medium loaf ciabatta,
cut into 2 buns and each cut
in half
12 small fresh basil leaves

For the pesto, in a food processor or blender, purée the basil, mint, Parmesan, pine nuts, garlic, and olive oil until smooth and season to taste with salt.

For the omelet, whisk together the eggs and heavy cream in a medium bowl and season to taste with nutmeg, salt, and pepper. In a small cast-iron pan or nonstick skillet, heat 1/2 teaspoon of butter over medium-high heat and sear the artichoke hearts, stirring occasionally, for about 2 minutes or until golden brown. Add 1/2 teaspoon of butter then pour the egg mixture into the pan and stir 3 to 4 times, scraping the egg mixture off the bottom of the pan. Mind not to scramble the eggs and to just fluff them up a bit; reduce the heat if they brown too quickly. When the bottom side is golden, flip the omelet and cook the other side for 1 to 2 minutes or until golden and just set. Take the pan off the heat and cut the omelet in half.

Arrange 1/2 of the arugula on the bottom of each bun and place an omelet half on top of each. Sprinkle with pesto, basil, and a little pepper. Place a top on each bun and serve.

There are many ways to cook fish soup, but there's always one very important rule to follow: Only use the freshest fish. Let your trusted fishmonger choose the tastiest bites from the sea. Firm and chunky fillets and steaks of halibut, cod, or monkfish are all perfect, and if you add a handful of prawns, they'll bring in sweetness. Mediterranean fish soup often shines with a subtle hint of tomato and fresh herbs. Here, heady saffron, vermouth, and pastis make it even more complex.

A Quick Fish Soup with Saffron, Vermouth, and Pastis

Serves 2 to 4

Olive oil
2 large cloves garlic,
cut into quarters
1 medium tomato,
roughly chopped
¼ cup (60 ml) French
anise-flavored spirit,
such as pastis, Ricard, or Pernod
¼ cup (60 ml) dry white vermouth,
such as Noilly Prat
(or dry white wine)
3¾ cups (900 ml) homemade
or quality store-bought fish
or lobster broth
1 small bunch fresh
flat-leaf parsley
8 medium sprigs fresh marjoram,
plus 1 tbsp leaves for serving
1 large bay leaf
½ tsp saffron threads
2 slices lemon
Fine sea salt
Finely ground pepper
18 ounces (500 g) thick firm
fish fillets, such as halibut, cod,
or monkfish, cut into 1½ x 1½-inch
(4 x 4 cm) chunks
4 medium peeled prawns
without heads

Picture page 249, top left

In a large pot, heat a splash of olive oil over medium heat, add the garlic, and sauté, stirring constantly, for 1 minute. Add the chopped tomato, stir, and cook over medium-high heat for 1 minute then add the anise-flavored spirit and vermouth and cook for 45 seconds. Add the broth, parsley, marjoram sprigs, bay leaf, saffron, and lemon slices and season to taste with salt and pepper. Bring to a boil then reduce the heat and simmer for 5 minutes. Add the fish and prawns then reduce the heat to medium-low and cook, just below simmering, for 5 minutes or until the fish is just cooked through. Season to taste with salt and pepper. Divide the fish soup among bowls, sprinkle with the marjoram leaves, and serve.

A plate of crespelle creates the same kind of happiness as pizza or lasagna. It's the magic of comfort food—the kind of meals you want to eat while snuggled into cushions, lazing on the sofa, and watching an old movie from the sixties. Filling these thin Italian crêpes with spinach and ricotta is the classic approach. Combining balsamic radicchio, potatoes, fresh marjoram, and aromatic Gruyère is a little more adventurous.

Crespelle with Radicchio, Potatoes, and Gruyère

Serves 2 to 4

For the béchamel sauce

2½ cups (600 ml) whole milk
1 large bay leaf
Nutmeg, preferably freshly grated
Fine sea salt
Finely ground pepper
2 tbsp (30 g) unsalted butter
¼ cup (30 g) all-purpose flour

For the crespelle

⅔ cups (150 ml) whole milk
2 large eggs
1 cup (130 g) all-purpose flour
¼ tsp fine sea salt
Unsalted butter

For the filling

Olive oil
1 (10-ounce / 280-g) cored
radicchio head, cut into quarters
and thickly sliced
2 tbsp balsamic vinegar
1 tbsp finely chopped
fresh marjoram leaves,
plus 2 tbsp for serving
Fine sea salt
Finely ground pepper
14 ounces (400 g) peeled
potatoes, cut into ½-inch
(1.25 cm) cubes, boiled, and
drained
4 ounces (110 g) Gruyère, Raclette,
or Comté, coarsely grated

Preheat the oven to 400°F (200°C).

For the béchamel sauce, combine the milk, bay leaf, $1/4$ teaspoon of nutmeg, $1/4$ teaspoon of salt, and a pinch of pepper in a medium saucepan and bring to a boil. Immediately take the pan off the heat, remove and discard the bay leaf, and set aside. To make the roux for the béchamel, melt the butter in a separate medium saucepan over medium-high heat and as soon as it's sizzling hot, whisk in the flour. Slowly pour the hot milk mixture into the roux and whisk until smooth. Simmer on low, whisking occasionally, for 2 to 3 minutes or until the texture starts to thicken. Season to taste with nutmeg, salt, and pepper then cover and set aside.

For the crespelle, in the bowl of a stand mixer fitted with the whisk attachment, whisk together the milk, eggs, flour, and salt until smooth. Let the batter sit for 10 minutes before you cook the crespelle.

In a large cast-iron pan or nonstick skillet, melt 1 teaspoon of butter over medium-high heat. Pour in $1/4$ of the batter, tilting and turning the pan, so that the batter spreads evenly and very thinly. Cook the crespelle for 30 to 60 seconds per side or until golden then transfer to a large plate. Use the remaining batter to make 3 more crespelle, adjusting the heat as necessary and adding 1 teaspoon of butter to the pan between crespelle.

For the filling, in a medium, heavy pan, heat a splash of olive oil over medium-high heat. Add the radicchio and sauté, stirring constantly, for 2 to 3 minutes or until the radicchio is golden and soft. Add the vinegar and marjoram, stir, and season to taste with salt and pepper.

Place the 4 crespelle on a work surface. Divide the radicchio and potatoes among the crespelle, spreading them evenly and leaving a thin border around the edges. Season to taste with salt and pepper and sprinkle each crespelle with $2 1/2$ tablespoons of béchamel sauce and $1/5$ of the Gruyère. Roll the crespelle into tight wraps and arrange them, side by side, in a medium baking dish. Sprinkle the remaining béchamel sauce and Gruyère over the crespelle and bake for 12 minutes or until golden and the sauce is set. To brown the cheese a little, switch on the broiler for the last 1 to 2 minutes.

Let the crespelle sit for 3 minutes then sprinkle with marjoram and serve.

A plain peach cake is a wonderful weekend baking project. The peaches sink deep into the spongy cake, spreading their juiciness, as soon as you push the fork through the crunchy cinnamon-sugar crust and into their soft, golden pulp. It's a beautiful cake for a Saturday brunch or teatime.

Peach Cake with Cinnamon-Sugar Crust

Serves 6 to 8

1 cup (130 g) all-purpose flour
¼ cup (30 g) cornstarch
1 ¼ tsp baking powder
½ tsp ground cinnamon,
plus ½ tsp for the topping
⅛ tsp fine sea salt
⅔ cup plus 1 tbsp (160 g) unsalted
butter, at room temperature
½ cup (100 g) granulated sugar,
plus 2 tbsp for the topping
3 large eggs
2 large peaches, pitted, cut into
quarters, and sliced crosswise

Preheat the oven to 350°F / 180°C (preferably convection setting). Butter an 8-inch (20 cm) springform pan.

In a medium bowl, whisk together the flour, cornstarch, baking powder, $1/2$ teaspoon of cinnamon, and the salt.

In the bowl of a stand mixer fitted with the paddle attachment, beat the butter and sugar for a few minutes or until fluffy. Add the eggs, 1 at a time, incorporating each egg before adding the next one, and continue beating for 2 minutes or until thick and creamy. Add the flour mixture and mix until combined. Scrape the batter into the prepared pan and arrange the peaches in circles on top, gently pushing them into the batter. Whisk together the remaining 2 tablespoons of sugar and $1/2$ teaspoon of cinnamon and sprinkle over the cake. Bake for 40 to 45 minutes (slightly longer if using a conventional oven) or until golden and firm on top. If you insert a skewer in the center of the cake, it should come out almost clean. Let the cake cool for a few minutes then take it out of the pan and transfer to a plate. Serve plain or with whipped cream.

Whenever my mother cooks a large roast with vegetables and herbs from her lush garden, the aromatic bouquet of rosemary, thyme, sage, and bay leaf, mingling with the meaty juices, takes over her house. While waiting impatiently, enveloped by this tempting cloud, you can almost taste the succulent meat and rich sauce that's soon to be on your plate.

Roasted Rosemary Lamb with Garlic and Tomatoes

Serves 3 to 4

3⅓ pounds (1.5 kg)
bone-in leg of lamb
5 large tomatoes, cut in half
2 bulbs garlic, cut in half crosswise,
plus 1 large crushed clove
⅓ cup (75 ml) olive oil
2½ tbsp chopped fresh rosemary
needles, plus 5 small sprigs
2½ tbsp chopped fresh
thyme leaves
Flaky sea salt
Coarsely ground pepper

Preheat the oven to 350°F (180°C).

Place the leg of lamb in a medium baking dish. Arrange the tomatoes (cut-side down) and garlic bulbs (cut-side up) around the meat. Whisk together the olive oil, crushed garlic clove, chopped rosemary, and thyme and sprinkle over the lamb, tomatoes, and garlic. Rub the herb-garlic oil into the lamb and arrange the rosemary sprigs underneath and around the meat. Season to taste with salt and pepper and roast for about 1 hour and 15 minutes, turning the garlic around after 45 minutes and spooning the juices from the baking dish over the meat twice.

Wrap the meat in a large piece of aluminum foil and let it rest for 8 minutes then cut into thick slices and serve with the garlic, tomatoes, and a fresh baguette or roasted potatoes.

Serves 2

1 avocado, peeled
½ small ripe Galia melon
(or cantaloupe), peeled
7 ounces (200 g) cored
fennel bulb
3 tbsp olive oil
1 tbsp white balsamic vinegar
1 tbsp freshly squeezed
lemon juice
Fine sea salt
Finely ground pepper
1 small handful small fresh
mint leaves

Picture page 249, top right

July is the official start to my salad season. I often skip warm dinners and indulge in simple, raw compositions of crisp greens and juice-dripping fruits tossed with a quick vinaigrette or just a dash of olive oil. Melon and fennel are a trusted duo in my salad repertoire, and ripe avocado makes this dish pleasantly rich.

Avocado, Melon, and Fennel Salad with Mint

Cut the avocado and melon into thin wedges and cut the fennel lengthwise into very thin slices.

In a small bowl, whisk together the olive oil, vinegar, and lemon juice and season to taste with salt and pepper.

Arrange the avocado, fennel, and melon in overlapping layers on a large plate. Drizzle with the dressing, sprinkle with mint leaves, and serve immediately.

Serves 2 to 3

Olive oil
1 ½ pounds (680 g) peeled
waxy potatoes, boiled, drained,
and dried
Flaky sea salt
Coarsely ground pepper
2 tbsp coriander seeds,
crushed with a mortar and pestle
5 ounces (140 g) soft chèvre,
crumbled
2 ½ tbsp fresh thyme leaves
2 tsp freshly grated lemon zest

Crispy potatoes eaten straight out of the pan are a pure and unbeatable delight. If you want to give this dish a Mediterranean touch, spice it up with crushed coriander seeds, lemon, chèvre, and thyme. It also goes very well with char-grilled meat.

Crispy Fried Coriander Potatoes with Chèvre, Thyme, and Lemon

Let the potatoes dry and cool completely on a wire rack then cut them into thick rounds.

In a large, heavy pan, heat a generous splash of olive oil over medium-high heat. Working in batches, add 1 layer of potatoes to the pan and fry, without moving, for a few minutes or until golden brown and crispy on the bottom. Carefully flip the potatoes over, 1 at a time, and fry for a few minutes or until golden brown and crispy on the other side. Season to taste with salt and pepper. Transfer to a large baking dish, cover, and keep warm. Repeat with the remaining potatoes, adding more oil if necessary. Transfer the last batch of potatoes to the baking dish then add a splash of olive oil and the coriander seeds to the pan and toast over medium heat for 15 seconds or until fragrant. Return the potatoes to the pan, stir gently, then sprinkle with the chèvre, thyme, and lemon zest and enjoy.

Serves 1

2 thick slices white
sourdough bread
High-quality olive oil
3 tsp fresh marjoram leaves
(or 1 tsp dried marjoram)
Flaky sea salt
Coarsely ground pepper

Toast a slice of sourdough bread in a hot pan, drizzle it with your best olive oil, and sprinkle the crusty warm top with fresh marjoram leaves and sea salt. I was introduced to this frugal breakfast during a farm holiday outside of Noto, a charming Baroque town in southern Sicily. It became one of my favorite weekday snacks and truly tastes like Sicilian summer.

Toasted Sourdough Bread with Marjoram and Olive Oil

Heat a large, heavy pan over medium-high heat. Brush the bread generously with olive oil on both sides and lay side by side in the hot pan. Sprinkle with 1/2 of the marjoram and toast for about 2 minutes or until golden brown then flip the bread and toast the other side until golden. Sprinkle with the remaining marjoram, season to taste with salt and pepper, and serve warm or cold.

Serves 2

2 medium zucchini,
cut in half lengthwise
Olive oil
Fine sea salt
Finely ground pepper
3 small sun-dried tomatoes,
preserved in salt or olive oil
1 ounce (30 g) pine nuts, toasted
7 ounces (200 g) feta,
mashed with a fork
1 large handful fresh basil leaves,
chopped, plus 10 small leaves
for the topping
1 tsp freshly grated orange zest

Maltese mamas and nannas master the art of stuffed vegetables. Their traditional recipes, passed from one generation to the next, are uncomplicated and honest. Sun-ripened zucchini, eggplant, and bell pepper are the dainty shells for meat, seafood, cheese, or vegetable fillings. The Maltese cook would always choose ricotta, but sometimes I like to sneak in saltier Greek feta.

Mediterranean Stuffed Zucchini with Feta, Basil, and Pine Nuts

Preheat the oven to 400°F (200°C).

Using a spoon, scrape out and discard the soft pulp of the zucchini. Arrange the zucchini, cut-side up, in a medium baking dish, brush with olive oil, and season to taste with salt and pepper.

If the sun-dried tomatoes are preserved in salt, cook them in a small pot of boiling water for 3 to 4 minutes or until soft. Drain, quickly rinse with cold water, and finely chop. If the sun-dried tomatoes are preserved in oil, finely chop them. Transfer the tomatoes to a medium bowl. Roughly chop 1/2 of the pine nuts and add to the bowl. Add the feta, chopped basil, orange zest, and 4 tablespoons of olive oil, mix and mash with a fork until well combined, and season to taste with pepper. Stuff the zucchini halves with the feta mixture, drizzle with a little olive oil, and sprinkle with the remaining pine nuts. Add a little water to cover the bottom of the dish and bake for about 45 minutes or until the zucchini are tender. Sprinkle with the basil leaves and serve warm, or let the zucchini cool to serve at a picnic.

201

Serves 1 to 2

4 tbsp olive oil
1 small zucchini,
cut into very small cubes
Fine sea salt
Finely ground pepper
1 tsp aniseed,
crushed with a mortar and pestle
8 small calamari, cleaned
2 tbsp French anise-flavored spirit,
such as pastis, Ricard, or Pernod
(or dry white wine)

The soothing aroma of aniseed smells like licorice mixed with the rugged soil cracking under the hot Mediterranean sun. These tiny seeds wrap pan-seared calamari and zucchini into a fragrant blanket, and turn them into a comforting, soul-warming dish.

Calamari with Aniseed and Zucchini

In a small, heavy pan, heat 2 tablespoons of the olive oil over medium-high heat. Add the zucchini and cook, stirring occasionally, for 3 minutes or until tender. Season to taste with salt and pepper and transfer to a plate, but leave the pan on the heat. Add the remaining 2 tablespoons of olive oil and heat over medium-high heat then add the aniseed and cook for 10 seconds. Add the calamari, season to taste with salt and pepper, and sear, stirring constantly, for about 2 minutes or until just cooked through—mind not to overcook the calamari or they become chewy. Add the anise-flavored spirit, stir, then return the zucchini to the pan and season to taste with salt and pepper. Divide the calamari and zucchini among plates and serve immediately.

202

Serves 4 to 6

10 apricots, pitted and cut in half
9 ounces (250 g) fresh blueberries
2 ⅓ cups (300 g) all-purpose flour
¾ cup (150 g) granulated sugar,
plus 2 tbsp for the topping
⅛ tsp fine sea salt
¾ cup plus 2 tbsp (200 g) unsalted
butter, at room temperature,
cut into cubes
1 tsp ground cinnamon,
for the topping
4 to 6 scoops vanilla ice cream,
for serving (optional)

A spontaneous baking session with my friend Cristina brought this fruity dish into my life. Apricots and blueberries are a lovely combination, but if you happen to find gooseberries at the farmers' market, use them instead to create a crumble that's even more on the sour side.

Apricot-Blueberry Crumble with Vanilla Ice Cream

Preheat the oven to 375°F / 190°C (preferably convection setting) and butter an oval 8 x 12-inch (20 x 30 cm) baking dish.

Spread the apricots and blueberries in the prepared baking dish.

In a large bowl, whisk together the flour, 3/4 cup (150 g) of sugar, and the salt. Add the butter and quickly mix with your fingers until it forms crumbles then spread on top of the fruit. Whisk together the remaining 2 tablespoons of sugar and the cinnamon and sprinkle over the crumbles. Bake for about 40 minutes (slightly longer if using a conventional oven) or until golden brown and crispy. Let the crumble cool for at least 10 minutes. Serve warm or cold with vanilla ice cream.

193

197

203

204

203

week 29 / sunday

Elegant meringues, lusciously filled with whipped honey mascarpone and ripe figs, look like Sunday teatime sweets coming out of the kitchen of an old palazzo. The large meringues are pale and crispy on the outside yet still a little soft inside. If you prefer your dessert a bit lighter, skip the mascarpone, and fill the shells with fruit compote instead.

Meringues with Honey Mascarpone and Figs

Makes 6 large meringues

For the meringues

3 large very fresh egg whites

⅛ tsp fine sea salt

½ tsp cider vinegar

1 cup (200 g) granulated sugar

For the filling

9 ounces (250 g) mascarpone

3 tbsp honey, preferably thyme or orange blossom

2 tbsp heavy cream

6 fresh figs, cut into quarters

Picture page 249, bottom left

Preheat the oven to 275°F (135°C) and line a baking sheet with parchment paper.

For the meringues, in the bowl of a stand mixer fitted with the whisk attachment, whisk the egg whites and salt for 1 minute then add the vinegar and continue whisking, gradually adding the sugar, for 12 minutes or until glossy and stiff.

Scoop 6 large mounds of egg white onto the lined baking sheet, leaving some space between the meringues, and gently swirl the tops. Bake for 2 hours or until pale and crispy and still a little soft inside. Let the meringues cool completely.

For the filling, whisk together the mascarpone, honey, and heavy cream until smooth. Cut a small top off each meringue and fill with a few spoonfuls of the mascarpone mixture and 1 fig. Place a top on each meringue and serve immediately.

If you have no idea what to do with a bunch of eggplant, slice and roast them in the oven, and marinate the smoky bites in olive oil. You can use them for sandwiches (*recipe no. 178*), or as a quick lunch topped with basil ricotta (*recipe no. 156*). Stirring eggplant into warm spaghetti isn't a bad idea either.

Spaghetti with Roasted Eggplant and Marjoram

Serves 2

1 medium eggplant, cut into
½-inch-thick (1.25 cm) circles
Olive oil
Flaky sea salt
Coarsely ground pepper
6 ounces (170 g) dried spaghetti
1 tbsp fresh marjoram leaves

Picture page 249, bottom right

Set the oven to broil (quicker method) or preheat to 500°F (260°C).

Set a wire rack on a rimmed baking sheet. Arrange the eggplant circles on the rack then brush both sides with olive oil and season to taste with salt and pepper. Broil, turning once, for about 7 minutes per side, or roast at 500°F (260°C) for 15 minutes then flip and continue roasting for another 6 minutes. The eggplant should be golden and partly brown and soft in the center. Watch it closely, as it tends to burn quickly. Stack the eggplant circles on a plate and set aside.

Bring a large pot of salted water to a boil and cook the spaghetti, according to the package instructions, until al dente. Drain the spaghetti and divide among bowls. Tear the eggplant circles in half and arrange on top of the pasta. Drizzle with a little olive oil, sprinkle with marjoram, and season to taste with salt and pepper. Serve immediately.

When you patiently sauté zucchini, eggplant, and bell pepper, one after the other, you spend a little more time at the stove, but the results are worth it. Each vegetable is tender yet has bite. Fold in creamy chèvre and crunchy coriander seed oil and then pile the colorful bunch on a thick slice of soft ciabatta. And if you happen to have hummus at hand (*recipe no. 292*), spread that onto the bread first—it tastes divine.

Sautéed Zucchini, Eggplant, and Bell Pepper with Chèvre and Coriander Oil

Serves 2 to 4

Olive oil
1 tbsp coriander seeds, crushed
with a mortar and pestle
7 ounces (200 g) zucchini,
cut into thin slices
Fine sea salt
Finely ground pepper
7 ounces (200 g) eggplant,
cut into very small cubes
1 medium red or yellow
bell pepper, cut into
very small cubes
12 small cherry tomatoes,
cut in half
4 ounces (110 g) soft chèvre
1 medium ciabatta bread,
for serving

In a small saucepan, heat 3 tablespoons of olive oil and the coriander seeds over medium-high heat until sizzling then take the pan off the heat and set aside.

In a medium, heavy pan, heat a splash of olive oil over medium-high heat. Add the zucchini and sauté, stirring constantly, for about 6 minutes or until golden brown and tender. Season to taste with salt and pepper and transfer to a plate, but leave the pan on the heat.

Add a generous splash of olive oil to the pan then add the eggplant and sauté, stirring constantly and adding a little more olive oil if necessary, for about 6 minutes or until golden brown and soft. Season to taste with salt and pepper and transfer to the plate with the zucchini, but leave the pan on the heat.

Add a splash of olive oil to the pan then add the bell pepper and sauté, stirring constantly, for about 3 minutes or until golden brown and al dente. Take the pan off the heat then add the zucchini, eggplant, tomatoes, and coriander oil, gently stir to combine, and season to taste with salt and pepper. Crumble the chèvre over the vegetables and serve warm or cold with ciabatta bread.

Bigilla is deeply woven into Maltese culinary tradition. Vendors used to sell this fava bean and herb dip from horse carts, loudly shouting and praising their product. There's no family feast on the islands without large loaves of white sourdough bread and a bowl full of bigilla on the table. You can also use this dip for pasta or salads.

Bigilla
Maltese Fava Bean-Parsley Dip

Serves 6 to 8

7 ounces (200 g) dried fava beans, soaked overnight*
1 ounce (30 g) fresh flat-leaf parsley leaves
3 large cloves garlic
½ to 1 medium, fresh red chile, seeded
¼ cup (60 ml) olive oil
2 tsp freshly squeezed lemon juice
1 tsp fine sea salt
Finely ground pepper

In a large saucepan, cover the soaked fava beans with plenty of (unsalted) water and bring to a boil. Reduce the heat and simmer for about 30 minutes or until the beans are soft. Reserve 1/2 cup (120 ml) of the cooking water then drain the beans, quickly rinse with cold water, and let cool for 3 minutes.

In a food processor or blender, purée the fava beans, parsley, garlic, 1/2 of the chile, the reserved fava bean cooking water, the olive oil, lemon juice, and salt until smooth. Season to taste with additional chile, salt, and pepper and transfer to a bowl.

Serve the dip with fresh sourdough bread or crostini, or with warm spaghetti.

* If you use peeled dried fava beans, the dip will be green. Unpeeled legumes lead to a more faded brown color.

207

When the skin is golden and crispy and the meat succulent and tender, nothing beats a whole roasted chicken. And when it comes to seasoning the chubby bird, there are no rules to obey. Sweet or sour, fruit- or veggie-focused, spiced up, or plain and salted, chicken can handle almost anything. Lemon butter tastes fresh, peaches lend sweet fruity juices, and rosemary brings in a woody aroma.

Lemon Butter Chicken with Peaches and Rosemary

Serves 2 to 3

¼ cup (60 g) unsalted butter
⅓ cup (75 ml) freshly squeezed lemon juice
1 (3 ⅓-pound / 1.5-kg) whole chicken
Flaky sea salt
Coarsely ground pepper
6 medium sprigs fresh rosemary
1 large lemon, cut into 8 wedges
3 large peaches, pitted and each cut into 8 wedges

Ovenproof cotton string

Preheat the oven to 375°F (190°C).

In a small saucepan, melt the butter and lemon juice over medium heat, whisking constantly, until combined then transfer to a baking dish, just large enough to fit the chicken.

Place the chicken in the baking dish and toss in the lemon butter until well coated. Season to taste with salt and pepper inside and out, lay 2 sprigs of rosemary inside the chicken, and tie the legs together with ovenproof cotton string. Arrange the remaining rosemary, lemon wedges, and peach wedges around the bird. Roast, spooning the juices from the baking dish over the chicken every 15 minutes, for about 1 hour and 15 minutes or until the juices run clear when you prick the thickest part of a thigh with a skewer. Turn on the broiler for the last 1 to 2 minutes or until the chicken skin is golden and starts sizzling. Take the chicken out of the oven and let it rest for a few minutes.

Carve the chicken then serve with the peach and lemon wedges and the juices from the baking dish.

A dollop of whipped arugula feta and a fresh focaccia from the bakery turn smoky bell peppers and cherry tomatoes into a proper meal. You can also serve them with oven-roasted potato wedges, or grilled coarse sausages.

Roasted Bell Peppers and Cherry Tomatoes with Whipped Arugula Feta

Serves 2 to 4

For the roasted vegetables

12 cherry tomatoes, on the vine
2 large bell peppers,
preferably 1 red and 1 yellow
Fine sea salt
Finely ground pepper

For the whipped feta*

7 ounces (200 g) feta
2 large handfuls arugula leaves
¼ cup (60 ml) olive oil
Finely ground pepper

For serving

1 medium focaccia

Set the oven to broil (quicker method) or preheat to 425°F (220°C).

Place the tomatoes in a small broiler-proof baking dish and broil for about 12 minutes, or roast at 425°F (220°C) for 35 to 45 minutes—their skins should turn partly black and start to burst. Leave the tomatoes on the vine, but divide them into 2 to 4 portions and set aside.

Place the bell peppers in a medium broiler-proof baking dish and roast, turning twice so they cook on 3 sides, until their skins turn partly black. The peppers need about 22 minutes using the broil setting or 30 minutes at 425°F (220°C). Remove the peppers from the oven and immediately cover with a wet paper towel—this will make peeling easier. Let them cool for 2 minutes. Use a sharp knife to peel the peppers then cut them in half, scrape out and discard any seeds and fibers, and cut into strips.

For the whipped feta, purée the feta, arugula, and olive oil in a food processor or blender until smooth. Season to taste with pepper.

Divide the bell peppers and tomatoes among plates and season to taste with a little salt and pepper. Serve with a generous dollop of the whipped arugula feta and thick slices of focaccia.

You can use leftover whipped feta for sandwiches.

Malta's Mediterranean climate and pace forces a rushed northerner like me to slow down—and this is also reflected in my cooking. If I want to spend a couple more hours at the beach, I keep dinner simple. This lovely sweet-and-savory tart is one of my lazy summer recipes. I usually don't use store-bought pastry, but I make an exception for puff pastry. The tart is topped off with peaches, chèvre, and rosemary, and only needs half an hour in the oven.

Peach and Chèvre Tart with Rosemary

Serves 4 to 6

11 ounces (310 g) high-quality frozen puff pastry, defrosted
5 large peaches, pitted and cut into thin wedges
5 ounces (140 g) soft, mild chèvre, crumbled
1¼ tbsp finely chopped fresh rosemary needles, plus 2 small sprigs for the topping
3 tbsp honey

Preheat the oven to 400°F (200°C).

Line an 11-inch (28 cm) tart pan with the puff pastry, pushing the pastry into the pan, especially along the edges, and freeze for 5 minutes.

Arrange the peaches in circles on top of the chilled pastry, sprinkle with the chèvre and chopped rosemary, and drizzle with the honey. Arrange the rosemary sprigs on top then bake for about 30 minutes or until the edges of the pastry are crispy—depending on the pastry, it may take more or less time. Enjoy warm or cold.

The famous *Zitronenrolle* (lemon Swiss roll) is a staple at traditional German bakeries. It's a rather heavy pleasure that was often brought to the Sunday coffee table when I was a child. The fluffy rolled sponge cake is fine and fragile, while the whipped cream inside makes it luscious and rich. My version features a cheesecake filling made of ricotta and cream cheese — it makes a cloudy bed for summery peaches and blackberries.

Ricotta Cheesecake Swiss Roll with Peaches and Blackberries

Serves 4 to 6

For the cake
2 large eggs, separated
⅛ tsp fine sea salt
¼ cup (50 g) granulated sugar,
plus 3 tbsp to roll the sponge cake
½ vanilla bean, split and scraped
¼ cup plus 1 tbsp (35 g)
all-purpose flour
2 tbsp (15 g) cornstarch

For the filling
4 ounces (110 g) fresh ricotta,
drained
4 ounces (110 g) cream cheese
2 tbsp granulated sugar
½ vanilla bean, split and scraped
1 large peach, peeled, pitted,
and cut into thin wedges
4 ounces (110 g) fresh
blackberries

Preheat the oven to 425°F (220°C). Line a baking sheet with parchment paper and sprinkle a large tea towel with 3 tablespoons of sugar for rolling the sponge cake.

For the cake, in the bowl of a stand mixer fitted with the whisk attachment, whisk the egg whites, salt, and 2 tablespoons (25 g) of the sugar for a few minutes or until stiff then transfer to a medium bowl.

In the same bowl of the stand mixer fitted with the whisk attachment, whisk the egg yolks, the remaining 2 tablespoons (25 g) of sugar, and the vanilla seeds for 2 minutes or until thick and creamy. With a wooden spoon, fold the egg whites into the egg yolk mixture. Sift and whisk together the flour and cornstarch then add to the egg mixture and gently fold until combined. Carefully scrape the batter onto the lined baking sheet and spread into a 12 x 6-inch (30 x 15 cm) rectangle. Bake on the middle rack for about 6 minutes or until spongy and lightly golden. Immediately flip the warm sponge cake onto the prepared tea towel then peel off the parchment paper. Starting on one of the shorter ends, use the towel to gently roll the cake into a 6-inch-long (15 cm) roll then let the cake, rolled up in the towel, cool completely.

For the filling, whisk together the ricotta, cream cheese, sugar, and vanilla seeds in a medium bowl until creamy.

Unwind the sponge roll and spread the filling on top of the cake, leaving a thin border. Sprinkle with the peach wedges and 2/3 of the blackberries then roll the cake up tightly. Transfer to a platter, decorate with the remaining blackberries, and serve immediately.

211

Serves 2

7 ounces (200 g)
dried spaghetti
Olive oil
1 medium zucchini,
cut into tiny cubes
Fine sea salt
Finely ground pepper
Tapenade* *(⅓ recipe no. 182)*

Dark tapenade lends exciting depth to sandwiches and pasta. The Provençal dip tastes earthy and potent, but if you pair it with golden sautéed zucchini, it treats the vegetable with respect and gives it the space it needs.

Spaghetti with Tapenade and Sautéed Zucchini

Bring a large pot of salted water to a boil and cook the spaghetti, according to the package instructions, until al dente. Drain the spaghetti and return it to the pot. Add a splash of olive oil and toss to coat.

In a medium, heavy pan, heat a splash of olive oil over medium-high heat, add the zucchini, and sauté, stirring occasionally, for 5 minutes or until golden and tender. Season to taste with salt and pepper.

Divide the spaghetti among plates, sprinkle with the tapenade and zucchini, and serve immediately.

* You can use any remaining tapenade for chicken (recipe no. 138), pizza (recipe no. 182), and mozzarella (recipe no. 296).

212

Serves 2 to 4

5 ounces (140 g) cored radicchio
6 ripe apricots, pitted
2 spring onions
3 tbsp olive oil
1 tbsp balsamic vinegar
1 tbsp white balsamic vinegar
1 tsp honey
½ to 1 tsp ground cardamom
Fine sea salt
Finely ground pepper
5 ounces (140 g) fresh raspberries

This salad gets the taste buds jumping. It's a firework of colors and textures, and sweet and bitter bites, tossed together on a plate.

Radicchio, Apricot, and Raspberry Salad with Cardamom and Spring Onion

Tear the radicchio into pieces, cut the apricots into quarters, and thinly slice the spring onions.

In a small bowl, whisk together the olive oil, both vinegars, the honey, and $1/2$ teaspoon of the cardamom. Season to taste with salt, pepper, and additional cardamom.

Divide the radicchio, apricots, raspberries, and spring onions among plates. Drizzle with the dressing and serve immediately.

August

Serves 2

1 (10-inch / 25-cm) rustic baguette,
cut in half horizontally
3 tbsp olive oil
3 ounces (85 g) aged chèvre,
preferably Sainte-Maure
de Touraine, thinly sliced
6 cherry tomatoes, cut in half
6 black olives, preferably Kalamata,
pitted
1 large clove garlic, thinly sliced
1 tbsp fresh thyme leaves
3 tbsp finely grated aromatic
cheese that melts well, such as
Raclette, Comté, or Gruyère
Coarsely ground pepper

Imagine a blossoming meadow, in the South of France, with hay-colored grass and red poppies dancing in the wind, and you sitting on an old bench, enjoying the quiet peace that has cast a blanket on the world around you. The first noisy bite of this crunchy baguette will disrupt such tranquility, but it quickly rewards you with the wonderful tastes of cherry tomatoes, chèvre, olives, garlic, and thyme.

Roasted Tomato and Chèvre Baguette with Thyme

Preheat the oven to 425°F (220°C) and line a baking sheet with parchment paper.

Place the bottom half of the baguette on the lined baking sheet, drizzle with 1 tablespoon of the olive oil then cover with the chèvre. Arrange the tomatoes and olives on top and drizzle with the remaining 2 tablespoons of olive oil. Sprinkle with the garlic, thyme, and grated cheese and season to taste with pepper. Roast for 10 to 15 minutes or until the cheese is melted and the tomatoes start to soften. Place the top on the baguette, cut in half, and enjoy.

Serves 2

6 small waxy potatoes,
preferably rainbow potatoes,
scrubbed and boiled
6 small spring onions,
cut in half lengthwise
6 large cloves garlic, unpeeled
Olive oil
Fine sea salt
Finely ground pepper
4 ounces (110 g) sour cream
1 tbsp freshly squeezed lime juice

You can prepare this dish in your kitchen, or turn it into an outdoor adventure, by heating the grill, and cooking spring onions, garlic, and foil-wrapped potatoes over smoldering coals. Sour cream whipped with roasted garlic also makes a refreshing dip for grilled steaks and spiced sausages.

Smashed Potatoes with Roasted Garlic Dip

Preheat the oven to 425°F (220°C). Smash the potatoes lightly with your palm.

Spread the spring onions in a medium baking dish and place the garlic in one corner of the same dish. Drizzle the spring onions with a little olive oil and season to taste with salt and pepper. Roast the spring onions for 15 minutes or until golden and soft then transfer to a plate. Roast the garlic for another 10 minutes or until soft enough to mash with a fork—mind that the garlic doesn't burn. Peel the garlic cloves, add to a medium bowl, and mash with a fork. Add the sour cream, lime juice, and 1 tablespoon of olive oil and whisk until smooth. Season to taste with salt and pepper. Divide the potatoes and spring onions among plates and serve with a dollop of the sour cream dip.

Meat can feel a little heavy during the hotter months of the year, but pork tenderloin spread with the dark juices of sun-ripened blackberries and spicy mustard is lighter than you might imagine. I use thin coppa di Parma to wrap it all up and balance the berries' sweetness with salty heartiness.

Pork Tenderloin Wrapped in Blackberries, Mustard, and Coppa di Parma

Serves 3 to 4

⅓ pound (150 g) fresh
blackberries
2 tsp honey
1 tbsp freshly squeezed
orange juice
1 tsp balsamic vinegar
6 juniper berries, lightly crushed
with a mortar and pestle
1 bay leaf
Fine sea salt
20 very thin slices coppa di Parma
(or prosciutto di Parma)
1 (1⅓-pound / 600-g)
pork tenderloin
Finely ground pepper
2 tsp Dijon mustard
Olive oil

Preheat the oven to 400°F (200°C).

In a medium, heavy pan, heat the blackberries, honey, orange juice, vinegar, juniper berries, bay leaf, and a pinch of salt over high heat and cook, stirring constantly, for 3 minutes or until the berries start to thicken. Let it cool for a few minutes then remove and discard the bay leaf and juniper berries.

Spread a piece of plastic wrap, large enough to wrap the tenderloin, on a work surface. Arrange the coppa di Parma on the plastic wrap, letting the slices overlap slightly and covering the entire piece of plastic wrap.

Season the pork generously with salt and pepper then rub with the mustard and spread the blackberry mixture all over the meat. Place the tenderloin on top of the coppa and roll it up tightly.

In a large, heavy ovenproof pan, heat a generous splash of olive oil over medium-high heat and sear the tenderloin, turning it gently, for 1 minute per side. Transfer the pan to the oven and roast the meat for 12 minutes—it should still be pink inside. Take the meat out of the oven, cover with aluminum foil, and let rest for 2 minutes.

Cut the tenderloin into thick slices and serve with *Mediterranean Lemon Mashed Potatoes (recipe no. 163)*.

Serves 2

3 tbsp (45 g) unsalted butter,
at room temperature
1 small handful fresh rosemary
needles, roughly chopped
1 small handful fresh
marjoram leaves,
plus 12 medium sprigs
Fine sea salt
Finely ground pepper
6 medium, whole sardines,
gutted and cleaned

Grilling whole fish is a little more adventurous than roasting fillets in the oven. When you go for firm and uncomplicated fish like sardines, you don't have to worry about the texture, as the rich meat softens tenderly over the dry heat of the coals. Stuffing them with marjoram-rosemary butter infuses the fish with the herbs' fragrant aroma.

Grilled Sardines Stuffed with Herb Butter

Heat the grill or preheat the oven to 400°F (200°C).

In a medium bowl, using a tablespoon, mix the butter, rosemary, marjoram leaves, and 1/8 teaspoon of salt.

Cut a piece of aluminum foil large enough to fit the sardines side by side, place on a work surface, and arrange the marjoram sprigs on top. Season the sardines, inside and out, with salt and pepper and stuff generously with the herb butter, reserving 1 tablespoon for the topping. Arrange the sardines on top of the marjoram and spread the reserved 1 tablespoon of herb butter on top. Transfer the foil to the barbecue grill and cook, preferably covered, for 6 minutes, or bake at 400°F (200°C) for 15 to 20 minutes or until you can lift the fillets off the bones.

Serves 6 to 8

⅔ cup (150 g) full-fat plain yogurt
⅔ cup (150 ml) mild olive oil
3 large eggs
1 cup (200 g) granulated sugar,
plus 2 tsp for the topping
½ tbsp freshly grated lemon zest
1¾ cups (230 g) all-purpose flour
2½ tsp baking powder
¼ tsp fine sea salt
⅔ pound (300 g) pitted dark
plums, each cut into 8 wedges
7 ounces (200 g) fresh figs,
cut into quarters
¼ tsp ground cardamom

This French classic is made with yogurt and olive oil instead of butter, which makes it lighter and slightly sour. It's the perfect cake for adding fruit. When I'm in Germany, I use greengage plums, but they are difficult to find in some places. If this small green stone fruit isn't available, I pick up figs and large dark plums from the farmers' market.

French Yogurt Cake with Figs, Plums, and Cardamom

Preheat the oven to 350°F / 180°C (preferably convection setting). Butter an 8-inch (20 cm) springform pan.

In a medium bowl, whisk together the yogurt, olive oil, eggs, 1 cup (200 g) of sugar, and the lemon zest until well combined. In the bowl of a stand mixer fitted with the whisk attachment, whisk together the flour, baking powder, and salt. Add the yogurt mixture and whisk for 1 minute or until well combined. Spread the batter in the prepared pan and arrange the plums and figs, standing, in circles on top, gently pushing them into the batter. Combine the remaining 2 teaspoons of sugar with the cardamom and sprinkle over the fruit. Bake for 60 to 65 minutes (slightly longer if using a conventional oven) or until golden brown and spongy. If you insert a skewer in the center of the cake, it should come out almost clean. Let the cake cool in the pan for a few minutes then transfer to a plate for serving.

I had my first camping experience quite late in life. I was a nonbeliever until my wise partner shared his dinner plans. We grilled a whole fish right by the sea—it was a gift from a fisherman in return for the tomatoes we gave his hungry vegetarian daughter. This experience changed my perspective. I developed an interest in outdoor culinary adventures: A plate of farfalle tossed with figs, mozzarella, velvety honey butter, and basil satisfies the longings of a gourmet who ends up off the beaten track.

Farfalle with Figs, Mozzarella, and Honey Butter

Serves 2

6 ounces (170 g) dried farfalle (bow-tie pasta)
3 tbsp (45 g) unsalted butter
2 tsp honey
2 large fresh figs, each cut into 8 wedges
4 ounces (110 g) mozzarella di bufala, drained and torn into pieces
1 small handful small fresh basil leaves
Fine sea salt
Coarsely ground pepper

Bring a large pot of salted water to a boil and cook the farfalle, according to the package instructions, until al dente. Drain the farfalle and transfer it to a medium bowl.

In the pot used to cook the farfalle, melt the butter and honey over medium-high heat and whisk until combined. Add the farfalle, toss to combine, and divide among plates. Arrange the figs, mozzarella, and basil on top, season to taste with salt and pepper, and serve immediately.

When August hits its boiling point in Malta, water in all its forms is the only savior. The cooling sea becomes a daily escape and on the culinary side, I try to defy the extreme weather conditions with juicy peaches, tomatoes, and melons. Watermelon combined with mozzarella, olive oil, basil, and mint is a delicious variation of the classic caprese salad.

Watermelon Caprese with Mozzarella di Bufala, Basil, and Mint

Serves 2 to 4

¼ medium watermelon, peeled and cut into thin triangles
4 ounces (110 g) mozzarella di bufala, drained and torn into bite-size chunks
Olive oil
16 small fresh basil leaves
8 small fresh mint leaves
Flaky sea salt
Coarsely ground pepper

Arrange the melon and mozzarella on a large platter or individual plates. Drizzle with olive oil, sprinkle with the basil and mint, and season to taste with salt and pepper. Enjoy.

A few things will never change when it's summer in Malta. The sky is blue and the sun scorching hot, I snorkel for hours until my fingers shrivel like prunes, and I eat too much *Ħobż biż-Żejt* on the beach. It's the simplest snack. All you need to do is brush thick slices of spongy sourdough bread with olive oil and concentrated tomato paste ("kunserva" in Maltese), then season to taste with salt and pepper and—for the advanced version—sprinkle with red onion, fresh basil, and mint. It's pure beach bliss.

Maltese Beach Sandwich with Tomato Paste, Red Onion, Basil, and Mint

Serves 2

2 to 4 large, thick slices
white sourdough bread
About 2 tbsp olive oil
2 tbsp concentrated tomato
paste, preferably Maltese
or Sicilian kunserva
Flaky sea salt
Coarsely ground pepper
¼ medium red onion,
very thinly sliced
1 small handful fresh basil
and mint leaves

Brush the bread generously with the olive oil and concentrated tomato paste. Season to taste with salt and pepper and sprinkle with onion, basil, and mint. Enjoy as an open sandwich or place a second slice of bread on top. Cut in half, take to the beach, and enjoy.

It's hard to believe that raw grated potatoes cooked in a pan for just ten minutes can taste so good. But rösti is a little kitchen miracle—and the ultimate comfort dish. Refining it with rosemary, lemon zest, and melted Raclette takes this Swiss mountain classic to new heights. It's a rustic lunch, but also makes a hearty side dish for grilled meat.

Raclette Rösti with Rosemary and Lemon

Serves 2

15 ounces (420 g) peeled waxy
potatoes, cut into thin matchsticks
1 tbsp freshly grated lemon zest
2 tsp finely chopped fresh
rosemary needles
Olive oil
Flaky sea salt
Coarsely ground pepper
2 ounces (60 g) aromatic cheese
that melts well, such as Raclette,
Comté, or Gruyère,
coarsely grated

In a medium bowl, use your fingers to mix the potatoes, lemon zest, and rosemary until well combined.

In a 10-inch (25 cm) cast-iron pan, heat 5 tablespoons of olive oil over high heat. Add the potatoes, spreading them evenly and gently pushing them down with a spatula. Turn the heat down to medium-high and cook for 5 minutes, reducing the heat if the potatoes brown too quickly. Using a spatula, loosen the rösti from the sides of the pan and lift gently off the bottom. Cover the pan with a large lid then carefully and quickly flip the pan over. Keep the rösti on the lid while you add 1 tablespoon of olive oil to the pan then slide the rösti off the lid into the pan. Cook for 5 minutes or until the potatoes are golden brown and crispy on the bottom. Take the pan off the heat and season the rösti to taste with salt and pepper. Sprinkle with the cheese, cover with a lid, and let it sit for 2 minutes or until the cheese starts to melt. Loosen the rösti from the sides and the bottom of the pan, slide it onto a large plate, and serve immediately.

222

week 32 / friday

Serves 2 to 4

4 whole chicken legs
Olive oil
Flaky sea salt
Coarsely ground pepper
1 tbsp fennel seeds, crushed
with a mortar and pestle
1 medium fennel bulb,
cut in half lengthwise, cored,
and cut into 8 wedges,
plus fennel fronds for serving
4 large dark plums, pitted
and cut into quarters
⅓ cup (75 ml) fruity white wine
2 tbsp maple syrup

When the concentrated juices of dark plums and white wine blend with fennel's aromatic bulb and seeds, the kitchen slowly fills with a sweet and heavy perfume. It's the taste of August, a fruitful time of year when nature gives plenty. It's also more than fitting for roasted chicken legs.

Roasted Chicken with Plums and Fennel

Preheat the oven to 425°F (220°C).

Cut off and discard any large chunks of fat from the chicken legs and arrange in a baking dish, just large enough to fit them in. Pour a generous splash of olive oil over the chicken and rub into the legs until well coated. Season to taste with salt and pepper then sprinkle with the fennel seeds and rub gently into the skin. Arrange the fennel wedges and plums in between the chicken legs and season to taste with salt and pepper. Whisk together the white wine and maple syrup and pour over the chicken. Roast, spooning the juices from the pan over the chicken every 10 minutes or so, for 25 to 30 minutes or until the juices run clear when you prick the thickest part of a thigh with a skewer. Turn on the broiler for 1 to 2 minutes or until the chicken skin is golden and starts sizzling. Take the baking dish out of the oven.

Roughly chop the fennel fronds, sprinkle over the meat, and serve.

223

week 32 / saturday

Serves 2

1 ¼ cups (300 ml) water, lukewarm
1 tbsp fine sea salt
12 medium shell-on langoustines
Olive oil
1 large lemon, cut into wedges
Extra-wide aluminum foil

Picture page 280, top left

One of my favorite restaurants in the world is tucked into a secluded bay in Gozo, on Malta's smaller sister island. Noel is a specialist when it comes to seafood and his fish and crustaceans cooked al *cartoccio* in seawater are a revelation. He cooks them on the grill, but the oven works just as well.

Seawater-Cooked Langoustines al Cartoccio from the Grill

Heat the grill or preheat the oven to 400°F (200°C).

Cut 2 pieces of extra-wide aluminum foil large enough to wrap the langoustines like a package and lay them on top of each other. Whisk together the water and salt until the salt dissolves. If you happen to live close to the sea, use the same amount of clean seawater. Place the langoustines in the middle of the foil and fold up the sides. Add the salted water (or seawater), a generous splash of olive oil, and the lemon wedges. Fold the sides over and twist both ends of the foil then fold the top twice to seal. Transfer the foil package to the barbecue grill and cook, preferably covered, for 3 to 5 minutes, or bake at 400°F (200°C) for 10 to 15 minutes or until the langoustines are cooked through. Serve immediately, preferably with a glass of chilled white wine.

French clafoutis is a moody dessert. You never really know what it's going to do when you take it out of the oven. Sometimes it's light and fluffy like a soufflé, but other times it's dense like a flan. Either way, it's the perfect bed for juice-packed summer fruit. Apricots or peaches are delicious, but blueberries and lemon-cardamom sugar is a thrilling, even more enticing combo.

Ricotta Clafoutis with Blueberries and Lemon-Cardamom Sugar

Serves 4 to 6

2 tbsp (30 g) unsalted butter
1 tbsp freshly grated lemon zest, plus ½ tbsp for the topping
1 tbsp freshly squeezed lemon juice
1 tsp ground cardamom, plus ¼ tsp for the topping
¾ cup (180 ml) whole milk
4 ounces (110 g) fresh ricotta, drained
4 large eggs
½ cup plus 2 tbsp (80 g) all-purpose flour
½ cup (100 g) granulated sugar, plus 1 tbsp for the topping
⅛ tsp fine sea salt
7 ounces (200 g) fresh blueberries

Preheat the oven to 350°F (180°C). Generously butter a 10-inch (25 cm) ovenproof skillet or baking dish.

In a small saucepan, melt 2 tablespoons (30 g) of butter over medium heat. Take the pan off the heat, add 1 tablespoon of lemon zest, the lemon juice, and 1 teaspoon of cardamom and whisk until combined. Transfer to a large bowl and let it cool for a few minutes then add the milk, ricotta, and eggs and whisk until combined.

In the bowl of a stand mixer fitted with the whisk attachment, whisk together the flour, 1/2 cup (100 g) of sugar, and salt. Add the milk mixture and mix for 1 to 2 minutes or until well combined.

Spread the blueberries in the prepared skillet, pour the batter over the fruit, and bake for 45 to 50 minutes or until the clafoutis is golden and set.

Whisk the remaining 1/2 tablespoon of lemon zest with the remaining 1/4 teaspoon of cardamom and 1 tablespoon of sugar and sprinkle over the warm clafoutis. Cut it into pieces and serve immediately.

I usually try to avoid adding ingredients to my recipes that I'll only use once a year. Orange blossom water may sound fussy, but you won't regret buying a bottle of this fragrant water. Be mindful to choose one of good quality and add it to summery salad dressings. The floral water is common for baking, but whisked into a simple vinaigrette, I find it even more compelling. It charms chickpeas and melon, and helps sautéed zucchini and peaches to outperform themselves.

Sautéed Zucchini with Peaches and Orange Blossom-Basil Vinaigrette

Serves 2 to 4

For the dressing

3 tbsp olive oil

1 tbsp balsamic vinegar

1 tbsp white balsamic vinegar

1 tbsp high-quality orange blossom water, preferably organic

1 handful fresh basil leaves, roughly chopped, plus 6 small leaves for the topping

Fine sea salt

Finely ground pepper

For the salad

Olive oil

7 ounces (200 g) zucchini, cut lengthwise into very thin slices on a mandoline

Fine sea salt

Finely ground pepper

3 large doughnut peaches (or regular peaches), pitted and each cut into 8 wedges

Picture page 280, top right

For the dressing, whisk together the olive oil, both vinegars, the orange blossom water, and chopped basil. Season to taste with salt and pepper.

For the salad, in a large, heavy pan, heat a splash of olive oil over medium-high heat. Working in batches, sauté a few zucchini slices, side by side, for 1 minute. Flip the slices over, season to taste with salt and pepper, and sauté for another 30 seconds or until golden and soft. Transfer to a plate and continue cooking the remaining slices, adding a small splash of olive oil between batches.

Arrange the zucchini and peaches on a large platter. Sprinkle with the dressing and basil leaves and serve immediately.

Traditional Greek moussaka is made with ground beef and topped off with a heavy béchamel sauce. Inspired by my second home, I leave the familiar track and feature vegetables and Malta's favorite dairy product. My moussaka is basically a caponata crowned with fluffy, soufflé-like lemon ricotta. It's much lighter and makes my vegetarian dinner party guests smile.

Zucchini, Bell Pepper, and Eggplant Moussaka with Lemon Ricotta

Serves 2 to 4

For the vegetables

1 medium eggplant,
cut into thin round slices
Fine sea salt
Olive oil
Finely ground pepper
1 medium red onion, cut into
quarters and very thinly sliced
1 medium red bell pepper,
thinly sliced lengthwise
3 large cloves garlic, thinly sliced
1 medium zucchini,
cut into thin round slices
2 tbsp balsamic vinegar,
plus more to taste
4 medium tomatoes,
roughly chopped
2 tbsp roughly chopped fresh
flat-leaf parsley leaves

For the topping

9 ounces (250 g) fresh ricotta,
drained
2 large eggs
1 ounce (30 g) Parmesan,
finely grated
30 large fresh basil leaves,
finely chopped
1 tsp freshly grated lemon zest
1 tsp freshly squeezed lemon juice
Nutmeg, preferably freshly grated
Fine sea salt
Finely ground pepper

Preheat the oven to 400°F (200°C).

For the vegetables, spread the eggplant on a large baking sheet and sprinkle with a little salt on both sides. Let the eggplant sit for 15 minutes then quickly rinse with cold water and dry with paper towels.

In a large, heavy pan, heat a splash of olive oil over medium-high heat. Working in batches, sauté the eggplant slices, side by side, for a few minutes per side or until golden and soft. Season to taste with salt and pepper and set aside.

In a large pot, heat a splash of olive oil over medium heat and sauté the onion, stirring occasionally, for 5 minutes or until golden and soft. Add the bell pepper and garlic and sauté for 2 minutes then add the zucchini and sauté for 3 minutes or until golden and soft. Add the vinegar and tomatoes, season to taste with salt and pepper, and cook, stirring occasionally, for 10 minutes or until thick. Add the parsley, stir, and season to taste with additional vinegar, salt, and pepper.

For the topping, whisk together the ricotta, eggs, Parmesan, basil, lemon zest, and lemon juice in a medium bowl and season to taste with nutmeg, salt, and pepper.

Transfer the vegetable mixture to a 7-inch (18 cm) casserole dish (or a dish of roughly this size) with a tight-fitting lid and arrange the eggplant on top. Spread the ricotta mixture over the eggplant, cover the baking dish, and bake for 35 to 45 minutes or until the ricotta is just set. Let the moussaka sit for 2 minutes then divide among plates and serve.

When my Maltese mama, Jenny, makes her fruity caponata, she takes out her largest pan in order to keep up with our Mediterranean tribe's appetite. This thick vegetable dish is a very convenient way to have a snack at hand when your house is constantly occupied by family and friends, and it tastes divine on thick slices of crusty Maltese bread. If you add chorizo sausage, it becomes heartier, and if you combine it with octopus (*recipe no. 243*) you have an elegant Palermo-style dinner.

Caponata Sandwich with Chorizo Sausage

Makes 4 to 6 sandwiches

For the caponata

Olive oil
7 ounces (200 g) eggplant,
cut into quarters lengthwise
and thinly sliced
Fine sea salt
Finely ground pepper
1 medium red onion,
cut into quarters and thinly sliced
3 large cloves garlic, thinly sliced
⅓ pound (150 g) bell peppers,
preferably a mix of green, red,
and yellow, cut into small cubes
7 ounces (200 g) zucchini,
cut in half lengthwise
and thinly sliced
6 cherry tomatoes, cut in half
1 ½ tbsp tomato paste
1 tbsp balsamic vinegar
1 tbsp capers,
preferably preserved in salt,
rinsed and dried

For the sandwiches

Olive oil
4 to 6 medium Mexican
chorizo sausages
1 large baguette,
cut into 4 to 6 buns
and each cut in half
1 small handful fresh
flat-leaf parsley leaves

For the caponata, heat a generous splash of olive oil in a large, heavy pan over medium-high heat and sauté the eggplant, stirring occasionally, for 7 minutes or until golden and soft. Season to taste with salt and pepper and transfer to a plate, but leave the pan on the heat.

Add a little more olive oil to the pan and sauté the onion and garlic, stirring occasionally, for 5 minutes or until golden and soft then scrape them to the sides of the pan and add some olive oil and the bell peppers. Sauté for 2 minutes then add the zucchini and cook for another 2 minutes. Add the tomatoes and the sautéed eggplant, season to taste with salt and pepper, and cook, stirring occasionally, for 15 minutes or until soft. Add the tomato paste, vinegar, and capers, stir, and cook for 1 minute then season to taste with salt and pepper. Take the pan off the heat, cover, and let the caponata sit for 10 minutes.

For the sandwiches, heat a generous splash of olive oil in a large, heavy pan over medium-high heat. Add the sausages, reduce the heat to medium, and cook, turning occasionally, for about 10 minutes or until golden brown and cooked through. Cut the sausages in half lengthwise.

Pile a few spoonfuls of caponata on the bottom of each bun, arrange the sausages on top, and sprinkle with parsley. Place a top on each bun, squeeze, and enjoy.

223

225

228

230

Serves 2 to 4

8 shallots, unpeeled
Olive oil
Flaky sea salt
1 tbsp balsamic vinegar
1 tbsp white balsamic vinegar
1 tsp honey
Fine sea salt
Finely ground pepper
4 large dark plums, pitted
4 fresh figs
6 very thin slices prosciutto di
Parma
2 ounces (60 g) Stilton, crumbled

Picture opposite, bottom left

Prosciutto and Stilton elevate a humble salad to culinary stardom. They can turn a bowl of arugula, Belgian endive, or even blanched leftover greens into a wonderful lunch, and if you pair the duo with roasted shallots and the season's ripest fruit, you'll have an elegant starter for a dinner party.

Figs and Plums with Prosciutto di Parma, Roasted Shallots, and Stilton

Preheat the oven to 425°F (220°C).

Cut the shallots in half lengthwise, toss with 2 tablespoons of olive oil and a little flaky sea salt in a medium baking dish, and roast for 15 minutes then turn them over and roast for 7 minutes or until soft. Let the shallots cool for a few minutes then peel them and set aside.

In a small bowl, whisk together 3 tablespoons of olive oil, both vinegars, and the honey. Season to taste with fine sea salt and pepper.

Cut the plums and figs into quarters and arrange, along with the prosciutto and shallots, on a large platter. Sprinkle with the Stilton and drizzle with the dressing just before serving.

Serves 3 to 4

¼ cup (60 ml) olive oil
⅔ pound (300 g) peeled
waxy potatoes, very thinly sliced
on a mandoline
3 medium tomatoes, thinly sliced
Fine sea salt
Finely ground pepper
3 medium salsiccia
(or any thick, coarse sausage),
cut in half crosswise
8 large cloves garlic, unpeeled
1 small bunch fresh thyme
3 long sprigs fresh rosemary

Layering the thinnest slices of potatoes, juicy tomatoes, salsiccia, and herbs in a baking dish, and roasting this rustic composition in the oven, is the summer interpretation of a cozy sausage casserole.

Potato, Tomato, and Sausage Casserole with Fresh Herbs

Preheat the oven to 400°F (200°C). Brush the bottom of a medium baking dish with 1 tablespoon of the olive oil.

Arrange the potatoes and tomatoes in overlapping layers in the prepared baking dish and season to taste with salt and pepper—mind that you season in between the layers. Pour the remaining 3 tablespoons olive oil over the vegetables and arrange the sausages, garlic, thyme, and rosemary on top. Roast for 40 minutes or until the potatoes are tender. To crisp the top, switch on the broiler for the last 1 to 2 minutes. Let the casserole sit for a few minutes before serving.

Ricotta and olive oil muffins are lighter than sweets made with butter. There's a subtle flowery hint of olive oil that's not very strong but present nonetheless. Topped with figs, it's a perfect bite for Saturday breakfast.

Ricotta and Olive Oil Muffins with Figs

Makes 12 muffins

2 ½ cups (325 g) all-purpose flour
⅔ cup (125 g) granulated sugar
1 tbsp baking powder
½ tsp baking soda
¼ tsp fine sea salt
9 ounces (250 g) fresh ricotta, drained
2 large eggs
⅓ cup plus 2 tbsp (100 ml) mild olive oil
2 tbsp freshly squeezed orange juice
6 fresh figs, cut in half lengthwise
3 tbsp honey, for the topping
12 paper muffin pan liners

Picture page 280, bottom right

Preheat the oven to 375°F / 190°C (preferably convection setting). Line a 12-cup muffin pan with paper liners.

In a large bowl, whisk together the flour, sugar, baking powder, baking soda, and salt.

In a medium bowl, whisk together the ricotta, eggs, olive oil, and orange juice. Add to the flour mixture and stir with a wooden spoon until the batter is lumpy with a few bits of flour here and there.

Spoon the batter into the muffin cups then place the fig halves, cut-side up, on top and gently push them into the batter. Drizzle with a little honey and bake for about 18 minutes (slightly longer if using a conventional oven) or until golden and baked through. If you prefer sweeter muffins, drizzle them with a little more honey. Let the muffins cool on a wire rack for 2 minutes before serving warm with butter.

Timpana is a rustic pasta pie found at every street corner on the Maltese islands. It's a filling lunch you can buy from the pastizzeria during the week, and on Sundays, you ask your nanna to bake it for you. While timpana is traditionally filled with penne and Bolognese sauce, I go for less pasta and more vegetables to give the dish a fresher soul: zucchini and eggplant for summer and asparagus and peas for spring *(recipe no. 112)*.

Summer Timpana
Maltese Pasta Pie with Zucchini, Eggplant, and Tomatoes

Serves 4 to 6

For the filling
Olive oil
1 large clove garlic, crushed
1½ pounds (680 g) tomatoes, chopped
1 tbsp tomato paste
1 tbsp balsamic vinegar
Fine sea salt
Finely ground pepper
16 large fresh basil leaves, thinly sliced
9 ounces (250 g) dried penne, cooked al dente
14 ounces (400 g) zucchini
10 ounces (280 g) eggplant
4 ounces (110 g) Parmesan, finely grated, plus 1 tbsp for the topping

For the pastry
2⅓ cups (300 g) all-purpose flour
1 tsp fine sea salt
⅔ cup (150 g) unsalted butter, cold
2 large egg yolks
2 tbsp water, cold

For the glaze
1 large egg yolk
1 tbsp whole milk
⅛ tsp fine sea salt

Picture page 284, top left

For the filling, in a large pot, heat a splash of olive oil over medium-high heat, add the garlic, and cook for 10 seconds then add the tomatoes, tomato paste, and vinegar. Season to taste with salt and pepper and cook for 10 minutes or until thick; let cool completely. Stir in the basil and cooked penne and season to taste with salt and pepper.

Cut the zucchini and eggplant into ¼-inch-thick (0.5 cm) round slices. In a large, heavy pan, heat a splash of olive oil over medium-high heat. Working in batches, sauté the zucchini slices, side by side, for 1 to 2 minutes per side or until golden and soft. Season to taste with salt and pepper and transfer to a plate. Add a splash of olive oil and cook the eggplant in the same way—mind that it will need to cook a little longer. Season to taste with salt and pepper and transfer to another plate.

For the pastry, combine the flour and salt in the bowl of a stand mixer fitted with the dough hook attachment. Add the butter and use a knife to cut it into the flour until there are just small pieces left. Quickly rub the butter into the flour with your fingers until combined. Add the egg yolks and cold water and mix with the hook until crumbly. Form the dough into a ball. Remove ⅓ of the dough and form it into a thick disc. Form the rest of the dough into a second disc. Wrap both discs in plastic wrap and freeze for 10 minutes.

Preheat the oven to 400°F (200°C). For the glaze, whisk together the egg yolk, milk, and salt.

On a work surface, place both discs of dough between 2 sheets of plastic wrap and use a rolling pin to roll each disc into a circle, the larger disc for the bottom and sides of an 8-inch (20 cm) springform pan and the smaller disc to close the pie. Line the pan with the larger disc of dough, pushing it into the dish, especially along the edges. Let the dough hang over the rim a little. Spread ⅓ of the penne mixture on top of the pastry, sprinkle with ⅓ of the Parmesan, and cover with ¾ of the eggplant. Spread ⅓ of the penne mixture on top, sprinkle with ⅓ of the Parmesan, and cover with ¾ of the zucchini. Spread the remaining penne mixture, Parmesan, and vegetables on top. Close the pie with the smaller disc of dough, gently pressing the edges of the pastry together to seal it. Use a skewer to make a few small holes in the top, brush with the glaze, and sprinkle with the remaining 1 tablespoon of Parmesan. Bake for 15 minutes then reduce the heat to 350°F (180°C) and continue baking for another 50 minutes or until the pie is golden and the pastry is baked through. Let the pie cool for at least 15 minutes before serving.

231

233

237

238

Spaghetti con polpette combines three things I love about Italian cuisine: pasta, tiny meatballs, and fruity tomato sauce.

Spaghetti with Coriander-Fennel Meatballs and Tomato Sauce

Serves 4

For the meatballs

18 ounces (500 g) ground beef
¼ cup (40 g) dry breadcrumbs
1 large egg
3 large cloves garlic, crushed
1 medium onion, finely chopped
1 small handful fresh flat-leaf
parsley leaves, roughly chopped
1 tbsp olive oil,
plus more to cook the meatballs
1 tbsp coriander seeds,
crushed with a mortar and pestle
1 tbsp fennel seeds,
crushed with a mortar and pestle
2 tsp fine sea salt
1 tsp black peppercorns,
crushed with a mortar and pestle
Unsalted butter

For the tomato sauce

1 large clove garlic, crushed
1 tbsp balsamic vinegar,
plus more to taste
1 tbsp tomato paste
1 ⅓ pounds (600 g) canned
whole peeled tomatoes, chopped
1 large bay leaf
Fine sea salt
Finely ground pepper

For the pasta

12 ounces (340 g) dried spaghetti
4 tbsp finely grated pecorino
1 small handful small fresh
basil leaves

For the meatballs, combine the ground beef, breadcrumbs, egg, garlic, onion, parsley, 1 tablespoon of olive oil, the coriander seeds, fennel seeds, salt, and crushed black peppercorns in a large bowl and mix with your hands until well combined. Form the mixture into 24 roughly 1½-inch (4 cm) meatballs.

In a large, heavy pan, heat 1 tablespoon of butter and a generous splash of olive oil over medium heat. Cook the meatballs, turning occasionally, for 5 minutes or until golden brown then transfer to a plate and set aside, but leave the pan on the heat.

For the tomato sauce, add the garlic to the pan used to cook the meatballs and sauté for 1 minute. Add the vinegar and tomato paste, stir, and cook for 15 seconds. Add the tomatoes and bay leaf, stir, and season to taste with salt and finely ground pepper. Return the meatballs to the pan, stir to coat with the sauce, and cook over medium-low heat for about 8 minutes or until the meatballs are cooked through. Season the sauce to taste with additional vinegar, salt, and pepper.

While the meatballs are cooking, cook the pasta: Bring a large pot of salted water to a boil and cook the spaghetti, according to the package instructions, until al dente.

Divide the spaghetti, meatballs, and sauce among plates, sprinkle with pecorino and basil, and enjoy.

233

Serves 2 to 4

¼ cup (60 ml) olive oil
1 tbsp maple syrup
½ tsp ground cumin
1 medium eggplant,
cut into ½-inch (1.25 cm)
round slices
3 large shallots,
cut lengthwise into quarters
6 firm apricots,
pitted and cut into quarters
Flaky sea salt
Coarsely ground pepper
16 small fresh basil leaves

Picture page 284, top right

Eggplant can seem plain and shy, but this purple beauty is versatile and complex enough to play with a broad range of flavors. Apricots, maple syrup, cumin, and shallots bring out another side of the underappreciated fruit. The composition is slightly unusual, but these little adventures spice up our kitchen life.

Fruity Eggplant, Apricot, and Shallot Casserole

Preheat the oven to 425°F (220°C).

Whisk together the olive oil, maple syrup, and cumin.

Spread the eggplant, shallots, and apricots in a medium baking dish, add the cumin oil, and toss with your fingers until combined. Season to taste with salt and pepper and roast for 30 to 40 minutes or until the fruit and vegetables are golden brown and soft.

Sprinkle with basil and serve warm for lunch, or cold as a salad with grilled meat or roasted chicken legs *(recipe no. 222)*.

234

Serves 2 to 4

12 large cloves garlic,
preferably young, unpeeled
4 ounces (110 g) soft, mild chèvre
4 black olives, preferably Kalamata,
pitted and roughly chopped
2 tsp olive oil
1 tsp balsamic vinegar
¾ tsp fresh thyme leaves
Fine sea salt
Finely ground pepper
1 baguette, for serving

The last time we visited my partner's American grandparents in sunny California, they made my mouth water when they mentioned a dip made with chèvre, garlic, and olives. You need this recipe when it's the peak of August and you feel like dining al fresco. Set up dinner outside, put a bowl of this dip, a fresh baguette, and a bottle of velvety red wine on the table, and celebrate a warm summer's night.

Chèvre Dip with Roasted Garlic, Black Olives, and Thyme

Preheat the oven to 425°F (220°C).

Spread the garlic cloves in a small baking dish and roast, turning occasionally, for about 25 minutes or until soft enough to mash with a fork—mind that the garlic doesn't burn. Let the garlic cool for a few minutes then peel the cloves, place in a medium bowl, and roughly mash with a fork. Add the chèvre, olives, olive oil, vinegar, and thyme and whisk until smooth. Season to taste with salt and pepper.

Spread the dip onto slices of crunchy baguette and enjoy.

235

Serves 1 to 2

1 large slice watermelon,
peeled and cut into chunks
Olive oil
½ medium lemon
Flaky sea salt
Coarsely ground pepper
1 (7-ounce / 200-g) grouper fillet
1 small handful small fresh
basil leaves
1 small handful small fresh
mint leaves

Sunday mornings in Malta often start with a creamy cappuccino in Marsaxlokk and a stroll through the market to see the local fishermen's catch. Cooking feels different when you leave the city behind, when the ingredients come fresh from the fields and the sea. The tastes are honest and pure, and it feels better to keep them that way—simple. Combining grouper with watermelon, basil, and mint tastes especially good under the Mediterranean sun.

Grouper with Watermelon, Basil, and Mint

Divide the watermelon among large plates, drizzle with olive oil and a little lemon juice, and season to taste with salt and pepper.

In a medium, heavy pan, heat a splash of olive oil over medium-high heat and sear the grouper for about 2 minutes per side or until you can flake the fish with a fork. Season to taste with salt and pepper and drizzle with a little lemon juice. Cut the fish in half and arrange next to the watermelon. Sprinkle the fish and fruit with basil and mint and serve immediately.

236

Serves 2

1 large handful fresh basil leaves,
roughly chopped, plus 10 small
leaves for the topping
1 tsp finely grated Parmesan,
plus 1 tsp for the topping
½ tsp freshly grated lemon zest
Olive oil
Fine sea salt
Finely ground pepper
1 large zucchini, cut into
½-inch (1.25 cm) round slices

Sautéed chunky zucchini slices are sweet and juicy. You get the most out of their taste when you allow them to touch the pan for only a few minutes. They should be firm inside and al dente, and then you only need to drizzle them with fragrant basil-lemon oil for a quick weekday lunch. And if your appetite calls for more, stir in some pasta.

Sautéed Chunky Zucchini with Basil-Lemon Oil

Whisk together the chopped basil, 1 teaspoon of Parmesan, the lemon zest, and 1/4 cup (60 ml) of olive oil and season to taste with salt and pepper.

In a large, heavy pan, heat a splash of olive oil over medium-high heat and sauté the zucchini, turning once, for 2 to 3 minutes per side or until golden brown and al dente. Season to taste with salt and pepper.

Arrange the zucchini on a large plate, drizzle with the basil-lemon oil, and sprinkle with basil leaves and Parmesan. Serve cold or warm.

There's something beautifully old-fashioned about cream puffs, called *Windbeutel* in German. Voluptuously shaped and filled with vanilla cream, figs, pears, and blackberries, they deserve a spot on a pretty coffee table.

Vanilla Cream Puffs with Figs, Pears, and Blackberries

Makes 12 cream puffs

For the vanilla custard

1 ½ cups (360 ml) milk
2 large egg yolks
⅓ cup plus 1 tbsp (80 g) granulated sugar
¼ cup (30 g) cornstarch
⅛ tsp fine sea salt
1 vanilla bean, split lengthwise
⅓ cup plus 2 tbsp (100 ml) heavy cream, whipped to stiff peaks

For the choux pastry

⅓ cup plus 1 tbsp (90 ml) whole milk
⅓ cup plus 1 tbsp (90 ml) water
⅓ cup plus 1 tsp (80 g) unsalted butter
1 ½ tbsp granulated sugar
⅛ tsp fine sea salt
1 cup (130 g) all-purpose flour, sifted
3 large eggs

For the filling

1 small pear, cored and cut into thin wedges
6 fresh figs, cut into thin wedges
1 small handful blackberries
Confectioners' sugar

Picture page 284, bottom left

For the vanilla custard, whisk ¼ cup (60 ml) of the milk with the egg yolks, sugar, cornstarch, and salt in a small bowl until well combined. In a medium saucepan, bring the remaining 1 ¼ cups (300 ml) of milk and the vanilla bean halves to a boil. Take the vanilla bean out and scrape the seeds from the pod into the milk. Whisking constantly, add the egg yolk mixture to the hot milk and bring to a boil. Take the saucepan off the heat and continue whisking for 2 minutes. Let it cool at room temperature then chill for at least 30 minutes or until cold. Fold the whipped cream into the cold vanilla custard and return to the refrigerator.

Preheat the oven to 400°F (200°C) and line a baking sheet with parchment paper.

For the choux pastry, in a medium pot, bring the milk, water, butter, granulated sugar, and salt to a boil. Reduce the heat to medium-low, add the flour, and stir vigorously with a wooden spoon until the dough is smooth and comes away from the sides of the pot. Transfer the dough to a bowl and let it cool for about 10 minutes. Add the eggs, 1 at a time, beating with a wooden spoon and incorporating each egg before adding the next one, and continue beating until well combined.

Transfer the dough to a piping bag with a wide tip and pipe 12 small puffs onto the lined baking sheet. Bake for 18 to 20 minutes or until golden and crisp; don't open the door while the choux pastry is baking. When the pastry is done, switch off the oven and leave the door closed for 5 minutes then prop the door partially open and leave the pastry inside for 5 more minutes. Transfer to a wire rack and let cool completely.

Just before serving fill the choux pastry: Cut off the tops of the puffs and fill the bottoms generously with the custard, followed by the pear wedges, fig wedges, and blackberries. Cover with the tops, dust with confectioners' sugar, and serve immediately.

This is one glorious focaccia and combines some of summer's best. The topping of ripe figs, soft chèvre, honey, and rosemary is lush and perfectly suited to breakfast, lunch, dinner, or a picnic. I could even eat it at teatime.

Fig and Chèvre Focaccia with Honey and Rosemary

Serves 3 to 6

3 ¾ cups plus 1 tbsp (500 g) all-purpose flour
1 (¼-ounce / 7-g) envelope fast-acting yeast
1 ½ tsp granulated sugar
1 tsp fine sea salt
1 cup plus 1 tbsp (255 ml) water, lukewarm
½ cup (120 ml) olive oil
6 fresh figs, cut in half
5 ounces (140 g) soft chèvre, crumbled
1 small handful fresh rosemary needles
Flaky sea salt
2 tbsp honey
Coarsely ground pepper

Picture page 284, bottom right

In the bowl of a stand mixer fitted with the dough hook attachment, combine the flour, yeast, sugar, and fine sea salt. Add the lukewarm water and ¼ cup (60 ml) of the olive oil and mix with the hook for 5 minutes or until well combined. If the dough is too sticky, add more flour. Transfer the dough to a work surface and continue kneading and punching it down with your hands for 4 minutes or until you have a smooth and elastic ball of dough. Place the dough back in the bowl, cover with a tea towel, and let rise in a warm place, or preferably in a 100°F (35°C) warm oven, for 60 minutes or until doubled in size.

Brush a baking sheet with olive oil. When the dough has doubled in size, punch it down, take it out of the bowl, and knead for 1 minute. On the prepared baking sheet, pull and stretch the dough into a 13 x 10-inch (33 x 25 cm) rectangle. Cover with a tea towel and let rise in a warm place for about 20 minutes or until puffy.

Preheat the oven to 425°F (220°C).

Using the bottom of a wooden spoon or your finger, push 6 rows of 7 holes into the dough. Pour the remaining ¼ cup (60 ml) of olive oil over the dough and into the holes. Arrange the figs, cut-side up, on top, gently pushing them into the dough. Sprinkle with the chèvre, rosemary, and a little flaky sea salt and drizzle with the honey. Bake for 20 minutes or until golden and spongy. Sprinkle with pepper and enjoy warm or cold.

The trilogy of spinach, ricotta, and tomato is a classic in Italian cuisine. Be it for lasagna, crespelle, or these cute shell-shaped conchiglioni, the tri-color combination calls to mind the Italian flag and always makes for a delicious dish. Green and white is reserved for the filling, while roasted red cherry tomatoes become the fruity bed for the pasta shells.

Spinach and Ricotta-Stuffed Conchiglioni with Roasted Tomatoes

Serves 3 to 4

18 ounces (500 g) cherry
tomatoes, on the vine
2 tbsp olive oil
1 tsp balsamic vinegar
Fine sea salt
Finely ground pepper
14 ounces (400 g) trimmed
spinach
7 ounces (200 g) fresh ricotta,
drained
Nutmeg, preferably freshly grated
About 25 dry conchiglioni
(large pasta shells),
cooked (al dente) and drained
3 ounces (85 g) Parmesan,
coarsely grated

Set the oven to broil (quicker method) or preheat to 425°F (220°C).

Place the tomatoes in a large broiler-proof baking dish and broil for about 12 minutes, or roast at 425°F (220°C) for 35 to 45 minutes—their skins should turn partly black and start to burst. Snip the tomatoes off the vine and transfer to a medium baking dish. Add the olive oil and vinegar, stir, and squeeze the tomatoes a bit with a tablespoon then season to taste with salt and pepper.

Bring a large pot of salted water to a boil and blanch the spinach for about 1 1/2 minutes or until tender. Transfer to a colander, drain, and quickly rinse with cold water. Leave the spinach in the colander to cool for 5 minutes then squeeze until it's quite dry. Roughly chop the spinach then transfer to a medium bowl, add the ricotta, and mix until combined. Season to taste with nutmeg, salt, and pepper.

Stuff the pasta shells with the spinach mixture and spread the pasta on top of the tomatoes, pushing the pasta gently into the tomatoes. Sprinkle with the Parmesan and a little pepper and put under the broiler, or roast at 425°F (220°C) for a few minutes or until the cheese starts to melt. Divide among plates and serve immediately.

My dear friend Chris is the chef and owner of Legligin in Malta's capital city of Valletta. Visiting his restaurant spoils the senses: The space is beautiful and cozy, the food and wine are divine, and late at night, when the streets are silent and the shutters are closed, the long chats we have create unforgettable memories. Chris features excellent Maltese tapas on the menu, but one year, he impressed me with a tomato soup packed with heat and lots of fresh cilantro. I reconstructed it in my own kitchen and it came out just as good as I remembered.

Spicy Tomato Soup with Cilantro and Chile

Serves 2 to 4

1 large clove garlic
Fine sea salt
Olive oil
½ to 1 medium, fresh red chile, seeded and very finely chopped
2 ¼ pounds (1 kg) tomatoes, roughly chopped
½ cup (120 ml) homemade or quality store-bought vegetable broth, hot
2 large handfuls fresh cilantro leaves and soft stalks, plus a few leaves for the topping
1 tbsp tomato paste
1 bay leaf
1 tbsp balsamic vinegar, plus more to taste
Finely ground pepper

Roughly chop the garlic then sprinkle with $1/4$ teaspoon of salt and use the side of a large knife to press and rub the garlic and salt into a smooth paste.

In a large pot, heat a splash of olive oil over medium heat. Add the garlic paste and $1/2$ of the chile and sauté, stirring occasionally, for 2 minutes. Add the tomatoes, bring to a boil, and cook over medium-high heat for 4 minutes. Add the hot broth, cilantro, tomato paste, bay leaf, and vinegar, stir, and season to taste with salt and pepper. Bring to a boil then reduce the heat and simmer for 5 minutes. Take the soup off the heat and remove and discard the bay leaf. In a food processor or blender, or with an immersion blender, purée the soup until smooth then season to taste with additional chile, vinegar, salt, and pepper.

Divide the soup among bowls, sprinkle with cilantro leaves, and serve immediately.

Makes 1 large sandwich

Olive oil

1 medium salsiccia (or any thick, coarse sausage)

1 sun-dried tomato, preserved in salt or oil

1 small loaf ciabatta, cut in half

4 cherry tomatoes, cut in half

½ medium red onion, thinly sliced

8 small fresh basil leaves

6 capers, preferably preserved in salt, rinsed, dried, and roughly chopped

4 green olives, pitted and thinly sliced

1 small clove garlic, very thinly sliced

Coarsely ground pepper

Maltese *ftira* celebrates the islands' tasty produce and lets tomatoes, capers, olives, onion, garlic, and basil sink into spongy sourdough bread—you really can't pack more summer flavor into a sandwich. The sandwich has the same name as the doughnut-shaped bread that it's made with. It's a perfect snack for the beach, and can easily become dinner when you stuff it with salsiccia.

Ftira—Maltese Summer Sandwich with Sausage

In a small, heavy pan, heat a splash of olive oil over medium-high heat. Add the sausage, reduce the heat to medium, and cook, turning occasionally, for about 10 minutes or until golden brown and cooked through. Remove the sausage from the pan, reserving the pan juices, and cut into thick slices.

If the sun-dried tomato is preserved in salt, cook it in a small pot of boiling water for 3 to 4 minutes or until soft. Drain, quickly rinse with cold water, and roughly chop. If the tomato is preserved in oil, roughly chop it.

Drizzle the bottom of the ciabatta with the juices from the pan used to cook the sausage and a little olive oil then arrange the sausage, tomatoes, and onion on top. Sprinkle with the sun-dried tomato, basil, capers, olives, and garlic. Season to taste with pepper then place the top on the ciabatta, squeeze, and enjoy.

Serves 1 to 2

6 ounces (170 g) trimmed green beans

2 tbsp (30 g) unsalted butter

½ large firm pear, cored and cut into thin wedges

1 tsp honey

1 tsp Dijon mustard, plus more to taste

2 tbsp dry white wine

Fine sea salt

Finely ground pepper

Green beans love pear and both love mustard and honey. It's a very harmonic quartet to enjoy for lunch, or as a side dish with heartier treats.

Pan-Roasted Green Beans with Pear, Honey, and Mustard

Bring a large pot of salted water to a boil and blanch the green beans for 4 to 5 minutes or until al dente. Drain and quickly rinse with cold water.

In a medium, heavy pan, heat the butter over high heat. When it starts sizzling, add the pear and sear for 1 to 1½ minutes per side or until golden brown. Add the honey and mustard, stir, then add the green beans and white wine. Toss to combine and cook for 15 seconds. Season to taste with salt, pepper, and additional mustard and serve as a warm salad or side dish.

In the capital city of Palermo, caponata is often topped with octopus and when you pair the fruity vegetables with tender seafood cooked in a star anise–fennel broth, the combination definitely stands out.

Sicilian Caponata alla Palermo with Star Anise-Fennel Octopus

Serves 4

For the octopus

2 large cloves garlic, cut in half

2 bay leaves

2 star anise

1 slice lemon

½ tsp fennel seeds

18 ounces (500 g) octopus, cleaned

For the caponata

Olive oil

7 ounces (200 g) eggplant, cut into quarters lengthwise and thinly sliced

Fine sea salt

Finely ground pepper

1 medium red onion, cut into quarters and thinly sliced

3 large cloves garlic, thinly sliced

⅓ pound (150 g) bell peppers, preferably a mix of green, red, and yellow, cut into small cubes

7 ounces (200 g) zucchini, cut in half lengthwise and thinly sliced

6 cherry tomatoes, cut in half

1½ tbsp tomato paste

1 tbsp balsamic vinegar

1 tbsp capers, preferably preserved in salt, rinsed and dried

1 small handful fresh flat-leaf parsley leaves, chopped

For the octopus, fill a large pot with salted water, add the garlic, bay leaves, star anise, lemon, and fennel seeds, and bring to a boil. Add the octopus, reduce the heat, and gently simmer for 45 to 60 minutes or until tender. Transfer the octopus to a plate and let it cool for a few minutes then cut into large pieces.

While the octopus is cooking, prepare the caponata: Heat a generous splash of olive oil in a large, heavy pan over medium-high heat and sauté the eggplant, stirring, for 7 minutes or until golden and soft. Season to taste with salt and pepper and transfer to a plate, but leave the pan on the heat. Add a little more olive oil to the pan and sauté the onion and garlic, stirring occasionally, for 5 minutes or until golden and soft then scrape them to the sides of the pan and add some olive oil and the bell peppers. Sauté for 2 minutes then add the zucchini and cook for another 2 minutes. Add the tomatoes and the sautéed eggplant, season to taste with salt and pepper, and cook, stirring occasionally, for 15 minutes or until soft. Add the tomato paste, vinegar, and capers, stir, and cook for 1 minute then season to taste with salt and pepper. Take the pan off the heat, cover, and let the caponata sit for 10 minutes.

Divide the caponata among plates, arrange the octopus on top, sprinkle with parsley, and enjoy warm or cold.

September

Grapes grow abundantly in my Maltese mother's garden. When I open the bedroom window, I can almost grab the plump fruits dangling from the vines, their skin stretched and ready to burst. Spoiled with lots of sun, they ripen quickly on the archipelago, and as September nears, it's time to snip them off their branches and turn them into a fruity tart. I use store-bought puff pastry for this recipe; it's a convenient solution if you're looking for a quick yet impressive picnic treat.

Grape and Rosemary Tart

Serves 4 to 6

11 ounces (310 g) high-quality
frozen puff pastry, defrosted
18 ounces (500 g) seedless
red grapes
⅔ cup (125 g) granulated sugar
1 tbsp freshly squeezed
lemon juice
1 ½ tbsp finely chopped
fresh rosemary needles

Preheat the oven to 400°F (200°C).

Line an 11-inch (28 cm) tart pan with the puff pastry, pushing it into the pan, especially along the edges, and freeze for 5 minutes.

In a large bowl, toss the grapes with the sugar and lemon juice then spread on top of the chilled pastry. Bake for 35 to 45 minutes or until the edges of the pastry are crisp—depending on the pastry, it may take more or less time. Sprinkle the tart with the rosemary and let it sit for at least 10 minutes. Serve warm or cold.

Fenkata is a Maltese feast celebrating the country's national dish: *stuffat tal-fenek*, rabbit stew. Family and friends gather around a large table to eat rabbit, drink, chat, and laugh until they drop. The meat is cooked in wine infused with aromatic herbs. It's an honor if you're the one who finds the rabbit's head on your plate. Traditionally, the stew's sauce is served with spaghetti as the first course, followed by the rabbit and roasted potatoes, but I like to combine the two into one dish and skip the potatoes.

Fenkata
Maltese Rabbit Stew

Serves 4

1 whole rabbit, cut into 8 pieces

1 small bunch fresh thyme

3 medium sprigs fresh rosemary

1 (750-ml) bottle full-bodied red wine

About 3 tbsp all-purpose flour

Olive oil

Fine sea salt

Finely ground pepper

3 medium carrots, thinly sliced

1 celery stalk, cut in half

2 medium onions, cut into quarters and thinly sliced

8 large cloves garlic, cut in half

2 tbsp tomato paste

3 large tomatoes, roughly chopped

6 allspice berries

6 juniper berries, crushed with a mortar and pestle

2 large bay leaves

⅓ pound (150 g) fresh or frozen peas

⅔ pound (300 g) dried spaghetti

In a large bowl, combine the rabbit, thyme, rosemary, and 1/2 of the red wine, cover, and marinate in the fridge for 2 to 4 hours. Reserve the marinade then dry the meat with paper towels and dust lightly with the flour.

In a Dutch oven large enough to fit the meat and with a tight-fitting lid, heat a generous splash of olive oil over high heat. Sear the rabbit, turning once, for 1 to 2 minutes or until evenly browned on all sides. Season to taste with salt and pepper and transfer to a large bowl. Reduce the heat to medium, add a splash of olive oil, the carrots, celery, onions, and garlic, and sauté, stirring occasionally, for 3 minutes. Add a splash of the red wine and deglaze the pan, using a spatula to scrape any bits and pieces off the bottom. Return the meat to the Dutch oven. Stir in the tomato paste then add the reserved marinade, the remaining red wine, the tomatoes, allspice berries, juniper berries, and bay leaves. Stir again and season to taste with salt and pepper. Cover the Dutch oven and bring to a boil then reduce the heat to medium-low and simmer for 1 hour. Remove and discard the herbs then add the peas and simmer for another 30 minutes or until the meat is tender. Transfer the rabbit to a large bowl, cover, and set aside. Remove and discard the celery then bring the sauce to a boil and reduce for 2 to 3 minutes or until it reaches the desired taste and texture. Season to taste with salt and pepper then return the meat to the Dutch oven, cover, and keep warm.

Bring a large pot of salted water to a boil and cook the spaghetti, according to the package instructions, until al dente. Drain the spaghetti, divide among plates, and serve with the rabbit and sauce.

Serves 2

20 cherry tomatoes, on the vine
Olive oil
1 ounce (30 g) guanciale,
cut into very small cubes
2 large cloves garlic, crushed
1¼ cups (250 g) drained
and rinsed canned giant
or butter beans
3 tbsp roughly chopped fresh
flat-leaf parsley leaves
1 tbsp water
1 to 2 tsp balsamic vinegar
Fine sea salt
Finely ground pepper

Picture page 303, top left

Bags of colorful dried beans pile up on my pantry shelves, but most of the time, I grab a can instead. During the week, I tend to throw my creations together spontaneously, so soaking legumes overnight is not part of my modus operandi. Combining roasted tomatoes with canned giant beans is a speedy variation of Greece's famous baked beans. You can keep it vegetarian, or mix in some guanciale or mild bacon, which lends heartiness.

Garlicky Butter Beans with Roasted Tomatoes and Guanciale

Set the oven to broil (quicker method) or preheat to 425°F (220°C).

Place the tomatoes in a large broiler-proof baking dish and broil for about 12 minutes, or roast at 425°F (220°C) for 35 to 45 minutes—their skins should turn partly black and start to burst. Remove the tomatoes from the oven, snip them off the vine, and set aside.

In a medium, heavy pan, heat a splash of olive oil over medium heat. Add the guanciale and garlic and cook, stirring occasionally, for 5 minutes or until the meat is golden. Add the beans, stir, and cook for 1 minute. Add 2 tablespoons of the parsley, the roasted tomatoes, water, and 1 teaspoon of the balsamic vinegar and season to taste with salt and pepper. Cover and cook over medium-low heat for 5 minutes. Season to taste with salt, pepper, and additional vinegar. Stir in 1 tablespoon of olive oil, sprinkle with the remaining parsley, and serve warm or cold, preferably with thick slices of spongy sourdough bread.

Serves 2

2 ounces (60 g) pitted
green olives
1 ounce (30 g) finely grated
Parmesan
1 small handful
unsalted pistachios
1 small handful fresh flat-leaf
parsley leaves
¼ cup (60 ml) olive oil
½ to 1 tsp freshly grated lime zest
1 tsp freshly squeezed lime juice
Fine sea salt
Finely ground pepper
7 ounces (200 g) dried spaghetti

You can only appreciate this pesto if you have a weak spot for green olives. Their presence is far from subtle—in fact, they dominate this culinary composition. Pistachios, parsley, Parmesan, and lime graciously play supporting roles.

Spaghetti with Green Olive-Pistachio Pesto and Lime

In a food processor or blender, purée the olives, Parmesan, pistachios, parsley, olive oil, ½ teaspoon of the lime zest, and the lime juice until smooth. Season to taste with salt, pepper, and additional lime zest.

Bring a large pot of salted water to a boil and cook the spaghetti, according to the package instructions, until al dente. Drain the spaghetti and return it to the pot. Add a splash of olive oil and toss to coat.

Divide the spaghetti among plates. Sprinkle with the pesto, some pepper and lime zest, and serve immediately.

The short transition between seasons is a rewarding gift for every cook. Fall is waiting in the wings, yet summer isn't quite ready to say goodbye, giving us two seasons to nurture our inspiration and cooking vocabulary. If I had to choose one flavor to describe September, it would be that of ripe plums. I love their concentrated late-summer fruitiness, but when you cook them with warming spices, you can taste autumn, plus a subtle hint of the year's fast-approaching festive season.

Ciabatta Sandwich with Cheese Omelet and Spiced Plums

Makes 2 sandwiches

For the caramelized plums

2 tbsp granulated sugar

2 tbsp (30 g) unsalted butter

1 tsp coriander seeds,
crushed with a mortar and pestle

½ tsp ground cinnamon

4 large dark plums,
pitted and cut into quarters

For the omelet

3 large eggs

¼ cup (60 ml) heavy cream

Nutmeg, preferably freshly grated

Fine sea salt

Finely ground pepper

Unsalted butter,
to cook the omelet

2 ounces (60 g) aromatic cheese
that melts well, such as Raclette,
Comté, or Gruyère,
coarsely grated

For the sandwiches

4 lettuce leaves

1 medium loaf ciabatta, cut
into 2 buns and each cut in half

1 tbsp fresh thyme leaves

Coarsely ground pepper

Picture opposite, top right

For the caramelized plums, heat the sugar, butter, coriander, and cinnamon in a medium, heavy pan over medium-high heat until sizzling. Immediately add the plums and cook, turning once, for 2 to 3 minutes per side or until golden brown. Set the pan aside.

For the omelet, in a medium bowl, whisk together the eggs and heavy cream and season to taste with nutmeg, salt, and finely ground pepper. In a small cast-iron pan or nonstick skillet, heat 1 teaspoon of butter over medium-high heat. Pour the egg mixture into the pan and stir 3 to 4 times, scraping the egg mixture off the bottom of the pan. Mind to not scramble the eggs and to just fluff them up a bit; reduce the heat if they brown too quickly. When the bottom side is golden, flip the omelet and cook the other side for 1 to 2 minutes or until golden and just set. Take the pan off the heat. Sprinkle the omelet with the cheese then cut it in half. Layer the two halves on top of each other and cut the omelet in half again so you have two stacked wedges.

For the sandwiches, divide the lettuce among the bottom halves of the buns and place the warm omelet on top. Divide the plums and their juices among the sandwiches and sprinkle with thyme and coarsely ground pepper. Place a top on each bun, squeeze a little, and enjoy.

246

248

249

250

When you cook fruit on high heat—just for a little while, it won't take long—it develops a deeper, more concentrated flavor. Seared apricots taste beautiful, and when seasoned with ground turmeric, they are spectacular. If you add crisp arugula and whipped honey chèvre, you have an exciting salad.

Turmeric Apricots with Arugula and Whipped Honey Chèvre

Serves 2 to 4

For the whipped chèvre

4 ounces (110 g) soft, mild chèvre
2 tbsp olive oil
1 ½ tsp honey
½ tsp ground turmeric
Fine sea salt

For the dressing

3 tbsp olive oil
1 tbsp white balsamic vinegar
1 tbsp freshly squeezed
orange juice
Fine sea salt
Finely ground pepper

For the salad

Olive oil
½ tsp ground turmeric
6 medium apricots,
pitted and cut in half
2 large handfuls arugula leaves

Picture page 303, bottom left

For the whipped chèvre, whisk together the chèvre, olive oil, honey, and turmeric and season to taste with salt.

For the dressing, whisk together the olive oil, vinegar, and orange juice and season to taste with salt and pepper.

For the salad, heat a splash of olive oil and the turmeric in a small, heavy pan over high heat. Add the apricots and sear for about 1 minute per side or until golden brown and partly charred.

Arrange the arugula in a medium bowl, drizzle with the dressing, and arrange the apricots on top. Sprinkle with the whipped chèvre and serve immediately.

Chicken and lemon is a safe combo, but if you replace the yellow fruit with green lime, you'll find flowery tones woven into the citrusy aroma.

Lime Chicken with Cherry Tomatoes and Potatoes

Serves 2 to 4

4 medium, peeled, waxy potatoes,
very thinly sliced
Flaky sea salt
Coarsely ground pepper
4 whole chicken legs
Olive oil
16 small cherry tomatoes,
cut in half
2 limes, each cut into 8 wedges
½ cup (120 ml) dry white wine

Picture page 303, bottom right

Preheat the oven to 425°F (220°C).

Bring a small pot of salted water to a boil and blanch the potatoes for about 5 minutes or until al dente. Drain the potatoes then spread them in a baking dish, just large enough to fit the chicken legs in, and season to taste with salt and pepper.

Cut off and discard any large chunks of fat from the chicken legs. Rub the chicken with a little olive oil, season to taste with salt and pepper, and place on top of the potatoes. Arrange the tomatoes and limes in between the chicken legs. Whisk together the white wine and 3 tablespoons of olive oil and pour over the chicken. Roast, spooning the juices from the pan over the chicken every 10 minutes or so, for 25 to 30 minutes or until the juices run clear when you prick the thickest part of a thigh with a skewer. Turn on the broiler for 1 to 2 minutes or until the chicken skin is golden brown and starts sizzling; serve immediately.

Think of Black Forest torte, take out the heaviness, and you have a rough idea of the taste of this extravagant beauty. This pie has all the fancy features of the famous southern German coffee table classic, including dark chocolate, Kirsch, and sweet cherries, but it's a tad lighter.

Cherry Chocolate Meringue Pie

Serves 6 to 8

For the cherry filling
1 ¼ pounds (560 g) pitted fresh cherries
½ cup (100 g) granulated sugar
1 tsp ground cinnamon
3 tbsp Kirsch
(German clear cherry brandy)
¼ cup (30 g) cornstarch

For the pastry
1 ¼ cups (160 g) all-purpose flour
½ cup (50 g) Dutch-process or natural unsweetened cocoa powder
3 tbsp granulated sugar
¼ tsp fine sea salt
½ cup (115 g) unsalted butter, cold
2 tbsp water, cold

For the meringue
3 large egg whites
⅛ tsp fine sea salt
⅓ cup plus 1 tbsp (80 g) granulated sugar

For the cherry filling, heat the cherries, sugar, and cinnamon in a medium saucepan over medium heat, stirring until the sugar dissolves. Add the Kirsch, cover, and simmer for 5 minutes or until the cherries soften. Transfer 3 tablespoons of the cherry juices to a small bowl, add the cornstarch, and whisk until smooth. Return the cornstarch mixture to the saucepan, bring to a boil, and cook, stirring constantly, for 30 seconds. Transfer to a large bowl and let cool completely.

For the pastry, combine the flour, cocoa powder, sugar, and salt in the bowl of a stand mixer fitted with the dough hook attachment. Add the butter and use a knife to cut it into the flour until there are just small pieces left. Quickly rub the butter into the flour with your fingers until combined. Add the cold water and mix with the hook until crumbly. Form the dough into a thick disc, wrap it in plastic wrap, and freeze for 15 minutes.

Preheat the oven to 400°F (200°C).

On a work surface, place the dough between 2 sheets of plastic wrap and use a rolling pin to roll out into a disc, large enough to line the bottom and sides of a 9-inch (23 cm) shallow pie dish. Fit the dough into the pie dish, pushing it into the dish, especially along the edges. Let the dough hang over the rim a little or trim with a knife. Use a fork to prick the dough all over. Bake for 15 minutes or until golden. If the dough bubbles up, push it down with a fork. Take the pie dish out of the oven and let it cool for at least 10 minutes.

For the meringue, whisk the egg whites and salt in the bowl of a stand mixer fitted with the whisk attachment for 30 seconds. Continue whisking, while gradually adding the sugar, for a few minutes or until stiff.

Pour the cherries on top of the pre-baked pastry and spread the egg white on top, forming peaks with a knife. Bake for 6 to 7 minutes or until the meringue is golden and crispy. Let the pie sit for at least 20 minutes before serving.

A quiche is like a good old friend. You can trust that it will bring joy and happiness to the table. It's comfort food, yet at the same time, there's something special about a buttery pastry base topped with a custardy filling. Reflecting the seasons is an easy task for quiche—artichokes, tomatoes, olives, thyme, and aromatic cheese scream late summer and make for a delightful Mediterranean picnic tart.

Artichoke and Tomato Quiche with Gruyère and Thyme

Serves 4 to 8

For the pastry

2 cups (260 g) all-purpose flour

1 tsp fine sea salt

½ cup plus 1 tbsp (130 g) unsalted butter, cold

1 large egg

For the filling

4 large eggs

¾ cup (175 g) sour cream (or crème fraîche)

½ cup (120 ml) heavy cream

3 tbsp fresh thyme leaves

1 tsp fine sea salt

Finely ground pepper

Nutmeg, preferably freshly grated

10 cherry tomatoes, cut in half

10 black olives, preferably Kalamata, pitted

3 large artichoke hearts, preserved in oil, cut in half lengthwise

3 tbsp finely grated aromatic cheese that melts well, such as Gruyère, Comté, or Raclette

For the pastry, combine the flour and salt in the bowl of a stand mixer fitted with the dough hook attachment. Add the butter and use a knife to cut it into the flour until there are just small pieces left. Quickly rub the butter into the flour with your fingers until well combined. Add the egg and mix with the hook until crumbly. Form the dough into a thick disc, wrap it in plastic wrap, and freeze for 10 minutes.

Preheat the oven to 400°F (200°C).

On a work surface, place the dough between 2 sheets of plastic wrap and use a rolling pin to roll out into a disc, large enough to line the bottom and sides of a 12-inch (30 cm) quiche dish. Fit the dough into the quiche dish, pushing it into the dish, especially along the edges. Let the dough hang over the rim a little or trim with a knife. Use a fork to prick the dough all over. Bake for 15 minutes or until golden. If the dough bubbles up, push it down with a fork. Take the quiche dish out of the oven and reduce the heat to 350°F (180°C).

For the filling, whisk together the eggs, sour cream, heavy cream, thyme, salt, and generous amounts of pepper and nutmeg.

Arrange the tomatoes, olives, and artichoke hearts on top of the pre-baked pastry. Slowly pour the egg mixture over the vegetables then sprinkle with the cheese and bake for 45 to 55 minutes or until the top is golden and firm. Let the quiche cool at least 10 minutes. Serve warm or cold.

I could eat spaghetti with tomato sauce almost every day, which is reason enough to come up with a variation once in a while. Crunchy bacon, fragrant fennel seeds, and salty-sharp capers definitely push red sauce in a new direction.

Spaghetti with Bacon and Fennel Tomato Sauce

Serves 2

Olive oil
3 ounces (85 g) thick-cut bacon,
cut into very small cubes
1 tsp fennel seeds,
crushed with a mortar and pestle
2 large cloves garlic, crushed
1 small dried chile
2 tbsp capers, preferably
preserved in salt, rinsed, dried,
and chopped
1 tbsp tomato paste
1 tbsp balsamic vinegar,
plus more to taste
½ tsp granulated sugar
14 ounces (400 g) canned whole
peeled tomatoes, chopped
Fine sea salt
Finely ground pepper
6 ounces (170 g) dried spaghetti

In a medium, heavy pan, heat a small splash of olive oil over medium-high heat and cook the bacon, stirring occasionally, for about 7 minutes or until golden brown and crispy. Scrape the bacon to the sides of the pan and add a little olive oil if the pan is dry. Add the fennel seeds, garlic, and chile and cook for 15 seconds then add the capers, tomato paste, vinegar, sugar, and tomatoes. Season to taste with salt and pepper and cook, stirring occasionally, for 7 to 10 minutes or until the sauce starts to thicken. Season to taste with additional vinegar, salt, and pepper.

Bring a large pot of salted water to a boil and cook the spaghetti, according to the package instructions, until al dente. Divide the spaghetti and tomato sauce among plates and serve immediately.

254

Serves 4 to 6

2 ¾ pounds (1.3 kg) trimmed rainbow chard (or regular chard)
¼ cup (60 ml) water
⅓ cup (75 ml) brandy
5 ounces (140 g) raisins
Olive oil
2 medium onions, finely chopped
2 ½ tsp ground cinnamon
2 ½ tsp ground cumin
2 tbsp balsamic vinegar
½ tsp freshly grated orange zest
¼ cup (60 ml) freshly squeezed orange juice
Fine sea salt
Finely ground pepper
4 ounces (110 g) pine nuts toasted

Sicilian dishes excite the palate with bold contrasts. The recipes from this southern Italian island aren't shy and they remind the skeptical cook to stay open-minded and playful. It's inspiring to taste sour-bitter balsamic chard and sweet raisins in one bite, and to feel the vegetable's soft leaves melt into crunchy pine nuts.

Sicilian Rainbow Chard with Pine Nuts and Brandy Raisins

Thinly slice the chard stalks and roughly chop the leaves.

In a saucepan, bring the water, brandy, and raisins to a boil, cover, and take the pan off the heat.

In a large, heavy pan, heat a splash of olive oil over medium-high heat and sauté the onions, stirring occasionally, for 7 minutes or until golden brown and soft. Add a little more oil and the cinnamon and cumin and cook for 15 seconds then add the chard stalks and sauté, stirring occasionally, for about 8 minutes or until al dente. Add the chard leaves and sauté, stirring occasionally, for 3 minutes, reducing the heat and adding more oil if necessary. Add the brandy-raisin mixture, vinegar, orange zest, and orange juice, season to taste with salt and pepper, and cook for about 2 minutes or until the chard stalks are tender. Sprinkle with the pine nuts and serve.

255

Makes 2 sandwiches

Olive oil
About ⅓ medium eggplant, cut into 18 very thin round slices on a mandoline
Fine sea salt
Finely ground pepper
1 tsp fennel seeds, crushed with a mortar and pestle
2 rustic white buns, cut in half
8 very thin slices salami, preferably Italian fennel salami
1 tbsp fresh oregano leaves

Sautéed eggplant slices drizzled with fragrant fennel oil taste divine. Add them to a salami sandwich and you'll have a scrumptious weekday lunch. You can prepare the oil and eggplant in advance and keep them in the fridge.

Sautéed Eggplant and Salami Sandwich with Fennel Oil

In a large, heavy pan, heat a generous splash of olive oil over medium-high heat. Working in batches, arrange the eggplant slices, side by side, in the pan and sauté for 45 to 60 seconds per side or until golden brown. If the eggplant browns too quickly, reduce the heat. Transfer the eggplant to paper towels to drain and season to taste with salt and pepper. Repeat to sauté the remaining eggplant, adding more oil between batches, and set aside.

In a small saucepan, heat 3 tablespoons of olive oil and the fennel seeds over medium heat until sizzling. Brush the bottom of each bun with the fennel oil then divide the salami and eggplant among the sandwiches. Sprinkle with the fennel seeds and the oregano, add a top to each bun, and enjoy.

Sautéed radicchio and leek turn sweet when they mingle in a pan. Together, they taste astonishingly like peas. This makes a pleasant side dish for seafood and if you top it off with a soft-boiled egg that's been marinated in balsamic vinegar, you won't need anything more to have a beautiful lunch.

Radicchio and Leek with Balsamic Soft-Boiled Eggs

Serves 2

For the eggs
2 to 4 large eggs
1 tbsp balsamic vinegar

For the vegetables
6 ounces (170 g) cored radicchio, cut into 1 ½-inch (4 cm) squares
Olive oil
½ medium leek (white and light green parts only), very thinly sliced
Fine sea salt
2 tbsp balsamic vinegar
1 tbsp honey
Coarsely ground pepper

For the eggs, bring a small saucepan of salted water to a boil and soft-boil the eggs over medium heat for 6 minutes. Rinse quickly with cold water then peel and transfer to a small bowl. Drizzle the vinegar over the warm eggs, gently toss to coat, and marinate while you cook the vegetables.

For the vegetables, rinse the radicchio with cold water and drain; it should be a bit wet when you cook it. In a large, heavy pan, heat a splash of olive oil over medium heat and sauté the leek for 2 minutes or until it starts to soften. Add the radicchio, season to taste with salt, and sauté, stirring occasionally, for 2 to 3 minutes or until the radicchio starts to wilt. Add the vinegar and honey and cook for 2 minutes then season to taste with salt. Divide the vegetables among plates and arrange the eggs on top. Season to taste with pepper and serve immediately.

The refreshing sweetness of green grapes finds a surprisingly perfect match in mussels. Gently steaming them in a Riesling broth with lots of fresh tarragon and marjoram infuses the tender orange meat with a colorful bouquet of aromas. It's a luscious lunch to slip into the weekend, and can be thrown together in no more than fifteen minutes.

Riesling Mussels with Grapes, Tarragon, and Marjoram

Serves 4

3⅓ pounds (1.5 kg) fresh mussels
1½ cups (360 ml) Riesling wine
⅔ cup (150 ml) freshly squeezed orange juice
1 tbsp elderflower syrup (or maple syrup)
⅔ pound (300 g) seedless green grapes
1 handful fresh tarragon sprigs
1 handful fresh marjoram sprigs
2 bay leaves
2 tsp fine sea salt

Rinse and scrub the mussels with cold water and cut off the beards. Discard any broken mussels.

In a large pot, combine the wine, orange juice, elderflower syrup, grapes, tarragon, marjoram, bay leaves, and salt, cover, and bring to a boil. Reduce the heat to medium and simmer for 5 minutes. Remove and discard the herbs then add the mussels, cover, and cook for 5 minutes or until the shells open. Shake the pot once or twice while the mussels are cooking or gently stir them with a slotted ladle or spoon. Discard any mussels that don't open.

Divide the mussels, grapes, and broth among bowls and serve with a crunchy baguette and a glass of chilled Riesling.

Zwetschgenknödel are fluffy potato dumplings made of gnocchi dough and filled with plums. The pillowy fruity balls are served with melted golden breadcrumb butter and lots of cinnamon sugar—it's a dessert wonderfully rich in taste and calories. My stepfather, Uli, introduced me to this traditional Swabian dish and taught me to keep the potato layer thin and soft to let the stone fruit shine. He was a meticulous instructor in the kitchen, watching every dumpling formed in my mother's and my hands.

Zwetschgenknödel Plum Dumplings with Cinnamony Breadcrumb Butter

Serves 4

For the potato dough

17 ounces (480 g) peeled starchy potatoes, cut into cubes

2 tbsp (30 g) unsalted butter

2 large egg yolks

1 cup (130 g) all-purpose flour

½ tsp fine sea salt

For the filling

About 25 fresh small purple plums, such as Italian prune plums (Empress plums) or damson, pitted (only cut halfway through each plum)

For the topping

¼ cup (50 g) granulated sugar

1 tsp ground cinnamon

⅓ cup plus 1 tbsp (90 g) unsalted butter

⅓ cup (50 g) dry breadcrumbs

For the potato dough, fill a medium pot with salted water, add the potatoes, and bring to a boil. Reduce the heat and simmer for 15 to 18 minutes or until the potatoes are soft. Transfer the potatoes to a colander and drain well then use a spoon to gently push out any water. Let the potatoes cool for 2 minutes then press them through a potato ricer into a large bowl. Add the butter and egg yolks, stir to combine, and let cool at room temperature for about 30 minutes or until completely cool.

For the topping, combine the sugar and cinnamon in a small bowl and set aside. In a small saucepan, heat the butter and breadcrumbs over medium-high heat until sizzling and golden brown; cover and keep warm.

Bring a large pot of water to a boil then add 3/4 teaspoon of salt and reduce the heat to a low simmer.

Add the flour and 1/2 teaspoon of salt to the potato mixture and, using a large spoon, quickly stir to combine. If it's too sticky, add a little more flour. Wet your hands then scoop 1 spoonful of the dough into your hand and form into a thin disc, large enough to wrap 1 plum. Place 1 plum, cut-side down, in the middle then gently wrap the dough around the fruit and use your fingers to squeeze the seam together and seal the plum inside. Transfer to a wire rack and repeat with the remaining plums and dough to create about 24 more dumplings. Before you cook the dumplings, using a wet finger, smooth out the marks made by the rack on the bottom of the dumplings.

Working in batches, add the dumplings to the water and cook, just below simmering, for 8 to 10 minutes or until they float to the top—mind that they don't stick to the bottom of the pot. Use a slotted ladle or spoon to scoop the dumplings out of the water, transfer to a large bowl, and cover. Cook the remaining dumplings, bringing the water back to a low simmer between batches.

Sprinkle the dumplings with the warm breadcrumb butter and cinnamon sugar and serve immediately.

My favorite English apple pie is dotted with blackberries, which makes the filling a little sharper than all-apple versions. It's a rustic sweet treat that helps us wave goodbye to summer.

Apple and Blackberry Pie

Serves 6 to 8

For the pastry

2 ⅓ cups (300 g) all-purpose flour

1 tbsp granulated sugar

½ tsp ground cinnamon

¼ tsp fine sea salt

⅔ cup (150 g) unsalted butter, cold

2 large egg yolks

2 tbsp water, cold

For the filling

⅓ cup (65 g) granulated sugar

1 tsp ground cinnamon

1 ⅓ pounds (600 g) peeled and cored tart baking apples, cut into quarters and very thinly sliced

2 tbsp all-purpose flour

7 ounces (200 g) fresh blackberries

For the glaze

1 tbsp whole milk

1 tsp granulated sugar

For the pastry, combine the flour, sugar, cinnamon, and salt in the bowl of a stand mixer fitted with the dough hook attachment. Add the butter and use a knife to cut it into the flour until there are just small pieces left. Quickly rub the butter into the flour with your fingers until combined. Add the egg yolks and cold water and mix with the hook until crumbly. Form the dough into a ball. Remove ⅓ of the dough and form it into a thick disc. Form the rest of the dough into a second disc. Wrap both discs in plastic wrap and freeze for 10 minutes.

Preheat the oven to 400°F (200°C).

On a work surface, place both discs of dough between 2 sheets of plastic wrap and use a rolling pin to roll each disc into a circle, the larger disc for the bottom and sides of an 8-inch (20 cm) springform pan or a 9-inch (23 cm) shallow pie dish and the smaller disc to close the pie. Line the springform pan or pie dish with the larger disc of dough, pushing it into the dish, especially along the edges. Let the dough hang over the rim a little.

For the filling, combine the sugar and cinnamon in a large bowl and toss with the apples. Arrange ⅓ of the apples on top of the pastry and sprinkle with 1 tablespoon of the flour and ½ of the blackberries. Add a second layer of apples and sprinkle with the remaining flour and blackberries. Cover with the remaining apples. Close the pie with the smaller disc of dough, gently pressing the edges of the pastry together to seal it. Use a skewer to make a few holes in the top, brush with the milk, and sprinkle with the sugar. Bake for 15 minutes then reduce the heat to 350°F (180°C) and bake for another 40 to 45 minutes or until golden and the pastry is baked through. Let the pie sit for at least 20 minutes before cutting into pieces and serving.

Panzanella is a brilliant dish, both simple and frugal. If you happen to have bread that's been lying around on your kitchen counter for a day or two, just pick some veggies, whisk together a quick vinaigrette, and make a Tuscan bread salad. The traditional recipe is made with white bread, but I'm hooked on sneaking in heartier northern-style dark spelt or rye bread. Panzanella is also nice with berries and bacon (*recipe no. 135*).

Green Bean and Tomato Panzanella with Dark Bread and Artichokes

Serves 2

For the salad

6 ounces (170 g) trimmed green beans

3 small artichoke hearts, preserved in oil, cut into quarters lengthwise

1 medium tomato, cut into wedges

1 medium red onion, cut in half and thinly sliced

1 large, thick slice dark spelt or rye bread, cut into cubes

For the dressing

3 tbsp olive oil

1 tbsp balsamic vinegar

1 tbsp white balsamic vinegar

Fine sea salt

Finely ground pepper

For the salad, bring a large pot of salted water to a boil and blanch the green beans for 4 to 5 minutes or until al dente. Drain the green beans, quickly rinse with cold water, and cut in half.

For the dressing, whisk together the olive oil and both vinegars. Season to taste with salt and pepper.

In a large bowl, combine the green beans, artichoke hearts, tomato, onion, and bread. Drizzle with the dressing, toss to combine, and let sit for 1 minute. If the salad is too dry, add a little more olive oil. Divide among plates and enjoy.

261

Serves 2

6 ounces (170 g) dried spaghetti
Olive oil
20 large fresh sage leaves
¾ pound (340 g) peeled
and seeded squash, preferably
butternut or Hokkaido,
cut into small cubes
½ cup (120 ml) freshly squeezed
orange juice
2 tbsp maple syrup
Fine sea salt
Finely ground pepper

Sweetening spaghetti with maple syrup may challenge the traditional pasta lover, but it makes sense if you fold in tender squash, orange juice, and crispy sage leaves.

Squash Pasta with Orange, Maple, and Sage

Bring a large pot of salted water to a boil and cook the spaghetti, according to the package instructions, until al dente. Drain the pasta and return it to the pot.

In a small saucepan, heat 1/4 cup (60 ml) of olive oil over high heat. Add the sage leaves and cook, stirring gently, for 10 to 20 seconds or until golden, green, and crispy—mind that the leaves don't burn. Transfer the sage leaves to a plate, reserving the sage oil.

In a large, heavy pan, heat a generous splash of olive oil over medium-high heat and cook the squash, stirring occasionally, for 10 minutes or until tender. Add the orange juice and maple syrup, stir, and season to taste with salt and pepper. Cook for 3 minutes then fold in the spaghetti and sage oil and season to taste with salt and pepper. Divide among plates, sprinkle with the sage leaves, and serve immediately.

262

Serves 4 to 6

1¾ pounds (800 g) small waxy
potatoes
1¾ pounds (800 g) trimmed
cauliflower, cut into 1¼-inch
(3 cm) wedges
⅓ cup plus 1 tbsp (90 ml) olive oil
Flaky sea salt
Coarsely ground pepper
5 ounces (140 g) aromatic cheese
that melts well, such as Raclette,
Comté, or Gruyère,
coarsely grated

Cauliflower tends to be a little bland if blanched, but roasting it works wonders, lending a subtle smoky touch that fills this rather shy veggie with confidence. Cauliflower isn't much of a solo performer, and only really shows its true potential if you let it mingle with bold flavors. Spices, herbs, ginger, or an aromatic cheese like Raclette, are excellent co-stars.

Cauliflower and Potato Gratin with Raclette

Preheat the oven to 425°F (220°C).

In a large pot, cover the potatoes with salted water and bring to a boil. Cover the pot, reduce the heat, and simmer for 15 minutes. Drain the potatoes and quickly rinse with cold water then let them dry on a wire rack for at least 15 minutes.

Peel the potatoes, cut them in half lengthwise, and transfer to a baking sheet. Add the cauliflower, drizzle with the olive oil, and toss to coat. Season to taste with salt and pepper, sprinkle with the cheese, and roast for about 40 minutes or until golden brown and crispy. Serve for lunch or as a side dish for hearty roasts.

Tomatoes and tapenade have opposing yet complementary qualities. The red fruit is bright and fresh, while the black olive dip, refined with parsley, onion, capers, and mustard, brings a dark, hearty character to the table. Monkfish is flavorful enough to embrace them both.

Monkfish with Tapenade and Tomatoes

Serves 2 to 4

For the tapenade*

7 ounces (200 g) pitted
black olives, preferably Kalamata
1 large handful fresh
flat-leaf parsley leaves
½ medium red onion
2 tbsp capers, preferably
preserved in salt, rinsed and dried
4 anchovy fillets, rinsed and dried
½ cup (120 ml) olive oil
2 tbsp freshly squeezed
lemon juice
2 tsp Dijon mustard
Finely ground pepper

For the monkfish

2 medium tomatoes, thinly sliced
Fine sea salt
Finely ground pepper
1 (¾-pound / 340-g) monkfish fillet,
preferably a thick center piece
2 slices lemon
2 tbsp dry white wine
2 tbsp olive oil

Preheat the oven to 400°F (200°C).

For the tapenade, in a food processor or blender, purée the olives, parsley, onion, capers, anchovy, olive oil, lemon juice, and mustard until smooth. Season to taste with pepper. Transfer 3/4 of the dip to a medium bowl, cover with olive oil then plastic wrap, and keep in the fridge for up to 3 days to use for other recipes. Transfer the remaining tapenade to a small bowl.

For the monkfish, spread the tomatoes in a medium baking dish and season to taste with salt and pepper. Using 1/2 of the tapenade in the small bowl, rub the tapenade into the monkfish until evenly coated then place the fish on top of the tomatoes and cover with the lemon slices. Whisk together the white wine and olive oil and pour over the fish and tomatoes. Sprinkle the tomatoes with the remaining tapenade. Bake for 20 to 25 minutes, depending on the thickness of the monkfish, or until the fish is just cooked through. Cut the monkfish into thick slices and divide among plates. Arrange a few tomato slices next to the fish, sprinkle with the juices from the baking dish, and serve.

* You'll only need about 1/4 of the tapenade. You can use any remaining tapenade for chicken (recipe no. 138), pizza (recipe no. 182), and pasta (recipe no. 211).

It takes time to turn pan-fried potatoes into golden bites of perfect crispiness. You have to be patient and cook them in batches, flipping them over, one by one, but every turn is worth the effort. Sautéed onions and crispy bacon turn fried potatoes into a cozy dinner for a misty cold night, but adding artichokes and fennel is a throwback to summer.

Crispy Fried Potatoes with Fennel and Artichokes

Serves 2 to 3

Olive oil
1 ½ pounds (680 g) peeled waxy potatoes, boiled, drained, and dried
Flaky sea salt
Coarsely ground pepper
6 small artichoke hearts, preserved in oil, cut in half lengthwise
1 (6-ounce / 170-g) fennel bulb, quartered, cored, and very thinly sliced lengthwise, plus 1 small handful roughly chopped fennel fronds for the topping
1 ½ tbsp fennel seeds

Let the potatoes dry and cool completely on a wire rack then cut them into thick rounds.

In a large, heavy pan, heat a generous splash of olive oil over medium-high heat. Working in batches, add 1 layer of potatoes to the pan and fry, without moving, for a few minutes or until golden brown and crispy on the bottom. Carefully flip the potatoes over, 1 at a time, and fry for a few minutes or until golden brown and crispy on the other side. Season to taste with salt and pepper. Transfer to a large baking dish, cover, and keep warm. Repeat with the remaining potatoes, adding more oil if necessary.

In the same pan, heat a generous splash of olive oil over medium-high heat. Add the artichoke hearts and sear for 1 minute per side or until golden brown then transfer to a plate. Reduce the heat to medium, add a small splash of olive oil and the fennel bulb, and sauté, stirring occasionally, for about 2 minutes or until golden and al dente. Scrape the fennel to the sides of the pan, add a splash of olive oil and the fennel seeds, and toast, stirring constantly, for 15 seconds. Return the potatoes and artichoke hearts to the pan, stir gently, and cook for 2 minutes. Season to taste with salt and pepper, sprinkle with the fennel fronds, and serve immediately.

Sunken apples create fruity pockets in this dainty loaf cake, ensuring that all their fragrant juices remain tucked inside the spongy weekend treat. The brown sugar-cardamom topping infuses the cake with a lovely sweet aroma, and while you can certainly use ground cardamom, if you can get a hold of the spice's much tastier pods, bring out the mortar and pestle and grind them by hand instead.

Sunken Apple Cardamom Cake

Serves 4 to 6

For the topping

1 tbsp light brown sugar
Seeds from 2 cardamom pods, crushed with a mortar and pestle (or ½ tsp ground cardamom)

For the cake

2 medium, tart apples, peeled, cut in half, and cored
¾ cup plus 1 tbsp (180 g) unsalted butter, at room temperature
1 cup (200 g) granulated sugar
½ vanilla bean, split and scraped
2 tbsp freshly squeezed orange juice
3 large eggs
1⅓ cups plus 1 tbsp (180 g) all-purpose flour
2 tsp baking powder
⅛ tsp fine sea salt

Preheat the oven to 350°F / 180°C (preferably convection setting). Butter a 9 x 4-inch (23 x 10 cm) loaf pan.

For the topping, combine the light brown sugar and cardamom.

For the cake, score the apple halves lengthwise 5 times on the rounded outsides.

In the bowl of a stand mixer fitted with the paddle attachment, beat the butter, granulated sugar, and vanilla seeds until light and fluffy. Add the orange juice and mix until combined. Add the eggs, 1 at a time, incorporating each egg before adding the next one, and continue beating for 2 minutes or until thick and creamy. Whisk together the flour, baking powder, and salt, add to the butter mixture, and mix until combined. Spread the batter in the prepared loaf pan and place the apples, scored-side up, on top, gently pushing them into the dough. Sprinkle the apples with the cardamom sugar and bake for 45 to 50 minutes (slightly longer if using a conventional oven) or until golden brown and spongy. If you insert a skewer in the center of the cake, it should come out almost clean. Let the cake cool for at least 10 minutes then transfer it to a large platter for serving.

Zucchini, eggplant, bell pepper, and tomato soften slowly in this colorful gratin. The perfume of thyme, rosemary, and marjoram escaping the oven is tempting, while the taste is the pure essence of a vegetable garden.

Provençal Vegetable Garden Gratin with Fresh Herbs

Serves 3 to 4

½ pound (225 g) eggplant, very thinly sliced
3 medium tomatoes, very thinly sliced
½ pound (225 g) zucchini, very thinly sliced
¼ pound (110 g) red and yellow bell peppers, cut into thin strips
10 black olives, preferably Kalamata
2 tbsp fresh thyme leaves
1 small handful fresh rosemary needles
1 small handful fresh marjoram leaves
⅓ cup plus 1 tbsp (90 ml) homemade or quality store-bought vegetable broth
⅓ cup (75 ml) olive oil
Flaky sea salt
Coarsely ground pepper

Preheat the oven to 400°F (200°C). Brush a 12-inch (30 cm) baking dish (or a dish of roughly this size) with olive oil.

Arrange the eggplant slices in a slightly overlapping circle along the outside rim of the oiled baking dish. Arrange the tomatoes in a slightly overlapping circle inside the circle of eggplant and slightly overlapping it. Moving inwards, continue with a circle of zucchini then spread the bell peppers in the middle of the baking dish. Sprinkle with the olives, thyme, rosemary, and marjoram. Whisk together the broth and olive oil and drizzle over the vegetables. Season to taste with salt and pepper and roast for 50 to 55 minutes or until the vegetables are golden and tender.

Let the gratin sit for a few minutes before serving.

Adding chopped rosemary needles, with their heady woody notes, into the dough of this spongy focaccia balances the sweetness of the grapes. If you're lucky to catch one of the last warm evenings of the season, set up your dinner table outside, spread out your favorite cheese, prosciutto, and this warm focaccia, and fill the glasses with a full-bodied Tuscan red wine.

Grape and Rosemary Focaccia

Serves 3 to 6

3 ¾ cups plus 1 tbsp (500 g) all-purpose flour

2 ½ tbsp finely chopped fresh rosemary needles, plus 7 medium sprigs for the topping

1 (¼-ounce / 7-g) envelope fast-acting yeast

1 ½ tsp granulated sugar

1 tsp fine sea salt

1 cup plus 1 tbsp (255 ml) water, lukewarm

½ cup (120 ml) olive oil

50 seedless red grapes

Flaky sea salt

In the bowl of a stand mixer fitted with the dough hook attachment, combine the flour, $2^{1}/_{2}$ tablespoons of finely chopped rosemary, the yeast, sugar, and fine sea salt. Add the lukewarm water and $^{1}/_{4}$ cup (60 ml) of the olive oil and mix with the hook for 5 minutes or until well combined. If the dough is too sticky, add more flour. Transfer the dough to a work surface and continue kneading and punching it down with your hands for 4 minutes or until you have a smooth and elastic ball of dough. Place the dough back in the bowl, cover with a tea towel, and let rise in a warm place, or preferably in a 100°F (35°C) warm oven, for 60 minutes or until doubled in size.

Brush a baking sheet with olive oil. When the dough has doubled in size, punch it down, take it out of the bowl, and knead for 1 minute. On the prepared baking sheet, pull and stretch the dough into a 13 x 10-inch (33 x 25 cm) rectangle. Cover with a tea towel and let rise in a warm place for about 20 minutes or until puffy.

Preheat the oven to 425°F (220°C).

Using the bottom of a wooden spoon or your finger, push 6 rows of 7 holes into the dough. Arrange the grapes in between the holes, gently pushing them into the dough. Pour the remaining $^{1}/_{4}$ cup (60 ml) of olive oil over the dough and into the holes. Sprinkle with the rosemary sprigs and a little flaky sea salt and bake for 20 minutes or until golden and spongy. Serve warm or cold.

Serves 2 to 4

Olive oil
Unsalted butter
4 medium, thick coarse sausages
½ medium red onion
4 large dark plums, pitted
2 tbsp granulated sugar
1 tsp coriander seeds,
crushed with a mortar and pestle

I can eat sausage for breakfast, lunch, and dinner—I'm German, after all, and we just love it. When the last plums plop off the trees, I turn the purple fruits into a thick caramelized sauce, refine it with coriander seeds, and let this deliciousness drip off the golden brown skin of fried coarse sausage.

Coarse Sausage with Caramelized Coriander Plums

In a large, heavy pan, heat a generous splash of olive oil and 1 tablespoon of butter over medium-high heat. Add the sausages, reduce the heat to medium, and cook, turning occasionally, for about 10 minutes or until cooked through.

Roughly chop the red onion and cut the plums into quarters. In a small, heavy pan, heat 2 tablespoons of butter, the sugar, onion, and coriander seeds over medium-high heat, stirring constantly, until sizzling. Add the plums and cook, stirring occasionally, for about 5 minutes or until soft but chunky.

Divide the sausages among plates, scoop a large spoonful of the caramelized plums on top, and serve immediately.

Makes 4 small sandwiches

5 ounces (140 g) trimmed
spinach leaves
Fine sea salt
Finely ground pepper
Nutmeg, preferably freshly grated
2 ounces (60 g) aged chèvre,
thinly sliced
2 large eggs
3 tbsp whole milk
3 tbsp all-purpose flour
4 slices soft white bread
Unsalted butter
Coarsely ground pepper

Picture page 329, top left

During a busy day in London, I found a minute of peace, while sitting on a park bench and munching spinach and chèvre in an *in carrozza*–style sandwich. The sunlight twinkled as it fell through the dancing leaves of a large chestnut tree and I thought to myself, if I ever write another cookbook, this recipe has to be included. The classic Italian in carrozza is filled with mozzarella *(recipe no. 66)*.

Spinach and Chèvre in Carrozza

Bring a medium pot of salted water to a boil and blanch the spinach for about 1 ½ minutes or until tender. Transfer to a colander, drain, and quickly rinse with cold water. Leave the spinach in the colander to cool for 5 minutes then squeeze until quite dry and roughly chop. Transfer the spinach to a small bowl and season to taste with salt, finely ground pepper, and nutmeg. Reserve 4 slices of chèvre for the topping then crumble the rest over the spinach and mix until combined.

In a shallow bowl, whisk together the eggs and milk and season to taste with salt and finely ground pepper. Spread the flour on a flat plate. Divide the spinach mixture among 2 slices of bread, leaving a thin border around the edges. Top each sandwich with a second slice of bread and press together. Dip both sides of each sandwich in the flour then carefully dip each sandwich in the egg mixture. In a large, heavy pan, heat 1 tablespoon of butter over medium-high heat and cook the sandwiches for a few minutes or until golden brown and crispy. Reduce the heat and add ½ tablespoon of butter then flip the sandwiches over and cook for 1 to 2 minutes or until golden brown. Place 2 slices of chèvre on top of each sandwich and cut them in half diagonally. Sprinkle with a little coarsely ground pepper and enjoy.

Serves 2

9 ounces (250 g) seedless
red grapes, on the vine
2 medium sprigs fresh rosemary
Olive oil
Flaky sea salt
4 ounces (110 g) burrata
(or mozzarella di bufala)
4 very thin slices
prosciutto di Parma
(or prosciutto di San Daniele)

Picture opposite, top right

When I roast grapes in the oven, I make use of their concentrated, bold flavor. They're not just a fruity snack—the shriveled fruit deserves more attention than that. Smooth polenta is a humble and comforting option (*recipe no. 278*), but combine roasted grapes with creamy burrata and prosciutto di Parma, and you'll have a stunner of a dish that's guaranteed to impress everyone at your next dinner party.

Roasted Grapes with Burrata and Prosciutto

Preheat the oven to 425°F (220°C).

Place the grapes and rosemary in a medium baking dish. Drizzle with 2 tablespoons of olive oil, gently toss to coat, and season to taste with salt. Roast for 30 to 35 minutes or until the grapes are soft and a little shriveled.

Tear the burrata in half and transfer to a platter. Arrange the prosciutto and grapes around the cheese and sprinkle with the roasted rosemary needles. Drizzle with a little olive oil and serve immediately.

Serves 2 to 4

⅓ cup (75 ml) olive oil,
plus more to taste
2 tsp coriander seeds,
crushed with a mortar and pestle
1¼ pounds (560 g) peeled
sweet potatoes, cut into cubes
Fine sea salt

This is the easiest recipe for mashed potatoes. It's light, as it's made with olive oil instead of milk or cream. And above all, it's delicious. You can use white potatoes and add lemon zest (*recipe no. 163*), or try this pairing of sweet potatoes and coriander. It's a cozy lunch on its own, or makes a quick side dish for meat and seafood.

Mashed Sweet Potatoes with Coriander

In a small saucepan, heat the olive oil and coriander seeds over medium heat for about 2 minutes or until fragrant. Take the pan off the heat and set aside.

In a large pot, cover the sweet potatoes with salted water and bring to a boil. Reduce the heat, cover, and simmer for about 10 minutes or until tender. Drain the sweet potatoes and return them to the pot.

Using a plain butter knife, break the sweet potatoes into chunks, while gradually adding the coriander seeds, coriander oil, and a little salt until the desired taste and texture is achieved—the mash should be smooth but a little chunky. If the potatoes are dry, add a little more olive oil. Season to taste with salt and serve warm or cold.

269

270

272

273

I'm a forest girl. I've always loved the sea, but I grew up in the countryside, so the fish from my region comes from lakes and rivers. Freshwater fish like trout tastes strong and earthy, and isn't as subtle as the Mediterranean catch I enjoy during our summers in Malta. Trout has a lot of character and requires its fellow ingredients to do more than just show up. Prosciutto and black olives are up to the challenge and a staple in my kitchen, but the tasty trio of artichokes, parsley, and juniper can't be ignored either.

Trout al Cartoccio with Artichokes, Parsley, and Juniper Berries

Serves 1 to 2

Olive oil
1 (12- to 14-ounce / 340- to 400-g)
whole trout, scaled, gutted,
and cleaned
Fine sea salt
Finely ground pepper
1 small bunch fresh
flat-leaf parsley, plus 1 small sprig
2 bay leaves
3 small artichoke hearts,
preserved in oil,
cut in half lengthwise
6 green olives
12 juniper berries,
crushed with a mortar and pestle
⅓ cup (75 ml) dry white wine
Parchment paper

Picture page 329, bottom left

Preheat the oven to 350°F (180°C).

Cut 2 pieces of parchment paper large enough to wrap the fish like a package and lay them on top of each other. Brush the top sheet with olive oil. Coat the trout with a little olive oil and season to taste with salt and pepper, inside and out. Stuff the bunch of parsley, along with 1 bay leaf, inside the trout. Place the trout in the middle of the parchment and tuck the remaining bay leaf underneath it. Arrange the artichoke hearts, olives, and juniper berries around and the parsley sprig on top of the trout then transfer the package to a baking dish. Fold the sides over and twist both ends of the parchment but leave a small opening on top of the fish. Pour the white wine through the opening onto the fish then close the parchment package and fold the top twice so it's well sealed. Bake for 20 minutes or until you can lift the fillets off the bones with a fork; mind that you don't overcook it.

Divide the trout into 2 fillets and serve with the artichoke hearts and olives. Drizzle with the juices from the parchment package, season to taste with salt and pepper, and serve immediately.

Buckwheat and ground hazelnuts replace wheat flour in this recipe and it makes for a cake that's less dainty and sweet. So, if you're up for a more rustic, earthy Sunday coffee table treat, take out the plums, chocolate, cinnamon, and cardamom, and fire up the oven.

Buckwheat and Hazelnut Cake with Plums, Chocolate, and Spices

Serves 8 to 12

2 cups (225 g) ground hazelnuts (or skin-on almonds)
1 ½ cups (225 g) buckwheat flour
4 ounces (110 g) bittersweet chocolate, finely chopped
1 ½ tbsp baking powder
1 ½ tbsp ground cinnamon, plus ¼ tsp for the topping
2 tsp ground cardamom
6 large eggs, separated
¼ tsp fine sea salt
1 cup plus 2 tbsp (250 g) unsalted butter, at room temperature
1 cup (200 g) granulated sugar, plus 2 tbsp for the topping
1 ⅓ pounds (600 g) pitted dark plums, cut into quarters

Picture page 329, bottom right

Preheat the oven to 350°F / 180°C (preferably convection setting). Butter a 10-inch (25 cm) springform pan.

In a medium bowl, combine the ground hazelnuts, buckwheat flour, chocolate, baking powder, 1 1/2 tablespoons of cinnamon, and the cardamom.

In the bowl of a stand mixer fitted with the whisk attachment, whisk the egg whites and salt for a few minutes or until stiff then transfer to a large bowl.

In the bowl of a stand mixer fitted with the paddle attachment, beat the butter and 1 cup (200 g) of sugar for a few minutes or until light and fluffy. Add the egg yolks, 1 at a time, incorporating each yolk before adding the next one, and continue beating for 2 minutes or until creamy. Using a wooden spoon, fold 1/3 of the egg whites into the butter mixture, followed by 1/3 of the hazelnut mixture. Repeat with the remaining egg whites and hazelnut mixture, gently mixing until combined. Spread the batter in the prepared pan and arrange the plums, standing, in circles on top, gently pushing them into the batter. Whisk together the remaining 2 tablespoons of sugar and 1/4 teaspoon of cinnamon and sprinkle over the cake. Bake for 45 to 50 minutes (slightly longer if using a conventional oven) or until golden brown and spongy. If you insert a skewer in the center of the cake, it should come out almost clean. Let the cake cool for at least 10 minutes before taking it out of the pan. Enjoy plain or with whipped cream on the side.

October

When a Mediterranean mama bakes lasagna, she always takes out the largest baking dish she can find on her shelves. This pasta casserole makes wonderful leftovers the next day, or you can cut it into handy portions for freezing. If you're up for switching up classic Bolognese, add earthy parsnip to the winey sauce.

Lasagna Bolognese with Parsnip

Serves 4 to 6

For the Bolognese sauce
Olive oil
1 medium onion, diced
6 ounces (170 g) peeled parsnip, cut in half lengthwise and thinly sliced
1 medium carrot, peeled and diced
1 large clove garlic, crushed
14 ounces (400 g) ground beef
2 tbsp tomato paste
2 cups (480 ml) full-bodied red wine, plus more as needed
14 ounces (400 g) canned whole peeled tomatoes, chopped
6 small sprigs fresh thyme
1 medium sprig fresh rosemary
1 bay leaf
Fine sea salt
Finely ground pepper

For the béchamel sauce
3 cups (720 ml) whole milk
1 large bay leaf
Nutmeg, preferably freshly grated
Fine sea salt
Finely ground pepper
2 tbsp (30 g) unsalted butter
¼ cup (30 g) all-purpose flour

For the lasagna
About 9 ounces (250 g) no-boil lasagna noodles
6 ounces (170 g) Parmesan (or pecorino), coarsely grated

Preheat the oven to 350°F (180°C). Butter a 10 x 8-inch (25 x 20 cm) baking dish (or a dish of roughly this size).

For the Bolognese sauce, in a large, heavy pan, heat a generous splash of olive oil over medium-high heat. Add the onion, parsnip, carrot, and garlic and sauté, stirring occasionally, for 4 minutes. Add the beef and a little more oil and cook, stirring to break up the meat, for a few minutes or until no more liquid comes out and the meat is browned. Add the tomato paste and cook, stirring, for 1 minute. Add the red wine and deglaze the pan, using a spatula to scrape any bits and pieces off the bottom, and let cook for 2 minutes. Add the tomatoes, thyme, rosemary, and bay leaf, season to taste with salt and pepper, and bring to a boil. Reduce the heat and simmer very gently, stirring occasionally and adding more wine if necessary, for 1 hour or until thick but still loose. Remove and discard the herbs then season to taste with salt and pepper.

For the béchamel sauce, combine the milk, bay leaf, ¼ teaspoon of nutmeg, ¼ teaspoon of salt, and a pinch of pepper in a medium saucepan and bring to a boil. Immediately take the pan off the heat, remove and discard the bay leaf, and set aside. To make the roux for the béchamel, melt the butter in a separate medium saucepan over medium-high heat and as soon as it's sizzling hot, whisk in the flour. Slowly pour the hot milk mixture into the roux and whisk until smooth. Simmer on low, whisking occasionally, for 2 to 3 minutes or until the sauce starts to thicken. Season to taste with nutmeg, salt, and pepper.

Reserve 3 tablespoons of the Bolognese and set aside. Arrange a layer of lasagna noodles on the bottom of the baking dish and spread with 1/3 of the Bolognese then sprinkle with ¼ of the béchamel and ¼ of the Parmesan. Repeat to make 2 more layers. Cover with a final layer of pasta then sprinkle with the remaining béchamel, Parmesan, and the reserved Bolognese. Bake for 35 to 45 minutes, depending on the lasagna package instructions, or until the pasta is al dente. To brown the cheese a little, you can switch on the broiler for the last 1 to 2 minutes. Let the lasagna sit for 5 to 10 minutes before serving.

Here's a five-minute lunch solution that let's you indulge in a fruity reminiscence of summer. Ripe figs, rapidly seared in the hottest pan until charred and smoky then deglazed with a little balsamic vinegar, make for a fabulous and scrumptious sweet bite. Place them gracefully atop a slice of baguette spread with candied date chèvre and you'll have an excellent midday snack.

Seared Balsamic Figs with Whipped Date Chèvre

Serves 2

5 ounces (140 g) soft, mild chèvre
Olive oil
2 large juicy dates, pitted
and roughly chopped
Fine sea salt
Finely ground pepper
4 fresh figs, cut in half
2 tsp balsamic vinegar
4 thick slices baguette (optional)
10 small fresh basil leaves

Whisk together the chèvre, 1 tablespoon of olive oil, and the dates, season to taste with salt and pepper, and transfer to a small bowl.

In a small, heavy pan, heat a splash of olive oil over high heat. Add the figs and sear for about 1 minute per side or until golden brown and partially charred but not burnt. Add the vinegar and gently stir then take the pan off the heat.

Serve the figs with the date chèvre or spread the whipped chèvre on the baguette slices and arrange the figs on top. Sprinkle with basil and a little pepper and enjoy.

The smell of mushrooms, of dark moist soil and falling leaves, is the essence of autumn. To treat their earthy taste and delicate texture with respect, mushrooms should only be cooked briefly over high heat. Keep them firm and pair with a thyme and Gruyère omelet—piled on a sandwich, it's a marvelous breakfast or lunch.

Thyme and Gruyère Omelet Sandwich with Seared Mushrooms

Makes 2 sandwiches

3 large eggs
¼ cup (60 ml) heavy cream
3 tbsp finely grated Gruyère
1 ½ tsp fresh thyme leaves
Nutmeg, preferably freshly grated
Fine sea salt
Finely ground pepper
Unsalted butter,
to cook the omelet
Olive oil
2 small handfuls small chanterelles
(or enoki mushrooms)
2 large king oyster mushrooms,
cut in half lengthwise
2 rustic white buns, cut in half

In a medium bowl, whisk together the eggs, heavy cream, cheese, and thyme and season to taste with nutmeg, salt, and pepper. In a small cast-iron pan or nonstick skillet, heat 1 teaspoon of butter over medium-high heat. Pour the egg mixture into the pan and stir 3 to 4 times, scraping the egg mixture off the bottom of the pan. Mind to not scramble the eggs and to just fluff them up a bit; reduce the heat if they brown too quickly. When the bottom side is golden, flip the omelet and cook the other side for 1 to 2 minutes or until golden and just set.

In a medium, heavy pan, heat a splash of olive oil over medium-high heat. Sear the chanterelles, stirring, for 1 minute or until golden and al dente, transfer to a plate, then add a little oil and cook the king oyster mushrooms for 45 to 60 seconds per side or until golden and al dente; transfer next to the chanterelles and season to taste with salt and pepper.

Cut the omelet in half and place on the bottom halves of the buns then arrange the mushrooms on top and place a top on each bun. Enjoy.

277

Serves 2

10 ounces (280 g) peeled parsnips
2 large clementines (or tangerines)
1 large blood orange
2 medium sprigs fresh thyme
¼ cup (60 ml) olive oil, plus more for serving
Flaky sea salt
Coarsely ground pepper

Picture opposite, top left

Parsnip and citrus may sound like an unusual combination, but they complement each other beautifully in both taste and texture.

Roasted Parsnips with Clementine, Blood Orange, and Thyme

Preheat the oven to 400°F (200°C). Cut the parsnips lengthwise into thin wedges. Peel the clementines and orange, removing the skin and white pith, and cut into thick slices.

In a medium baking dish, drizzle the parsnips and thyme with the olive oil, toss to combine, and season to taste with salt and pepper. Roast, flipping the parsnips twice, for about 35 minutes or until golden brown and tender.

Spread the clementine and blood orange slices on a large platter. Arrange the parsnips and thyme on top, drizzle with a little olive oil, and season to taste with salt and pepper. Serve warm or as a cold salad.

278

Serves 2

For the grapes
⅔ pound (300 g) seedless red grapes, on the vine
2 medium sprigs fresh rosemary
2 tbsp olive oil
Flaky sea salt

For the polenta
1 cup (240 ml) whole milk
1 cup (240 ml) water, plus more as needed
1 tsp fine sea salt
2 tbsp olive oil, plus more for serving
¾ cup (120 g) fine polenta
Coarsely ground pepper

If you roast double the amount of grapes for this recipe, you can use them as a sticky topping for creamy polenta first and then snip them over a luscious antipasto of burrata and prosciutto (*recipe no. 270*) the next day.

Polenta with Roasted Grapes and Rosemary

Preheat the oven to 425°F (220°C).

For the grapes, in a medium baking dish, drizzle the grapes and rosemary with the olive oil, gently toss to coat, and season to taste with flaky sea salt. Roast for 30 to 35 minutes or until the grapes are soft and a little shriveled.

While the grapes are roasting, make the polenta: Bring the milk, water, and fine sea salt to a boil in a medium saucepan. Take the pan off the heat, add the olive oil and polenta, and whisk until combined. Place the saucepan over the lowest heat setting and cook the polenta like a risotto, stirring occasionally and adding a little more water whenever the polenta starts to thicken, for 10 minutes or until smooth and creamy. Season to taste with fine sea salt and divide among bowls. Arrange the grapes (on the vine) and a few roasted rosemary needles on top, sprinkle with pepper, drizzle with a little olive oil, and serve.

277

279

280

281

Thanks to my partner's American roots, there's always a pumpkin pie on our German Thanksgiving table. I fell for it right from the start, though I thought the sweet nutmeg-scented squash filling could use a little extravagance. I've tried meringue and boozy toppings, but golden caramel blended with fragrant coriander seeds is my favorite. Using homemade squash purée boosts the pleasure of this pie tremendously.

Pumpkin Pie with Coriander Caramel

Serves 8 to 12

For the pastry
2 cups (260 g) all-purpose flour
1½ tbsp granulated sugar
¼ tsp fine sea salt
½ cup plus 1 tbsp (130 g) unsalted butter, cold
2 tbsp water, cold

For the filling
18 ounces (500 g) seeded and peeled squash, preferably butternut or Hokkaido, cut into 1-inch (2.5 cm) cubes (or 14 ounces / 400 g canned pumpkin purée)
1 cup (240 ml) whole milk, lukewarm
2 large eggs
⅓ cup (75 g) light brown sugar
1 ¼ tsp freshly grated ginger
1 tsp ground cinnamon
¼ tsp ground mace (or nutmeg)
¼ tsp fine sea salt
⅛ tsp ground cloves
Parchment paper

For the coriander caramel
½ cup (100 g) granulated sugar
¼ cup (60 ml) water
1 tsp coriander seeds, lightly crushed with a mortar and pestle
⅓ cup plus 1 tbsp (90 ml) heavy cream

Picture page 337, top right

Preheat the oven to 400°F (200°C).

For the pastry, combine the flour, granulated sugar, and salt in the bowl of a stand mixer fitted with the dough hook attachment. Add the butter and use a knife to cut it into the flour until there are just small pieces left. Quickly rub the butter into the flour with your fingers until combined. Add the water and mix with the hook until crumbly. Form the dough into a thick disc, wrap it in plastic wrap, and freeze for 10 minutes.

For the filling, if using fresh squash, spread the cubes in a large baking dish and cover the bottom with a little water. Soak a large piece of parchment paper with water, squeeze it, and then use to cover the squash. Roast for 20 to 30 minutes or until soft then purée in a food processor or blender until smooth. Measure 14 ounces (400 g) and set aside; use any remaining squash for other recipes.

In a medium bowl, whisk together the squash purée, the lukewarm milk, the eggs, light brown sugar, ginger, cinnamon, mace, salt, and cloves.

On a work surface, place the dough between 2 sheets of plastic wrap and use a rolling pin to roll out into a disc, large enough to line the bottom and sides of a 12-inch (30 cm) quiche dish. Fit the dough into the quiche dish, pushing it into the dish, especially along the edges. Let the dough hang over the rim a little or trim with a knife. Use a fork to prick the dough all over. Bake for about 10 minutes or until golden. If the dough bubbles up, push it down with a fork. Take the quiche dish out of the oven and increase the heat to 425°F (220°C). Pour the squash filling on top of the pre-baked pastry and bake for 10 minutes then reduce the heat to 350°F (180°C) and bake for another 15 to 20 minutes or until the pie is golden and just set. Remove from the oven and let cool completely.

For the coriander caramel, bring the granulated sugar and water to a boil in a medium, heavy pan and cook, without stirring, until golden brown and caramelized. Take the pan off the heat and add the coriander seeds then slowly whisk in the heavy cream, stirring until smooth. Bring the caramel to a boil and cook, whisking constantly, for 1 to 2 minutes or until it reaches the desired texture. Let it cool for 2 minutes then sprinkle the cooled pie with the caramel and serve immediately.

Roasted pork is the kind of hearty dish you want to pull out of the oven when the days get colder and shorter. Crunchy, golden crackling and tender, spice-infused meat are the core of this German classic. Hard cider, apples, and sweet potatoes make it a little fruity and highlight the bounty of autumn's produce.

Slow-Roasted Pork Shoulder with Cider, Apples, and Spices

Serves 4 to 6

1 ¼ tbsp fine sea salt
30 whole cloves, finely crushed
with a mortar and pestle,
plus 8 cloves for the sauce
20 allspice berries, finely crushed
with a mortar and pestle
7 to 8 pounds (3.2 to 3.6 kg)
bone-in pork shoulder,
with the fat scored*
2 cups (480 ml) hard apple cider
6 medium red onions,
cut into quarters
2 large, tart baking apples, peeled,
cored, and each cut into 8 wedges
1 large sweet potato, peeled
and cut into chunky cubes
Coarsely ground pepper

Picture page 337, bottom left

Preheat the oven to 400°F (200°C).

Combine the salt, crushed whole cloves, and allspice berries, sprinkle onto the scored surface of the pork, and rub into the scores with your fingers.

Place the meat, scored-side up, in a large, deep roasting pan and roast for 30 minutes then reduce the heat to 325°F (160°C) and roast for 1 hour. Take the pan out of the oven then pour the cider over the meat, arrange the onions, apples, sweet potato, and the remaining 8 whole cloves around the meat, and sprinkle with pepper. Roast, spooning the juices from the pan over the meat every hour, for another 2 hours and 45 minutes or until the meat is tender. Turn on the broiler for the last 1 to 2 minutes or until most of the crackling is crispy, but mind that it doesn't burn. Remove the pork from the oven, cover with aluminum foil, and let it sit for about 10 minutes.

Cut the pork into 1/2-inch (1.25 cm) slices then divide the pork, fruit, and vegetables among plates. Sprinkle with the juices from the roasting pan and serve.

Ask the butcher to do this or use a very sharp knife to create a diamond pattern.

Beluga lentils look like beautiful tiny black pearls, have a nutty-earthy flavor, and cook quickly, all qualities that never cease to inspire me. Seared red cherry tomatoes and fir-green cilantro-pistachio pesto shine vibrantly on top of the dark legumes and turn them into a satisfying lunch.

Beluga Lentils with Tomatoes and Cilantro-Pistachio Pesto

Serves 3 to 4

For the lentils

1 ¼ cups (280 g) lentils,
preferably beluga
(no soaking required)
1 small bunch fresh thyme
1 bay leaf
Olive oil
Fine sea salt
Finely ground pepper

For the pesto

1 ounce (30 g) salted pistachios
1 ounce (30 g) fresh cilantro leaves
3 tbsp finely grated Parmesan
⅓ cup (75 ml) olive oil
Fine sea salt

For the tomatoes

Olive oil
16 cherry tomatoes

Picture page 337, bottom right

Place the lentils in a medium saucepan with plenty of (unsalted) water, add the thyme and bay leaf, and bring to a boil. Reduce the heat and simmer, adding more water if necessary, for about 20 minutes or until al dente (or follow the package instructions). There should be a little cooking liquid left when the lentils are done. Remove and discard the herbs, add a splash of olive oil, and season to taste with salt and pepper.

For the pesto, purée the pistachios, cilantro, Parmesan, and olive oil in a food processor or blender until smooth and season to taste with salt.

For the tomatoes, heat a small splash of olive oil in a small, heavy pan over high heat. Add the tomatoes and sear, stirring occasionally, for $1\frac{1}{2}$ to 2 minutes or until soft but still holding their shape and partially charred.

Divide the lentils and a little of their cooking liquid among bowls, arrange the tomatoes on top, and sprinkle with the pesto; serve immediately.

Heaven and earth—*Himmel und Erde*—is a traditional dish that's popular in Western Germany, where I grew up. It consists of mashed potatoes with apple compote and gets its name from the fact that one ingredient grows under the earth's surface, while the other grows into the sky. I use this frugal dish as the inspiration for a cozy soup made of parsnip and pear—the ingredients differ, but the sentiment is the same.

Parsnip and Pear Soup with Mascarpone

Serves 2 to 4

Olive oil
1 medium onion, chopped
⅔ pound (300 g) peeled parsnip,
roughly chopped
7 ounces (200 g) peeled
and cored firm pear,
roughly chopped
3 large cloves garlic,
cut into quarters
3⅓ cups (800 ml) homemade
or quality store-bought
vegetable broth, hot
1 bay leaf
1 small bunch fresh thyme
1 sprig fresh rosemary
Nutmeg, preferably freshly grated
Fine sea salt
Finely ground pepper
¼ cup (60 ml) heavy cream
4 heaping tsp mascarpone,
for the topping
1 to 2 tbsp fresh marjoram leaves,
for the topping

In a large pot, heat a splash of olive oil over medium heat and sauté the onion for 5 minutes or until soft and golden. Add the parsnip, pear, and garlic and sauté, stirring constantly, for 1 minute. Add the hot broth, bay leaf, thyme, and rosemary and season to taste with nutmeg, salt, and pepper. Bring to a boil then reduce the heat and simmer for 25 minutes or until the parsnip is tender. Remove and discard the herbs. In a food processor or blender, or with an immersion blender, purée the soup until smooth. Whisk in 2 tablespoons of the heavy cream, adding more if necessary, then season to taste with salt and pepper. Divide the soup among bowls then top with a spoonful of mascarpone and a little marjoram and pepper and serve immediately.

282
week 41 / tuesday

Velvety smooth winter squash is packed with flavor and practically destined to be turned into pesto. You can use canned pumpkin purée, but homemade always tastes better. Refine it with orange and thyme to add some excitement. I'm sure stirring it into warm spaghetti would be scrumptious, but I prefer to spread this golden pesto on a sandwich and finish it off with juicy dates and aged Sainte-Maure de Touraine chèvre.

Squash-Pesto Sandwich with Dates and Chèvre

Makes 2 to 3 sandwiches

For the pumpkin pesto

¾ pound (340 g) seeded
and peeled squash, preferably
butternut or Hokkaido,
cut into 1-inch (2.5 cm) cubes
2 tbsp pumpkin seeds
2 tbsp olive oil
¼ to ½ tsp freshly grated
orange zest
1 tbsp freshly squeezed
orange juice
1½ tsp fresh thyme leaves
Fine sea salt
Parchment paper

For the sandwiches

2 to 3 spelt or rye buns, cut in half
3 ounces (85 g) aged chèvre,
preferably Sainte-Maure
de Touraine, thinly sliced
4 large juicy dates, pitted
and cut into quarters
1 tbsp pumpkin seeds
1 tsp fresh thyme leaves
Coarsely ground pepper

Preheat the oven to 400°F (200°C).

Place the squash in a medium baking dish and cover the bottom of the dish with a little water. Soak a large piece of parchment paper with water, squeeze it, and then use to cover the squash. Roast for 20 to 30 minutes or until soft then transfer to a food processor or blender. Add the pumpkin seeds, olive oil, 1/4 teaspoon of the orange zest, the orange juice, and thyme and purée until smooth. Season to taste with additional orange zest and salt and transfer to a small bowl.

Spread the pumpkin pesto generously on the bottom half of each bun, top with the chèvre, and sprinkle with the dates, pumpkin seeds, thyme, and pepper. Place a top on each bun and enjoy.

Serves 2 to 4

¾ pound (340 g) trimmed
green beans
Olive oil
3 ounces (85 g) thick-cut bacon,
cut into very small cubes
Unsalted butter, to cook the apple
1 large, tart baking apple,
cored and cut into thin wedges
1 tsp honey
1 tbsp white balsamic vinegar
2 tbsp fresh thyme leaves
Fine sea salt
Finely ground pepper

Green beans and apple wedges tossed in bacon fat make a comforting meal. You can add a fried egg or coarse herb sausage if your appetite asks for more.

Green Beans
with Bacon, Apple, and Thyme

Bring a large pot of salted water to a boil and blanch the green beans for 4 to 5 minutes or until al dente. Drain and quickly rinse with cold water.

In a medium, heavy pan, heat a small splash of olive oil over medium-high heat and cook the bacon, stirring occasionally, for about 4 minutes or until golden brown and crispy. Transfer the bacon to a plate, but leave the fat in the pan. Add 1 tablespoon of butter and the apple to the pan and sear, turning once, over medium-high heat for 1½ minutes per side or until golden brown. Add the honey, green beans, and bacon, stir, and then add the vinegar and 1 tablespoon of the thyme and cook for 1 minute. Season to taste with salt and pepper, sprinkle with additional thyme, and serve warm.

Serves 2 to 3

1 (3⅓-pound / 1.5-kg)
whole chicken
Olive oil
Flaky sea salt
Coarsely ground pepper
1 small bunch fresh thyme
1¼ pounds (560 g) seedless
grapes on the vine
10 large cloves garlic, unpeeled
2 bay leaves
⅔ cup (150 ml) fruity white wine
2 tbsp (30 g) unsalted butter,
cut into cubes

Ovenproof cotton string

Roasted chicken with grapes and white wine is a winner. At first, I was uncertain if adding a generous amount of garlic would conflict with the fruits' mellow juices, but the very first bite proved there was no need to worry—the dish is balanced and the bird tastes divine.

Roasted Chicken
with Grapes and Garlic

Preheat the oven to 375°F (190°C).

Place the chicken in a medium baking dish, rub the skin with a little olive oil, and season to taste with salt and pepper inside and out. Fill the chicken with 1/3 of the thyme then tie the legs together with ovenproof cotton string. Arrange the grapes, garlic, the remaining thyme, and the bay leaves around the chicken. Whisk the white wine with 2 tablespoons of olive oil and pour over the chicken and grapes. Place the butter on top of the chicken then roast, spooning the juices from the pan over the chicken every 15 minutes, for about 1 hour and 15 minutes or until the juices run clear when you prick the thickest part of a thigh with a skewer. Turn on the broiler for the last 1 to 2 minutes or until the skin is golden and starts sizzling. Take the chicken out of the oven and let it rest for a few minutes.

Carve the chicken and divide the meat, grapes, and garlic among plates. Drizzle with the juices from the baking dish and serve immediately.

The first time I saw a babka in a cookbook I was mesmerized by its beauty. Lusciously filled and artistically twisted and braided, the yeast loaf looks like an edible piece of art. Dark chocolate is a very common filling, but you should try poppy seeds and white chocolate (recipe no. 62), or lemony cream cheese and blueberries. And if you start preparing the dough on a Saturday, you can enjoy your own piece of art for brunch on Sunday morning.

Blueberry and Lemon Cream Cheese Babka

Serves 6

For the dough

2 cups plus 2 tbsp (275 g)
all-purpose flour
¼ cup (50 g) granulated sugar
1 ½ tsp fast-acting yeast
¼ tsp fine sea salt
¼ cup (60 ml) whole milk,
lukewarm
1 large egg
1 large egg yolk
⅓ cup (75 g) unsalted butter,
at room temperature,
cut into cubes
Sunflower oil, to grease the bowl

For the filling

2 large egg whites,
plus 1 large egg yolk
⅛ tsp fine sea salt
½ pound (225 g) cream cheese,
drained
2 tbsp granulated sugar
½ vanilla pod, split and scraped
2 tsp freshly grated lemon zest
5 ounces (140 g) fresh blueberries

For the glaze

1 large egg yolk
1 tbsp whole milk

For the dough, whisk together the flour, sugar, yeast, and salt in the bowl of a stand mixer fitted with the dough hook attachment. Whisk together the lukewarm milk, egg, and egg yolk then add the milk mixture and butter to the flour mixture and mix with the hook for 5 minutes or until smooth and well combined. Transfer to a work surface and continue kneading with your hands for 5 minutes or until you have a soft and silky ball of dough. If the dough is too sticky, add a little more flour, but mind that it stays soft. Brush a large bowl with a little sunflower oil, add the dough, cover with plastic wrap, and leave it in the fridge overnight, or for about 8 hours (don't be alarmed, the dough will only rise a little). Take the dough out of the fridge and let it sit at room temperature for about 60 minutes.

For the filling, in the bowl of a stand mixer fitted with the whisk attachment, whisk the egg whites and salt until stiff. In a large bowl, whisk together the cream cheese, egg yolk, sugar, vanilla seeds, and lemon zest until smooth. Gently fold in the egg whites.

Butter a 9 x 4-inch (23 x 10 cm) loaf pan and line the bottom with a piece of parchment paper. Punch the dough down, take it out of the bowl, and knead for 30 seconds. Lightly flour a work surface and roll the dough with a rolling pin into a 16 x 11-inch (40 x 28 cm) rectangle. Spread the filling on top of the dough, leaving a 3/4-inch (2 cm) border, then sprinkle with the blueberries. Starting from one long side, carefully roll the dough up into a log. Use your fingers to squeeze the overlapping dough. Gently stretch and bend the log and close it to form a ring, tucking one end into the other and pushing the ends together to seal the filling inside. Gently push the 2 sides of the ring together to form an oval-like shape. Starting from the middle, carefully twist the roll about 3 times on one side and 3 times on the other side to form a thick double spiral that looks like a screw (don't worry if it tears a bit). Quickly transfer the babka to the prepared pan. Cover with a tea towel and let rise in a warm place for 60 to 90 minutes or until puffy.

Preheat the oven to 375°F (190°C).

Whisk together the egg yolk and milk and brush on top of the babka. Bake for 35 minutes then cover loosely with aluminum foil and bake for another 20 to 30 minutes or until golden brown and spongy. If you insert a skewer in the center of the babka, it should come out almost clean. Let the babka cool for at least 20 minutes before removing from the pan. Enjoy warm or cold.

There's a reason why there are so many quiche recipes in this book. It was one of the first dishes that I learned to bake and eventually master, as I moved out into the world during my university years. Quiche has been a reliable companion throughout my life and it's helped me celebrate the ups and overcome the downs. It's the best comfort food I know, plus adaptable to moods and seasons. At the peak of autumn, squash, Taleggio, and sage are an unbeatable combination.

Squash and Taleggio Quiche with Crispy Sage

Serves 4 to 8

For the filling

1 ⅓ pounds (600 g) seeded squash, preferably peeled butternut or Hokkaido with skin, cut into 1-inch (2.5 cm) wedges

1 tbsp olive oil

Flaky sea salt

Finely ground pepper

3 large eggs

¾ cup (175 g) sour cream (or crème fraîche)

½ cup (120 ml) heavy cream

1 tsp fine sea salt

Nutmeg, preferably freshly grated

5 ounces (140 g) mild, sweet cheese that melts well, such as Taleggio, fontina, or Robiola, diced

3 tbsp (45 g) unsalted butter

50 large fresh sage leaves

For the pastry

2 cups (260 g) all-purpose flour

1 tsp fine sea salt

½ cup plus 1 tbsp (130 g) unsalted butter, cold

1 large egg

Picture book cover

Preheat the oven to 400°F (200°C).

For the filling, spread the squash in a large baking dish, drizzle with the olive oil, and toss to combine. Season to taste with flaky sea salt and pepper and roast for 15 minutes then flip the squash and continue roasting for 10 to 15 minutes or until golden and tender; set aside.

For the pastry, combine the flour and fine sea salt in the bowl of a stand mixer fitted with the dough hook attachment. Add the butter and use a knife to cut it into the flour until there are just small pieces left. Quickly rub the butter into the flour with your fingers until combined. Add the egg and mix with the hook until crumbly. Form the dough into a thick disc, wrap it in plastic wrap, and freeze for 10 minutes.

On a work surface, place the dough between 2 sheets of plastic wrap and use a rolling pin to roll out into a disc, large enough to line the bottom and sides of a 12-inch (30 cm) quiche dish. Fit the dough into the quiche dish, pushing it into the dish, especially along the edges. Let the dough hang over the rim a little or trim with a knife. Use a fork to prick the dough all over. Bake for 15 minutes or until golden. If the dough bubbles up, push it down with a fork. Take the quiche dish out of the oven and reduce the heat to 350°F (180°C).

In a medium bowl, whisk together the eggs, sour cream, heavy cream, and fine sea salt and season to taste with pepper and a generous amount of nutmeg.

Arrange the squash in a circle on top of the pre-baked pastry and sprinkle with the cheese. Pour the egg mixture over the squash and bake for 45 to 55 minutes or until golden brown and firm. Take the quiche out of the oven and let it sit at least 10 minutes.

In a large saucepan, heat the butter over medium-high heat, add the sage, and cook, stirring gently, for 20 to 30 seconds or until golden, green, and crispy—mind that the leaves don't burn. Spread the sage on top of the quiche, sprinkle with a little pepper, and serve warm or cold.

Sicilian arancini are little saffron-scented rice balls that shine bright like a Mediterranean sunset. Stuffed with mozzarella, then breaded and fried, they aren't the lightest of all treats, but if you serve them on top of a crisp fennel, arugula, and orange salad, no one will notice.

Sicilian Saffron-Mozzarella Arancini with Fennel and Orange Salad

Serves 4 to 6

For the arancini

½ cup (120 ml) white wine
⅛ tsp saffron threads
Olive oil
1 medium onion, finely chopped
7 ounces (200 g) risotto rice
About 2 ½ cups (600 ml) home-made or quality store-bought vegetable broth
Fine sea salt
Finely ground pepper
2 large egg yolks, plus 3 large eggs, beaten
1 ounce (30 g) Parmesan, finely grated
7 cups (1.6 liters) sunflower oil
About 1 cup (130 g) all-purpose flour
About 1 ½ cups (220 g) dry breadcrumbs
3 ounces (85 g) mozzarella, cut into small cubes

For the salad

2 medium fennel bulbs
2 large oranges
1 large handful fresh arugula
3 tbsp olive oil
1 tbsp balsamic vinegar
1 tbsp white balsamic vinegar
Fine sea salt
Finely ground pepper

For the arancini, whisk together the white wine and saffron. In a large pot, heat a splash of olive oil over medium heat and sauté the onion, stirring occasionally, for 3 minutes or until golden. Add the rice and cook, stirring constantly, for 1 minute. Add the saffron-white wine mixture and a ladle of the broth to cover the rice then cook, stirring occasionally and adding more broth when necessary to keep the rice covered, until the broth is fully absorbed and the rice is al dente. The texture should be thicker than risotto, not soupy; only add an additional small ladle of water, if the rice is undercooked. Take the pan off the heat then season to taste with salt and pepper, cover, and let sit for 2 minutes. Remove the lid then add the 2 egg yolks and the Parmesan, mix until combined, and let cool completely.

In a large, heavy pot, heat the sunflower oil over medium-high heat.

Place the flour, the 3 beaten eggs, and the breadcrumbs in 3 separate deep, wide plates. Divide the mozzarella into 16 portions.

Wet your fingers and scoop a heaping tablespoon of the rice mixture into your hand. Form it into a thick disc and place 1 portion of mozzarella cubes in the middle then roll into a round dumpling, sealing the mozzarella inside. Gently roll the dumpling in the flour then quickly roll it in the eggs, followed by the breadcrumbs, and transfer to a large baking dish. Repeat with the remaining rice mixture to make about 15 more arancini.

To see if the oil is hot enough, dip the bottom of a wooden spoon into the oil; tiny bubbles should form around it. Start with 1 arancina to test the oil. Carefully drop the arancina into the hot oil and fry, turning occasionally, for $1^1/2$ to 3 minutes or until golden and firm, reducing the heat to medium if the arancina browns too quickly. Using a slotted ladle or spoon, transfer the arancina to paper towels. Working in batches, repeat to fry the remaining arancini.

For the salad, cut the fennel bulbs in half then core and very thinly slice them lengthwise. Peel the oranges, removing the skin and white pith, and cut into thick slices. Divide the fennel, oranges, and arugula among plates. Whisk together the olive oil and both vinegars, season to taste with salt and pepper, and drizzle over the salad. Arrange the warm arancini on top and serve immediately.

As winter squash season begins, orange, green, and yellow butternut, acorn, and Hokkaido squash take over our kitchen's windowsill and I need to have a pile of recipes at hand to keep the fresh supply under control. I often chop up a whole squash, roast it in the oven, and use it for quiche *(recipe no. 287)*, pesto *(recipe no. 283)*, crespelle *(recipe no. 316)*, or hearty salads. When you toss the tender flesh with roasted shallots, radicchio, and Stilton, you can enjoy a light lunch or dinner that's bursting with color and flavor.

Roasted Squash, Shallot, and Radicchio Salad with Stilton

Serves 2 to 4

For the salad
¾ pound (340 g) seeded squash,
preferably peeled butternut
or Hokkaido with skin,
cut into 1-inch (2.5 cm) wedges
8 shallots, unpeeled,
cut in half lengthwise
⅓ cup (75 ml) olive oil
Flaky sea salt
Finely ground pepper
5 ounces (140 g) radicchio,
soft leaves only, torn into pieces
1 large, firm pear, cored
and cut into thin wedges
2 ounces (60 g) Stilton, crumbled
1 tbsp fresh thyme leaves

For the dressing
3 tbsp olive oil
1 tbsp balsamic vinegar
1 tbsp white balsamic vinegar
1 tsp honey
Fine sea salt
Finely ground pepper

Preheat the oven to 400°F (200°C).

For the salad, spread the squash on one side of a large baking dish and the shallots on the other side. Drizzle with the olive oil and toss to combine, keeping the squash and shallots separate. Season generously with flaky sea salt and pepper and roast for 15 minutes. Flip the squash and shallots over and continue roasting for 10 to 15 or until golden and tender. Transfer the squash to a plate. Let the shallots cool for a few minutes then peel and add to the squash.

For the dressing, whisk together the olive oil, both vinegars, and the honey and season to taste with fine sea salt and pepper.

Divide the radicchio, pear, squash, and shallots among plates, arranging them in overlapping layers. Sprinkle with the Stilton and thyme, drizzle with the dressing, and serve immediately.

290

Makes 2 sandwiches

3 tbsp olive oil
1 small handful fresh
rosemary needles
4 very thin slices Italian
rosemary ham (or plain ham)
2 rustic white buns, cut in half
4 thick slices aromatic cheese
that melts well, such as Raclette,
Comté, or Gruyère
Coarsely ground pepper

A rustic ham-and-cheese sandwich can be plain and frugal and still be the best sandwich of your life. If you go for Italian rosemary ham and melted Raclette cheese, you'll up your game.

Raclette and Rosemary Ham Sandwich

Set the oven to broil (quicker method) or preheat to 500°F (260°C).

In a small saucepan, heat the olive oil and rosemary over medium-high heat until the oil is sizzling and the rosemary is golden and crispy but still green. Take the pan off the heat.

Layer 2 slices of ham on the bottom half of each bun and top with the cheese. Put the sandwiches under the broiler, or roast at 500°F (260°C) for a few minutes or until the cheese starts to melt. Sprinkle with the rosemary and pepper, drizzle with the rosemary oil, and place a top on each bun. Squeeze and enjoy.

291

Serves 1 to 2

Olive oil
5 ounces (140 g) peeled kohlrabi,
thinly sliced on a mandoline
Fine sea salt
½ tsp seeded and finely chopped
fresh red chile

I always fail miserably at frying kohlrabi chips, so I sauté the thinly sliced cabbage instead, and add fresh chile for some heat. Kitchen failures can be rewarding and sometimes lead to dishes that are even better than the original idea...sometimes.

Sautéed Kohlrabi with Chile

In a medium, heavy pan, heat a splash of olive oil over medium-high heat and sauté the kohlrabi, turning occasionally, for 6 to 7 minutes or until golden and tender. Season to taste with salt, sprinkle with the chile, and serve immediately.

The deep blue Mediterranean Sea around the islands of Malta is home to the best prawns I've ever had. They're so good that you want to keep their taste pure by not adding flavors that are too confident and distracting. But, if you serve them with pan-roasted potatoes and hummus spiced up with cinnamon, cloves, and cumin, you'll actually manage to enhance the pink crustaceans' sweetness.

Pan-Roasted Prawns and Potatoes with Spiced Hummus

Serves 2 to 4

For the hummus
1 ¼ cups (250 g) drained
and rinsed canned chickpeas
⅔ cup (150 g) light tahini
⅓ cup (75 ml) water
4 tbsp freshly squeezed
lemon juice
1 large clove garlic, crushed
1 tsp fine sea salt
¾ tsp ground cinnamon
¼ tsp ground cumin
2 whole cloves, finely crushed
with a mortar and pestle

For the prawns and potatoes
Olive oil
12 small waxy potatoes,
scrubbed, boiled, cooled,
and cut in half lengthwise
Flaky sea salt
Coarsely ground pepper
8 large shell-on prawns
without heads

Picture page 355, top left

For the hummus, purée the chickpeas, tahini, water, lemon juice, garlic, fine sea salt, cinnamon, cumin, and cloves in a food processor or blender until smooth. Season to taste with fine sea salt and transfer to a small bowl.

In a large, heavy pan, heat a generous splash of olive oil over medium-high heat. Add the potatoes and cook, turning occasionally, for 5 to 7 minutes or until golden brown and crispy. Season to taste with flaky sea salt and pepper and transfer to a large plate, but leave the pan on the heat. Add a splash of olive oil and the prawns to the pan, increase the heat to high, and sear the prawns, turning occasionally, for 3 to 5 minutes or until golden brown and cooked through. Return the potatoes to the pan, stir, and cook for 1 minute. Divide the potatoes and prawns among plates and serve with a generous dollop of the hummus.

I appreciate a buttery pie all year round, but there's something particularly satisfying about this dish on a cold autumn evening. Just imagine coming home after a walk through the pouring rain, with your bones cold and clothes wet, and then you smell this golden beauty filled with potatoes, apples, onion, and Taleggio.

Potato, Apple, and Onion Pie with Taleggio

Serves 3 to 4

For the filling

¼ cup (60 ml) heavy cream

1 tbsp chopped fresh
thyme leaves

Fine sea salt

Finely ground pepper

Nutmeg, preferably freshly grated

¾ pound (340 g) peeled potatoes,
boiled, cooled, and diced

1 large shallot, thinly sliced

2 tart baking apples, peeled,
cut into quarters, cored,
and thinly sliced

3 ounces (85 g) mild,
sweet cheese that melts well,
such as Taleggio, fontina,
or Robiola, cut into cubes

For the pastry

2⅓ cups (300 g) all-purpose flour

1 tsp fine sea salt

⅔ cup (150 g) unsalted butter,
cold

2 large egg yolks

2 tbsp water, cold

For the glaze

1 large egg yolk

1 tbsp whole milk

⅛ tsp fine sea salt

Picture opposite, top right

For the filling, in a large bowl, whisk together the heavy cream, thyme, $1/4$ teaspoon of salt, and pinches of pepper and nutmeg. Add the potatoes and toss to combine. Season to taste with salt, pepper, and nutmeg.

For the pastry, combine the flour and salt in the bowl of a stand mixer fitted with the dough hook attachment. Add the butter and use a knife to cut it into the flour until there are just small pieces left. Quickly rub the butter into the flour with your fingers until combined. Add the egg yolks and cold water and mix with the hook until crumbly. Form the dough into a ball. Remove $1/3$ of the dough and form it into a thick disc. Form the rest of the dough into a second disc. Wrap both discs in plastic wrap and freeze for 10 minutes.

Preheat the oven to 400°F (200°C). For the glaze, whisk together the egg yolk, milk, and salt.

On a work surface, place both discs of dough between 2 sheets of plastic wrap and use a rolling pin to roll each disc into a circle, the larger disc for the bottom and sides of a 9-inch (23 cm) shallow pie dish or an 8-inch (20 cm) springform pan and the smaller disc to close the pie. Line the pie dish or springform pan with the larger pastry disc, pushing it into the dish, especially along the edges. Let the dough hang over the rim a little. Spread the potato mixture on top of the pastry and cover with the shallot, apples, and cheese. Close the pie with the smaller disc of dough, gently pressing the edges of the pastry together to seal it. Use a skewer to make a few holes in the top and brush with the glaze. Bake for 15 minutes then reduce the heat to 350°F (180°C) and continue baking for another 45 minutes or until golden and the pastry is baked through. Let the pie cool at least 15 minutes before cutting into pieces and serving.

292

293

295

296

We celebrate exuberantly when it's time for Santa. But why am I writing about this at the end of October? Because now's the time to test recipes! For me, there needs to be a proper duck on the table on Christmas Eve—it's my tradition—and I always slowly roast it for four hours in a sauna-like oven set to 175°F (85°C). I like the idea of combining the bird with figs, chestnuts, spices, and elderflower syrup, but there's still enough time to play with different variations (*recipe no. 358*).

Spiced Duck with Elderflower, Figs, and Chestnuts

Serves 3 to 4

Olive oil
1 (5½-pound / 2.5-kg) duck
2 tsp flaky sea salt
1 tsp black peppercorns,
crushed with a mortar and pestle
3 tbsp elderflower syrup
(or honey)
10 allspice berries,
crushed with a mortar and pestle
10 whole cloves,
crushed with a mortar and pestle
1 tsp ground cinnamon
3 medium red onions,
cut into quarters
1 small bunch fresh thyme
10 ounces (280 g) fresh figs,
cut into quarters
1 handful vacuum-packed
whole cooked chestnuts

Ovenproof cotton string

Preheat the oven to 175°F (85°C).

In a large, heavy pan, heat a splash of olive oil over high heat and sear the duck, turning, for a few minutes or until golden brown on all sides. Transfer the duck to a medium baking dish and carefully pour the fat from the pan into a small bowl. Season the duck, inside and out, with the salt and crushed black peppercorns and rub into the skin. Whisk together the elderflower syrup, allspice berries, cloves, and cinnamon, pour over the duck, and rub into the skin. Stuff 1/2 of the onions and 1/2 of the thyme inside the duck and arrange the remaining onion and thyme around the bird. Tie the legs together with ovenproof cotton string. Arrange the figs and chestnuts around the duck and roast, spooning a little of the reserved duck fat and the juices from the baking dish over the duck every hour, for 4 hours. After 4 hours, check to see if the duck is done by pricking the thickest part of a thigh with a skewer—the juices should run clear. Turn on the broiler for the last 1 to 2 minutes or until the skin is golden brown and partially crispy, but mind that it doesn't burn.

Let the duck rest for a few minutes then carve it and serve the meat with the figs, chestnuts, onions, and the juices from the baking dish.

Split peas and squash love to mingle in a cozy soup. It's a nutty, heart-warming meal, and when you top it off with maple onions, whipped Gorgonzola, and marjoram, it becomes a lavish starter for a dinner party with friends.

Split Pea and Squash Soup with Maple Onions, Gorgonzola, and Marjoram

Serves 3 to 6

For the soup
Olive oil
1 medium onion, finely chopped
2 large cloves garlic, cut in half
14 ounces (400 g) seeded
and peeled squash,
preferably butternut or Hokkaido,
cut into very small cubes
1 cup (210 g) yellow split peas
(no soaking required)
6 ½ cups (1.5 liters) unsalted
vegetable broth, hot
2 bay leaves
2 whole cloves
1 small bunch fresh
marjoram sprigs,
plus 2 tbsp marjoram leaves
for the topping
Fine sea salt
Finely ground pepper

For the onions
Olive oil
2 large red onions,
cut in half and thinly sliced
2 tbsp maple syrup
1 tsp balsamic vinegar

For the whipped Gorgonzola
2 ounces (60 g) Gorgonzola
2 ounces (60 g) mascarpone
⅓ cup (75 ml) heavy cream
⅛ tsp fine sea salt

Picture page 355, bottom left

For the soup, heat a splash of olive oil in a large pot over medium heat. Add the onion and garlic and sauté, stirring occasionally, for 3 minutes or until golden and soft. Add the squash and sauté, stirring constantly, for 1 minute. Add the yellow split peas, hot broth, bay leaves, cloves, and marjoram sprigs. Bring to a boil, cover, then reduce the heat and simmer for 35 minutes or until the squash and split peas are soft. Remove and discard the bay leaves, cloves, and marjoram sprigs then season to taste with salt and pepper. Cover and keep warm.

For the onions, heat a generous splash of olive oil in a medium, heavy pan over medium heat and cook the onions, stirring occasionally, for 10 minutes. Add the maple syrup and vinegar and cook for 10 minutes or until golden brown and soft.

For the whipped Gorgonzola, whisk together the Gorgonzola, mascarpone, heavy cream, and salt until smooth.

Divide the soup among bowls and top with the onions and a dollop of the whipped Gorgonzola. Sprinkle with the marjoram leaves and serve immediately.

It's worth keeping mozzarella, tapenade, and preserved lemons in the fridge just for this recipe. A scrumptious lunch or starter can't be put together any quicker.

Mozzarella with Tapenade and Preserved Lemon

Serves 2 to 4

For the tapenade*

7 ounces (200 g) pitted
black olives, preferably Kalamata
1 large handful fresh
flat-leaf parsley leaves
½ medium red onion
4 anchovy fillets, rinsed and dried
2 tbsp capers, preferably
preserved in salt, rinsed and dried
½ cup (120 ml) olive oil
2 tbsp freshly squeezed
lemon juice
2 tsp Dijon mustard
Finely ground pepper

For the salad

2 (4-ounce / 110-g) balls
mozzarella di bufala, drained
and torn in half
2 tbsp olive oil
¼ preserved lemon,
very thinly sliced
(or 1 ½ tsp freshly grated
lemon zest)
Coarsely ground pepper

Picture page 355, bottom right

For the tapenade, in a food processor or blender, purée the olives, parsley, onion, anchovy, capers, olive oil, lemon juice, and mustard until smooth. Season to taste with finely ground pepper. Transfer 3/4 of the dip to a medium bowl, cover with olive oil then plastic wrap, and keep in the fridge for up to 3 days to use for other recipes. Transfer the remaining tapenade to a small bowl.

For the salad, divide the mozzarella among plates, drizzle with the olive oil, and sprinkle with the preserved lemon and a spoonful of the tapenade. Season to taste with coarsely ground pepper and serve immediately.

* You'll only need about 1/4 of the tapenade. You can use any remaining tapenade for chicken (recipe no. 138), pizza (recipe no. 182), and pasta (recipe no. 211).

297

week 43 / wednesday

Makes 4 sandwiches

2 medium, tart baking apples
3 tbsp (45 g) unsalted butter
1½ tbsp granulated sugar
1½ tbsp fresh thyme leaves,
plus 1 tsp for the topping
4 ounces (110 g) mild Camembert
3 ounces (85 g) cream cheese
1 tbsp heavy cream
Fine sea salt
Finely ground pepper
1 handful arugula leaves
4 large, thick slices rustic
dark bread, such as spelt or rye

Following the Bavarian tradition, you normally finish *Obatzda* with caraway seeds or fresh herbs (*recipe no. 150*), but this creamy Camembert dip tastes superb when you introduce fruit. The sweetness of apple wedges caramelized in thyme butter is smooth and subtle and it's the perfect contrast to hearty rye or spelt bread.

Bavarian *Obatzda* with Caramelized Apples and Thyme Butter on Dark Bread

Peel and core the apples and cut each into 8 wedges. In a medium, heavy pan, heat the butter and sugar over medium-high heat until golden brown and sizzling. Add the apples and thyme and cook, turning the apples, for 2 to 3 minutes per side or until golden brown and tender. Take the pan off the heat.

Transfer 3 apple wedges to a food processor or blender, add the Camembert, cream cheese, and heavy cream and purée until smooth. Season to taste with salt and pepper and transfer to a medium bowl.

Divide the arugula among the slices of bread and arrange the caramelized apples on top. Sprinkle with the Obatzda and thyme leaves and enjoy.

298

week 43 / thursday

Serves 3 to 4

2 medium onions
1 large, firm pear,
cut in half and cored
¾ pound (340 g) seedless
green grapes, on the vine
1⅔ pounds (750 g) medium,
waxy potatoes, scrubbed
1 small handful fresh
rosemary needles
3 tbsp olive oil
1 tbsp dry white wine
1 tbsp freshly squeezed
lemon juice
1 tbsp maple syrup
Flaky sea salt
Coarsely ground pepper

With the right food you can appreciate each season to the fullest. As October is coming to an end and winter is rapidly approaching, the dishes we eat naturally turn richer and heartier. So, let's enjoy fresh produce as long as we can and put autumn's fruity beauties into the spotlight on top of a savory potato casserole.

Potato Casserole with Grapes, Pear, and Onion

Preheat the oven to 425°F (220°C). Cut each onion into 10 wedges, cut the pear into 8 wedges, and snip the bunch of grapes into 8 to 10 portions (on the vine).

In a large pot, cover the potatoes with salted water and bring to a boil. Cover the pot, reduce the heat, and simmer for 10 minutes. Drain the potatoes, quickly rinse with cold water, and let them dry on a wire rack for at least 15 minutes then cut each potato into 6 wedges.

Spread the potatoes, grapes, onions, pear, and rosemary in a medium baking dish. Whisk together the olive oil, white wine, lemon juice, and maple syrup, pour over the potato mixture, and toss to combine. Season to taste with salt and pepper and roast for about 55 minutes or until golden brown and tender. Snip the grapes off the vines and serve immediately.

Fluffy gnocchi are addictive little bites—you always end up eating far more than you intended. While you can never go wrong serving these potato pillows the classic way, with sage brown butter, at this time of year, try a nutty walnut-parsley pesto brightened with a hint of mustard.

Potato Gnocchi with Walnut-Parsley Pesto

Serves 2 to 3

For the pesto

3 ounces (85 g) walnuts,
plus 1 small handful chopped
walnuts for the topping
1 small handful fresh
flat-leaf parsley leaves
1 large clove garlic
1 tbsp finely grated pecorino,
plus 2 tbsp for the topping
½ tsp Dijon mustard
⅓ cup (75 ml) olive oil
Fine sea salt
Finely ground pepper

For the gnocchi

1 pound (450 g) peeled
starchy potatoes, cut into cubes
2 tbsp (30 g) unsalted butter
2 large egg yolks
1 cup (130 g) all-purpose flour
1½ tsp fine sea salt
½ tsp nutmeg,
preferably freshly grated
Finely ground pepper

For the pesto, in a food processor or blender, purée 3 ounces (85 g) of walnuts, the parsley, garlic, 1 tablespoon of pecorino, the mustard, and olive oil and season to taste with salt and pepper.

For the gnocchi, cover the potatoes with salted water in a medium pot and bring to a boil. Cover the pot, reduce the heat, and simmer the potatoes for 15 to 18 minutes or until soft. Transfer the potatoes to a colander, drain, and use a spoon to gently push out any remaining water. Leave to dry in the colander for 2 minutes then press through a potato ricer into a large bowl. Add the butter and egg yolks, stir to combine, and let cool at room temperature for 30 minutes or until completely cool, or refrigerate for about 15 minutes.

Bring a large pot of salted water to a boil.

Once the potato mixture is completely cool, add the flour, salt, nutmeg, and a generous amount of pepper and quickly stir to combine. If the mixture is too soft and not firm enough to roll into a log, gradually add more flour. Lightly dust your hands and a work surface with flour. Roll 1/4 of the dough into a 1-inch-thick (2.5 cm) log. Cut the log into 1-inch (2.5 cm) pieces and transfer to a well-floured baking sheet. Repeat with the remaining dough to make more gnocchi.

Working in batches, add the gnocchi to the boiling water and simmer, reducing the heat if necessary, for 3 to 4 minutes or until they float to the top—mind that they don't stick to the bottom of the pot. Use a slotted ladle or spoon to scoop the gnocchi out of the water then quickly drain and place them in an ovenproof dish. Cover and keep in a warm oven while you cook the remaining gnocchi, bringing the water back to a boil between batches.

Divide the gnocchi among plates and drizzle with a little olive oil. Sprinkle with the pesto, chopped walnuts, pecorino, and a little pepper and serve immediately.

The day after the New York launch of my first cookbook, I strolled around the Bryant Park Holiday Market with my editor, Holly La Due. The moment I spotted screaming-pink beet and ricotta doughnuts at a little stand, I was smitten. Those were fried, while mine are baked and sprinkled with orange zest and pistachios. They're lighter and less oily, but that's just a personal preference.

Beet and Ricotta Doughnuts with Pistachios

Makes 16 doughnuts

For the doughnuts

2 ½ cups (325 g) all-purpose flour
¼ cup (50 g) granulated sugar
1 ¼ tsp fast-acting yeast
½ tsp fine sea salt
½ tsp freshly grated orange zest
⅔ cup (150 ml) whole milk, lukewarm
1 ½ tbsp (20 g) unsalted butter, melted and cooled
1 large egg
½ vanilla bean, split and scraped
9 ounces (250 g) fresh ricotta, drained and whipped

For the topping

2 cups (200 g) confectioners' sugar
¼ cup (60 ml) beet juice
1 small handful unsalted pistachios, chopped
1 to 2 tbsp freshly grated orange zest

For the doughnuts, in the bowl of a stand mixer fitted with the dough hook attachment, combine the flour, granulated sugar, yeast, salt, and orange zest. In a separate bowl, whisk together the lukewarm milk, the butter, egg, and vanilla seeds, add to the flour mixture, and mix with the hook for 5 minutes or until smooth and well combined. Transfer the dough to a work surface and continue kneading and punching it down with your hands for 5 minutes or until you have a soft and silky ball of dough. If the dough is too sticky, add a little more flour. Place the dough back in the bowl, cover with a tea towel, and let rise in a warm place, or preferably in a 100°F (35°C) warm oven, for about 60 minutes or until almost doubled in size.

Line 2 baking sheets with parchment paper. When the dough has almost doubled in size, punch it down, take it out of the bowl, and knead for 1 minute. On a lightly floured work surface, use a rolling pin to roll out the dough until it's about 1/2-inch thick (1.25 cm). Using a 3-inch (7.5 cm) cookie cutter or glass, cut out discs and transfer to the lined baking sheets. Using a 1 1/3-inch (3.5 cm) cookie cutter, cut out circles in the middle of each disc and arrange next to the doughnuts on the baking sheets. Cover with a tea towel and let rise for about 30 minutes or until puffy.

Preheat the oven to 375°F (190°C).

Bake the doughnuts, 1 sheet at a time, for 6 to 8 minutes or until light golden, spongy, and just baked through. Transfer to a cooling rack and let cool completely. Cut the doughnuts in half horizontally, spread the bottom of each with a spoonful of ricotta, and return the tops to the doughnuts.

For the topping, whisk the confectioners' sugar with the beet juice until smooth and sticky. Drizzle the doughnuts and doughnut holes with the glaze, and sprinkle with the pistachios and a little orange zest. Let the glaze dry and serve.

Tyrolean apple strudel is a weekend project—and a little tricky. The strudel is filled with lots of apples, as you want it to be fruity and juicy. The pastry is buttery-soft and a bit crumbly, and sometimes it can't deal with all that fruit and starts to crack. Just stay calm, close the cracks with a spoon, and continue baking. It'll work out. This strudel tastes so unbelievably good that I bake it for most of our dinner parties, despite the hassle it can cause. If you have time, serve the strudel with warm vanilla custard (recipe no. 6), which you can prepare in advance.

Tyrolean Apple Strudel

Serves 8 to 12

For the pastry

2⅓ cups (300 g) all-purpose flour

¾ cup (150 g) granulated sugar

1½ tsp baking powder

1 tsp ground cinnamon

⅛ tsp fine sea salt

⅔ cup (150 g) unsalted butter, cold

1 large egg, beaten

For the strudel

1 ¼ pounds (560 g) peeled and cored tart baking apples, each cut into 8 wedges and very thinly sliced crosswise

3 ounces (85 g) raisins

⅓ cup (50 g) dry breadcrumbs, toasted

1¼ tbsp freshly grated orange zest

2 ½ tsp ground cinnamon

1 ½ tsp freshly grated lemon zest

2 tbsp Kirsch (German clear cherry brandy)

1 tbsp freshly squeezed lemon juice

1 tbsp freshly squeezed orange juice

½ vanilla bean, split and scraped

¼ cup (50 g) granulated sugar

1 large egg, beaten

Confectioners' sugar

For the pastry, combine the flour, granulated sugar, baking powder, cinnamon, and salt in the bowl of a stand mixer fitted with the dough hook attachment. Add the butter and use a knife to cut it into the flour until there are just small pieces left. Quickly rub the butter into the flour with your fingers until combined. Add the egg and mix with the hook until crumbly. Form the dough into a thick disc, wrap it in plastic wrap, and freeze for 18 minutes.

Preheat the oven to 350°F/180°C (preferably convection setting).

For the strudel, in a large bowl, combine the apples, raisins, breadcrumbs, orange zest, cinnamon, lemon zest, Kirsch, lemon juice, orange juice, and vanilla seeds and toss to combine.

On a work surface, place the dough between 2 sheets of plastic wrap and use a rolling pin to roll out into a 14 x 12-inch (35 x 30 cm) rectangle. Remove the top plastic wrap and replace with a large piece of parchment paper. Flip the pastry over and remove the second plastic wrap. Spread the apple mixture evenly on the pastry, leaving a 1-inch (2.5 cm) border then sprinkle with ¼ cup (50 g) of granulated sugar. Using the parchment paper, gently fold up one of the long sides toward the middle of the rectangle until it reaches just past the middle. Pull the parchment away from the pastry then fold up the opposite side, letting the edges of the pastry overlap in the middle; pull the parchment away from the second side. Use your fingers to push the pastry together and seal the fold and both ends of the strudel. Place a second piece of parchment paper on top of the strudel and, holding the strudel from underneath with your hand, quickly flip the strudel and parchment over and place on a baking sheet. Quickly brush the top with the beaten egg and bake for 35 to 40 minutes (slightly longer if using a conventional oven) or until golden brown and crispy. Watch the strudel closely in the first 10 minutes—if the pastry cracks, close the cracks with the backside of a spoon. Let the strudel cool on the baking sheet for 15 minutes then dust with confectioners' sugar and serve warm or cold, preferably with warm vanilla custard.

Squash, feta, and pistachios are a tasty trio, and roasting the vegetable on top of a thick slice of the Greek cheese for half an hour turns it into a quick after-work dinner. Double the recipe and you can stir leftovers into a bowl of warm spaghetti.

Roasted Squash Wedges with Feta, Cumin Oil, and Pistachios

Serves 2 to 3

Olive oil
1 ½ tsp ground cumin
1 ⅓ pounds (600 g) seeded squash,
preferably peeled butternut
or Hokkaido with skin,
cut into 1-inch (2.5 cm) wedges
1 (5-ounce / 140-g) slice feta
Flaky sea salt
Coarsely ground pepper
1 ounce (30 g) salted pistachios,
roughly chopped

Preheat the oven to 400°F (200°C).

In a large bowl, whisk together ⅓ cup (75 ml) of olive oil and the cumin. Add the squash and toss to combine.

Place the feta in the middle of a medium baking dish and arrange the squash on top of and around the cheese. Drizzle with 2 tablespoons of olive oil and season to taste with salt and pepper then roast for about 30 minutes or until the squash is golden and tender. Sprinkle with the pistachios and serve warm or cold.

This is the kind of dish you long for after a silent walk through the misty woods, when your body craves caressing warmth on the outside and inside.

Green Lentil and Borlotti Bean Soup with Salsiccia

Serves 3 to 4

¾ cup (170 g) small green
or French Puy lentils
(no soaking required)
1 small bunch fresh thyme,
plus 1 tbsp fresh thyme leaves
1 small sprig fresh rosemary
1 bay leaf
Olive oil
3 large cloves garlic, crushed
1 tbsp balsamic vinegar,
plus more to taste
4 medium tomatoes, chopped
1 ¼ cups (250 g) drained
and rinsed canned borlotti
(cranberry) or pinto beans
Fine sea salt
Finely ground pepper
2 large salsiccia
(or any thick, coarse sausage)

Place the lentils in a medium saucepan with plenty of (unsalted) water, add the bunch of thyme, the rosemary, and bay leaf, and bring to a boil. Reduce the heat and simmer, adding more water if necessary, for about 20 minutes or until al dente (or follow the package instructions). There should be a little cooking liquid left when the lentils are done. Remove and discard the herbs and set the lentils aside.

In a large pot, heat a splash of olive oil over medium heat and sauté the garlic, stirring constantly, for 1 minute then add the vinegar and tomatoes and cook, stirring, for 1 minute. Add the lentils, borlotti beans, and 2/3 of the thyme leaves, stir, and season to taste with salt and pepper. Add the salsiccia, and a small ladleful of water if the lentil mixture is too dry, then cover and bring to a boil. Reduce the heat and simmer gently for about 10 minutes or until the sausages are cooked through. Transfer the sausages to a cutting board, cut into thick slices, and return to the pot. Season to taste with salt, pepper, and additional vinegar. Divide the soup among bowls, sprinkle with the remaining thyme leaves, and serve warm.

304

week 44 / wednesday

Grapes and blue cheese always taste divine together, but if you roast the fruit first, the combination is truly sublime.

Roasted Grapes and Stilton Tartine with Rosemary

Makes 4 tartines

¼ pound (110 g) seedless
red grapes, on the vine
1 medium sprig fresh rosemary
Olive oil
Flaky sea salt
4 slices ciabatta
4 ounces (110 g) Stilton
(or any crumbly blue cheese)
Coarsely ground pepper

Preheat the oven to 425°F (220°C).

Place the grapes and rosemary in a medium baking dish. Drizzle with 2 tablespoons of olive oil, gently toss to coat, and season to taste with salt. Roast for 30 to 35 minutes or until the grapes are soft and a little shriveled.

Brush the ciabatta with a little olive oil then crumble the Stilton on top. Snip the grapes off the vine and divide among the tartines. Sprinkle with the roasted rosemary, season to taste with pepper, and serve immediately.

November

My friend Emiko Davies introduced me to Florentine *gnudi* when I visited her beautiful home neatly tucked into the soft hills just outside Florence. A Tuscan specialty, gnudi are "naked" dumplings, which means they're fluffy balls of ravioli filling without any pasta wrapped around them. It's common to make gnudi with spinach, ricotta, and sage brown butter, but at home in Germany, I go for sauerkraut, ricotta, and juniper butter instead.

Sauerkraut-Ricotta Gnudi with Juniper Butter

Serves 2

For the juniper butter

3 tbsp (45 g) unsalted butter
14 juniper berries, lightly crushed
1 bay leaf

For the gnudi

18 ounces (500 g) canned
or jarred sauerkraut
6 ounces (170 g) ricotta, drained
Fine sea salt
Finely ground pepper
Nutmeg, preferably freshly grated
1 large egg, beaten
About ¾ cup (100 g) all-purpose
flour, to dust the gnudi

For the juniper butter, heat the butter, juniper berries, and bay leaf in a medium, heavy pan over high heat until sizzling. Take the pan off the heat and push the juniper berries into the butter with the backside of a spoon; cover and set aside.

For the gnudi, bring a large pot of salted water to a boil.

Drain the sauerkraut then squeeze it until no more liquid comes out; it should be quite dry. Measure 6 ounces (170 g) of the sauerkraut, finely chop it, and transfer to a large bowl; use any remaining sauerkraut for other recipes. Add the ricotta, season to taste with salt, pepper, and nutmeg then add the egg and mix until well combined.

Spread the flour on a large baking sheet. Wet your hands and form the gnudi mixture into $1^1/_2$-inch (4 cm) balls then roll the gnudi in the flour until well coated and transfer to a large platter.

Working in batches, add the gnudi to the boiling water and simmer, reducing the heat if necessary, for 3 to 4 minutes or until they float to the top—mind that they don't stick to the bottom of the pot. Use a slotted ladle or spoon to transfer the gnudi to a large platter. When all the gnudi are done, add them to the juniper butter and cook over medium-high heat, turning, for about 1 minute or until golden. Divide among plates and serve immediately.

Braised lamb shanks are succulent, tender, and tasty. They need to cook for about two hours, but you can prepare them a day in advance. Imagine coming home after work and indulging in the shanks and their fragrant, dark sauce infused with orange, herbs, and spices. The preparation is easy and while the meat is slowly tenderizing in the simmering juices, you can sit on the sofa and relax.

Braised Lamb Shanks with Orange, Herbs, and Spices

Serves 3 to 4

Olive oil
3 to 4 lamb shanks,
about 2 ¾ pounds (1.3 kg) total
Fine sea salt
Finely ground pepper
2 tsp coriander seeds,
crushed with a mortar and pestle
1 tsp aniseed,
crushed with a mortar and pestle
10 allspice berries
2 bay leaves
4 medium carrots,
cut lengthwise into 8 wedges
2 celery stalks, thinly sliced
1 medium onion, finely chopped
4 cloves garlic, cut in half
2 cups (480 ml) dry white wine
14 ounces (400 g) canned
whole peeled tomatoes, chopped
1 orange, cut into 8 wedges
1 clementine (or tangerine),
cut into 8 wedges
1 small bunch fresh thyme
1 small sprig fresh rosemary
Boiled potatoes or baguette,
for serving

Preheat the oven to 325°F (160°C).

In a Dutch oven, large enough to fit the meat and with a tight-fitting lid, heat a splash of olive oil over high heat. Add the lamb shanks and sear, turning, for a few minutes or until browned on all sides. Season to taste with salt and pepper. Remove the meat from the pan and set it aside. Add a little more olive oil to the Dutch oven and place over medium-high heat. Add the coriander seeds, aniseed, allspice berries, and bay leaves and cook, stirring constantly, for 15 seconds or until fragrant. Add the carrots, celery, onion, and garlic and sauté, stirring, for 2 minutes or until golden. Return the lamb to the Dutch oven and stir to mix it with the vegetables and spices. Add the white wine and tomatoes and season to taste with salt and pepper. Add the orange, clementine, thyme, and rosemary and bring to a boil. Cover the Dutch oven, transfer to the oven, and cook for 2 hours or until the meat is tender and you can easily pull it off the bone with a fork.

If you prefer a thicker sauce, remove the meat from the Dutch oven, cover, and keep warm. Place the Dutch oven over medium-high heat and reduce the sauce until it reaches the desired taste and texture. Remove and discard the herbs then season the sauce to taste with salt and pepper. Serve the meat with the sauce and potatoes or crunchy baguette.

307

week 44 / saturday

Serves 2

1 (14-ounce / 400-g) whole
mackerel, gutted and cleaned
Olive oil
Fine sea salt
Finely ground pepper
12 large sprigs fresh tarragon,
plus 3 tbsp finely chopped
tarragon leaves
⅔ cup (150 ml) dry white wine
3 tbsp (45 g) unsalted butter
1½ tbsp Dijon mustard

Picture opposite, top left

Although it's neglected by many cooks, mackerel is ready for the spotlight. This underestimated fish is oily and rich, and won't dry out when you cook it. The taste and texture is far from delicate, making mackerel ripe for experimentation, so stuff a whole fish with fresh tarragon and dip the meat into spicy mustard butter.

Oven-Roasted Mackerel with Tarragon and Mustard Butter

Preheat the oven to 425°F (220°C) and brush a medium baking dish with olive oil.

Using a sharp knife, slash the skin in parallel lines on both sides of the mackerel. Rub the fish with a little olive oil and season to taste with salt and pepper. Stuff the mackerel with 1/2 of the tarragon sprigs and transfer to the prepared baking dish. Arrange the remaining tarragon sprigs under and around the mackerel then pour about 1/2 of the white wine over the fish (the bottom of the dish should be covered) and roast for about 20 minutes or until you can lift the fillets off the bones with a fork. In a small saucepan, heat the butter over high heat until sizzling then immediately add the mustard and chopped tarragon and whisk thoroughly—it might curdle a little. Add 1/4 cup (60 ml) of white wine and a pinch of salt and whisk until smooth. Cook for 10 seconds, stirring constantly, then take the pan off the heat. Divide the fish into 2 fillets and serve with the mustard butter.

308

week 44 / sunday

Makes 12 muffins

1 ½ cups (200 g) all-purpose flour
¾ cup plus 2 tbsp (175 g)
granulated sugar
2 ½ tsp baking powder
½ tsp baking soda
⅛ tsp fine sea salt
⅔ cup (150 g) unsalted butter,
melted and cooled
3 large eggs
1 ½ tbsp freshly grated
orange zest
⅓ cup plus 1 tbsp (90 ml) freshly
squeezed orange juice
4 ounces (110 g) bittersweet
chocolate, roughly chopped
12 paper muffin pan liners

My Maltese granny, Edith, bakes a bittersweet chocolate and orange sponge cake that is fluffy, buttery, and fragrant. These muffins are a miniature version of her Mediterranean masterpiece.

Mediterranean Bittersweet Chocolate and Orange Muffins

Preheat the oven to 400°F / 200°C (preferably convection setting). Line a 12-cup muffin pan with paper liners.

In a large bowl, whisk together the flour, sugar, baking powder, baking soda, and salt.

In a medium bowl, whisk together the butter, eggs, orange zest, and orange juice. Add to the flour mixture and stir with a wooden spoon until the batter is lumpy with a few bits of flour here and there. Gently fold in the chocolate. Mind that if you mix the batter too much, the muffins will lose their light texture.

Spoon the batter into the muffin cups and bake for about 15 minutes (slightly longer if using a conventional oven) or until golden and baked through.

307

309

310

313

Swabian potato noodles, called *Schupfnudeln* in German, are exactly what my home country is famous for: comforting food that's good for the soul. The finger-thick noodles are similar to gnocchi, but unlike the Italian specialty, they're shaped like small cigars, less pillowy, and often served with rich meat and dark, heavy sauces. I find a topping of sautéed parsnips and mushrooms more thrilling, especially for a cozy dinner in November.

Potato Noodles with Parsnips and Mushrooms

Serves 4 to 5

For the noodles

15 ounces (420 g) peeled starchy potatoes, cut into cubes
1 tbsp (15 g) unsalted butter
1 large egg yolk
2 cups (260 g) all-purpose flour
2 ½ tsp fine sea salt
½ tsp nutmeg, preferably freshly grated
Finely ground pepper

For the topping

Olive oil
3 small parsnips, peeled and cut into very thin round slices
¼ cup (60 g) unsalted butter
1 ¼ pounds (560 g) trimmed cremini mushrooms, cut into ¼-inch (0.5 cm) slices
½ pound (225 g) trimmed king trumpet mushrooms, cut in half lengthwise
Fine sea salt
Finely ground pepper
1 tbsp fresh thyme leaves

Picture page 377, top right

For the noodles, cover the potatoes with salted water in a medium pot and bring to a boil. Cover the pot, reduce the heat, and simmer the potatoes for 15 to 18 minutes or until soft. Transfer the potatoes to a colander, drain, and use a spoon to gently push out any remaining water. Leave to dry in the colander for 2 minutes then press through a potato ricer into a large bowl. Add the butter and egg yolk, stir to combine, and let cool at room temperature for 30 minutes or until completely cool, or refrigerate for about 15 minutes.

Bring a large pot of salted water to a boil.

Once the potato mixture is completely cool, add the flour, salt, nutmeg, and a generous amount of pepper and quickly mix with your hands until combined. Lightly dust your hands with flour. Scoop a small spoonful of dough into one hand, roll it into a ball and then into a finger-thick, 2 $1/_2$-inch-long (6 cm) noodle with points on both ends. Transfer to a floured baking sheet and repeat with the remaining dough to make more noodles.

Working in batches, add the noodles to the boiling water and simmer, reducing the heat if necessary, for 3 to 4 minutes or until they float to the top—mind that they don't stick to the bottom of the pot. Use a slotted ladle or spoon to scoop the noodles out of the water then quickly drain and spread them on a wire rack to dry. Finish cooking the noodles, bringing the water back to a boil between batches.

For the topping, heat a generous splash of olive oil in a large, heavy pan over medium-high heat and sauté the parsnips, stirring occasionally, for about 5 minutes or until golden brown and al dente. Transfer the parsnips to a large platter, but leave the pan on the heat. Add a splash of olive oil and 1 tablespoon of the butter and sauté the cremini mushrooms, turning occasionally, for 2 to 3 minutes or until golden and al dente then add to the plate with the parsnips. Add 1 tablespoon of the butter to the pan and sauté the king trumpet mushrooms for 1 minute per side or until al dente then add to the plate with the parsnips and mushrooms and season to taste with salt and pepper. Add the remaining 2 tablespoons of butter and the thyme to the pan then add the potato noodles and cook, turning, for a few minutes or until golden brown. Season to taste with salt and pepper. Return the parsnips and mushrooms to the pan, stir gently, and cook for 1 minute then divide among plates and serve immediately.

310

week 45 / tuesday

Serves 2

Olive oil
4 large sprigs fresh tarragon
1 (⅔-pound / 300-g) halibut fillet
(or any firm white fish,
such as monkfish or cod),
about 1-inch thick (2.5 cm)
Fine sea salt
Finely ground pepper
1 pink grapefruit, peeled
(skin and white pith removed)
and cut into segments
2 tbsp dry white wine
1 tbsp freshly squeezed
orange juice
Parchment paper

Picture page 377, bottom left

Tucked inside a sealed parchment paper package—*al cartoccio*—halibut is infused with the flavor of pink grapefruit and tarragon in this unusual combination. The citrus fruit and powerful herb pleasantly present themselves in each bite, while also complementing each other.

Halibut al Cartoccio with Grapefruit and Tarragon

Preheat the oven to 400°F (200°C).

Cut 2 pieces of parchment paper large enough to wrap the fish like a package and lay them on top of each other. Brush the top sheet with olive oil, place 2 tarragon sprigs in the middle, and lay the halibut on top. Season to taste with salt and pepper then lay the remaining tarragon on top and arrange the grapefruit segments around the fish. Whisk together the white wine, 2 tablespoons of olive oil, and the orange juice and pour over the fish. To close the package, fold the sides over, twist both ends of the parchment, and fold the top twice so it's well sealed. Place the parchment package in a baking dish and bake for about 15 minutes or until you can flake the fish with a fork. If the fish isn't cooked through, close the parchment and continue baking for up to 5 minutes. The cooking time can vary depending on the kind of fish and the fillet's thickness, but mind that you don't overcook it.

Divide the halibut fillet among plates and serve with the grapefruit, tarragon, and cooking juices.

311

week 45 / wednesday

Makes 2 sandwiches

Olive oil
2 small heads Belgian endive,
cut in half lengthwise
Fine sea salt
Finely ground pepper
4 large, thin slices ham
2 large, thick slices white
sourdough bread
½ large, firm pear, cored
and cut into thin wedges
3 ounces (85 g) aromatic cheese
that melts well, such as Raclette,
Comté, or Gruyère, thinly sliced

Endive and ham is a familiar combination, but imagine them paired with Raclette and pear, piled onto sourdough bread, and put under the broiler. It'll impress every sandwich lover.

Belgian Endive with Ham, Raclette, and Pear on Sourdough

Set the oven to broil (quicker method) or preheat to 500°F (260°C).

In a medium, heavy pan, heat a splash of olive oil over medium-high heat and sauté the endives for 1 1/2 to 2 minutes per side or until golden brown and al dente but still firm in the middle. Season to taste with salt and pepper.

Layer 2 slices of ham on each slice of sourdough bread then carefully spread the pear and endive on top. Cover with the cheese and put the sandwiches under the broiler, or roast at 500°F (260°C) for a few minutes or until the cheese starts to melt. Sprinkle with a little pepper and serve immediately.

Serves 2

4 tbsp freshly squeezed
orange juice
3 tbsp olive oil
Fine sea salt
Finely ground pepper
1¼ cups (250 g) drained
and rinsed canned butter
or cannellini beans
2 spring onions, thinly sliced
2 tsp fresh thyme leaves
½ to 1 tsp freshly grated
orange zest

My mother served this salad at one of her garden parties and although there were far more lavish treats on the buffet table, I couldn't stop thinking about this frugal dish of butter beans, spring onions, orange peel, and thyme. It's a light lunch for busy days and you can easily keep it in a lunch box.

Butter Bean Salad with Spring Onions, Orange Peel, and Thyme

In a large bowl, whisk together the orange juice and olive oil and season to taste with salt and pepper. Add the beans, spring onions, thyme, and $1/2$ teaspoon of the orange zest and toss to combine. Season to taste with salt, pepper, and additional orange zest, divide among plates, and enjoy.

Serves 4 to 6

8 ounces (225 g) fresh ricotta
1 ounce (30 g) Parmesan,
finely grated
1½ tbsp fresh thyme leaves
1½ tbsp freshly grated lemon zest
1 tbsp freshly squeezed
lemon juice
1 tsp fine sea salt
Finely ground pepper
2¾ pounds (1.25 kg) boneless,
skin-on suckling pig loin and belly,
butterflied*
Olive oil
Flaky sea salt
About ½ cup (120 ml)
dry white wine
Ovenproof cotton string

Picture page 377, bottom right

A whole suckling pig roasting on a spit over a barbecue grill or open fire is a traditional German ritual often celebrated at village feasts in the countryside. I don't use a spit in my kitchen, nor do I roast a whole pig. And on top of that, I mellow the meat's hearty qualities with a Maltese ricotta stuffing.

Ricotta-Stuffed Pork Roast with Lemon and Parmesan

Preheat the oven to 450°F (230°C).

In a medium bowl, whisk together the ricotta, Parmesan, thyme, lemon zest, lemon juice, and fine sea salt and season to taste with pepper.

Place the meat, skin-side down, on a work surface and season to taste with fine sea salt and pepper. Spread the ricotta mixture on top of the meat, leaving a 1-inch (2.5 cm) border. Starting from one long side, gently roll up the meat and tie with ovenproof cotton string at $1 1/2$-inch (4 cm) intervals. Rub the skin with a little olive oil, transfer to a medium baking dish, and sprinkle with flaky sea salt. Roast for 15 minutes then add enough white wine to cover the bottom of the dish, reduce the heat to 325°F (160°C), and roast the pork for another 50 to 60 minutes or until the meat is juicy and cooked through. Turn on the broiler for the last 2 to 3 minutes or until the skin is golden brown and starts to crackle. Transfer the meat to a large piece of aluminum foil, wrap it, and let it rest for 10 minutes. Cut the pork into slices and serve immediately.

* Ask your butcher to butterfly the meat, keeping it in 1 piece.

For me, baking is a perfect antidote and mood lifter for gloomy, nasty weekend weather. Cookies are a great way to create instant happiness and you can even store this feeling in a jar.

Ginger-Spice Cookies with Cinnamon-Oat Crunch

Makes about 20 cookies

For the cookie dough
2 ¾ cups (360 g) all-purpose flour
1 tsp baking soda
1 tsp whole cloves, ground
with a mortar and pestle
1 tsp ground cinnamon
½ tsp fine sea salt
⅛ tsp allspice berries,
ground with a mortar and pestle
½ cup plus 1 tbsp (130 g) unsalted
butter, at room temperature
¾ cup plus 2 tbsp (175 g)
granulated sugar
1 ½ tbsp freshly grated ginger
¼ cup (80 g) sugar beet syrup
(or dark molasses)
3 tbsp (60 g) honey
1 large egg

For the oat crunch
1 cup (90 g) rolled oats
½ cup (100 g) granulated sugar
1 tsp ground cinnamon
¼ cup (60 g) unsalted butter,
at room temperature,
cut into small pieces

For the cookie dough, combine the flour, baking soda, cloves, cinnamon, salt, and allspice in a medium bowl.

In the bowl of a stand mixer fitted with the paddle attachment, beat the butter, sugar, and ginger until fluffy. Add the sugar beet syrup, honey, and egg and mix for 1 minute or until creamy. Add the flour mixture and quickly mix until just combined. Scrape the dough together, cover, and refrigerate for at least 30 minutes.

Preheat the oven to 350°F / 180°C (preferably convection setting). Line 2 baking sheets with parchment paper.

For the oat crunch, combine the oats, sugar, and cinnamon in a medium bowl, add the butter, and quickly mix with your fingers until crumbly.

Roll spoonfuls of the dough into 1 1/2-inch (4 cm) balls and arrange them on the lined baking sheets, leaving a roughly 1 1/2-inch (4 cm) space in between them. Lightly flatten the balls with an espresso mug or a spoon and scoop a spoonful of the oat crunch on top. Bake, 1 baking sheet at a time, for about 13 minutes (slightly longer if using a conventional oven) or until golden and still a bit soft.

Let the cookies cool completely then store in a cookie jar for up to 1 week.

Buttery shortbread topped with puréed jelly-like persimmons and crunchy crumble makes the most delicious streusel bars. They'll get you in the mood for next month's festive baking.

Persimmon Streusel Bars

Serves 4 to 6

For the filling
18 ounces (500 g) peeled
ripe persimmons
2 tbsp freshly squeezed
orange juice
1 tbsp honey
¼ vanilla bean, split and scraped
⅛ tsp fine sea salt

For the pastry
3 cups plus 1 tbsp (400 g)
all-purpose flour
1 cup (200 g) granulated sugar
¼ vanilla bean, split and scraped
¼ tsp fine sea salt
1 cup (225 g) unsalted butter,
at room temperature
1 large egg, beaten

Preheat the oven to 350°F / 180°C (preferably convection setting). Butter an 11 x 9-inch (28 x 23 cm) baking dish.

For the filling, purée the persimmons, orange juice, honey, vanilla seeds, and salt in a food processor or blender until smooth.

For the pastry, combine the flour, sugar, vanilla seeds, and salt in a large bowl. Add the butter and use a knife to cut it into the flour until there are just small pieces left. Add the egg and quickly mix the butter and egg into the mixture with your fingers until crumbly.

Transfer about 2/3 of the crumbles to the prepared baking dish, spread evenly, and push it into the baking dish, especially along the edges, until it creates a firm layer. Spread the persimmon filling on top and sprinkle with the remaining crumbles. Bake for 50 to 55 minutes (slightly longer if using a conventional oven) or until golden brown and crunchy. Let cool for about 15 minutes before cutting into 12 large or 24 small streusel bars.

The streusel bars taste best on the first and second day after they are baked.

Roasted squash paired with ricotta, creamy béchamel, Parmesan, and crispy sage makes the most addictive autumn crespelle. It's a bit more labor-intensive than lasagna—you have to bake the thin crêpes first—but every single bite proves the effort is worth it.

Squash-Ricotta Crespelle with Sage

Serves 2 to 4

For the filling

1¼ pounds (560 g) seeded squash, preferably peeled butternut or Hokkaido with skin, cut into ½-inch (1.25 cm) cubes
Olive oil
Fine sea salt
Finely ground pepper
2 tbsp (30 g) unsalted butter
40 large fresh sage leaves
4 heaping tbsp fresh ricotta
4 ounces (110 g) Parmesan, coarsely grated

For the béchamel sauce

2½ cups (600 ml) whole milk
1 large bay leaf
Nutmeg, preferably freshly grated
Fine sea salt
Finely ground pepper
2 tbsp (30 g) unsalted butter
¼ cup (30 g) all-purpose flour

For the crespelle

⅔ cup (150 ml) whole milk
2 large eggs
1 cup (130 g) all-purpose flour, sifted
¼ tsp fine sea salt
Unsalted butter, to cook the crespelle

Preheat the oven to 400°F (200°C) and line a medium baking dish with parchment paper.

For the filling, spread the squash in the lined baking dish. Drizzle with 2 tablespoons of olive oil, season to taste with salt and pepper, and toss to coat. Roast for 25 minutes or until tender.

For the béchamel sauce, combine the milk, bay leaf, ¼ teaspoon of nutmeg, ¼ teaspoon of salt, and a pinch of pepper in a medium saucepan and bring to a boil. Immediately take the pan off the heat, remove and discard the bay leaf, and set aside. To make the roux for the béchamel, melt the butter in a separate medium saucepan over medium-high heat and as soon as it's sizzling hot, whisk in the flour. Slowly pour the hot milk mixture into the roux and whisk until smooth. Simmer on low, whisking occasionally, for 2 to 3 minutes or until the texture starts to thicken. Season to taste with nutmeg, salt, and pepper then cover and set aside.

For the crespelle, in the bowl of a stand mixer fitted with the whisk attachment, whisk together the milk, eggs, flour, and salt until smooth. Let the batter sit for 10 minutes before you cook the crespelle. In a large cast-iron pan or nonstick skillet, melt 1 teaspoon of butter over medium-high heat. Pour in ¼ of the batter, tilting and turning the pan, so that the batter spreads evenly and very thinly. Cook the crespelle for 30 to 60 seconds per side or until golden then transfer to a large plate. Use the remaining batter to make 3 more crespelle, adjusting the heat as necessary and adding 1 teaspoon of butter to the pan between crespelle.

For the filling, in a small saucepan, heat 2 tablespoons of butter over medium-high heat and cook the sage leaves, stirring gently, for 20 to 30 seconds or until golden, green, and crispy—mind that the leaves don't burn.

Place the 4 crespelle on a work surface. Divide the squash cubes among the crespelle, spreading them evenly and leaving a thin border around the edges. Sprinkle each crespelle with 2 1/2 tablespoons of béchamel sauce, 1 heaping tablespoon of ricotta, 5 crispy sage leaves, and 1/5 of the Parmesan. Season to taste with salt and pepper. Roll the crespelle into tight wraps and arrange them, side by side, in a medium baking dish. Sprinkle the remaining béchamel sauce and Parmesan over the crespelle and bake for 12 minutes or until golden and the sauce is set. To brown the cheese a little, switch on the broiler for the last 1 to 2 minutes. Sprinkle with the remaining crispy sage leaves and serve.

317

Misty November days call for bright dishes like this fruity tomato soup refined with saffron and mussels. With excitement, I always look forward to when this orange-colored shellfish finally returns to the fishmongers' displays after its long summer break.

Mussel-Tomato Soup with Saffron

Serves 3 to 4

For the mussels

2 ¼ pounds (1 kg) fresh mussels
Olive oil
1 medium onion, finely chopped
2 large cloves garlic, thinly sliced
¾ cup plus 1 tbsp (200 ml)
dry white wine
2 bay leaves
⅛ tsp saffron threads
½ tsp fine sea salt
Finely ground pepper

For the tomato soup

Olive oil
2 ¼ pounds (1 kg) tomatoes,
very finely chopped
1 large clove garlic, thinly sliced
Fine sea salt
Finely ground pepper
1 ½ tbsp chopped fresh flat-leaf
parsley leaves, for the topping

For the mussels, rinse and scrub the mussels with cold water and cut off the beards. Discard any broken mussels.

Heat a splash of olive oil in a large pot over medium heat and sauté the onion and garlic for a few minutes or until golden and soft. Add the white wine, bay leaves, saffron, salt, and a generous amount of pepper and bring to a boil. Add the mussels then reduce the heat to medium, cover, and cook for 5 minutes or until the shells open. Shake the pot once or twice while the mussels are cooking or gently stir them with a slotted ladle or spoon. Use the slotted ladle or spoon to transfer the mussels to a large bowl, discarding any that don't open. Reserve 1 ⅔ cups (400 ml) of the mussel broth, along with the onions and garlic, and set aside for the soup. Reserve 8 mussels in their shells for the topping then peel the remaining mussels from their shells and set aside.

For the tomato soup, heat a splash of olive oil in a large pot over medium-high heat. Add the tomatoes and garlic and cook, stirring occasionally, for 4 minutes then add the reserved mussel broth, onions, and garlic and bring to a boil. Reduce the heat and simmer for about 7 minutes or until the soup starts to thicken. Season to taste with salt and pepper. If you prefer a smoother soup, purée it in a food processor or blender, or with an immersion blender. Add the mussel meat to the soup, stir, and divide among bowls. Sprinkle with the parsley, top with the mussels in shells, and serve immediately.

Makes 2 sandwiches

6 small shallots, unpeeled
1 tbsp olive oil
Unsalted butter, to cook the apple
1 medium, tart baking apple,
peeled, cored,
and cut into 8 wedges
3 ounces (85 g) aromatic cheese
that melts well, such as Raclette,
Comté, or Gruyère,
coarsely grated
2 white buns, cut in half
Coarsely ground pepper

Roasted shallots and seared apple sink smoothly into a grilled cheese sandwich—they melt into the cheese like butter.

Grilled Cheese Sandwich with Shallots and Apple

Preheat the oven to 425°F (220°C).

In a small baking dish, toss the shallots with the olive oil and roast, turning once, for 30 minutes or until soft. Remove the baking dish from the oven and set the oven to broil (quicker method) or increase the heat to 500°F (260°C).

In a small, heavy pan, heat 1 tablespoon of butter over high heat until sizzling. Add the apple wedges and sear for 45 to 60 seconds per side or until golden brown and al dente. If the apple browns too quickly, reduce the heat.

Divide the cheese among the bottom halves of the buns. Put the sandwiches under the broiler, or roast at 500°F (260°C) for a few minutes or until the cheese starts to melt. Spread the apple wedges on top of the cheese then cut the ends off the shallots and squeeze them out of their skins and onto the apples. Sprinkle with pepper, place a top on each bun, and enjoy.

Serves 2 to 4

Fine sea salt
1 pound (450 g) cored white
or green cabbage, shredded
3 tbsp olive oil
1 tbsp freshly grated ginger, plus
more to taste
1 medium sprig fresh rosemary
1 tsp honey
2 to 3 tsp white balsamic vinegar
Finely ground pepper
2 small oranges, peeled
(skin and white pith removed)
and cut into segments

Shredded cabbage salad with caraway seeds, bacon, and vinegar is an evergreen German classic. It's a beloved companion for both barbecued meats in summer and rich roasts in winter. Introducing the crisp cabbage to orange and ginger wakes it up a bit and makes this cozy salad a bit more complex.

Cabbage and Orange Salad with Ginger and Rosemary

In a large bowl, sprinkle $1/2$ teaspoon of salt over the cabbage and rub it in with your fingers for about 1 minute. Let it sit for 10 minutes to soften the cabbage.

In a small saucepan, heat the olive oil, ginger, and rosemary over high heat until sizzling. Take the pan off the heat and remove and discard the rosemary. Add the honey and 2 teaspoons of the vinegar, whisk until smooth, and pour over the cabbage. Toss to combine and season to taste with additional ginger, vinegar, salt, and pepper. Gently fold the orange segments into the cabbage, divide among plates, and serve.

When I lived close to the French border, not far from the Alsace region, I used to visit winegrowers on both sides of the border as soon as they started producing their first young wines of the year, like Alsatian vin nouveau or *Federweisser* in the Pfalz area, on the German side. Many villages celebrate the harvest season with a traditional feast, pouring lots of wine and serving *Zwiebelkuchen*. It's a scrumptious savory pie with a juicy onion and bacon filling. Baked on top of the filling and not inside, the smoky meat turns golden and crispy.

Zwiebelkuchen
Onion Pie with Crispy Bacon

Serves 4 to 6

For the pastry
1 ½ cups (200 g) all-purpose flour
¼ tsp fine sea salt
⅓ cup plus 2 tbsp (100 g) unsalted butter, cold
2 tbsp water, cold

For the filling
Olive oil
1 ½ tbsp (20 g) unsalted butter
1 ½ pounds (680 g) onions, cut in half and thinly sliced
1 ¼ tbsp all-purpose flour
¾ cup plus 1 tbsp (200 ml) heavy cream
⅔ cup (150 ml) whole milk
Fine sea salt
Finely ground pepper
Nutmeg, preferably freshly grated
3 large eggs, beaten
2 ounces (60 g) thick-cut bacon, cut into very small cubes

For the pastry, combine the flour and salt in the bowl of a stand mixer fitted with the dough hook attachment. Add the butter and use a knife to cut it into the flour until there are just small pieces left. Quickly rub the butter into the flour with your fingers until combined. Add the cold water and mix with the hook until crumbly. Form the dough into a thick disc, wrap it in plastic wrap, and freeze for 10 minutes.

Preheat the oven to 400°F (200°C).

For the filling, in a large, heavy pan, heat a generous splash of olive oil and the butter over medium heat and cook the onions, stirring occasionally, for about 15 minutes or until golden brown and soft. Add the flour and cook, stirring constantly, for 1 minute. In a separate bowl, whisk together the heavy cream and milk then add to the onions. Bring to a boil then reduce the heat to medium-high and cook, stirring, for about 3 minutes or until thick. Take the pan off the heat, season to taste with salt, pepper, and nutmeg then add the eggs and stir until combined.

On a work surface, place the dough between 2 sheets of plastic wrap and use a rolling pin to roll out into a disc, large enough to line the bottom and sides of a 12-inch (30 cm) quiche dish. Fit the dough into the quiche dish, pushing it into the dish, especially along the edges. Let the dough hang over the rim a little or trim with a knife. Use a fork to prick the dough all over. Bake for 10 minutes or until golden. If the dough bubbles up, push it down with a fork. Spread the onion filling on top of the pre-baked pastry and sprinkle with the bacon. Bake for 10 minutes then reduce the heat to 350°F (180°C) and bake for another 30 minutes or until golden brown and set.

Let the pie cool at least 10 minutes. Serve warm or cold with a glass of vin nouveau.

My mother often cooked liver with apples and onions for me, and her mother used to do the same for her. This traditional dish, rural and unassuming, originated in a time when all cuts and pieces of an animal were used and nothing was wasted. It's either a childhood nightmare or a favorite, and for me, it's the latter. I always loved the combination of sweet, earthy flavor and velvety texture. Mixing the apple and onion with fresh marjoram and chunky mashed potatoes makes for an inventive and delicious twist.

Veal Liver with Apple-Onion Mashed Potatoes

Serves 2

For the mashed potatoes
¾ pound (340 g) peeled
waxy potatoes
Olive oil
2 medium onions,
cut in half and thinly sliced
1 tbsp elderflower syrup
(or maple syrup)
Unsalted butter, to cook the apple
1 medium, tart apple, peeled,
cored, and cut into 8 wedges
Fine sea salt
Finely ground pepper
2 tsp fresh marjoram leaves

For the liver
Unsalted butter, to cook the liver
Olive oil
1 (10-ounce / 280-g) slice veal liver
Fine sea salt
Finely ground pepper

For the mashed potatoes, in a medium pot, cover the potatoes with salted water and bring to a boil. Cover the pot, reduce the heat, and simmer for about 20 minutes or until tender. Drain the potatoes and return them to the pot.

In a medium, heavy pan, heat a splash of olive oil over medium heat. Add the onions and cook, stirring occasionally, for 15 minutes or until golden brown and soft. Add the elderflower syrup, stir, and set aside.

In a small, heavy pan, heat 1 tablespoon of butter over medium-high heat and sear the apple wedges for about 2 minutes per side or until golden brown and al dente.

Place the pot with the potatoes over medium heat, add $1/4$ cup (60 ml) of olive oil, $1/2$ of the onions, and $1/2$ of the apple and use a plain knife to break the potatoes and apples into chunks. Continue chopping until the mash is smooth but partially chunky, adding more olive oil if the mixture is too dry, then season to taste with salt and pepper.

For the liver, heat 1 tablespoon of butter and a splash of olive oil in a medium, heavy pan over medium-high heat. Add the liver, reduce the heat to medium, and cook for 1 to $1 1/2$ minutes per side or until just cooked through and still a little pink in the center. Season to taste with salt and pepper, cut in half, and divide among plates. Add a large spoonful of the mashed potatoes, sprinkle with the marjoram, and serve with the remaining onions and apple wedges.

Creating fiddly lattice tops for pies is not an easy task for the impatient baker, but you will definitely impress your guests—especially if there happens to be a filling of spiced chestnuts and apples slumbering underneath.

Spiced Chestnut and Apple Pie

Serves 6 to 8

For the pastry

2⅔ cups (350 g) all-purpose flour

¾ tsp fine sea salt

¾ cup plus 2 tbsp (200 g) unsalted butter, cold

3½ tbsp water, cold

1 tsp cider vinegar

For the filling

5 medium, tart baking apples

2 whole cloves

2 allspice berries

2 tsp freshly grated orange zest

1 tsp ground cinnamon

⅛ tsp nutmeg, preferably freshly grated

7 ounces (200 g) vacuum-packed whole cooked chestnuts

½ cup (100 g) granulated sugar

¼ cup (60 ml) freshly squeezed orange juice, plus 3 tbsp for the apples

1 large egg

2 tbsp all-purpose flour

1 tbsp (15 g) unsalted butter, cut into small pieces

For the topping

1 large egg yolk

1 tbsp whole milk

⅛ tsp fine sea salt

1 tbsp granulated sugar

For the pastry, combine the flour and salt in the bowl of a stand mixer fitted with the dough hook attachment. Add the butter and use a knife to cut it into the flour until there are just small pieces left. Quickly rub the butter into the flour with your fingers until combined. Add the cold water and the vinegar and mix with the hook until crumbly. Form the dough into a ball, divide it in half, and form 2 thick discs. Wrap both discs in plastic wrap and freeze for 15 minutes.

Preheat the oven to 400°F (200°C).

For the filling, peel and core the apples and cut each apple into 8 wedges. Grind the cloves and allspice berries with a mortar and pestle then transfer to a small bowl, add the orange zest, cinnamon, and nutmeg, and whisk until combined. In a food processor or blender, purée the chestnuts until smooth then transfer to a large bowl. Add $1/2$ of the spice mixture, $1/4$ cup (50 g) of the sugar, $1/4$ cup (60 ml) of orange juice, and the egg and whisk until combined. In a medium bowl, toss the apples with the remaining 3 tablespoons of orange juice, the flour, the remaining $1/4$ cup (50 g) of sugar and the remaining spice mixture.

On a work surface, place both discs of dough between 2 sheets of plastic wrap. Use a rolling pin to roll out 1 of the discs into a circle, large enough to line the bottom and sides of a 9-inch (23 cm) shallow pie dish. Line the pie dish with the dough, pushing it into the dish, especially along the edges. Let the dough hang over the rim a little. Roll out the second disc into a 10 x 10-inch (25 x 25 cm) square and cut it into 8 ($1 1/4$-inch / 3-cm) strips.

Spread the chestnut purée on top of the pastry in the pie dish, arrange the apples on top, and sprinkle with the butter. Quickly arrange the pastry strips in a lattice pattern on top of the filling, gently pressing the edges of the pastry together to seal it.

For the topping, whisk together the egg yolk, milk, and salt, brush on the lattice top, and sprinkle with the sugar. Bake for 15 minutes then reduce the heat to 350°F (180°C) and bake for another 45 minutes or until golden brown. Let the pie cool at least 15 minutes before cutting it into pieces and serving.

Choosing green, black, red, or yellow lentils is more than a matter of aesthetics, as they each have their own unique tastes and qualities. Beluga lentils turn the simplest meal into a stunner (recipe no. 67 and no. 281). If you cook tender pear wedges in star anise–thyme butter and let them melt into the dark legumes, along with some crumbly blue cheese, you'll have an extravagant dish that's perfect for a romantic evening or an elegant dinner party.

323

Serves 3 to 4

1 cup (220 g) lentils, preferably
beluga (no soaking required)
1 small bunch fresh thyme,
plus 4 tbsp thyme leaves
1 small sprig fresh rosemary
1 slice lemon
1 bay leaf
Fine sea salt
Finely ground pepper
¼ cup (60 g) unsalted butter
3 star anise
1 large, firm pear, cored
and cut into thin wedges
4 ounces (110 g) Stilton
(or any crumbly blue cheese),
crumbled

Picture page 397, top left

Beluga Lentils with Stilton, Pear, and Star Anise–Thyme Butter

Place the lentils in a medium saucepan with plenty of (unsalted) water, add the bunch of thyme, the rosemary, lemon, and bay leaf, and bring to a boil. Reduce the heat and simmer, adding more water if necessary, for about 20 minutes or until al dente (or follow the package instructions). There should be a little cooking liquid left when the lentils are done. Remove and discard the herbs and lemon and season to taste with salt and pepper.

In a medium, heavy pan, heat the butter, thyme leaves, and star anise over medium-high heat until sizzling. Add the pear and sauté, turning once, for about 4 minutes or until golden brown and tender. Season to taste with salt and pepper.

Divide the lentils among bowls, arrange the pear wedges on top, and drizzle with the star anise–thyme butter. Sprinkle with the Stilton and a little pepper and serve immediately.

324

Serves 3 to 6

1 pound (450 g) seeded squash,
preferably peeled butternut
or Hokkaido with skin
¾ pound (340 g) sweet potatoes,
scrubbed
⅓ cup plus 1 tbsp (90 ml) olive oil
Flaky sea salt
Coarsely ground pepper
3 ounces (85 g) Stilton, crumbled
1 small bunch fresh thyme

This is such an easy weekday gratin. Just pile up the squash and sweet potato in a baking dish then relax and let the oven and the aromatic cheese take care of the rest. The melted Stilton is present, but it doesn't dominate the vegetables—it just makes them a little tastier than they are on their own.

Squash and Sweet Potato Gratin with Stilton

Preheat the oven to 400°F (200°C). Cut the squash into 1/2-inch (1.25 cm) wedges and cut the sweet potatoes into 1/4-inch-thick (0.5 cm) circles.

In a 12-inch (30 cm) quiche dish, drizzle the squash and sweet potatoes with the olive oil and toss to combine. Arrange the vegetables in overlapping layers, season to taste with salt and pepper, and sprinkle with the Stilton and thyme sprigs. Roast for about 40 minutes or until the vegetables are golden and tender. Serve warm as a main or as a side dish for hearty roasts and poultry.

325

Makes 2 sandwiches

5 ounces (140 g) peeled celeriac, cut into small cubes
2 ounces (60 g) fresh ricotta, drained
1 tsp balsamic vinegar
½ tsp maple syrup
¼ tsp ground cinnamon
Fine sea salt
Finely ground pepper
Olive oil
4 slices bacon
2 large slices rustic dark bread, such as rye or spelt

Celeriac is an underestimated root, usually reserved for soups, sauces, or broth. But when it's only allowed to blend in and lend its distinctive, nutty taste to more complex creations, the knobbly vegetable barely gets the chance to show its full potential. So, this sandwich is dedicated to unpretentious celeriac, a veggie that helps others shine, while never demanding the spotlight for itself.

Celeriac-Ricotta Dip and Bacon on Rye Bread

Bring a small pot of salted water to a boil and blanch the celeriac for about 6 minutes or until tender. Drain the celeriac then transfer to a food processor or blender, add the ricotta, vinegar, maple syrup, and cinnamon, and purée until smooth. Season to taste with salt and pepper and transfer to a small bowl.

In a medium, heavy pan, heat a splash of olive oil over medium-high heat and cook the bacon, turning occasionally, for a few minutes or until golden brown and crispy.

Generously spread the celeriac-ricotta dip on the bread and top with the bacon. Sprinkle with a little pepper and enjoy.

326

Serves 2 to 4

Olive oil
2 tbsp freshly squeezed orange juice
2 tsp high-quality orange blossom water, preferably organic
Fine sea salt
Finely ground pepper
¾ cup (150 g) drained and rinsed canned chickpeas
1 tbsp balsamic vinegar
2 large handfuls arugula leaves
2 blood oranges, peeled (skin and white pith removed) and cut into segments

Chickpeas plus orange blossom water is a magical combination that turns a quick arugula and blood orange salad into a delicious and healthy lunch break.

Chickpea, Blood Orange, and Arugula Salad with Orange Blossom Dressing

In a small bowl, whisk together 3 tablespoons of olive oil, the orange juice, and orange blossom water and season to taste with salt and pepper.

Heat a splash of olive oil in a small, heavy pan over medium-high heat and sauté the chickpeas, stirring occasionally, for 3 minutes or until golden and crispy. Add the vinegar, stir, and cook for 1 minute then season to taste with salt.

Arrange the arugula, blood orange segments, and chickpeas in a large bowl, drizzle with the dressing, and serve immediately.

Serves 3 to 4

½ cup (100 g) pearl barley
¾ tsp coriander seeds
½ tsp allspice berries
½ tsp fennel seeds
½ tsp ground cumin
¼ tsp ground cardamom
Olive oil
5 ounces (140 g) feta,
cut into cubes
2 tbsp honey
12 kumquats, cut in half
lengthwise and seeds removed
(or 2 small oranges, peeled
and cut into segments)
½ cup (120 ml) freshly squeezed
orange juice
1 medium fennel bulb, quartered,
cored, and very thinly sliced
Fine sea salt
Finely ground pepper
1 small handful fresh mint leaves

Picture opposite, top right

After years of banishing it from my kitchen, a recipe from Yotam Ottolenghi and Sami Tamimi's *Jerusalem* cookbook finally opened up my taste buds to barley. Seeing the chefs add feta marinated in za'atar oil to a barley salad made me rethink my prejudices and finally enjoy the grain. I use cardamom, cumin, coriander, allspice, and fennel seeds instead of the Middle Eastern dried herb mixture and sneak in fennel bulb and caramelized kumquats. It's the freshest winter salad.

Barley and Fennel Salad with Spiced Feta and Caramelized Honey Kumquats

Bring a large pot of salted water to a boil and cook the barley, according to the package instructions, until al dente. Drain the barley and transfer to a large bowl.

Grind the coriander seeds, allspice berries, fennel seeds, cumin, and cardamom with a mortar and pestle and transfer to a medium bowl. Add 1/3 cup (75 ml) of olive oil, whisk, then add the feta and toss to combine.

In a small, heavy pan, heat the honey over high heat until bubbling. Add the kumquats and 1/4 cup (60 ml) of the orange juice and cook, turning once, for 3 to 4 minutes or until golden brown and soft—mind that they don't burn.

Add the fennel bulb, the remaining 1/4 cup (60 ml) of orange juice, the feta, and spiced oil to the barley and gently stir until combined. Season to taste with salt and pepper and if the salad is dry, add more olive oil. Arrange the kumquats on top, sprinkle with mint, and serve warm or cold.

Serves 1

6 to 9 fresh French oysters,
preferably from Cap Ferret,
freshly shucked, on the half shell
½ lemon
6 to 9 small fresh mint leaves,
very finely chopped

I met Alison at Cap Ferret in France, at the tip of the idyllic headland separating the Atlantic Ocean form the Arcachon Bay. We sat in the garden of Chez Boulan, with the oyster banks spread out in front of us, and the smell of wet sand and seaweed woven into the salty air. Alison, who manages the restaurant that specializes in oysters, told me to try one with fresh mint—I obeyed and fell in love.

French Oysters with Fresh Mint

Arrange the oysters on a large plate. Drizzle 1 oyster at a time with 1 to 2 drops of lemon juice, add a pinch of mint, and enjoy immediately.

323

327

329

331

As November comes to an end, it's time to herald the festive baking season that'll sweeten our weekends and the smell of our kitchens in the weeks to come. Chocolate and orange panettone is a very satisfying project and it's a treat that never manages to meet expectations unless it's homemade.

Chocolate and Orange Panettone

Makes 1 panettone

3¾ cups plus 1 tbsp (500 g) all-purpose flour
½ cup (100 g) granulated sugar
2 tbsp freshly grated orange zest
2 (¼-ounce / 7-g) envelopes fast-acting yeast
½ tsp fine sea salt
⅛ tsp nutmeg, preferably freshly grated
¾ cup plus 3 tbsp (225 ml) whole milk, lukewarm
¾ cup (170 g) unsalted butter, melted and cooled
5 large egg yolks
4 ounces (110 g) bittersweet chocolate, cold, roughly chopped
1 tbsp heavy cream
4 almonds
Confectioners' sugar

Picture page 397, bottom left

In the bowl of a stand mixer fitted with the dough hook attachment, whisk together the flour, granulated sugar, orange zest, yeast, salt, and nutmeg. In a separate bowl, whisk together the lukewarm milk, the melted butter, and egg yolks and add to the flour mixture then mix with the hook for 5 minutes or until smooth and well combined. Transfer the dough to a work surface and continue kneading with your hands for 5 minutes or until you have a soft and silky ball of dough. Place the dough back in the bowl, cover with a tea towel, and let rise in a warm place, or preferably in a 100°F (35°C) warm oven, for about 1 hour and 30 minutes or until doubled in size.

Butter a 7-inch (18 cm), roughly 4-inch-tall (10 cm) ovenproof dish or metal pot. Line the sides of the pot with a piece of parchment paper that exceeds the height of the pot by 2 inches (5 cm) and is buttered on the inside.

When the dough has doubled in size, punch it down, take it out of the bowl, and knead for about 30 seconds. Add the cold chocolate and quickly mix until well combined. Form the dough into a ball then transfer to the lined pot, cover with a tea towel, and let rise in a warm place for another 60 minutes or until doubled in size.

Preheat the oven to 400°F / 200°C (preferably convection setting).

Brush the dough with the heavy cream and use a sharp knife to cut a cross in the top then decorate with the almonds. Bake for 10 minutes then reduce the heat to 350°F (180°C) and bake for 30 minutes, covering the panettone with a piece of aluminum foil if it browns too quickly. Reduce the heat to 325°F (160°C) and bake for another 10 minutes (slightly longer if using a conventional oven) or until golden brown and firm. Let the panettone cool in the pot for at least 30 minutes or until stable enough to cool on a wire rack. When it's completely cool, dust with confectioners' sugar, and serve plain or with butter.

The panettone tastes best on the first and second day after it's baked.

The winter months bring roots and all their deeply colored shades and earthy-sweet flavors back to the menu. Roasting roots in the oven unfolds their full depth and when you merge the firm bites with a vibrant dip made of sheep's milk yogurt whipped with turmeric, cardamom, cinnamon, and cayenne pepper, they make for an exciting brunch, lunch, or dinner.

Roasted Turnips and Beets with Spiced Sheep's Milk Yogurt

Preheat the oven to 425°F (220°C).

For the roots, whisk together the olive oil, blood orange juice, honey, cinnamon, and star anise and pour into a medium baking dish. Add the yellow turnips and beets, toss to combine, and season generously with flaky sea salt and coarsely ground pepper. Roast for 20 minutes then stir and continue roasting for another 20 minutes or until golden brown and al dente.

For the dip, in a small bowl, whisk together the yogurt, blood orange juice, turmeric, cardamom, cinnamon, and cayenne pepper and season to taste with fine sea salt.

Serve the roasted roots warm or cold with a generous dollop of the yogurt dip.

Serves 2

For the roots

3 tbsp olive oil

2 tbsp freshly squeezed
blood orange juice
(or regular orange juice)

1 tsp honey

½ tsp ground cinnamon

3 star anise

1¼ pounds (560 g) peeled
yellow turnips (or white turnips)
and beets, each cut into 8 wedges

Flaky sea salt

Coarsely ground pepper

For the dip

1 cup (240 g) Greek
sheep's milk yogurt (or regular
full-fat plain Greek yogurt)

2 tbsp freshly squeezed
blood orange juice
(or regular orange juice)

¾ tsp ground turmeric

¼ tsp ground cardamom

⅛ tsp ground cinnamon

⅛ tsp ground cayenne pepper

Fine sea salt

331

week 48 / tuesday

Serves 2 to 4

1 large pink grapefruit
⅔ cup (160 g) full-fat plain Greek
yogurt
2 tbsp olive oil
½ tsp freshly grated orange zest
¼ cup (60 ml) freshly squeezed
orange juice
1½ tbsp freshly squeezed
lime juice
Fine sea salt
Finely ground pepper
½ pound (225 g) peeled celeriac
1 small handful fresh
cilantro leaves

Picture page 397, bottom right

The combination of grapefruit and cilantro is one to remember. You can keep it simple and toss the bitter, juicy fruit and bright fresh herb with a quick vinaigrette, or use them as a contrasting topping for a smooth celeriac salad. Either way, the vibrant pink and green pairing will successfully lift November's grey monotony.

Celeriac Salad with Pink Grapefruit and Cilantro

Peel the grapefruit, removing the skin and white pith, and cut into segments.

In a small bowl, whisk together the yogurt, olive oil, orange zest, orange juice, and lime juice and season to taste with salt and pepper.

Coarsely grate the celeriac and transfer to a medium bowl. Add the yogurt dressing and toss until well combined. Arrange the grapefruit and cilantro on top and serve immediately.

332

week 48 / wednesday

Makes 4 tartines

9 ounces (250 g) fresh ricotta
1 tsp high-quality orange
blossom water, preferably organic,
plus more to taste
6 tbsp freshly squeezed
orange juice
2½ tbsp honey
Fine sea salt
Finely ground pepper
12 kumquats, cut in half
lengthwise and seeds removed
4 thick slices ciabatta
1 small handful unsalted
pistachios, roughly chopped

The culinary excitement of my early days in Malta revolved around ricotta, orange blossom water, and citrus fruits, and this scrumptious tartine brings them all together.

Orange Blossom-Ricotta Tartine with Caramelized Kumquats

In a medium bowl, whisk together the ricotta, orange blossom water, 2 tablespoons of the orange juice, and 1/2 tablespoon of the honey. Season to taste with salt, pepper, and additional orange blossom water.

In a small, heavy pan, heat the remaining 2 tablespoons of honey over high heat until bubbling. Add the kumquats and the remaining 4 tablespoons of orange juice and cook, turning once, for 3 to 4 minutes or until golden brown and soft—mind that they don't burn.

Spread the ricotta mixture on the bread and top with the kumquats. Drizzle with the honey juices from the pan, sprinkle with the pistachios, and enjoy.

333

I ate tangerine jam for the first time on warm buttered toast in Sicily. The color of the chunky spread was as bright and warm as the Mediterranean sun, a beautiful deep orange. It tasted unbelievably good—sweet and sour with bitter hints—and immediately became my favorite jam and the one you'll always find in my pantry all year round. It's also a fantastic filling for gooey brownies (recipe no. 70).

Tangerine Jam

Makes 4 jars

2⅔ pounds (1.2 kg) thin-skinned organic tangerines
(or clementines), scrubbed
2 medium lemons, cut in half
3 cups (600 g) granulated sugar
80-proof (40%) spirit,
to sterilize the jars*

Bring a large pot of water to a boil. Add the tangerines then reduce the heat, cover, and simmer for 20 minutes. Reserve $1/2$ cup (120 ml) of the cooking water and transfer the tangerines to a cutting board. Trim and discard the ends then cut the tangerines into quarters and set aside. Remove the tangerine seeds and the lemon seeds and place the seeds in a small saucepan. Add the reserved cooking water and bring to a boil. Reduce the heat and simmer for 5 minutes to extract the pectin from the seeds. Strain and discard the seeds and set the cooking water aside.

Transfer the quartered tangerines to a food processor or blender and pulse until roughly chopped then transfer to a tall, large pot. Juice the lemons and add their juice, along with the sugar and the reserved cooking water, to the tangerines. Gently bring to a boil, stirring, until the sugar dissolves. Continue boiling, stirring occasionally, for 18 to 20 minutes or until thick. Divide the jam among sterilized jars, fill the jars to the top and close them tightly, then let them cool completely. You can keep the jam in the pantry for at least 1 year. Once opened, the jars should be stored in the refrigerator.

* Sterilize 4 (1¼-cup / 300-ml) jam jars and their screw tops for 5 minutes in boiling water then rinse them out with 80-proof (40%) spirit just before filling them with jam.

I learned to make this southern German classic from a spaetzle master, my Swabian stepfather. He taught me how to make the best crowd-pleaser I know, a heavenly cheesy noodle and onion gratin. Uli's spaetzle rules were strict but simple: never add water to the batter and layer the spaetzle with lots of onions and just the right amount of aromatic cheese. The kitchen creates some of the most precious memories and I'm grateful I got to spend so many years next to this man both at the stove and at the table.

Raclette and Onion Spaetzle

Serves 4 to 6

For the onions

Olive oil

10 medium onions,
cut in half and thinly sliced

For the spaetzle

About 1¾ cups (230 g)
all-purpose flour

About 1 cup (180 g) coarse durum
wheat semolina

Fine sea salt

8 large eggs

Coarsely ground pepper

11 ounces (310 g) aromatic cheese
that melts well, such as Raclette,
Comté, or Gruyère,
coarsely grated

You'll need a spaetzle or potato ricer for this recipe, or use a colander with 1/4-inch (0.5 cm) holes and a flexible spatula.

For the onions, heat a generous splash of olive oil in a large, heavy pan over medium heat. Add the onions and cook, stirring occasionally, for about 30 minutes or until golden brown and very soft then cover and set aside.

For the spaetzle, in a large bowl, whisk together the all-purpose flour, durum wheat semolina, and 1 1/2 teaspoons of salt. Add the eggs and beat with a wooden spoon (or use a stand mixer fitted with the paddle attachment) until the batter is smooth and forms bubbles. When you lift a spoonful of the batter, it should slowly drip off the spoon in heavy drops. If it's too loose and not thick enough, add more all-purpose flour and durum wheat semolina. Let the batter sit for 10 to 20 minutes.

Preheat the oven to 275°F (135°C) and place a large ovenproof bowl inside. Fill your largest pot with salted water and bring to a boil.

Working in batches, fill about 2/3 of the spaetzle ricer with about 1/4 of the batter. When the water is boiling, hold the spaetzle ricer close to the top of the water and squeeze the batter into the water then quickly cut the spaetzle off with a large knife and swirl the knife in the water. Cook the spaetzle for 30 to 45 seconds or until firm. Using a slotted ladle or spoon, transfer the spaetzle to a colander, drain, and transfer to the bowl in the oven. Season to taste with salt and pepper, sprinkle with 1/4 of the cheese and 1/4 of the onions, and return the bowl to the oven. Repeat to make 3 more layers, bringing the water back to a boil between batches. When the last layer is added, keep the bowl in the oven for about 3 minutes or until all the cheese has melted.

Scoop large spoonfuls of the spaetzle onto plates, season to taste with salt and pepper, and serve with a simple green salad on the side.

December

December is a good month. We sing along to Christmas carols, eat too many cookies, and enjoy far too much mulled wine. We dare to skip our duties to share a few more precious moments with the ones we love. The festive perfume of fir and spices mixes with the buttery smell of baked goods and turns the house into the coziest place on earth. A golden spinach and Gorgonzola quiche is just the right dish to begin a month of exuberant feasting.

Spinach and Gorgonzola Quiche

Serves 4 to 8

For the pastry

2 cups (260 g) all-purpose flour

1 tsp fine sea salt

½ cup plus 1 tbsp (130 g) unsalted butter, cold

1 large egg

For the filling

18 ounces (500 g) trimmed spinach leaves

5 large eggs

¾ cup (175 g) sour cream (or crème fraîche)

½ cup (120 ml) heavy cream

1 tsp fine sea salt

Finely ground pepper

Nutmeg, preferably freshly grated

3 ounces (85 g) Gorgonzola, cut into small pieces

For the pastry, combine the flour and salt in the bowl of a stand mixer fitted with the dough hook attachment. Add the butter and use a knife to cut it into the flour until there are just small pieces left. Quickly rub the butter into the flour with your fingers until combined. Add the egg and mix with the hook until crumbly. Form the dough into a thick disc, wrap it in plastic wrap, and freeze for 10 minutes.

Preheat the oven to 400°F (200°C).

For the filling, bring a large pot of salted water to a boil and blanch the spinach for about 1 1/2 minutes or until tender. Transfer to a colander, drain, and quickly rinse with cold water. Leave the spinach in the colander to cool for 5 minutes then squeeze until it's quite dry and roughly chop.

On a work surface, place the dough between 2 sheets of plastic wrap and use a rolling pin to roll out into a disc, large enough to line the bottom and sides of a 12-inch (30 cm) quiche dish. Fit the dough into the quiche dish, pushing it into the dish, especially along the edges. Let the dough hang over the rim a little or trim with a knife. Use a fork to prick the dough all over. Bake for 15 minutes or until golden. If the dough bubbles up, push it down with a fork. Take the quiche dish out of the oven and reduce the heat to 350°F (180°C).

In a medium bowl, whisk together the eggs, sour cream, heavy cream, salt, and generous amounts of pepper and nutmeg.

Spread the spinach on top of the pre-baked pastry and cover with the egg mixture. Sprinkle with the Gorgonzola and bake for about 40 minutes or until golden and firm. Let the quiche cool for at least 10 minutes. Serve warm or cold.

Weekend baking is pure meditation. All you need is a quiet kitchen and time to reflect on life while the mixer is purring in the background like a sleepy cat. Easy recipes with spectacular results are the best, especially if cake decorating isn't your forte—it's definitely not one of my talents. This spongy tangerine-scented Madeira cake is perfect and the caramelized citrus fruit topping looks dramatic. Despite the title, this English cake is not made with Madeira, but traditionally is accompanied by a glass of the sweet Portuguese wine, which led to its name.

Madeira Cake with Caramelized Tangerines

Serves 6 to 8

For the cake

2 cups (260 g) all-purpose flour

2 tbsp freshly grated tangerine zest (or clementine zest)

1 tsp baking powder

¼ tsp ground cinnamon

⅛ tsp fine sea salt

¾ cup plus 2 tbsp (200 g) unsalted butter, at room temperature

1 cup (200 g) granulated sugar

3 large eggs

3 tbsp freshly squeezed tangerine juice (or clementine juice)

For the topping

4 small thin-skinned tangerines (or clementines), very thinly sliced

½ cup (100 g) granulated sugar

¼ cup (60 ml) water

Preheat the oven to 350°F / 180°C (preferably convection setting). Butter a 7-inch (18 cm) springform pan.

For the cake, combine the flour, tangerine zest, baking powder, cinnamon, and salt in a medium bowl.

In the bowl of a stand mixer fitted with the paddle attachment, beat the butter and sugar for a few minutes or until fluffy. Add the eggs, 1 at a time, incorporating each egg before adding the next one, and continue beating for a few minutes or until thick and creamy. Add the flour mixture and tangerine juice and quickly mix until well combined. Spread the batter in the prepared pan and bake for 50 to 60 minutes (slightly longer if using a conventional oven) or until golden and spongy. If you insert a skewer in the center of the cake, it should come out clean. Let the cake cool in the pan for 10 minutes then transfer to a large plate and let it cool completely.

For the topping, divide the tangerines, sugar, and water among 2 medium pots and bring to a boil. Cook over high heat for 3 to 5 minutes or until golden and caramelized—mind that the tangerines don't burn. Quickly arrange the tangerines in overlapping circles on top of the cake—mind that you work quickly, as the fruit will harden within seconds. Cut the cake with a sharp knife, divide among plates, and serve.

Even the most festive and lavish month of the year needs a simple, comforting pasta. A bowl of warm spaghetti with lemon-pistachio pesto and mozzarella is a splendid lunch and can be thrown together in less than fifteen minutes.

Spaghetti with Lemon-Pistachio Pesto and Mozzarella di Bufala

Serves 2

For the pasta

6 ounces (170 g) dried spaghetti
Olive oil
4 ounces (110 g) mozzarella di
bufala, drained and torn
into chunks
Fine sea salt
Coarsely ground pepper

For the pesto

4 tbsp freshly grated lemon zest,
plus 1 tsp for the topping
4 tbsp finely grated Parmesan,
plus 1 tbsp for the topping
1 tbsp finely chopped
unsalted pistachios,
plus 1 tbsp for the topping
3 tbsp olive oil
Fine sea salt

For the pasta, bring a large pot of salted water to a boil and cook the spaghetti, according to the package instructions, until al dente. Drain the spaghetti and return it to the pot. Add a splash of olive oil and toss to combine.

For the pesto, in a medium bowl, whisk together the 4 tablespoons of lemon zest, 4 tablespoons of Parmesan, 1 tablespoon of pistachios, and the olive oil. Use the back of a spoon to press the Parmesan into the oil until well combined then season to taste with salt.

Divide the spaghetti and mozzarella among plates and drizzle with the pesto. Sprinkle with the lemon zest, Parmesan, and pistachios, season to taste with salt and pepper, and serve immediately.

338

week 49 / tuesday

If you're already thinking about your Christmas menu and pondering how to please your vegetarian guests, here's a recipe that will put an end to your worries and make meat lovers jealously spy on their neighbor's plate.

Potato and Apple-Stuffed Cabbage Rolls with Walnut Butter and Gruyère

Serves 2 to 4

For the cabbage rolls
⅔ pound (300 g) peeled potatoes,
boiled and cut into small cubes
1 medium, tart baking apple,
peeled, cored,
and cut into small cubes
1 tbsp fresh thyme leaves
3 ounces (85 g) mascarpone
(or sour cream or ricotta)
2 tbsp finely grated
aromatic cheese that melts well,
such as Gruyère, Raclette,
or Comté
1 large egg
Fine sea salt
Coarsely ground pepper
Nutmeg, preferably freshly grated
8 large white or green
cabbage leaves
About ½ cup (120 ml)
dry white wine

For the topping
¼ cup (60 g) unsalted butter
1 ounce (30 g) walnuts,
roughly chopped
2 tbsp finely grated
aromatic cheese that melts well,
such as Gruyère, Raclette,
or Comté
1 tbsp fresh thyme leaves
Coarsely ground pepper

Preheat the oven to 400°F (200°C). Butter a baking dish just large enough to fit 4 cabbage rolls.

For the cabbage rolls, combine the potatoes, apple, and thyme in a large bowl. Whisk together the mascarpone, grated cheese, and egg and add to the potato mixture. Stir to combine and season to taste with salt, pepper, and nutmeg.

Bring a large pot of salted water to a boil and blanch the cabbage leaves for 5 to 8 minutes or until tender. Drain and quickly rinse with cold water then dry with paper towels and cut out the thick, hard stalks (just at the bottom). Spread the 4 largest cabbage leaves on a work surface and season to taste with salt and pepper. Divide the potato filling among the leaves, placing it in the center of each cabbage leaf, then fold up both sides and roll into a wrap; use the remaining cabbage leaves to fix any holes and cracks.

Transfer the cabbage rolls, seam-side down, to the prepared baking dish and add enough white wine to cover the bottom of the dish. Bake for 30 to 35 minutes or until golden and firm.

While the cabbage rolls are baking, prepare the topping: In a small saucepan, melt the butter over high heat until sizzling. Add the walnuts, reduce the heat to medium, and cook for 10 to 20 seconds or until golden.

Divide the cabbage rolls among plates and drizzle with the walnut butter. Sprinkle with the cheese, thyme, and pepper and serve.

Pesto, dips, and hummus are a convenient and exciting way to modify a few classic weekday meals. Smooth puréed herbs and vegetables turn pasta, sandwiches, potatoes, and salads into tasty bites. Keep your mind open and use ingredients in unusual ways. Even lentils can be turned into a fabulous hummus, especially if you pair them with roasted garlic cloves.

Dark Bread with Green Lentil Hummus, Roasted Garlic, and Mozzarella

Makes 6 sandwiches

For the lentil hummus

14 large cloves garlic, preferably young, unpeeled

¾ cup (170 g) small green or French Puy lentils (no soaking required)

1 bay leaf

6 medium sprigs fresh thyme

1 medium sprig fresh rosemary

¼ cup (60 g) light tahini, plus 2 tbsp for the topping

1 tsp freshly grated lemon zest, plus 1 tbsp for the topping

3 tbsp freshly squeezed lemon juice

3 tbsp water

2 tbsp olive oil

Fine sea salt

Finely ground pepper

For the sandwiches

6 large, thick slices crusty dark bread, such as spelt or rye

8 ounces (225 g) mozzarella di bufala, drained and cut into small cubes

Preheat the oven to 425°F (220°C).

For the hummus, spread the garlic cloves in a small baking dish and roast, turning occasionally, for about 25 minutes or until soft enough to mash with a fork—mind that the garlic doesn't burn. Let the garlic cool for a few minutes then peel the cloves.

Place the lentils, bay leaf, thyme, and rosemary in a medium saucepan with plenty of (unsalted) water and bring to a boil. Reduce the heat and simmer, adding more water if necessary, for about 20 minutes or until the lentils are al dente (or follow the package instructions). Drain the lentils and let cool for 5 minutes; remove and discard the herbs.

Transfer the lentils to a food processor or blender, add the roasted garlic, 1/4 cup (60 g) of tahini, 1 teaspoon of lemon zest, the lemon juice, water, and olive oil and purée until smooth. Add more water and olive oil if necessary then season to taste with salt and pepper and transfer to a medium bowl.

Spread the lentil dip on the bread, sprinkle with mozzarella and lemon zest, and drizzle with a little tahini. Enjoy.

Serves 1

1 large orange, peeled
(skin and white pith removed)
and sliced
High-quality olive oil
1 tsp fresh marjoram leaves
(or ½ tsp dried marjoram)
Flaky sea salt

I discovered this quickest of salads on a Sicilian breakfast table at a farm in Noto, and I've been holding on to it dearly ever since. It's a good choice when you need a refreshing break from all that holiday feasting, eating, cooking, and baking.

Sicilian Orange Salad with Olive Oil, Marjoram, and Flaky Sea Salt

Arrange the orange slices on a plate, drizzle with olive oil, and sprinkle with marjoram and a little salt. Enjoy in peace and quiet.

Makes about 60 cookies

¾ cup plus 2 tbsp (200 g) unsalted
butter, at room temperature
1 ½ ounces (45 g) high-quality
marzipan, at room temperature
⅔ cup (125 g) granulated sugar,
plus ¼ cup (50 g) for the topping
1 ¼ tbsp finely chopped
fresh rosemary needles,
plus ½ tsp for the topping
2 tsp freshly grated lemon zest,
plus 2 tsp for the topping
½ tsp fine sea salt
2 cups (260 g) all-purpose flour

Picture page 415, top left

Let December's cookie craziness begin and fill the jars with a German Christmas classic. *Heidesand* is a crumbly shortbread cookie refined with marzipan. I deviate from tradition, and add lemon zest and rosemary. It's a perfect recipe for the lazy baker, as there are no cookie cutters or decorating involved—you simply slice rounds of dough, bake, and enjoy.

German Heidesand Cookies with Rosemary and Lemon

Preheat the oven to 375°F / 190°C (preferably convection setting). Line 2 baking sheets with parchment paper.

In the bowl of a stand mixer fitted with the paddle attachment, beat the butter, marzipan, 2/3 cup (125 g) of sugar, 1 1/4 tablespoons of rosemary, 2 teaspoons of lemon zest, and the salt until smooth. Add the flour and quickly mix until combined. Divide the dough in half, transfer each portion to a piece of plastic wrap, and roll into a 1 1/2-inch-thick (4 cm) log. Wrap the logs in the plastic wrap and freeze for 15 minutes or until firm enough to cut with a knife.

Combine 1/4 cup (50 g) of sugar, 2 teaspoons of lemon zest, and 1/2 teaspoon of rosemary and spread on a cutting board. Remove the plastic wrap from the logs of dough and roll them in the lemon-rosemary sugar until evenly coated. Cut the rolls into 1/4-inch-thick (0.5 cm) slices and transfer to the lined baking sheets. Bake, 1 sheet at a time, for 8 to 9 minutes (slightly longer if using a conventional oven) or until golden. Let the cookies cool for a few minutes then transfer to a wire rack to cool completely. Store the cookies in airtight containers for up to 1 week.

Braised beef shanks are succulent and tender. Although the preparation isn't labor-intensive, it does take time—about five hours—to tenderize and infuse the marbled meat with vibrant spices and full-bodied red wine. If you braise the shanks the day before Christmas, the flavors will deepen considerably and you won't be left with much work during the festivities. The leftovers make a wonderful meat pie, or a quick pasta dish: pappardelle with Neapolitan beef ragu.

Christmassy Braised Beef Shanks with Spices and Red Wine

Serves 4

Olive oil

4 beef shanks, about 4 pounds (1.8 kg) total

Fine sea salt

Finely ground pepper

14 allspice berries

6 whole cloves

2 large bay leaves

About 2 tsp ground cinnamon

About 1 tsp ground cardamom

8 large cloves garlic

4 medium red onions, cut into quarters

4 large carrots, thickly sliced

1 (750-ml) bottle full-bodied red wine

1 ¾ pounds (800 g) canned whole peeled tomatoes, chopped

1 small bunch fresh thyme

Picture opposite, top right

Preheat the oven to 350°F (180°C).

In a Dutch oven, large enough to fit the meat and with a tight-fitting lid, heat a splash of olive oil over high heat. Working in batches, sear the beef shanks for 1 to 2 minutes per side or until evenly browned. Season to taste with salt and pepper and transfer to a plate. Reduce the heat to medium, add a splash of olive oil and the allspice, cloves, bay leaves, cinnamon, and cardamom, stir, and cook for 15 seconds. Add the garlic, onions, and carrots and sauté, stirring occasionally, for 3 minutes. Add a splash of red wine and deglaze the Dutch oven, using a spatula to scrape any bits and pieces off the bottom. Add the tomatoes, return the meat to the Dutch oven, and add the remaining wine and the thyme. Season to taste with salt and pepper, cover the Dutch oven, and place it in the oven. After 45 minutes, reduce the temperature to 275°F (135°C) and cook for 3 to 4 hours or until the meat is tender. Remove and discard the thyme and bay leaves and season the sauce to taste with salt, pepper, cinnamon, and cardamom.

Serve the beef shanks with a large spoonful of the sauce, plus potato dumplings (*recipe no. 26*), roasted Brussels sprouts (*recipe no. 344*), or sautéed parsnips (*recipe no. 354*).

341

342

343

345

343

week 49 / sunday

Lemon adds just the right amount of sourness to the silky-smooth filling of this crème brûlée tart. The fact that it sits inside crunchy, buttery pastry makes this dessert even more tempting, while the caramelized lemon slices atop the blistered golden sugar crust give it a very festive look.

Lemon Crème Brûlée Tart

Serves 6 to 8

For the pastry

1 ½ cups (200 g) all-purpose flour
⅓ cup (65 g) granulated sugar
⅛ tsp fine sea salt
⅓ cup plus 2 tbsp (100 g)
unsalted butter, cold
2 large egg yolks

For the filling

2 large eggs plus 2 large egg
yolks
⅓ cup plus 2 tbsp (100 ml)
heavy cream
3 tbsp sour cream
(or crème fraîche)
½ cup (100 g) granulated sugar
¼ tsp ground cardamom
⅛ tsp fine sea salt
3 tbsp freshly grated lemon zest
3 tbsp freshly squeezed
lemon juice

For the topping

1 medium lemon, very thinly sliced
¼ cup (50 g) granulated sugar,
plus 2 tbsp to caramelize the top
¼ cup (60 ml) water

Picture page 415, bottom left

For the pastry, combine the flour, sugar, and salt in the bowl of a stand mixer fitted with the dough hook attachment. Add the butter and use a knife to cut it into the flour until there are just small pieces left. Quickly rub the butter into the flour with your fingers until combined. Add the egg yolks and mix with the hook until crumbly. Form the dough into a thick disc, wrap it in plastic wrap, and freeze for 12 minutes.

Preheat the oven to 400°F (200°C).

On a work surface, place the dough between 2 sheets of plastic wrap and use a rolling pin to roll out into a disc, large enough to line the bottom and sides of a 9-inch (23 cm), preferably loose-bottom, tart pan. Fit the dough into the tart pan, pushing it into the pan, especially along the edges. Trim the dough with a knife then use a fork to prick the dough all over. Bake for 10 minutes or until golden. If the dough bubbles up, push it down with a fork. Take the tart pan out of the oven and reduce the heat to 350°F (180°C).

For the filling, in the bowl of a stand mixer fitted with the whisk attachment, whisk the eggs, egg yolks, heavy cream, sour cream, sugar, cardamom, and salt for 2 minutes or until smooth. Add the lemon zest and juice and mix until well combined. Pour the lemon filling on top of the pre-baked pastry and bake for about 25 minutes or until set. Let the tart cool completely.

For the topping, in a large, heavy pan, bring the lemon slices, 1/4 cup (50 g) of sugar, and the water to a boil and cook over medium-high heat for 6 to 10 minutes or until soft and golden brown—mind that the lemon doesn't burn. Arrange the lemon slices on top of the tart, sprinkle the remaining 2 tablespoons of sugar over the entire surface, and use a kitchen torch (or the oven's broiler) to caramelize the sugar. Serve immediately.

Serves 4

1⅓ pounds (600 g) trimmed
Brussels sprouts, cut in half
1 large, tart baking apple,
cored and cut into 12 wedges
1 medium bunch fresh marjoram
⅓ cup (75 ml) olive oil
2 tbsp freshly squeezed
orange juice
1 tbsp honey
Flaky sea salt
Coarsely ground pepper

Picture page 420, top left

Once the choices are made for a feast's roasts and meats, it's time to focus on the vegetables. Brussels sprouts roasted with honey, apples, and marjoram taste almost too good to be just a side dish, so let's view them as a fabulous cozy weekday dinner as well.

Roasted Brussels Sprouts with Honey, Apples, and Marjoram

Preheat the oven to 425°F (220°C).

Spread the Brussels sprouts, apple, and marjoram in a medium baking dish. Whisk together the olive oil, orange juice, and honey, pour over the Brussels sprouts and apples, and toss to combine. Season generously with salt and pepper. Roast for 10 minutes, stir, and continue roasting, stirring every 5 minutes or so, for 15 to 20 minutes or until golden brown, crispy, and al dente. Serve as a main or as a side dish for roasts and poultry.

Serves 2 to 4

Olive oil
3 small heads Belgian endive,
cut in half lengthwise
Fine sea salt
Finely ground pepper
6 thin slices prosciutto di Parma
(or prosciutto di San Daniele)
2 tbsp balsamic vinegar
3 tbsp (45 g) unsalted butter,
cut into small pieces
1 tbsp fresh marjoram leaves
⅛ tsp granulated sugar

Picture page 415, bottom right

One of the recipes in my first cookbook, *Eat In My Kitchen*, that got a lot of love and attention, is in fact very simple. Sautéed Endive with Balsamic Butter and Marjoram took palates by storm and quickly found many fans. This recipe is a little heartier and raises the dish to the next level with one single addition: prosciutto di Parma.

Prosciutto-Wrapped Endive with Balsamic-Marjoram Butter

In a medium, heavy pan, heat a splash of olive oil over medium-high heat and sauté the endive for 1½ to 2 minutes per side or until golden brown and al dente—it should stay firm in the middle. Season to taste with salt and pepper, transfer to a plate, and tightly wrap each endive half in a slice of prosciutto. Return to the pan and sauté over medium-high heat for 1 minute per side or until golden.

In a small saucepan, bring the vinegar to a boil then reduce the heat and simmer gently for 1 minute. Take the pan off the heat and add the butter in 4 batches, letting it melt before adding more and whisking well to bind the sauce. Whisk in the marjoram and sugar and season to taste with salt and pepper. Don't let the sauce sit for too long without whisking or it will separate.

Divide the endive among plates, drizzle with the balsamic butter, and serve.

Makes 2 sandwiches

20 large cloves garlic,
preferably young, unpeeled
Fine sea salt
2 ciabatta buns, cut in half
4 ounces (110 g) aromatic cheese
that melts well, such as Raclette,
Gruyère, or Comté, thinly sliced
Coarsely ground pepper
1 small handful watercress

A roasted garlic sandwich is an energy booster. Ten cloves on a bun ensure that nature's healing powers put a weak body and soul back on track. Adding melted, aromatic Raclette is a game changer and will make you go for seconds and thirds.

Roasted Garlic and Raclette Sandwich

Preheat the oven to 425°F (220°C).

Spread the garlic cloves in a medium baking dish and roast, turning occasionally, for about 25 minutes or until soft enough to mash with a fork—mind that the garlic doesn't burn. Remove the garlic from the oven and set the oven to broil (quicker method) or increase the heat to 500°F (260°C).

Let the garlic cool for a few minutes then peel the cloves, mash them with a fork until smooth, and season to taste with salt. Spread the garlic paste on the bottom half of each bun, cover with the cheese, and put under the broiler, or roast at 500°F (260°C) for a few minutes or until the cheese starts to melt. Sprinkle with a little pepper and watercress, place a top on each bun, and enjoy.

Serves 4

1⅓ pounds (600 g) cored
red cabbage, cut into thin wedges
⅓ pound (150 g) kumquats,
cut into very thin rounds
and seeds removed (or 2 small
oranges, cut into thin wedges)
¼ cup (60 ml) olive oil
¼ cup (60 ml) freshly squeezed
orange juice
2 tbsp maple syrup
Flaky sea salt
Coarsely ground pepper
1 small bunch fresh thyme

Picture page 420, top right

When the meat, sauce, and carbs are rich and heavy, roasted red cabbage wedges and kumquats lighten up the meal with citrusy and smoky tones.

Roasted Red Cabbage Wedges with Kumquats

Preheat the oven to 400°F (200°C). Line a baking sheet with parchment paper.

Spread the cabbage and kumquats on the lined baking sheet. Whisk together the olive oil, orange juice, and maple syrup, pour over the cabbage and kumquats, and gently toss to combine—mind that the cabbage wedges don't fall apart. Season to taste with salt and pepper and sprinkle with the thyme. Roast for 15 minutes then use two forks to gently turn the cabbage wedges and roast for another 15 minutes or until the cabbage is just tender. Serve immediately or prepare a few hours ahead and warm in the oven just before serving.

When you purée preserved artichoke hearts, olive oil, and garlic, you witness a little kitchen miracle. The dip looks, feels, and tastes almost like aïoli, without the eggy heaviness of the Mediterranean-style mayonnaise. It's scrumptious on crostini and tastes heavenly when you drip it onto seared halibut fillet.

Seared Halibut with Artichoke-Garlic Dip

Serves 1 to 2

For the dip
4 ounces (110 g) artichoke hearts,
preserved in olive oil, drained
and squeezed
2 large cloves garlic
¼ cup (60 ml) olive oil
1 tsp freshly grated lemon zest
1 tsp freshly squeezed lemon juice
Fine sea salt
Finely ground pepper

For the halibut
Olive oil
1 (7-ounce / 200-g) halibut fillet
Fine sea salt
Finely ground pepper
6 large fresh flat-leaf
parsley leaves, thinly sliced
1 small loaf ciabatta, sliced
and toasted, for serving

For the dip, purée the artichoke hearts, garlic, olive oil, $1/2$ teaspoon of the lemon zest, and the lemon juice in a food processor or blender until smooth. Season to taste with salt and pepper.

For the halibut, heat a splash of olive oil in a medium, heavy pan over medium-high heat. Add the halibut and sear for $1\,1/2$ to 2 minutes per side or until you can flake the fish gently with a fork. Season to taste with salt and pepper and transfer to a plate. Sprinkle with the parsley, the remaining lemon zest, and a little pepper and serve with the ciabatta and a spoonful of the artichoke dip.

344

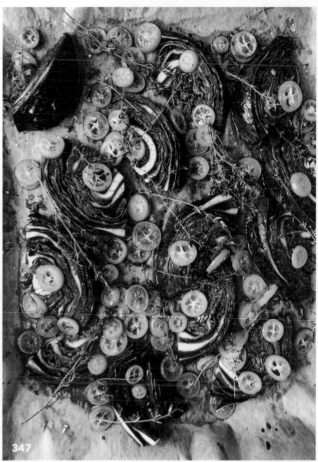

347

349

350

Duck legs baked in a casserole dish filled to the brim with the bird's fat is called *confit de canard* and is a fantastic way to cook the dark meat to succulent perfection. Later, when you roast the tender legs with potatoes, chestnuts, prunes, and star anise–infused fat, they develop the crispiest of skin. It's a perfect Christmas Eve dinner, if you plan it properly. First, you dry-cure the legs, then you slowly cook them in duck fat and at the end you roast them. Spread the preparation over two or three days and it's less daunting than one would think.

Duck Confit with Roasted Potatoes, Chestnuts, and Prunes

Serves 4

For the duck confit

4 duck legs

1 ½ tbsp flaky sea salt

1 ½ tsp black peppercorns, crushed with a mortar and pestle

1 small bunch fresh thyme

2 ¼ pounds (1 kg) rendered duck or goose fat

1 large, tart baking apple, peeled, cored, and cut into thin wedges

2 bay leaves

For the roasted duck

8 medium, waxy potatoes, peeled and thinly sliced on a mandoline

7 ounces (200 g) vacuum-packed whole cooked chestnuts

5 ounces (140 g) dried plums

3 large cloves garlic, thinly sliced

1 small bunch fresh thyme

3 star anise

Flaky sea salt

Coarsely ground pepper

Picture opposite, bottom left

For the duck confit, place the duck legs in a medium baking dish. Whisk together the salt and crushed black peppercorns then sprinkle over the duck and rub into the skin. Arrange ½ of the thyme underneath the legs and ½ of the thyme on top. Cover with plastic wrap and refrigerate for 5 hours, or preferably overnight (*day 1*).

Preheat the oven to 250°F / 120°C (*day 2*).

Reserve the thyme sprigs and rub the salt and pepper off the duck legs with paper towels. In a large Dutch oven, melt the duck fat over medium heat then add the duck legs, the reserved thyme sprigs, the apple wedges, and bay leaves. Transfer to the oven and bake for about 2 ½ hours or until the meat starts to shrink off the bones and the juices run clear when you prick the thickest part of a leg with a skewer. If you plan to roast the duck legs immediately, transfer them to a plate then measure 3/4 cup (180 ml) of the fat and keep it warm and liquid. Pour any remaining fat into sterilized jars; you can keep the jars closed in the fridge for months. Alternatively, place the meat in a terrine mold or covered dish, cover completely with the fat, keep in the fridge, and roast in the next few days.

Preheat the oven to 425°F / 220°C (*day 3*).

For the roasted duck, spread the potatoes, chestnuts, dried plums, garlic, thyme, and star anise on a large baking sheet. Add the reserved 3/4 cup (180 ml) of duck fat, season to taste with salt and coarsely ground pepper, and toss to combine. Roast for 10 minutes then stir and roast for another 10 minutes. Arrange the duck legs, skin-side up, on top of the potatoes and roast, stirring the potatoes every 10 minutes, for 25 to 30 minutes or until the potatoes and duck legs are golden brown and crispy. Divide the duck, potatoes, prunes, and chestnuts among plates and serve immediately.

This tart is a bit like millionaire's shortbread, but instead of a firm caramel layer sandwiched between pastry and chocolate, the buttery caramel drips lusciously off the silky bittersweet filling. It's the ultimate dessert for a dinner party.

Chocolate Tart with Butter Caramel

Serves 12

For the pastry
1⅓ cups (175 g) all-purpose flour
¼ cup (50 g) granulated sugar
⅛ tsp fine sea salt
⅓ cup plus 1 tbsp (90 g) unsalted butter, cold
1 large egg yolk
1 tbsp water, cold

For the chocolate filling
⅓ cup (75 ml) heavy cream
3 tbsp whole milk
5 ounces (140 g) bittersweet chocolate
1 tbsp (15 g) unsalted butter
1 tbsp granulated sugar
⅛ tsp fine sea salt
1 large egg, beaten

For the butter caramel*
¾ cup plus 1 tbsp (200 ml) heavy cream
1¾ cups (175 g) confectioners' sugar
⅓ cup plus 1 tbsp (90 g) unsalted butter, cut into pieces
Fine sea salt

Picture page 420, bottom right

For the pastry, combine the flour, granulated sugar, and salt in the bowl of a stand mixer fitted with the dough hook attachment. Add the butter and use a knife to cut it into the flour until there are just small pieces left. Quickly rub the butter into the flour with your fingers until combined. Add the egg yolk and cold water and mix with the hook until crumbly. Form the dough into a thick disc, wrap it in plastic wrap, and freeze for 10 minutes.

Preheat the oven to 350°F (180°C).

For the chocolate filling, in a small saucepan, bring the heavy cream and milk to a boil. Take the pan off the heat, add the chocolate, butter, granulated sugar, and salt, and whisk until smooth. Transfer to a medium bowl, add the egg, and whisk until combined.

On a work surface, place the dough between 2 sheets of plastic wrap and use a rolling pin to roll out into a disc, large enough to line the bottom and sides of a 9-inch (23 cm), preferably loose-bottom, tart pan. Fit the dough into the tart pan, pushing it into the pan, especially along the edges. Trim the dough with a knife then use a fork to prick the dough all over. Bake for 11 minutes or until golden. If the dough bubbles up, push it down with a fork. Pour the chocolate mixture on top of the pre-baked pastry and bake for 10 to 15 minutes or until set. Let the tart cool for at least 15 minutes.

For the butter caramel, heat the heavy cream in a small pot over medium-high heat until hot but not boiling. In a medium saucepan, melt the confectioners' sugar over medium heat, whisking occasionally, for about 5 minutes or until golden brown and caramelized. Slowly add the hot heavy cream, whisking constantly, then add the butter and 1/3 teaspoon of salt and continue whisking until smooth. Season to taste with salt.

Cut the tart into thin slices and drizzle with the butter caramel.

* You can use any leftover caramel for crêpes (recipe no. 77), ice cream, muffins, or waffles.

A puréed soup made of squash, sweet potato, and parsnip looks like liquid gold. It's a quick recipe that you can easily turn into a splendid starter if you top it off with roasted grapes, rosemary, and whipped orange mascarpone. To keep the mood and schedule relaxed at Christmas, you can prepare the grapes and soup up to a day ahead.

Squash, Parsnip, and Sweet Potato Soup with Roasted Grapes and Mascarpone

Serves 2 to 4

For the topping
9 ounces (250 g) seedless
red grapes, on the vine
2 medium sprigs fresh rosemary
2 tbsp olive oil
Flaky sea salt
4 ounces (110 g) mascarpone
3 tbsp freshly squeezed
orange juice
⅛ tsp fine sea salt

For the soup
Olive oil
½ medium onion,
roughly chopped
½ pound (225 g) seeded squash,
preferably peeled butternut
or Hokkaido with skin,
cut into cubes
⅓ pound (150 g) peeled parsnip
and sweet potato, cut into cubes
2 ½ cups (600 ml) homemade
or quality store-bought
vegetable broth, hot
6 medium sprigs fresh thyme
1 bay leaf
Fine sea salt
Finely ground pepper

Preheat the oven to 425°F (220°C).

For the topping, place the grapes and rosemary in a medium baking dish. Drizzle with the olive oil, gently toss to coat, and season to taste with flaky sea salt. Roast for 30 to 35 minutes or until the grapes are soft and a little shriveled.

For the soup, heat a splash of olive oil in a large pot over medium heat. Add the onion and sauté for a few minutes or until golden and soft. Add the squash, parsnip, and sweet potato and sauté, stirring constantly, for 1 minute. Add the hot broth, thyme, and bay leaf, season to taste with fine sea salt and pepper, and bring to a boil. Reduce the heat, cover, and simmer for 15 to 20 minutes or until the vegetables are tender. Remove and discard the bay leaf and thyme. In a food processor or blender, or with an immersion blender, purée the soup until smooth then return it to the pot and bring to a boil. Cook, stirring, for about 1 minute or until it reaches the desired taste and texture. Season to taste with fine sea salt and pepper.

For the topping, in a medium bowl, whisk together the mascarpone, orange juice, and fine sea salt.

Divide the soup among bowls, top with a spoonful of the orange mascarpone and the roasted grapes (snipped or on the vine), and sprinkle with a little roasted rosemary and pepper.

352

Serves 2 to 4

For the salad
Fine sea salt
13 ounces (370 g) cored
red cabbage, shredded
1 large ripe persimmon,
peeled and torn into chunks
3 ounces (85 g) soft,
mild chèvre, crumbled
1 tbsp fresh marjoram leaves

For the dressing
3 tbsp olive oil
1 tbsp balsamic vinegar
1 tbsp white balsamic vinegar
1 tsp freshly squeezed
orange juice
Finely ground pepper

Peppery red cabbage paired with juice-dripping persimmon brings bold contrast to the table. Soft chèvre and fresh marjoram give this vibrant salad an almost Mediterranean touch.

Red Cabbage and Persimmon Salad with Chèvre and Marjoram

For the salad, in a large bowl, sprinkle 1/2 teaspoon of salt over the cabbage, rub it in with your fingers for about 1 minute, and let it sit for 10 minutes to soften the cabbage.

For the dressing, whisk together the olive oil, both vinegars, and the orange juice and season to taste with pepper. Add to the cabbage, toss to combine, and season to taste with salt.

Divide the cabbage among plates and arrange the persimmon chunks and chèvre on top. Sprinkle with marjoram and serve immediately.

353

Makes 4 sandwiches

4 thick slices white
sourdough bread (or ciabatta)
7 ounces (200 g) smoked
Scamorza (or any lightly
smoked cheese), thinly sliced
1 to 2 medium white
or black truffles, freshly grated
or very thinly sliced with a truffle
slicer
Coarsely ground pepper

When the year comes to an end, I like to spoil my loved ones—and myself—with a simple yet sumptuous meal. If New Year's Eve is already on your mind, consider a truffle and smoked Scamorza sandwich. It will put a smile on your guests' faces and that's the way to end a year. You could use truffle oil, but that spoils the fun.

Truffle and Smoked Scamorza on Sourdough

Set the oven to broil (quicker method) or preheat to 500°F (260°C).

Divide the Scamorza among the bread and put the sandwiches under the broiler, or roast at 500°F (260°C) for a few minutes or until the cheese starts to melt. Arrange the truffle on top of the warm cheese, sprinkle with pepper, and enjoy.

Sometimes a recipe surprises the mind and senses and the satisfaction it creates exceeds expectations. Sautéed parsnips with candied date butter is that kind of recipe. The first time I made it, there was silence at the table, as we experienced the root's sweet yet earthy complex flavor combined with the sticky butter. It's a beautiful warm salad or side dish for December's hearty roasts.

Sautéed Parsnips with Maple-Date Butter

Serves 2 to 4

Olive oil
⅔ pound (300 g) peeled parsnips, very thinly sliced lengthwise on a mandoline
Fine sea salt
Finely ground pepper
2 tbsp (30 g) unsalted butter
1 tsp maple syrup
2 large juicy dates, pitted and finely chopped

Heat a splash of olive oil in a large, heavy pan over medium-high heat. Working in batches, sauté the parsnip slices side by side, turning once or twice, for 2 to 3 minutes or until golden and soft. Season to taste with salt and pepper, arrange the parsnips on a platter, and cover to keep warm. Repeat to sauté the remaining parsnips, adding a splash of olive oil between batches.

In a small, heavy pan, melt the butter, maple syrup, and dates over high heat until sizzling. Immediately take the pan off the heat then stir for 10 seconds. Sprinkle the maple-date butter over the parsnips and serve warm.

Blood orange, turmeric, and thyme are a powerful trio, and salmon is the perfect fish for such a vibrant fusion of flavors. Baked and sealed in a thick salt crust, the fish fillets stay perfectly juicy and tender. You can also replace the citrus and yellow spice with dill and juniper berries *(recipe no. 89)*.

Salt-Baked Salmon with Blood Orange, Turmeric, and Thyme

Serves 2 to 3

For the salt crust

2 ¼ pounds (1 kg) flaky sea salt

¾ cup (100 g) all-purpose flour

¼ cup (30 g) cornstarch

2 large egg whites

About ⅓ cup (75 ml) water, cold

For the salmon

1 tsp black peppercorns, crushed with a mortar and pestle

½ tsp ground turmeric

2 (10-ounce / 280-g) skin-on salmon fillets

2 small blood oranges, thinly sliced

1 small bunch fresh thyme

Ovenproof cotton string

Preheat the oven to 400°F (200°C). Line a medium baking dish with parchment paper.

For the salt crust, combine the salt, flour, cornstarch, egg whites, and cold water in a large bowl and use your fingers or a tablespoon to quickly mix until combined. Spread a thin layer of the salt mixture, roughly the size of 1 salmon fillet, in the middle of the lined baking dish.

For the salmon, whisk together the crushed black peppercorns and turmeric and rub the mixture into the pink side of each salmon fillet then spread the blood orange slices, slightly overlapping, on top. Arrange the thyme on top of 1 salmon fillet and top with the second fillet, so that the skin side of each fillet is on the outside. Tie the salmon fillets together with ovenproof cotton string and arrange on top of the salt mixture in the baking dish. Using your fingers, gently pack the remaining salt mixture over and around the salmon until it's covered. If the salt mixture is too dry, add a little more water. The salt may slide down a little and have some cracks, but that's fine—just try to seal the fish inside the crust as much as possible. Bake for 55 minutes or until a metal skewer, poked through the crust into the thickest part of the salmon, is warm to the touch when you pull it out of the salmon.

Let the salt crust cool for 2 minutes then carefully break it open with a sharp bread knife. Scrape the salt off the salmon, divide the fillets and orange slices among plates, and serve immediately.

Baumkuchen is a delicious attraction at German Christmas markets. Traditionally, it's baked on a spit next to a broiler or open fire, with up to twenty layers of batter brushed onto the cake and baked one after the other. The layers resemble growth rings of a tree, hence the name Baumkuchen, meaning "tree cake" in German. I bake my marzipan-scented Baumkuchen in a cake pan under the broiler and cut it into small squares that I drizzle with chocolate.

German Baumkuchen
Layered Marzipan Cake
with Bittersweet Chocolate

Makes about 20 small squares

For the cake

6 large eggs, separated
⅛ tsp fine sea salt
½ cup (65 g) all-purpose flour
¼ cup (30 g) cornstarch
¾ cup plus 2 tbsp (200 g) unsalted butter, at room temperature
1 cup (200 g) granulated sugar
4 ounces (110 g) high-quality marzipan, at room temperature, finely chopped
2 tbsp brandy
1 vanilla bean, split and scraped
1 tsp freshly grated orange zest
¼ tsp ground cinnamon

For the topping

4 ounces (110 g) bittersweet chocolate
1 tsp unsalted butter
About 2 tbsp freshly grated orange zest

Set the oven to broil (quicker method) or preheat to 425°F (220°C). Butter the bottom and sides of an 8-inch (20 cm) springform pan, or a tall 8 x 6-inch (20 x 15 cm) cake pan, and line the bottom and sides with parchment paper.

For the cake, in the bowl of a stand mixer fitted with the whisk attachment, whisk the egg whites and salt until stiff and scrape into a large bowl. Combine the flour and cornstarch and sift into a medium bowl.

In the bowl of a stand mixer fitted with the paddle attachment, beat the butter, sugar, marzipan, brandy, vanilla seeds, orange zest, and cinnamon until smooth and well combined. Add the egg yolks and continue mixing for another 3 minutes or until fluffy. Add the flour mixture and fold until well combined. Gently fold in the egg whites. Using about 3 generous tablespoons of batter, spread a thin layer on the bottom of the prepared pan. Place the pan in the top third of the oven and bake for 3 to 4 minutes or until deep golden and set. Carefully remove the pan from the oven, brush another thin layer of batter on top of the cake, and return to the oven. Repeat with the remaining batter to bake about 11 more layers. When the last layer is done, let the cake cool in the pan for at least 10 minutes then transfer to a wire rack and let it cool completely.

For the topping, in a small saucepan, heat the chocolate and butter over low heat, whisking until smooth; let it cool for a few minutes. Cut the cake into little squares, drizzle with the melted chocolate, and sprinkle with a little orange zest. Let the chocolate cool or serve immediately.

I have a sweet mantra: Desserts deserve pastry. My crème brûlée lies on top of a short crust shell (recipe no. 343) and even an elegant Pavlova becomes more dramatic when it's a tart rather than just a meringue and whipped cream dessert. If you want to add more culinary excitement to your upcoming Christmas celebrations, you can refine the Pavlova with a hint of rosewater and sprinkle the lush beauty with crunchy pistachios and pomegranate seeds, plus a concentrated syrup made from the pink fruit's juices.

Pomegranate Pavlova Tart with Pistachios and Rosewater

Serves 6 to 8

For the pastry

1 ½ cups (200 g) all-purpose flour
⅓ cup (65 g) granulated sugar
⅛ tsp fine sea salt
⅓ cup plus 2 tbsp (100 g)
unsalted butter, cold
2 large egg yolks

For the topping

¼ cup (60 ml) pomegranate juice
Granulated sugar
¾ cup plus 2 tbsp (200 ml) heavy
cream, whipped to stiff peaks
1 tsp high-quality rosewater,
preferably organic,
plus more to taste
Seeds from ½ large pomegranate
1 small handful unsalted
pistachios, chopped

For the meringue

4 large egg whites
⅛ tsp fine sea salt
½ tsp cider vinegar
1 cup (200 g) granulated sugar
1 ½ tsp cornstarch
2 tsp rosewater, plus more to taste

For the pastry, combine the flour, sugar, and salt in the bowl of a stand mixer fitted with the dough hook attachment. Add the butter and use a knife to cut it into the flour until there are just small pieces left. Quickly rub the butter into the flour with your fingers until combined. Add the egg yolks and mix with the hook until crumbly. Form the dough into a thick disc, wrap it in plastic wrap, and freeze for 12 minutes.

Preheat the oven to 400°F (200°C).

On a work surface, place the dough between 2 sheets of plastic wrap and use a rolling pin to roll out into a disc, large enough to line the bottom and sides of a 9-inch (23 cm), preferably loose-bottom, tart pan. Fit the dough into the tart pan, pushing it into the pan, especially along the edges. Trim the dough with a knife then use a fork to prick the dough all over. Bake for 10 minutes or until golden. If the dough bubbles up, push it down with a fork. Take the tart pan out of the oven and reduce the heat to 350°F (180°C). Let the pastry cool completely.

For the topping, in a small saucepan, bring the pomegranate juice and 1 1/2 tablespoons of sugar to a boil and cook for 1 1/2 minutes or until syrupy; let cool completely.

For the meringue, in the bowl of a stand mixer fitted with the whisk attachment, whisk the egg whites and salt for 1 minute then add the vinegar and continue whisking, gradually adding the sugar, for 12 minutes or until glossy and stiff. Whisk in the cornstarch and 2 teaspoons of rosewater. Gently spread the meringue on the pre-baked pastry and swirl the top a little. Bake for 5 minutes then reduce the heat to 275°F (135°C) and bake for another 60 minutes or until pale and crispy. Turn off the oven, prop the door partially open, and leave the tart inside for another 15 minutes. Take the tart out of the oven and let it cool completely.

Add 1 teaspoon of rosewater and a little sugar to the whipped cream, whisk, and adjust to taste, then arrange the whipped cream in the middle of the meringue. Drizzle with the pomegranate syrup, sprinkle with the pomegranate seeds and pistachios, and serve immediately.

358

week 52 / monday

We celebrate two Christmases. Following the German tradition, we first clink glasses and fill the table with far too much food on Christmas Eve. Then, thanks to my partner and his Maltese and American roots, the festivities continue on the 25th. We always plan the two menus individually. I'm a traditionalist and my main course is always the same: slow-roasted duck. Figs and elderflower syrup make it sweet and fruity (*recipe no. 294*), while duck à l'orange with lingonberry-port gravy is a more classic approach. Merry Christmas!

Slow-Roasted Duck à l'Orange with Lingonberry-Port Gravy and Chestnuts

Serves 3 to 4

Olive oil

1 (5 ½-pound / 2.5-kg) duck, with neck and giblets reserved

2 tsp flaky sea salt

1 tsp black peppercorns, crushed with a mortar and pestle

3 medium onions, cut into thin wedges

2 medium, tart baking apples, peeled, cored, and cut into wedges

1 large orange, cut into thin wedges

1 handful vacuum-packed whole cooked chestnuts

1 small bunch fresh thyme

10 fresh sage leaves

1 bay leaf

¼ cup (60 ml) port (or brandy)

¼ cup (60 ml) full-bodied red wine

2 tbsp freshly squeezed orange juice

1 tbsp lingonberry jam, plus more to taste

Fine sea salt

Finely ground pepper

Ovenproof cotton string

Preheat the oven to 175°F (85°C).

In a large, heavy pan, heat a splash of olive oil over high heat and sear the duck, turning, for a few minutes or until golden brown on all sides. Transfer the duck to a medium baking dish and carefully pour the fat from the pan into a small bowl. Season the duck, inside and out, with the flaky sea salt and crushed black peppercorns and rub into the skin. Stuff the duck with some of the onion, apple, and orange wedges, $1/3$ of the chestnuts, $1/2$ of the thyme, $1/2$ of the sage, and the bay leaf and tie the legs together with ovenproof cotton string. Arrange the remaining onion, apple, and orange wedges, the chestnuts, thyme, and sage around the duck and roast, spooning a little of the reserved duck fat and the juices from the baking dish over the duck every hour, for 4 hours. After 4 hours, check to see if the duck is done by pricking the thickest part of a thigh with a skewer—the juices should run clear. Turn on the broiler for the last 1 to 2 minutes or until the skin is golden brown and partially crispy, but mind that it doesn't burn.

Let the duck rest for a few minutes while you make the gravy: Heat 2 teaspoons of the reserved duck fat in a large, heavy pan over medium-high heat and sear the neck and giblets, turning, for 2 minutes. Add the port, stir, and then add the red wine and orange juice and bring to a boil. Remove the neck and giblets, whisk in the lingonberry jam, and season to taste with additional lingonberry jam, fine sea salt, and finely ground pepper.

Carve the duck and serve the meat with the gravy, onions, apples, oranges, and chestnuts.

A marvelous dinner in Rome introduced my palate to this beautiful dish that focuses on only four ingredients. Creamy burrata, salty bottarga (dried and cured mullet roe), olive oil, and lemon zest are a revelation and one of the quickest starters the Christmas table has ever seen.

Burrata with Bottarga

Serves 2

7 ounces (200 g) burrata
(or mozzarella di bufala)
3 to 4 tbsp (about 35 g)
freshly grated bottarga
High-quality olive oil
Freshly grated lemon zest

Break the burrata into large chunks and divide among plates. Sprinkle with the bottarga, a few drops of olive oil, and a pinch of lemon zest and serve immediately.

When Christmas is over and leftovers occupy every corner of the fridge, it's time to think of a sandwich. Easy comfort food feels right after days of passionate feasting, so pile thin slices of leftover poultry, pork, or beef on ciabatta, and top it off with creamy chestnut purée and star anise–infused pear wedges.

Leftover Roast Meat Sandwich with Chestnut Purée and Sautéed Star Anise Pear

Makes 4 sandwiches

7 ounces (200 g) vacuum-packed
whole cooked chestnuts
About ⅓ cup (75 ml) heavy cream
3 tbsp freshly squeezed
orange juice
2 tbsp port (or brandy)
¼ tsp ground cinnamon
Fine sea salt
Finely ground pepper
3 tbsp (45 g) unsalted butter
2 tbsp granulated sugar
1 heaping tbsp fresh thyme leaves
3 star anise
1 large, firm pear, cored
and cut into thin wedges
8 slices ciabatta
8 thin slices leftover roast meat,
such as duck, turkey, chicken,
pork, or beef

In a food processor or blender, purée the chestnuts, heavy cream, orange juice, port, and cinnamon until smooth. Add a little more heavy cream if it's too firm then season to taste with salt and pepper.

In a medium, heavy pan, heat the butter, sugar, thyme, and star anise over high heat until sizzling. Add the pear wedges, reduce the heat to medium-high, and sauté, turning once, for 3 to 4 minutes or until golden brown and tender.

Spread the chestnut purée on 4 ciabatta slices, arrange the roast meat and pear wedges on top, and drizzle with the buttery pear juices from the pan. Place a slice of ciabatta on top of each sandwich, squeeze, and enjoy.

Leftover meat can be turned into delicious sandwiches (*recipe no. 360*), but flat leftover Champagne is just as useful for creating new dishes. If it happens to be pink, even better. Whisk together a smooth Champagne butter, toss with warm spaghetti, and top it off with seared scallops and pomegranate seeds. It can be a treat just for you before the year comes to an end, or you can increase the amounts, and share with your loved ones.

361
week 52 / thursday

Spaghetti with Scallops, Pink Champagne Butter, and Pomegranate

Serves 1

3 ounces (85 g) dried spaghetti
4 large sea scallops,
side muscle removed
Olive oil
2 tbsp (30 g) unsalted butter
Fine sea salt
Coarsely ground pepper
¾ cup (180 ml) leftover pink
Champagne (or any dry
sparkling wine)
3 tbsp pomegranate seeds
1 tsp elderflower syrup
(or maple syrup)
1 small handful small
fresh basil leaves

Bring a large pot of salted water to a boil and cook the spaghetti, according to the package instructions, until al dente. Drain the spaghetti and return it to the pot.

Pat the scallops dry with paper towels.

In a small, heavy pan, heat a splash of olive oil and 1 tablespoon of the butter over high heat. Add the scallops, reduce the heat to medium-high, and sear the scallops for 1 minute per side or until golden brown and just cooked through. Season to taste with salt and pepper. Transfer the scallops to a plate and keep warm, but leave the pan on the heat. Add the Champagne and deglaze the pan, using a spatula to scrape any bits and pieces off the bottom, then add the pomegranate seeds and elderflower syrup. Simmer for 4 to 5 minutes or until the sauce reaches the desired taste and texture. Take the pan off the heat, add the remaining 1 tablespoon of butter, and whisk until smooth. Season to taste with salt and pepper, add the spaghetti, and toss to combine. Transfer to a plate then arrange the scallops on top, sprinkle with basil and a little pepper, and enjoy.

Once you make your own ravioli, you'll never be able to buy them from a store again. You do need a pasta machine and it's a rather labor-intense project but one that will make everybody at the dinner table very happy. Preserved artichokes, ricotta, and orange make a light Mediterranean filling, perfect for a starter. To keep the end of the year stress free, cook the ravioli a day ahead and warm them in the butter just before serving.

Artichoke, Ricotta, and Orange Ravioli

Serves 2 to 4

For the pasta dough

1¼ cups (160 g) all-purpose flour
¾ cup plus 2 tbsp (150 g)
fine durum wheat flour, plus more
for the baking sheet
¼ tsp fine sea salt
3 large eggs plus 1 large egg yolk
1 tbsp olive oil

For the filling

6 ounces (170 g) artichoke hearts,
preserved in olive oil, drained
and squeezed
5 ounces (140 g) fresh ricotta,
drained
1 ounce (30 g) Parmesan,
finely grated
1 tbsp olive oil
½ tsp freshly grated orange zest
Fine sea salt
Finely ground pepper

For serving

¼ cup (60 g) unsalted butter
2 large artichoke hearts,
preserved in olive oil, drained
and each cut into 6 wedges
Finely grated Parmesan
Freshly grated orange zest
Coarsely ground pepper

For the pasta dough, in the bowl of a stand mixer fitted with the dough hook attachment, combine the all-purpose flour, durum wheat flour, and salt. Add the eggs, egg yolk, and olive oil and mix with the hook for about 5 minutes or until well combined. If the mixture is too dry, add 1 tablespoon of water. Transfer to a work surface and continue kneading patiently with your hands for about 15 minutes or until well combined and firm but smooth. Form the dough into a ball, wrap it in plastic wrap, and refrigerate for 1 hour.

For the filling, in a food processor or blender, purée the artichoke hearts, ricotta, Parmesan, olive oil, and orange zest until smooth and season to taste with salt and pepper.

Divide the dough into 4 to 8 portions (depending on the width and power of your pasta machine) and cover with plastic wrap. On a work surface, use a rolling pin to roll out 1 portion until thin enough to fit through the pasta machine. Using the thickest setting, pull the dough through the pasta machine twice then fold it in the middle. Rotate the dough by 90° and pull through the pasta machine another 2 to 3 times. Repeat, using one thinner setting after the other and pulling the dough through the machine about 3 times before changing the setting, until you can see your hand through the dough. If the dough is sticky, add a little durum wheat flour; don't use all-purpose flour. Sprinkle the pasta sheets with durum wheat flour, fold loosely, and cover with plastic wrap. Repeat to roll out the remaining portions of dough.

Sprinkle a baking sheet with durum wheat flour. Bring a large pot of salted water to a simmer.

Using a 3-inch (7.5 cm) round cutter, cut discs out of the pasta sheets. Place 1 teaspoon of filling in the middle of half of the pasta discs then wet the borders with a little cold water and cover each with a second pasta disc, pressing the edges together to seal the filling inside. With the prongs of a fork, press the edges again then transfer the filled ravioli to the prepared baking sheet. This makes 20 to 24 ravioli.

→

Working in batches, simmer the ravioli for 2 to 3 minutes or until al dente—mind that they don't stick to the bottom of the pot. Use a slotted ladle or spoon to scoop the ravioli out of the water, drain, and transfer to a large baking dish. Spread them, side by side, and then finish cooking the remaining ravioli.

For serving, in a large, heavy pan, heat the butter over high heat until golden brown. Add the artichoke hearts and sauté, turning once, for 1 minute. Add the ravioli and toss gently then divide among plates. Sprinkle with a little Parmesan, orange zest, and coarsely ground pepper and serve immediately.

363
week 52 / saturday

Serves 4

For the walnut butter
2 ounces (60 g) walnuts
¼ cup (60 g) unsalted butter,
at room temperature
1 tsp Dijon mustard
Flaky sea salt

For the beets
2 large beets, scrubbed
2 large bay leaves

For serving
Olive oil
4 (5-ounce / 140-g) beef fillets,
each about 1½- to 2-inch thick
(4 to 5 cm)
2 tbsp (30 g) unsalted butter
Flaky sea salt
Coarsely ground pepper
1 small handful walnuts,
roughly chopped

December is filled with fireworks for the taste buds. The food is exciting and festive and there's plenty of it. This month is all about colorful flavors, complex compositions, and extravagant treats—until it's time to slow down. The most tender fillet of beef, topped off with walnut butter and served with sweet and earthy beets, proves that simplicity does taste best sometimes.

Fillet of Beef with Walnut Butter and Beets

Take the meat out of the refrigerator about 1 hour before you want to start cooking. Dry the fillets with paper towels just before you sear them in the pan.

For the walnut butter, purée the walnuts, butter, mustard, and a little salt in a food processor or blender until smooth and season to taste with salt. Scrape the butter onto a piece of plastic wrap and roll it into a thick log. Refrigerate for 45 minutes or freeze for 10 minutes or until firm.

For the beets, bring a medium pot of salted water to a boil and add the beets and bay leaves then reduce the heat, cover, and simmer for 45 to 50 minutes or until tender. Drain the beets and quickly rinse with cold water. When they are cool enough to handle, peel off the skin and cut into chunky cubes.

For serving, in a large, heavy pan, heat a generous splash of olive oil over high heat and sear the beef fillets for 1 minute per side. Reduce the heat to medium, add the butter, and continue cooking the fillets, turning once and spooning the buttery juices over the meat twice, for another 1½ minutes per side for medium-rare. Season to taste with salt and pepper then transfer the fillets to a plate, wrap in aluminum foil, and let rest for 2 minutes. Reserve the juices in the pan.

Divide the beets among plates, drizzle with a little olive oil, and sprinkle with the walnuts and a little salt. Place the beef fillets next to the beets, top with a slice of walnut butter, drizzle with the juices from the pan, and serve immediately.

This recipe will make you squeal with joy. It tastes divine, feels silky-smooth, and is easy to prepare. When life gives you lemons, make Limoncello Panna Cotta—it's that simple.

Limoncello Panna Cotta

Serves 2 to 4

2 ½ (3 × 4-inch / 7.5 x 10-cm) gelatin sheets
(or 2 ½ tsp powdered gelatin)
1 cup (240 ml) heavy cream
½ cup (120 ml) whole milk
¼ cup (60 ml) Limoncello liqueur
2 long strips fresh lemon peel (white pith removed)
2 tbsp granulated sugar
⅛ tsp fine sea salt
4 very thin lemon slices (optional)
8 small fresh mint leaves (optional)

Soak the gelatin sheets in cold water for about 5 minutes.

In a small saucepan, bring the heavy cream, milk, Limoncello, lemon peel, sugar, and salt to a boil. As soon as the mixture is bubbling, take the pan off the heat. Squeeze the excess water from the soaked gelatin sheets, crumble into the warm cream mixture, and whisk thoroughly. Remove the lemon peel and let the mixture cool in the pan, whisking occasionally.

Once the cream mixture is at room temperature—it will still be liquid—divide it between 4 (4-ounce / 120-ml) ramekins. Cover the ramekins with plastic wrap and refrigerate for 1 hour. Transfer the ramekins to the freezer and chill for 35 to 45 minutes or until set but not frozen. Alternatively, leave the ramekins in the refrigerator for 2 to 3 hours or overnight.

Decorate the panna cotta with lemon slices and mint just before serving.

There are many ways to end a year. To say goodbye to the last twelve months with spaghetti carbonara and truffle is not only simple but also a feast. The traditional Tuscan dish is all about comfort and coziness, pure honest flavors, and time spent with special ones around the table. It's about good food and beloved people embracing the past together and welcoming what's yet to come tomorrow and in the next 365 days. It's a meal where the wine should be exceptional and the music cheerful. Happy New Year!

Tuscan Truffle Carbonara

Serves 2

Olive oil
2 ounces (60 g) guanciale
(or mild bacon),
cut into matchsticks
7 ounces (200 g) dried spaghetti
2 very fresh large eggs,
at room temperature
2 very fresh large egg yolks,
at room temperature
Fine sea salt
Coarsely ground pepper
2 ounces (60 g) pecorino,
finely grated
1 medium or 2 small white
or black truffles, freshly grated
or very thinly sliced with
a truffle slicer

In a small, heavy pan, heat a splash of olive oil over medium-high heat and cook the guanciale for 1 to 2 minutes or until soft and translucent. (If using bacon, it will need a little longer and should be golden brown and crispy.) Set the pan aside.

Bring a large pot of salted water to a boil and cook the spaghetti, according to the package instructions, until al dente.

While the pasta is cooking, in a large bowl, whisk together the eggs, egg yolks, and a pinch of salt and season generously with pepper. Stir in 2/3 of the pecorino.

When the pasta is done, drain quickly and transfer to the bowl with the egg mixture. Add the guanciale and toss quickly to combine. Divide the pasta among plates, sprinkle with the remaining pecorino, the truffle, and a little pepper and serve immediately. Buon appetito!

Index

Acknowledgments

A big hug to all the people who inspired, encouraged, and supported me to turn 365 recipes into a book.

Jamie, for being there 365 days and nights for so many years, for being with me on this journey, helping me overcome every obstacle, and reminding me to celebrate every second of it. Your love is boundless.

My Mama, for all our phone calls and talks about food and wine; for taking my hand and guiding me through recipes and life; for your extraordinary, unbreakable will to enjoy life. For being at my side, always.

My family and friends, for catching me when I fall, inspiring me when my mind is starving, and—above all—for making me laugh. Your patience is a gift and so is your appetite, especially while I tested hundreds of recipes.

Holly La Due, for diving into 365 together with me since we first spoke about it over a coffee on Broadway. Everybody at Prestel in New York, London, and Munich, for standing forcefully behind our vision.

Lauren Salkeld and Djan Sauerborn for polishing my words, Jen Endom for editing my pictures, and Tanja Kapahnke and Sven Lindhorst-Emme for shaping the looks of this book.

Seb Tanti Burlò, for sharing your bay leaf drawing (page 5) and keeping the memory of Daphne Caruana Galizia and her work alive. (The political cartoonist and artist started drawing bay leaves doubling up as quills as a series after the Maltese journalist's assassination in 2017, when her sons delivered pizza along with bay leaves from the family's garden to support protesters.)

I cook, style, and shoot all my recipes, but 365 recipes felt too overwhelming to cope with on my own. Thank you Marlon Bertzbach, for always making me believe that I'd manage. For shopping, chopping, and stirring together with me for months, and for bringing your joy and the best playlists to my kitchen.

The readers of my blog and followers of my work in the endless space of social media, our fruitful dialogue brought me to the place where I am today.

Broste Copenhagen and Hering Berlin, for filling my kitchen shelves with your beautiful plates. All the small producers who bring their exceptional products to my kitchen table, for respecting nature, and creating food that is tasty and good for us.

Thank you.